27

W9-CCV-423

Antiquing in New Jersey

and Bucks County, Pennsylvania

Very fine 1790 Hepplewhite two-part Dutch cupboard. Walnut and poplar with cove molding and French bracket feet; original H-hinges and oval brasses. Inside: pink luster pitchers, pewter serving spoons. The tea set is Gaudy ironstone. *Courtesy Mayfair House, Inc., Lambertville*

Antiquing
in New Jersey
and Bucks County, Pennsylvania

Muriel Jacobs
Doris Ballard

Rutgers University Press
New Brunswick, New Jersey

LIBRARY OF CONGRESS CATALOGING IN PUBLICATION DATA

Jacobs, Muriel.
  Antiquing in New Jersey and Bucks County, Pennsylvania.

  Bibliography: p.
  Includes index.
    1. Antiques—New Jersey—Directories.   2. Antiques—
Pennsylvania—Bucks Co.—Directories.   I. Ballard,
Doris, joint author.   II. Title.
NK835.N45J33   338.4'7'741525749   78-9471
ISBN 0-8135-0853-3
ISBN 0-8135-0863-0 pbk.

Copyright © 1978 by Muriel Jacobs and Doris Ballard
Manufactured in the United States of America

NK
835
N45
J33

To Sanford S. Jacobs; and to
Andrew, Edward, and Anne Gweneth,
who always help

To Allan G. Ballard, Jr.
because whatever there is of an I *in this*
book is mostly we, *and to Douglas and*
Jeffrey Ballard, who could always be
counted on to be encouraging all along
the way

Contents

Antique Shops

Spanning Skyline to Ridgeline: The Northern Counties

In the Hills and Beyond: The Central Counties

From the Pine Barrens to the Shore: The Southern Counties

Across the Delaware: Urbane and Rural Byways

Prefatory Note

One of the many pleasures of antiquing in New Jersey and Bucks County is the availability of so much so close to home. Tucked away throughout this area are unexpected discoveries for the antiques connoisseur and for the weekend enthusiast.

In addition to the urban establishments and malls, there are many intriguing shops in unlikely places—less obvious collections found in basements, barns, stables, carriage houses, garages, front parlors, and occasionally at a "shop-within," revealed at the proprietor's discretion.

Profiles of a dozen regional artisans and masters of early commercial enterprise are sketched in the introduction to this volume. The legacy of their exceptional craftsmanship is also available to knowledgeable collectors.

With a small amount of planning, one can enjoy any number of rewarding cross-state excursions that take less than a day.

But where to go? And when? What will you find when you get there? How much should you expect to spend? What services are available? Will children be welcome?

The answers to these questions, plus detailed information about repair and restoration specialists, auctioneers, and principal antiques shows, are contained in the nearly two thousand listings in this book.

The authors have personally visited the shops and spoken with the proprietors and specialists. While every effort has been made to provide a guide that is both comprehensive and accurate, it is recommended that in addition to taking along a magnet and magnifying glass, one should be equipped with a good map, a compass, and a dime or two for calling ahead.

———————◆———————

The authors have attempted to be as comprehensive and accurate as possible in listing the many antiques shops in New Jersey and Bucks County, Pennsylvania. Dealers and specialists who have opened shops since the authors' initial interviews, or those who might have been inadvertently omitted or who have changed address, are asked to fill out and return the questionnaire on page 439 so that their shops may be included in subsequent editions.

Acknowledgments

The authors wish to express their gratitude to those persons who were especially helpful during the preparation of this book. Our sincere appreciation to Kay Addison, Museum Registrar, and Don Pettifer, Village Curator, Wheaton Historical Association; Elaine Bernstein; Harmony Coppola, University Archives, Rutgers University; Phillip Curtis, Curator of Decorative Arts, Kenneth L. Gosner, Curator of Zoology, and Helen Olsson, Research Library, Newark Museum; William J. Dane, Supervising Librarian, Art and Music Department, Newark Public Library; Arthur Livingston; Ella Morier and Somers Corson, Cape May Historical and Genealogical Society; Esther I. Schwartz; Donald Sinclair, Curator, Special Collections, Alexander Library, Rutgers University; Pauline Stothoff, Research Assistant, Hunterdon County Historical Society; Howard Wiseman, Curator, New Jersey Historical Society; and Sadie Zainy, Secretary, Fine Arts Collection, Rutgers University Extension Division.

The reference staffs of the New Jersey Collection and Archives Department, Alexander Library, Rutgers University; the New Jersey Room, Somerset County Library, and the staffs of the Berkeley Heights, Plainfield, Warren and Watchung libraries were most cooperative and helpful when we used their facilities.

We are indebted, too, to the dealers and private collectors who generously provided many of the photographs that illustrate this book and to those who graciously allowed us to photograph antiques in their shops or in their homes.

New Jersey and Bucks County Profiles

Early Artisans and Innovators

Pale aquamarine Wistarberg pitcher with delicate thread decoration around the neck and graceful applied handle. Ht. 6⅞ in. *Courtesy The Newark Museum*

The Wistar Glassworks

On a rural road just outside Alloway, in Salem County, New Jersey, a state historical marker reads: "Wistarburg (*sic*) Glass Works—Alloway— Here Caspar Wistar began the manufacture of glass in 1739. His son Richard carried on the business till the Revolution made it unprofitable. This was the beginning of an industry important in South Jersey for 150 years." There is nothing else on that country road to suggest the bustling village of Wistarberg and the site of the first successful glassworks in America.

The tradition of South Jersey glass, which later spread to glasshouses in New York, New England, Pennsylvania, and Ohio, began at Alloway Creek, where over a period of time, Caspar Wistar purchased 2,000 acres of land to start a glassworks. Attempts had been made at Jamestown in 1608 and 1620, at Salem, Massachusetts, between 1638 and 1642, and in New York in the mid-1600s—all with brief or at best faltering survival rates. Caspar Wistar, a button manufacturer from Philadelphia, succeeded.

Wistar arrived in Philadelphia from Germany in 1717. He was twenty-two and practically penniless. Menial jobs sustained him for a time, but he must have been a very enterprising young man because he was soon engaging in real estate ventures that enabled him to amass enough capital to start his own business—the making of brass buttons, which he confidently advertised as being "warranted for seven years."

His astute business sense must have told him that glassmaking could also be a profitable venture in a country that was in great need of glass products—windowpanes, bottles of all kinds, and common household articles. The land that he purchased in South Jersey was ideal for the undertaking: sands with practically no impurities, lots of timber to fuel the furnaces, and a navigable stream to the Delaware River for the transportation of his products. One important ingredient remained: the artisans who would create the product. Before opening his glassworks, he enticed four expert glassmen from the Palantine, the area of Germany from which he had come, to join the venture. The incentive was that he would make them partners if they would teach him and his son the art of glassmaking. He offered them passage to America, homes, fuel, food, and, most important of all, one-third of the profits. They came.

It was apparently a successful enterprise for all, for the Wistarberg glassmaking establishment was profitable for forty years. The main products were utilitarian—windowpanes and bottles of varying sizes and shapes. Individual craftsmen made the more fanciful pieces in their spare time—bowls, vases, candlesticks, pitchers—and these are the pieces that have come to be known as South Jersey glass.

As the glassworks prospered, more and more glassmen were brought from Europe to work the furnaces. These later workers were not so fortunate as the first four Palantines. Many were indentured for long periods to repay their passage money. There were frequent runaways, and the Wistars advertised in local journals for their return. A typical advertisement of the day reads:

> Ten Dollars Reward. Run away from the Subscriber's Glass House in Salem County, West Jersey, a Dutchman named Adrian Brust, about 27 years of Age, 5 feet 7 or 8 inches High of a pale Complexion has short light hair, two Moles on his left Cheek and on his right temple a Scar, also on one of his Feet near his Ancle which is but lately healed, and the Shoe mended where the Cut was. Had on when he went away an old Felt Hat, a lightish coloured Upper Jacket with Brass Buttons, this Country make, about half worn with a Patch on one of the hind Flaps where there was a Hole burnt. Leather Breeches, Grey Yarn Stockings, good shoes with Brass Buckles, A good Shirt, and generally wears the Bosom Part behind.

The Wistars apparently kept detailed records of their employees and their personal idiosyncracies.

Over the years, Wistar workers, including some of the runaways, moved on to the other glasshouses that began to emerge in South Jersey, carrying with them and passing on to their children the manner of glassmaking begun at Wistarberg. It was free blown rather than blown in molds. Glass was used to decorate itself, with superimposed designs applied to the main body—loops, swirls, and a distinctively American appliqué known as the lily pad, which looks more like waves surrounding the main body than lily pads. Thin threads of glass were wound around the necks of bottles for decorative effect; very often, ornamental crimping or fluting was used on the bases of vessels, and the handles were looped back and crimped. Principal colors of the early glass, made from bottle and window glass, ranged from pale aqua to olive green and shades of amber.

The tradition of South Jersey glass, begun at Alloway Creek and practiced at glasshouses throughout South Jersey in the 1800s, is being perpetuated today

Highly collectible glass, typical of South Jersey, was being freeblown as late as 1930 at Clevenger Brothers in Clayton. Representative of the early South Jersey tradition but produced at this later period are (left to right): an aqua pitcher and creamer with superimposed lilypad design, an aqua tumbler, a 10 in. aqua lilypad pitcher with applied crimped foot, a ruby camphor jug, a deep green mug, and a brown "end of day" lilypad. *Courtesy The Wheaton Historical Association, Millville*

at Wheaton Village in the glassmaking town of Millville, in Cumberland County. The re-created Victorian community, with a replica of the 1880s Wheaton glass factory at its hub, was established "to preserve the history of glassmaking and the skills of handcrafting glass in the typical South Jersey style." The village is maintained as a nonprofit foundation by the Wheaton Historical Association. Here the early methods of blowing glass are demonstrated by longtime gaffers like Henry William Davis, who worked at the Victor Durand glassworks with Ralph Barber, and by students who are being taught the art of free-blown glass. The Museum of Glass at the village has an outstanding collection of early glass to fascinate the collector.

Nineteenth-century cherry linen press reflecting earlier Dutch influence. Attributed to
Matthew Egerton, Jr., ca. 1825. *Courtesy The Hudson Shop, Inc., Red Bank*

Matthew Egerton

Three Generations of Cabinetmakers

Very fine American period furniture was crafted by lesser known cabinet-makers whose work was a unique combination of personal and regional motifs imposed on traditional English design. Notable among these early artisans were the three generations of Egertons, distinguished contemporaries of John Goddard of Newport, William Savery of Philadelphia, and Duncan Phyfe of New York.

Sometime prior to the Revolution, "MATTHEW EGERTON, CABINET-MAKER, IN BURNET STREET. NEW BRUNSWICK, (N. J.)," became established. Examples of the mid to late 18th-century Hepplewhite style secretaries, sideboards, chests, and desks he is known to have made are uncommon, and his work is more often attributed than identified. Egerton's furniture was never signed and has rarely been found with the (oval) label quoted above intact. His later works especially are also frustratingly indistinguishable from those of his son.

Egerton worked in mahogany with great artistry, using the beautifully grained wood to enhance the grace of English design. Veneers, bands of satinwood, and delicate foliate inlay are typical, as are the dominant oval inlays on drawer and cabinet fronts. While exquisite care was taken with the obvious, Egerton was considerably more pragmatic about interiors. Here the main concern appears to have been structural; the joints are carefully strengthened with blocks, but interior finishing is often less refined than might be expected. Like most American craftsmen, Egerton also used native woods. An inventory which appeared in the *New Brunswick Advertiser* of September 2, 1803, to announce the dispersal of the cabinetmaker's estate includes "a large stock of excellent seasoned stuff, consisting of mahogany, cherry, black walnut and bilsted boards [as well as] a small pile of chestnut rails."

LEFT: Rare Sheraton style corner wash-stand with crotch mahogany veneer, brass pulls; ca. 1800. ABOVE: Duplicate of the label on the washstand. The label was used by Matthew Egerton and by Matthew Egerton, Jr. after his father's death in 1802. From an end table at the Old Dutch Parsonage in Somerville, New Jersey, exhibited at The Newark Museum. Above: *Courtesy The Newark Museum.* Left: *Courtesy H. & R. Sandor, Inc., New Hope. Photo: Helga Photo Studio.*

A patriot of probable English lineage, Matthew Egerton was born in 1739 and was a private in the State Militia during the Revolution. In later years he was warden, then vestryman of Christ Church in New Brunswick. Married to Catelyna (Catherine) Voorhees, Egerton was father of two daughters and three sons, one of whom became a cabinetmaker. Another son, Luke, matriculated at Queen's College (now Rutgers University) and became a teacher. When Matthew Egerton died on May 3, 1802, his estate contained the effects of a comfortable existence: "a complete set of cabinetmaker's tools of every description, some very valuable household furniture," a small collection of books, a "gin case with four square bottles (valued at fifty cents)," a coffee mill, several properties, and the heritage of his fine skills.

Like his father, Matthew Egerton, Jr. was a superb craftsman. He began his own distinguished career in cabinetmaking alongside his father in 1785 and remained at the Burnet Street address for more than fifty years. He was also a landowner, a person of means and prominence. During his father's lifetime, the patronymic *Jr.* was used on the octagonal and scalloped edge labels on which he styled himself "joiner and cabinetmaker." On the oval labels used afterward, the *Jr.* is dropped, compounding the difficulty of distinguishing between the generations.

The late 18th- and early 19th-century furniture "MADE and SOLD by MATTHEW EGERTON, Junior, Joiner and Cabinetmaker, New-Brunswick, NEW-JERSEY.—No.—" was in the manner of Chippendale, Sheraton, and Hepplewhite, as well as in the Empire style and the old Dutch tradition. Cellarettes, sideboards, and demi-lune tables were made in suites of excellent mahogany. The numerous secretaries, sewing tables, bureaus, chests, bedsteads, tall clock cases (for Leslie & Williams of New Brunswick and Joakim Hill of Flemington), and the great Dutch clothespress known as a *kas* were variously of mahogany, finely grained cherry (the Dutch kas often with walnut moldings), and other fruitwoods. No chairs were made. During this period, the furniture of the two Egertons evolved into more distinctive form. Small knobs gradually

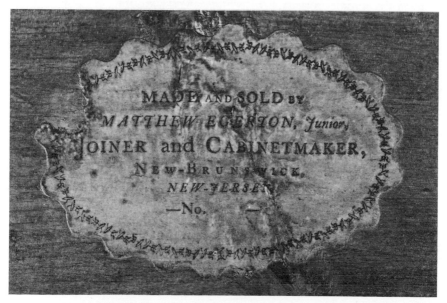

Hepplewhite-style mahogany demi-lune dining tables with satinwood banding and castors. Matthew Egerton, Jr., 1790s. Ht. 29 in., length 47 in., depth 23 in. DETAIL: scalloped-edge label used by Matthew Egerton, Jr. during his father's lifetime. *The New Jersey State Museum Collection, Trenton*

supplanted oval brasses, drops became more original, graduated diamond banding was introduced on the tapered furniture legs, diamond-shaped insets protected keyhole surrounds, and an element of restrained classicism became evident in the use of colored urn inlays.

Carving, the extensive use of native woods, and a certain diversity of enterprise are most apparent in the third generation, knowledge of which is largely derived or inferred from old records and inventories. No labeled pieces from this time have been found.

Of Matthew Jr.'s three sons, two became cabinetmakers, surviving their father's death in 1837 by only a year. The eldest, John Bergan Egerton, was independently established, though not within the scope of the 1829 map and directory of New Brunswick landholders and proprietors. An insight into the materials he used and the nature of his life is provided by an inventory of his "goods and chattels," presented to Rutgers University in the 1920s by a prominent New Brunswick attorney. In this listing are quantities of the mahogany, cherry, walnut, and bilsted (sweet-gum) woods used earlier, as well as curled maple, poplar, white pine, walnut coffin materials, carving tools, glass and brass knobs, and castors. Augmented by "rights and credits & personal property," bonds, notes, and shares of stock in the New Brunswick Fire Insurance Company, the appraised value of John Bergan's estate in 1838 was $5,612.31.

Evert Egerton, the younger son, continued to make furniture at Burnet Street

Hepplewhite-style late 18th-century serpentine-front sideboard; mahogany with delicate satinwood inlay and banding. Attributed to Matthew Egerton, New Brunswick. No label. *Courtesy Dr. and Mrs. Edward Bloustein* and *Rutgers, the State University. Photo: Andrew Jacobs*

after his father's death. The partnership with his father was known as Matthew Egerton (Jr.) & Son until 1825, and as Egerton & Son thereafter. The furniture produced by this member of the family was, however, less in the tradition of fine cabinetmaking. Simpler pieces were executed, and the crafting of parts in quantity foretold the beginning of the Industrial Revolution. Old records and accounts disclose further divergence from the past, in the billing for a walnut coffin "rais'd. and lined" and in payment by Rutgers College to "M. Egerton & Son" for the papering of rooms.

With the deaths of Matthew Egerton, Jr. in 1837 and of John Bergan and Evert in the following year, an era had truly passed. The workshop in Burnet Street was acquired by Isaac G. Sillcocks, whose solicitation of "a share of patronage [on] as good terms as at any other establishment in this city, or EXCHANGE FOR COUNTRY PRODUCE" appeared in the New Brunswick press. In the 1970s the sturdy but derelict brick structure and almost all trace of Burnet Street were removed for highway expansion.

Traditional paneled Dutch *kas* (clothespress) with octagonal Matthew Egerton, Jr. label used prior to 1802. Late 18th century. *Courtesy Monmouth County Historical Association, Freehold.* *Photo: Helga Photo Studio*

Rocking chair of cherry and maple made by Dan Ware, son of Maskell Ware. Seat is "checkered" style of rushing typical of Dan Ware chairs. *Courtesy The Newark Museum*

The Ware Chairmakers

A brief article datelined "Mays Landing, N. J., Feb. 24" and picked up by the New York *Herald Tribune* in 1934 carried the headline: "Last of Four Generations of Chairmakers to Quit; No Heirs Left to Carry On at Jersey Handicraft Plant." The announcement brought an end to more than 150 years of expert chairmaking by the Ware family of Roadstown, in Cumberland county.

The making of the sturdy but handsome rush-bottom, slat-backed chairs, so honored by collectors today, began with Maskell Ware, who was born in southern Jersey in 1766. As a young man, he was apprenticed to John Lanning, chairmaker of Salem, New Jersey. Once he had learned his craft, he opened his own shop in Roadstown. He was such a meticulous craftsman that even the final rubbing of his chairs was often done with the palm of his hand because the oil of the skin gave a fine patina.

In 1790 Maskell Ware married Hannah Simpkins and purchased land for a farm in Roadstown from John Lanning for 20 shillings. Here they raised four daughters and seven sons. The sons were apprenticed to their father and five of them—Thomas, John, William, Reuben, and Dan—followed their father's occupation and became master chairmakers.

Each of the Ware craftsmen left his hallmark on his work. Maskell used globular, ball-like turnings on the front rungs and on the finials that finish the back posts. Other Wares used oval or pear-shaped finials. William made the lightest chair of all the Wares. After interviewing the family members in 1926, Mabel Crispin Powers reported in her article, "The Ware Chairs of South Jersey," that the consensus was that "Uncle William made a dainty chair."

Maskell Ware side chair ca. 1790 with globular, ball-like turnings on the front rung and on the finials that finish the back posts. *Courtesy The Newark Museum. Photo: Armen Photographers*

Dan Ware was more experimental in the use of woods. All of the brothers used swamp maple, plain or curly, as their father did, but Dan also used cherry or walnut and sometimes combined different woods in the same chair.

While the turnings of the front rungs and the shapes of the finials differed with the individual taste of each Ware chairmaker, the manner of working remained constant. Native wood, which Maskell and his sons obtained from the area surrounding their home, was always used. The three-sided rushes for the seats were personally gathered from nearby marshes in summer, carried home in bundles, and carefully cured. Nails were never used in Ware chairs. The wood for the frames was allowed to become dry on the outside but left slightly green inside. The rungs were made from completely dry wood, and as the green posts shrank on the dried rungs, an extremely tight fit was achieved.

The Wares used two styles of rushing for the seats: "straight," with each strand overlapping another; and "checker," with four strands overlapping the next four and forming a checkered diagonal. Dan Ware was known for using only the checker-type rushing.

The Wares made many kinds of slat-back chairs: dining chairs, handsome rockers with broad arms, children's chairs, ladies' sewing chairs, armchairs, junior desk chairs, and even highchairs. Rockers, an American invention dating back to 1772, were added to the straight chairs beginning with Maskell.

Known for their excellent proportions and unsurpassed comfort, Ware chairs, which graced many South Jersey farmhouses and village homes, are highly valued today. An early Ware tradition was the making of chairs as wedding gifts for family members, and some of these fine pieces may still be scattered in parts of South Jersey.

Fortunately for the collector, the Ware brothers apprenticed their own sons, and the chairmaking tradition continued through four generations. With the retirement in 1934 of George Ware, the great-grandson of Maskell, the tradition ended. The chairs, some of which have survived intact since the late 1700s, are testimony to Ware craftsmanship.

TOP: "Deers Chase." Exuberantly detailed sgraffito plates of overlapping design. David Spinner, ca. 1800–1810. BOTTOM LEFT: Youthful Continental soldiers with fife and drum, rather more woebegone appearing than stalwart. Pennsylvania sgraffito plate. David Spinner, ca. 1800. BOTTOM RIGHT: A pensive young couple on a garden stroll depicted with formality and grace in sgraffito. David Spinner, ca. 1810. *Given by John T. Morris. Courtesy Philadelphia Museum of Art*

Pennsylvania Sgraffito

David Spinner

In country homes where there was no porcelain or pewter to grace a mantel or fill a cupboard shelf, the Pennsylvania redware pottery called sgraffito often could be found. Known in Germany from the late 16th century, this type of earthenware became especially popular with the German–Swiss population of eastern Pennsylvania during the mid 18th and early 19th centuries. Decorative rather than functional, the pottery's naturally warm and attractive reddish-brown hue was a result of iron oxide impurities released during the firing process. A luxury frequently given as a gift, sgraffito-ware suggested gentility and, like all folk art, indicated pride of place and tradition.

The word "sgraffito," from the Italian *sgraffiare* (to scratch), refers to the method by which the design was incised through a light-colored slip to expose portions of the underlying redware. The design itself was either stencil traced or hand drawn with a quill. Borders were a common embellishment, as were sentiments, usually lettered in the old native German. Popular motifs included numerous depictions of the Continental soldier, which may have been a stylized adaptation of the German cavalier. Blossoming flowers, birds, tulip designs, animals, and patterns were also common. However, the charm of sgraffito was perhaps best expressed in the renderings of country life and its pleasures: hounds and the hunt, or a mount well sat. The designs were enlivened by bold and subtle flourishes of color derived from naturally occurring metal oxides. Reds, oranges, and browns were obtained from iron salts; other browns came from manganese dioxide; shades of green from copper salts (the residue of scrap copper burned in the kiln); and a strong blue from oxides of cobalt, which intensified to a lustrous black when applied directly to unglazed redware.

More than fifty potters are known to have made sgraffito in Bucks, Berks, and Montgomery counties. One of the foremost of these craftsmen was David Spinner—a prominent citizen, justice of the peace, and facile artist. Of Swiss descent, Spinner was born in Pennsylvania on May 16, 1758. His beautifully sketched and detailed sgraffito plates, sometimes paired and of overlapping or connecting design, were made at the pottery on his farm at Willow Creek in Milford Township, Bucks County.

Spinner's plates are notable for their considerable sophistication within the context of traditional folk design. In the hunting scenes especially, the manners, mores, attitudes, and dress of the gentry are captured with engaging spontaneity

Pennsylvania redware sgraffito plate; folk art modeled after traditional design. Pictured, an ingenuous Federal bird and shield motif crowned by an eagle head whimsically suggesting Franklin's turkey. Highly collectible. Artist unknown, ca. 1820s. *Courtesy Mitchell and Susan Bunkin, Pipersville. Photo: Christian Mattheson*

and wealth of detail, providing a uniquely interesting record of late 18th- and early 19th-century rural society. The earliest authenticated Spinner plates date to around 1800, the last to 1811, the year of his death. When signed, the plates are inscribed in English "David Spinner his Make [or] David Spinner Potter," in a gracefully disciplined 18th-century hand.

Though Spinner's work is rare, many fine examples of sgraffito, slip-decorated pottery, brush-painted work, spatter- and spongeware are to be found in antique shops in Bucks County and elsewhere, and at public sale. Among the many potters who excelled in this genre were Andrew Headman, Georg Hübener, Christian Klinker, Johannes Neesz (probably at one time an apprentice to Spinner), and Jacob Taney of Pennsylvania. Philip Durell, John McCulley, and the Prudens were respected sgraffito potters in New Jersey.

Tall clock with works by Joakim Hill, Flemington. Mahogany case attributed to Matthew Egerton, Jr., New Brunswick, ca. 1800. Ht. 94½ in., w. 19¼ in., finials missing. *Courtesy The Newark Museum. Photo: Armen Photographers*

Joakim Hill
The Country Clockmaker

During the 18th and early 19th centuries, when noting time was less a preoccupation than an art and individual workshops flourished, a number of excellent clockmakers were located in New Jersey and Bucks County.

One of the most prolific was Joakim Hill of Hunterdon County, a figure remembered as much for the imprint of his personality as for his abilities in fabricating the tall, dignified timepieces of the day. Less innovator than craftsman, Hill was a country clockmaker who worked with components largely furnished by others. In the final assemblage, however, his skills are most enduringly apparent, and his fine eight-day case clocks bear the mark of the artisan as well as his name.

In the small brick building near Copper Hill, purchased about 1814 and equipped with large bellows and what was by all accounts a very "pretty" engine he had fashioned himself, Hill worked with brass parts that had been roughly cast in English machine shops. Here he meticulously refined, polished, and assembled the rack and snail mechanisms, improving the tone of the strike with an opening directly behind the gong. Though his small workshop was no farther from home than across the road, Hill was nevertheless said to have established his bailiwick in the family dining room. An aspect of life not unheard of today, it was more remarkable for the eventual presence of three sons and four daughters.

The many clocks on which Hill labored have similar characteristics. The moon-phase dials, typically English and representative of the era, may have been imported. Their origin is not known. All bear the name of the Flemington

Joakim Hill Hepplewhite-style mahogany case clock, ca. 1820. Moon phase dial with concise, ornate signature and scroll. *From the original in the New Jersey Historical Society, Newark. Photo: Jack Sheehan*

clockmaker in prominent black letters across the lower portion of the face. The Hepplewhite-style mahogany cases—inlaid, columned, scrolled, and surmounted by brass spheres—are prime examples of the cabinetmaker's art and cherished by collectors. Though most commonly unsigned, they are known to have been crafted by John Tappen (Tappan) of Flemington, John Scudder (Westfield), James Topping (Chester), a one-time apprentice of Scudder, and Oliver Parsell of New Brunswick. A tall case has also been tentatively attributed to Matthew Egerton, Jr., the New Brunswick cabinetmaker whose work is discussed elsewhere in the introduction.

Though details of the clockmaker's early life and apprenticeship are lost, an extraordinary recollection by Flemington resident Judiah Higgins (made in 1892 and recounted in a 1922 article in the weekly *Hunterdon County Democrat*) places young Hill in the Flemington shop of Thomas Williams, a clockmaker, sometime around the year 1800. Shortly after this and in the two decades following, Hill established his reputation. In an interview written in 1905, Hill was said by his daughter Martha to have attributed the later decline in popularity of his stately clocks to "Yankee" trade incursions; and it is true that by 1820 or 1825 demand was for the new flexibility and sophistication of mantel and banjo clocks, early products of the Industrial Revolution.

Records indicate that Joakim Hill was born to Isaac and Mary Hunt Hill at their farm in Amwell on November 25, 1783. On September 4, 1813, he married Martha Barcroft of Kingwood, leaving the Presbyterian church, of which he was a comparatively recent member (and his father an elder), to worship as his wife wished in the new Methodist congregation. "His clocks, however," observed the unknown writer in the December 14, 1922 edition of the *Democrat*, "were neither Presbyterian nor Methodist, just keeping time and leaving matters of salvation and the soul to other members of the household."

The couple, who had seven children, farmed and purchased parcels of land as the years passed. The "ten acres, one quarter and three perches" of one such property, measured in chains and links, is recorded in an 1830 certificate of indenture (a deed and mortgage) extant in the archives of the Hunterdon County Historical Society.

Hill was a familiar sight in the rural Hunterdon countryside for more than a half-century after his most prolific years as a clockmaker were ended. Precise, individualistic to the verge of eccentricity, he is affectionately limned by Alex B. Allen in the May 1905 issue of *The Jerseyman*: a figure of short stature, black haired even into advancing age, "trudging along on his little brown mare, a sheepskin for a saddle and a small supply of tools for repairing clocks." This he accomplished by simple means. Hill first removed the works and cleansed them in a mixture of ashes and boiling water. A hickory nut clasped in heated tongs released drops of oil exactly where needed to lubricate the mechanism.

Joakim Hill Hepplewhite-style mahogany case clock, ca. 1815. Moon phase dial with gracefully expansive signature; unembellished. *From the original in the New Jersey Historical Society, Newark. Photo: Jack Sheehan*

The date of repair and Hill's signature were written in white chalk inside the door of the case, an interesting record still visible in a number of old timepieces.

During his last years, Hill lived at the home of his daughter Martha at 76 Orchard Street in Newark, a narrow row building no longer standing, where he died April 12, 1869. He is buried beside his wife in the cemetery of the Presbyterian Church in Flemington.

A full-winged eagle and panoply of thirteen stars detailed in the center of an exceptional machine-woven cotton spread. Made by the Rutgers Factory, Paterson. *From a private collection. Photo: The Smithsonian Institution*

Col. Henry Rutgers and
the Rutgers Factory

Of the textiles that survive the era of the first cotton mills, none is more intriguing than the handsome machine-woven spread acquired by a prominent New Jersey collector in 1951 at an antiques show in Westchester County, New York. An outstanding example of early power-loom weaving, it is still more remarkable for the tantalizing threads of New Jersey history woven into its graceful design.

Patterned in stylized flowers and foliage reminiscent of crewel work, the heavy 99" x 107" cream-colored spread has a full-winged eagle and the thirteen stars of the new Republic at its center. Beneath the formal tasseled swag along the spread's perimeter, the name of Col. Henry Rutgers and the year 1822 are woven into a simple border. Equally conspicuous, though more perplexing, is the attribution to Rutgers Factory.

Considerably more is known about the owner of the factory than about the counterpane itself. One of the most celebrated figures in New Jersey history, Col. Henry Rutgers was a New Yorker widely esteemed for his philanthropy. An aristocrat of Dutch lineage, he was born October 7, 1745, was an early graduate of King's College (Columbia), and served as an officer throughout the Revolution. He also occupied the position of elder in the Reformed Dutch Church, was a member of the New York Assembly, and an active participant in the political affairs of his day.

The benefactor of numerous religious and humanitarian endeavors, Col. Rutgers is lastingly associated with the state university at New Brunswick, established by the Dutch Church in 1766. Chartered as Queens College, after the consort of George III, it was a foundering institution in 1825 when its trustees and the General Synod successfully petitioned the New Jersey State Legislature for a change in name to Rutgers College "as a mark of their respect for his character, and in gratitude for his numerous services rendered the Reformed Dutch Church." Along with a new infusion of spirit, Col. Rutgers subsequently gave the sum of $200 for the purchase of the college bell and endowed the annual award of a gold medal for excellence in the then existent medical school. In a codicil to his will dated March 9, 1826, Rutgers declared his intention of bequeathing a $5,000 bond and the 6 percent interest accruing from it. This provision was, however, withdrawn on March 27. The sum was instead bestowed during his lifetime and administered by the General Synod for the immediate benefit of the college.

A man of independent wealth, Rutgers augmented his considerable fortune through the long-term leasing of his real estate holdings, having at the time of his death 429 lots appraised at $907,949. One of these properties may indeed have been the cotton mill in Paterson, New Jersey, developed by others on a lease arrangement.

The facts may only be surmised from a unique religious and industrial *Census of Paterson, New Jersey,* undertaken between 1825 and 1832 by the Reverend Samuel Fisher, D.D. In 1825, the mill was recorded as "Rutger's Cotton Factory, Shaw, Cross & Berry"; in 1827, as "Rutgers Cotton Factory, John W. Berry & Co."; in 1829, as "Rutgers Cotton Factory, J. W. Berry"; and in 1832, two years after Col. Rutgers' death, as "The Cotton Mill of John W. Berry." In 1825, there were as many as 100 persons employed at the mill, which was an important commercial enterprise in early Paterson; 45 power looms were in use by 1827—with "capital in buildings, machinery, &c.," amounting to $60,000; 510,000 yards of cloth were woven in 1829, valued at $38,250.

The background and duration of Rutgers' association with the mill are unknown. Only twenty shares of stock are mentioned in his will. These were established in a trust fund of ten shares each for two minors, James Van Horn Lawrence and Samuel Forbert, Junior, with the hope that young Forbert "will follow the business of spinning and weaving at that Factory or some other." Though Rutgers probably did not engage in the everyday affairs of the business, he contributed a respected name and perhaps financial underwriting as well. Major production at the mill was undoubtedly profitably utilitarian. Hitherto, textiles had been laboriously woven at home or imported at great expense from England or France. The beautiful signed spread, representative of the highest quality of manufacture, may be the very same "counterpane offered by Col. Rutgers, wrought with much taste, [which] claimed the attention of the committee" at the annual cattle show and fair in New York, described in the November 20, 1822 *Paterson Chronicle.*

Rutgers died February 17, 1830, at the age of nearly eighty-five. A bachelor,

Detail of the 99 in. × 107 in. cream-colored counterpane, enigmatically signed "Col. Henry Rutgers" and dated 1822. Documented by The Smithsonian Institution. *From a private collection. Photo: The Smithsonian Institution*

he left the greatest portion of his estate to William B. Crosby, the grandson of his sister Catherine. During his long life, he not only regally entertained Washington and Lafayette but also welcomed the chiefs of the Creek Nation to a parade of militia on the grounds of his mansion in Rutgers Place. He was a longtime regent of the University of the State of New York, president of the Free School Society, and a trustee of Rutgers College and of Princeton University. As a Republican elector, he was also instrumental in the election of Jefferson and Burr. He was vigorously opposed to slavery and a member of the 1819 committee of correspondence founded to stop its spread. Rutgers' will, drafted in 1823, makes known his "desire & Will that my negro Wench slave named Hannah being superannuated be supported out of my estate." A virtually unknown codicil, dated March 21, 1828, written during a "long and protracted illness [gives and bequeathes] to my Executors in trust and for the use of the Colonization society at Washington whether incorporated or not and by whatsoever name it may be called and known, the sum of $1,000 for the purpose of transporting free People of Colour to Liberia in Africa, and in no event to be directed from that object."

Hound-handled stoneware pitcher, ca. 1829–1833, from D. & J. Henderson displays hunting scenes in relief on the body and a hound with its head resting on its paws forming
the handle. *Courtesy The New Jersey State Museum Collection, Trenton. Gift of J. Lion-
berger Davis. Photo: Joe Crilley*

The Hendersons of Jersey City

Little is known about David Henderson and even less about his brother, known only as J. Henderson, but the firm they established at Jersey City was so innovative that it has been called "the cradle of the pottery industry in the United States."

The brothers were born in Scotland in the late 1700s. Nothing else is known about them until 1828, when they purchased the failing, three-year-old Jersey Porcelain and Earthenware Company. The name was changed to D. & J. Henderson, and the new owners adopted a mark with the name and "Jersey City" imprinted in a circle. Only two years later they were awarded a silver medal at the Franklin Institute for their exhibition of flint stoneware of "superior quality." A price list of the period shows that they were producing "pitchers, coffee pots, tea pots, flower pots, butter boxes, spittons, mugs, jars with covers, tea tubs, pipkins, nursery lamps, water coolers, ink stands, and assorted toys." Today's collector might well blanch at the prices. Coffeepots commanded the highest price at $15 a dozen, and the now-prized toby pitchers sold for $9 a dozen.

It was this small company that first introduced the concept of producing stoneware in molds. The Hendersons were also the first to bring out a fine quality rockingham, a brown-glazed earthenware that is sometimes spattered before firing to produce a mottled effect. By using molds rather than relying on the individualized work of the potter, elaborate pieces designed by expert modelers could be produced inexpensively and in quantity.

In 1833, the company was reorganized and the name changed to The American Pottery Manufacturing Company. David Henderson was still at its

Stoneware toby jug made by D. & J. Hendrson, ca. 1829. The jugs, named for an
English character, Sir Toby Belch, became popular in America in the 1800s and were
produced in quantity by many potteries. *Courtesy The Brooklyn Museum, Dick S. Ramsay
Fund*

head, but J. was no longer mentioned in any of the company's records. Two new
marks were adopted at this time: one is a flag, with the name of the firm,
"Am. Pottery Manufg. Co.," imprinted inside it; the second is an elliptical
design, with the name and address imprinted around the edge.

A series of designers, many of them from England, was employed by Henderson to create the models for his wares. One of the best known was Daniel

Greatbach, a brilliant modeler who came from Staffordshire in 1839. It was in Jersey City that he created the first of the famous rockingham hound-handled pitchers, adapted from an English piece. The pitcher has as the handle a hound with its head resting on its paws and elaborate hunting scenes in relief on the body.

The pitchers, as well as toby mugs designed by Greatbach, became so popular in the mid-1800s that they were copied by modelers in other potteries. Greatbach himself went to Bennington, Vermont, where he designed hound-handled pitchers for the United States Pottery Company. Because a high-quality rockingham ware was produced in quantity at Bennington, the ware is sometimes erroneously called Bennington ware. But rockingham of fine quality was made earlier at Jersey City.

As little is known about David Henderson's death as is known about his personal life. He was killed in 1845 in an accidental shooting incident in the Adirondacks. After his death, the firm passed into new hands, and only white earthenware was produced. The days of innovation at the Jersey City company were over.

Rockingham teapot made in Jersey City between 1838 and 1845, the period that Daniel Greatbach was with the American Pottery Company. *Courtesy The Newark Museum.* *Photo: Armen Photographers*

Baby Paterson. Colt pocket pistol serial no. 22; .34 caliber, 4½ in. barrel, cased. Including walnut-headed bullet mold, blued steel combination tool, brass cylindrical flask and key. Bequest of Mrs. Samuel Colt (Elizabeth Hart Jarvis). *Courtesy Wadsworth Atheneum, Hartford. Photo: E. Irving Blomstrann, Photographer*

Samuel Colt

"Colt's Patent. Paterson, N.J."

Colt firearms, one of the romantic legends of the early West, were first manufactured in Paterson, New Jersey. From 1836 to 1842, anywhere from two thousand to as many as five or six thousand repeating revolvers and longarms were produced at the "Gun Mill" on Van Houten and Mill Streets by the Patent Arms Manufacturing Company, founded by Samuel Colt. Now part of the Great Falls Historic District, the old four-story brownstone structure was an easily distinguished landmark from its earliest days with its picket fence of wooden guns and gilded rifle emblazoned on the weathervane atop its bell tower.

During the six years the Paterson factory remained in business, a succession of Colt repeating revolvers, rifles, carbines, shotguns, and some muzzle-loaders was made. These were the weapons of the last generation of fur trappers and traders, the Texas Navy and Texas Rangers, soldiers in the Seminole War, and any civilian or Indian fighter looking for the advantage of being able to fire at least five shots without reloading. Along the Santa Fe Trail, wagon trains led by Kit Carson were defended with Colt arms.

All Colt Paterson firearms were made with the revolving breech mechanism on which the patents were based. Models included the .28, .31, .34, and .36 caliber single-action pistols; a later heavier .36 caliber pistol with a nine-inch barrel; the eight-shot rifles of .34, .44, and .47 caliber; a .52 caliber six-shot rifle; and a .69 caliber seven-shot rifle. Standard guns were of blued steel with polished wood grips. Custom models were optionally engraved and inlaid, embellished with precious metals, and fitted with ivory or pearl stocks.

Samuel Colt, born at Lord's Hill in Hartford, Connecticut on July 19, 1814, was the son of Christopher and Sarah Caldwell Colt. His father was a respected

TOP: Colt Paterson carbine serial no. 118; .525 caliber, 6 shots, 24⅜ in. barrel. Standard decoration by W. L. Ormsby; roll engraved on cylinder. Bequest of Mrs. Samuel Colt (Elizabeth Hart Jarvis). BOTTOM: Colt Paterson rifles: (above) serial no. 125; .36 caliber, 8 shots, 32¼ in. barrel; refinished; (below) serial no. 189; .34 caliber, 8 shots, 31⅞ in. barrel. Engraved silver Colt horse heads inlay on stock cheek pieces. Bequest of Mrs. Samuel Colt (Elizabeth Hart Jarvis). *Courtesy Wadsworth Atheneum, Hartford. Photos: E. Irving Blomstrann, Photographer*

merchant and proprietor of a mercantile factory at Ware, Massachusetts. Colt's early achievements were impressive. Motherless before the age of seven, and perhaps not greatly impeded in his childhood enthusiasms, he had by the age of eleven devised a submarine mine which successfully capsized a raft on Ware Pond. A torpedo launched four years later on the Fourth of July precipitated his departure from the Academy at Amherst, ending his formal education.

The first model of the repeating revolver was carved in wood by the sixteen-year-old Colt aboard the East Indiaman *Corvo* during a year-long voyage from Boston to Calcutta intended to temper adventure with mental discipline. Assisted by his father on his return from the sea, Colt commissioned Anson Chase of Hartford to make a prototype revolver. Its explosion on firing was a costly failure, and Colt left the factory at Ware to raise additional funds. This departure occasioned the following timeless letter (excerpted from *The Book of Colt Firearms* by R. Q. Sutherland and R. L. Wilson):

> MY DEAR SON: You are once more on the move to seek your fortune, and must remember that your future prospects and welfare depend on your own exertions. Should you seek diligently until you find some kind of useful employ, I have no doubt but you may do well. Do not despond, my son, but be resolute and go forward. It matters but little what employ you embark in, if it is but an honest one and well followed up, with a determination to excel in whatever you undertake. This will enable you to obtain a good living, and to command respect.
>
> Your affectionate father,   C. Colt
> March 30th, 1832

For the next three years, the determined inventor donned spectacles and metamorphosed as "Dr. Coult," a successful traveling showman who lectured and demonstrated the wonders of nitrous oxide (laughing gas) to audiences across the country and in Canada. Nearly six feet tall, lean, well spoken, heroically incautious, the "Dr." was said to have been called upon to treat cholera victims aboard a Mississippi riverboat on which he was performing. The treatment of the disease, then new to this country, was at best speculative; Colt responded (harmlessly) with the means at hand, thus providing perhaps the only known effective treatment with nitrous oxide!

Colt's first patents, obtained in England and France in 1835, were followed by American patents granted on February 25, 1836. Colt was then twenty-one. Eight days later, on March 5, the Patent Arms Manufacturing Company was

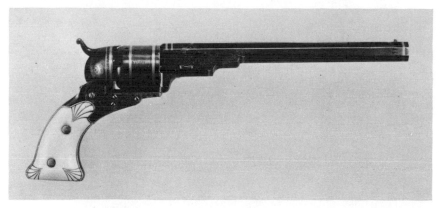

Colt Paterson holster pistol serial no. 984; .36 caliber, 9 in. barrel. A presentation piece with ivory handle, silver inlay, and engraving. Bequest of Mrs. Samuel Colt (Elizabeth Hart Jarvis). *Courtesy Wadsworth Atheneum, Hartford. Photo: E. Irving Blomstrann, Photographer*

chartered by the New Jersey Legislature. In April, the company announced a proposed capitalization of $230,000; and production began that summer.

Though Paterson was an early center of industrialization and members of the Colt family had long been prominent there, only about 60 percent of the stock was sold. The lack of government contracts also presaged the fiscal difficulties which ended in the company's bankruptcy in 1842. Reincorporated in 1848 in Hartford, where it is still very much in existence, the armory went on to renown after the Civil War (and Colt's death in 1862), manufacturing the Single Action Army Colt of the 1870s. It is this model, the gun that won the West, that is lastingly associated with Wyatt Earp, Bat Masterson, Billy the Kid, Wild Bill Hickok, Calamity Jane, and George Armstrong Custer.

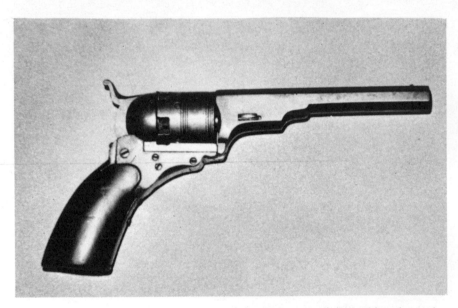

Rare Colt Paterson pocket pistol model 1836, .31 caliber. Blued steel with walnut grip, concealed trigger. *From a private collection. Photo: Sanford Jacobs*

Paperweights at Millville

Druggists' and physicians' bottles, vials, and patent medicine bottles were the main products of the Whitall Tatum glassworks at Millville, New Jersey in the 1800s. The highly sought after by-products were the creative work of the talented glassblowers who used their spare hours, usually the lunch hours, to produce unique decorative glass. Among the most ardently sought of these "offhand" pieces is the Ralph Barber rose, often called the Millville rose.

Born into a glassblowing family in Manchester in 1869, Barber and his family came to the United States when he was a young boy. His father first joined a glasshouse in Pennsylvania then moved his family to Millville when he took a job at Whitall Tatum & Co.

The young Barber soon joined his father at the Millville glasshouse. His older brother George, an experienced glassblower, worked in an Ohio plant and was later to attempt to help Ralph perfect his rose weight by sending him first ruby cullet from that state and in later years green cullet from Pennsylvania. But the colored glass that was most compatible with the clear glass at Millville came from E. P. Gleason Co. in Brooklyn. It is recorded that Barber ordered ruby glass, green, and opalescent from them, which helped make possible the beautiful rose weights so admired today.

Ralph Barber spent many hours studying the roses from his garden and an even longer time perfecting the crimps—metal tools shaped like roses—that would produce a lifelike rose inside the clear crystal ball. It was several years before he was satisfied that he had a good rose, and his best roses were created at Whitall Tatum from 1904 to 1912.

Most of the Barber weights have the rose upright, nestled in three opaque green leaves; occasionally the rose is tilted or suspended on its side. Colors of

the Barber rose are pale pink, rose pink, white, yellow, or deep ruby. The
weights have circular, footed pedestals, with a collar between the foot and the
rose.

Millville rose paperweight attributed to Ralph Barber. The rose inside the clear crystal
ball is deep pink and is nestled in three opaque green leaves. The best of the rose weights
were produced at the Whitall Tatum & Company glassworks, Millville, between 1904 and
1912. *Courtesy The Wheaton Historical Association, Millville*

During the time that Ralph Barber worked at Whitall Tatum, his talented coworkers were glassblowers Emil Stanger, Marcus Kuntz, John Ruhlander, and Michael Kane, all of whom made beautiful weights in the offhour time they had. In addition to the rose, the Millville lily was produced at Whitall Tatum. Earlier artisans experimented with the fountain, devil's fire, the swirl, and some plain, flat weights. Horses, dogs, eagles, and boats encased in the globe also came out of Millville.

An interesting account related by Edward Minns in *American Collector* magazine in 1938 offers one explanation as to why paperweight-making ended at Whitall Tatum. Most of the glasshouses of the day supplied all the clear glass, pots, and tools that the men used in their offhour blowing, and Whitall Tatum was no exception. The "offhand" pieces were fired in the same furnaces used for the regular orders of glassware. One night a thief broke into the ovens to steal the paperweights. When the oven doors were opened, the company's products, as well as the paperweights, were destroyed because they were exposed to the outside air prematurely. Whether or not this was the reason that precipitated the company's policy against "offhand" blowing, it was not the reason Ralph Barber's roses stopped appearing.

In 1912, Barber left Whitall Tatum to become plant superintendent at the Vineland Flint Glass Works, owned by Victor Durand. Here he supervised the exacting work of making tubes for vacuum bottles; later, when the Durand glasshouse was acquired by Kimble glass, he had an even more demanding task— supervising the production of precision X-ray tubes. Perhaps because of the exigencies of his position, he attempted few paperweights at Vineland.

Ralph Barber died in 1936. During his lifetime his reputation as a great American glassblower was attained because of his skill at blowing perfect X-ray tubes. The rose weights that he made in his spare hours are now cherished by collectors and museums. Today's collector might well wish that he had had more spare hours to create his perfect roses.

Exquisite 9 in. high Parian pitcher in the form of a child seated on a seashell and holding a ribbon that forms a handle. Designed by Walter Scott Lenox in 1887. *Courtesy Lenox, Inc., Trenton*

Walter Scott Lenox

Lenox porcelain, produced at Trenton, was the first American-made dinnerware to be used in the White House. It was purchased in 1913 during Woodrow Wilson's administration and is still used today by American Presidents. Before Wilson's time, White House dinnerware was imported from England, France, and Germany. Lenox, a lustrous, cream-colored porcelain that competes with any made in the world today, is the result of Walter Scott Lenox's dedication to quality and represents a triumph over the American preference in the late 1800s for European imports.

Walter Lenox was born in Trenton, a center of pottery-making, in 1859. Even as a young boy, he was fascinated by the art of fashioning beautiful objects from clay and observed the potters at work in a small factory near his home. Later he became an apprentice at Ott and Brewer, another Trenton pottery, where belleek, a thin, luminous porcelain originally made at Belleek in Ireland, was first produced in this country. While learning the practical skills of the potter, Lenox experimented with artistic and decorative effects. His creativity led to his becoming art director at Ott and Brewer.

By 1889 he was ready to open his own pottery, which was organized in partnership with Jonathan Coxon, Sr. and known as the Ceramic Art Company. When he acquired sole ownership in 1894, the little company was producing decorative belleek pieces. Lenox was always striving for a better product, and with the aid of financial backers, he started a larger factory in 1906 which became known as Lenox, Inc. Apparently, some of his backers were doubtful about the success of the enterprise because one of the stipulations was that the factory building be constructed so that it could be converted into a tenement if the pottery failed.

Delicately executed belleek basket designed by James Sheldon at Walter Scott Lenox's Ceramic Art Company, ca. 1900. Ht. 3 in., diam. 6¾ in. *Courtesy The Newark Museum Collection*

Success did not come easily; it took many years to attain the quality Lenox demanded. He was sometimes urged by friends to give up and manufacture cheaper, easily salable china. He was determined, however, to produce an American porcelain that could compete with the best of the European imports— imports which were so favored in the United States that many American manufacturers of the period stamped their ware with English marks. From the beginning, Lenox insisted on using his own mark.

In 1895, Lenox was stricken with blindness and paralysis. With the aid of associate Harry A. Brown, he continued his work, even though the company was not yet a financial success. Finally, after years of experimentation, a fine dinnerware made from belleek was produced; it became increasingly popular with the American public, and the company began to prosper.

Lenox died in 1920. He had not seen the porcelain that he had struggled to perfect, but he had realized his ideal, described by George Sanford Holmes in 1924 as "elevating American ceramic art to a place of primary importance."

His insistence on quality remains. Even now, any imperfect piece of his ware is destroyed before it gets to the marketplace.

Harry V. Shourds

Master Decoy Carver

The town of Tuckerton, a coastal community just west of Little Egg Harbor, in Ocean County, New Jersey, was the center of an area favored by sportsmen and wildfowl hunters during the late 1800s and early 1900s. In addition to the individual hunters, market gunners—men who killed the birds to be sold in America's markets—were extremely active and the shore bird population was in danger of becoming extinct.

During this period, before Congress passed the Migratory Bird Treaty Act prohibiting the killing of shore birds, the demand for handmade decoys was at its peak. One of the master decoy carvers of the time was Harry V. Shourds, who was born in Tuckerton in 1861.

A house painter by trade, Shourds as a young man began to whittle the likenesses of the ducks, geese, and shore birds that made their periodic migrations along the coastal flyway. Eventually he was to devote full time to this early avocation, producing thousands of expertly carved decoys that are now avidly sought by collectors.

The museum pamphlet *Decoys at the Shelburne Museum* relates that "because of Shourds' efforts, Tuckerton may be said to have been the handmade decoy capital of the United States." Records from the little railroad station at Tuckerton reveal that crates of Shourds' decoys were shipped up and down the Atlantic Coast from Maine to Georgia. The demand attests to the skill of the master carver.

Shourds had an expert knowledge of wood and was an artisan in realistically fashioning and painting the birds that were to be used to lure their real-life counterparts. Intimate attention to detail, grace in body structure, beautiful coloring, and superb carving skill combined to establish his reputation. He also must have had detailed knowledge of wildfowl habits—how they floated on the water, what proportion of the body was above the surface, how they looked when

lix

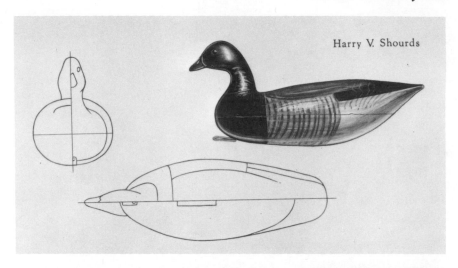

Harry V. Shourds

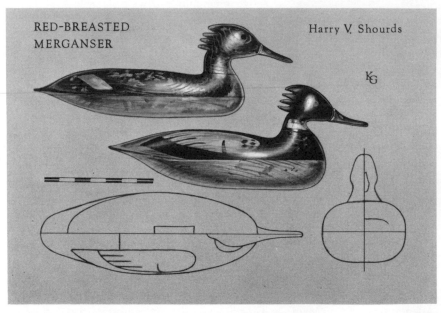

RED-BREASTED
MERGANSER

Harry V. Shourds

TOP: Harry V. Shourds' Brant. BOTTOM: Shourds' Red-Breasted Merganser drake (above) and hen. Drake: *Collection of Murray Mitterhoff*. Hen: *Collection of Pam and Armand Carney*. Brant: *Collection of Isabelle and John Hillman. Drawings by Kenneth L. Gosner, Curator of Zoology, The Newark Museum*

feeding—for his decoys were always properly weighted and rode in the water exactly right. Shourds' grandson, Harry V. Shourds, said that they floated perfectly, "like little boats."

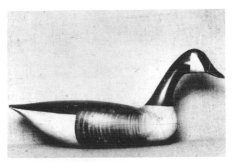

LEFT: Harry V. Shourds' shore bird, a Curlew. RIGHT: Shourds' Canada Goose. Curlew: *Collection of Murray Mitterhoff. Photo: Mary Sue Sweeney.* Canada Goose: *Collection of Isabelle and John Hillman. Photo: Kenneth L. Gosner, Curator of Zoology, The Newark Museum*

Shourds insisted on doing everything himself—no mean task considering the volume of fine decoys he produced. He chose the wood, usually cedar, fashioned, sanded, painted, weighted, and even managed the sale of his birds. William Mackey, in his book, *American Bird Decoys,* reports that during the height of the season, when practically every room in the Shourds house was crammed with decoys, he might occasionally ask one of his daughters to do some sanding. But, on the whole, his was a one-man undertaking.

Shourds died in Tuckerton in 1920, but his manner of carving was carried on by his son, Harry M. Shourds of Ocean City. His decoys, also highly collectible, are somewhat lighter and smaller than his father's and his output was on a much smaller scale. It was only a spare-time involvement, and he maintained his job as a painting contractor.

While most of the working decoys made today are mass produced in factories and are made of plastic, a few artisans carry on the tradition of hand-carving. Harry V. Shourds, named for his grandfather, practices the art in Seaville in Cape May County, hand-carving decoys and birds of all kinds with the skill inherited from two generations of wood sculptors. And along the coast at West Creek in Ocean County, a young house painter named Robert Daley makes them in his spare time. In 1977, his white swan confidence decoy won first prize at the World Championship Decoy Carving Competition.

Today, Shourds' decoys are no longer used as working lures. They are too valuable as examples of American folk art and are coveted by collectors. The hand-carved decoys that started out to work the marshes and bays along the Jersey coast are now more likely to be resting on mantelpieces or in museum cases.

(Left) a beguilingly pretty baby doll from the era of World War I. Bisque head made by the Fulper Pottery Company, Flemington; body from the Horsman Company, Trenton. The vertical Fulper mark is incised at the back of the head. (Right) German china doll in original dress, ca. 1860. Ht. 24 in. *Courtesy Raggedy Ann Antique Doll and Toy Museum, Flemington. Photo:* Hunterdon County Democrat

Fulper Dolls

World War I American Bisque

F
U
L
P
E

The vertical R trademark and distinguishing "Made in U.S.A.," are well known to doll collectors. Between 1918 and 1921, when trade with Germany was curtailed, the Fulper Pottery Company of Flemington, New Jersey manufactured thousands of hand-painted bisque doll heads, principally for the Amberg and Horsman Companies.

The pottery at Flemington, one of the oldest in the country, was founded by Abraham Fulper in 1805. It had been prosaically manufacturing quality tiles, vases, bowls, and crocks for more than a century when J. M. Stangl was brought in as ceramic engineer. It was Stangl who perfected the glazes for and introduced the distinctive art pottery that made the Fulper Company famous. It was also Stangl who prior to 1918 arranged to use the beautiful doll-head molds of the Armand Marseille Company, a German firm with a Gallic name.

Collectors identify the origin of these European-appearing dolls principally by the quality and tone of the bisque, which is not truly comparable to that of the most finely crafted French and German dolls of the period. Two rounded teeth are also typical of the American dolls. The Fulper name is incised vertically at the back of the head. "Made in U.S.A." is stamped into the base of the shoulders, which also contain two small holes through which the body was

LEFT: Porcelain and bisque *"Peterkin"* doll modeled after the character in the 19th-century Howard Pyle children's stories. Made by the Fulper Pottery Company, Flemington, 1920. Ht. 11 in. RIGHT: Popular "Kewpie" bisque doll. Designed by Rose O'Neill, impressed Fulper. Ht. 9 in. *Courtesy The Newark Museum. Photos: Armen Photographers*

sewn. Additional markings may indicate the name of the company for which the doll was made, as well as the head size and style.

In all, the Fulper Company produced at least 22 varieties of the bisque heads, including baby dolls, boy and girl dolls, and life-size mannequins for children's wear shops. Among the rare all-bisque dolls are "Peterkin," from the Howard Pyle children's story of the last century, and Rose O'Neill's immortal Kewpie.

The Fulper bisque head dolls, although inspired by foreign sources, are an excellent representation of their time and notable for being American made in an era when Europe dominated the market.

Antiquing in New Jersey
and Bucks County, Pennsylvania

Antique Shops

Key to the Listings

A (Antiques)	Conforming to U.S. Customs age criteria: 100 years for general articles; 50 years for "ethnographic objects made in traditional aboriginal styles." Equally important are consideration of design, workmanship, and materials; cultural and historic context.
C (Collectibles)	Items of collectible interest not of current manufacture.
PM	Prices marked.
Consignments	Consigned articles accepted for sale; terms and provisions by agreement.
Authentication	A signed notation on the bill of sale affirming representation of the article, date, and place of origin.

———— ◆ ————

For substantial acquisitions, a formal statement on business letterhead certifying attribution and date, provenance, physical characteristics, materials employed, and the presence of repairs or restoration.

Spanning Skyline to Ridgeline
The Northern Counties

Beautifully proportioned electroplated silver coffee pot with engraved foliate design, ribbed body and lid. Tiffany & Co., Newark, ca. 1885. Ht. 10 in. *Courtesy The Newark Museum. Photo: Armen Photographers*

Sussex County

Andover 07821

ANDOVER JUNCTION ANTIQUES & CRAFTS, Rt. 206, southbound (opp. Texaco Sta.).

Hours: 7 days 10–5

Primitives; jelly and jam cupboards, pie safes, blanket chests, hutches, tables. Civil War uniform accessories. Handcrafts on consignment; handicraft supplies. Also see Buttzville, Warren County.

A—PM. Wide range. Consignments. Authentication.

Prop. Jane Hoernlen, Susan Elizabeth Hauser   201–786–5800

THE FURNITURE EMPORIUM, INC., 139 Main St. (Rt. 206, southbound, intersection Rt. 517). *Also see* Repair and Restoration listing.

Hours: Mon. thru Fri. 8–6; Sat. 8–2 (flexible, call ahead suggested)

Primarily repair and restoration; cabinetry. Some antiques; a Jenny Lind cradle, early painted arrowback chairs, a 1910 wicker rocker. Unusual mill artifacts; enormous wood gears and screws; ox-cart wheels from South America at least a century old, crafted of rosewood, teakwood, lignum vitae.

A/C—Some prices marked. Wide range. Consignments. Authentication; age and value of furniture.

Prop. Dan Weldon   201–786–5118

THE GREAT ANDOVER ANTIQUE COMPANY, 124 Main St. (Rt. 206).
Hours: Daily 11–5. Closed Tues. & Wed.

Large collection, mostly American antiques. Primitives, early 19th- to early 20th-century furniture (including oak), in ready-to-use condition. Including cupboards, hutch tables, jam cupboards, pie safes, old baskets, crocks, and an old slant-back planked wooden bathtub, once copper lined. Delivery service. The residence dates to 1879; both stories filled.

A/C—PM. Wide range.

Prop. Patricia Heitman   201–786–6384

JEAN'S ANTIQUES, Main St. (Rt. 206, southbound; opp. Andover Hotel).
Mailing address: R. D. 1, Box 482, Newton 07860.

Hours: Winter: Sat. & Sun. 10–5. Summer: Thurs. thru Sun. 10–5

Oak and walnut furniture, turn-of-the-century to the '20s; some wicker. Located at Oak House Antiques.

C—PM. Wide range. Authentication.

Prop. Jean Doty   201–786–5969

LAKELAND GALLERIES, Rt. 206, southbound. *Also see* Auctioneers listing.
Hours: Thurs. thru Sun. 12–5

"Unusual antiques" preferred. Late 19th- and early 20th-century Oriental rugs. General line, including furniture, silver, some jewelry, glass. Weekly auctions outside; antiques auctions indoors once a month. Weekend flea market, rain or shine (antiques inside).

A/C—Most prices marked. Wide range. Authentication.

Prop. Tom Dwyer, Robert Larsen   201–786–6004

OAK HOUSE ANTIQUES, Main St. (Rt. 206, southbound; opp. Andover Hotel).

Hours: Winter: Sat. & Sun. 10–5. Summer: Thurs. thru Sun. 10–5

Twentieth-century furniture, prints, pictures. Shares premises with Jean's Antiques.

C—PM. Affordable/wide range.

Prop. Dale Long   201–786–5993

OLD MILL BOOKS, Rt. 206, southbound (opp. Texaco Station). Mailing address: P. O. Box 77, Stillwater 07875.

Hours: Sat. & Sun. 11–5

OLD MILL BOOKS *continued*

Specializing in used and rare books; emphasis on New Jersey, books on the South Pacific. Some antiques, small collectibles. Search service for books; mail orders. Libraries appraised. In a turn-of-the-century greengrocer's.

C/A—PM. Wide range. Consignments. Authentication.

Prop. Sam Tomlin, George Loukides   201–786–5344
                                                       383–5924

Culvers Lake 07875

RANDI ROLESON'S CULVER LAKE ANTIQUE BARN, Rt. 206, southbound. Mailing address: Box 55, Stillwater 07875.

Hours: Shop: Tues. thru Fri. 11–5; Sat., Sun., hols. 10–6. Closed Mon.
Flea Market: Sat., Sun., hols. 10–6; weather permitting

General line; furniture, china, crocks, books, bottles, and oddities. Selection of new books on antiques.

C—PM. Affordable. Authentication when possible.

Prop. Randi Roleson   201–948–9960

Frankford Twp. 07826

THE BLUE VASE, Rt. 206, southbound (at Lake Owassa turnoff). Mailing address: R. D. 2, Box 543, Branchville 07826.

Hours: 7 days 1–5

Sterling, silverplate, early American and English pewter; furniture, especially blanket chests. In a sixty-year-old former church. The quotation introducing the Auctioneers section is used courtesy of the Van Syckles.

A/C—PM. Wide range. Authentication when possible.

Prop. L. George Van Syckle   201–875–4296

Franklin 07416

1750 HOUSE, Franklin.

Hours: By appt.

General line in the red barn of the oldest house in Franklin. Primitives, porcelains from 1600 to 1890, paintings (primarily 19th century), Oriental antiquities. Legal and museum appraisals. New books on antiques. Oriental pieces purchased.

Prop. Marilyn Pardo   201–827–5018

A/C—PM. Wide range. Consignments. Authentication.

Fredon 07860

TRASH & TREASURES, Rt. 94, eastbound (6 mi. from Newton and from Blairstown). Mailing address: R. D. 2, Box 589, Newton 07860.

Hours: By chance or call ahead

Glass and china; Victorian furniture, oak, some early pieces; some old tools, wagon and carriage seats; general line. Also displayed, Mrs. Buchanan's hand-made lampshades, macramé, needlepoint, dried flower pictures and notepaper, theorem painting. Browsing invited.

A/C—PM. Wide range. Authentication.

Prop. K. Buchanan   201–383–6162

Lafayette 07848

BOGWATER JIM ANTIQUES, Rt. 15 and Beaver Run Rd. *Also see* Repair and Restoration listing.

Hours: Sat., Sun., hols. 9:30–6; weekdays by chance or appt.

Primitives, country furniture, accessories, unusual pieces. New and restored stained glass; stained glass repair. Caning, rushing; handmade splint baskets. Selection of dried flowers.

A/C; also new—PM. Wide range. Authentication when possible.

Prop. Don and Karen Kihlstrom   201–383–8170

LAMP LIGHTERS OF LAFAYETTE, Rt. 15. Mailing address: P. O. Box 64.

Hours: Mon. thru Sat. 10–6; Sun. 1–6. Closed Wed.

Victorian, oil and converted lamps. Also new lamps, decorator lampshades, lamp supplies.

C; also new—Some prices marked. Selective.

Prop. Betty and Don Platt   201–383–5513

PUMLEYE'S, Rt. 15.

Hours: Sun.; call ahead suggested

Country, in-the-rough, and formal period furniture, including Allison, Duncan Phyfe, Chippendale. Primarily antiques, some bric-a-brac.

A/C (some)—Most prices marked. Wide range. Authentication on request.

Prop. John Pumleye   201–383–2114

Montague 12771

CARPENTER'S ANTIQUES, Deckertown Tpk. (off Rt. 206, northbound at Clove Rd.).

Hours: Fri. thru Mon. 9–5

A country store and recreated barber shop; country store advertising and barber shop items a specialty. Some glassware, trade signs, Ohr pottery (Biloxi, Miss., 1885–1906). Furniture in-the-rough in the rear shed. Appraisals. "Absolutely no smoking."

C—PM. Affordable/Wide range.

Prop. James Carpenter   201–293–7297

CORNER ANTIQUES, Rt. 206, southbound (2 mi. east of Milford, Pa.).

Hours: After Memorial Day: Tues. thru Sun. 10–5. Closed Mon. Oct. 1– Dec. 31: Sat. & Sun. 10–5. Closed Jan., Feb., Mar.

American primitives; Pennsylvania Dutch pine, Pennsylvania redware, baskets, old quilts. Also glassware, Art Nouveau, Art Deco. Located at Old Colony Antiques.

A/C—Prices not marked. Wide range. Authentication when possible.

Prop. Sonia Gatzke   201–293–7312

OLD COLONY ANTIQUES, off Rt. 206, southbound. Mailing address: Box 554, R. D. 1, Port Jervis, N. Y. 12771. *Also see* Repair and Restoration listing.

Hours: After Memorial Day: Tues. thru Sun. 10–5. Closed Mon. Oct. 1– Dec. 31: Sat. & Sun. 10–5. Closed Jan., Feb., Mar.

American weight clocks from the 1830s, some earlier. Tall case and wall clocks, furniture; general line. Clocks purchased. Repair and restoration of clocks and antique furniture; furniture crafted of old wood. Also coffee, snacks, and country gifts at this congenial spot. Dealers welcome. Member Nat'l. Assoc. of Watch & Clock Collectors. On a pre-1800 farm. Also see Corner Antiques above.

A/C—PM. Wide range. Consignments. Authentication when possible.

Prop. Robert Pollara   201–293–7312 (bus.)
                                                          293–7359 (res.)

Newton 07860

THE CHURN ANTIQUES. Mailing address: R. D. 6, Box 495.
Hours: By appt.

THE CHURN ANTIQUES *continued*

Primitives, iron, pressed glass, silver, jewelry, lamps, and hanging fixtures; general line.

A/C—PM. Affordable. Authentication when possible.

Prop. Herb and Nancy Hallman   201–383–1593

THE CURIOSITY SHOP, 192 Spring St.

Hours: Mon. thru Sat. 12–5; Fri. 'til 9

General line of collectibles. Jewelry, old post cards, bottles, china, glassware, old signs, records. A small, in-town shop.

C—Most prices marked. Affordable. Consignments. Authentication.

Prop. Helen Terwilliger   201–383–4218

Sparta 07871

CENTURY HOUSE ANTIQUES, 24 Main St.

Hours: 7 days 10–5

Primarily European Victorian furnishings and accessories; marble-top furniture, antique wall clocks, cut and colored glass, bisque, majolica; reproductions and giftware. Occupying a stately gray and white Victorian residence and carriage house built in 1883 by a former Civil War colonel. The double entry doors are carved chestnut.

C; also new/A—PM. Affordable/Wide range. Authentication.

Prop. James E. Kinley, Chester B. Dick   201–729–5420

COBWEB CORNER, Rt. 15. *Also see* Repair and Restoration listing.

Hours: Sat. & Sun. 9–sundown; weekdays by chance

A hobby expanded into a charming shop. Early and later country furniture, lamps, crocks, jugs; general line in a pre-1820 carriage house. Repair and restoration of lamps and furniture.

A/C—PM. Wide range. Authentication.

Prop. Betty Grosch   201–383–1952

CONNIE'S ACCENT HOUSE, 9 Main St.

Hours: Mon. thru Sat. 10–4:30

Antiques the decorative accent, "anything beautiful and unique." Small pieces: china, stoneware, cut glass, crystal, small lamps; tapestries and embroideries

CONNIE'S ACCENT HOUSE *continued*

(when available). Courtesy decorating services. A gracious shop. Member Nat'l. Home Fashions League.

A/C—PM. Wide range. Authentication when possible.

Prop. Constance Dickman   201–729–2423

RETURN ENGAGEMENT, 20 Main St.

Hours: Mon. thru Sat. 10–5; Sun. 1–5. Closed Wed.

Nice older things on consignment in a large, airy shop. Oak furniture, silver, china, cut and pressed glass displayed with care. Browsing invited.

C—PM. Affordable/Wide range. All-consignment. Authentication.

Prop. Philip Washichek   201–729–5515

Stanhope 07857

BOB'S ANTIQUES, Rt. 183, northbound (just south of Economy Dept. Store).

Hours: 7 days 9–4; call ahead suggested

A deceptively intriguing shop at the side of the highway. Antique, new, and used Oriental rugs, Victorian furnishings, American Indian artifacts, children's furniture. General line; antique and used furniture, oak; glass, china, weapons, trunks, crocks, lamps, stained glass. Oriental rugs purchased, cleaned, and repaired by arrangement. Congenial shop with wide-ranging interests; good reference library.

C/A—Some prices marked. Wide range. Consignments. Authentication.

Prop. Catherine Bott   201–347–9883 (bus.)
                                                                     691–9234 (res.)

CAMEO ANTIQUES, 44 Main St. *Also see* Repair and Restoration listing.

Hours: Mon., Thurs. thru Sat. 11–5; open Sun. Closed Tues. & Wed.

Quality antiques and collectibles. Primitives; early American chairs, tables, coffers, chests. Eighteenth- to 20th-century furniture, lighting; some porcelain, glass, American paintings, an early tricycle from a long-ago childhood. Appraisals. Estate sales. Porcelain repair. Off-street parking in the lot next door. Browsers welcome.

A/C—PM. Wide range. Authentication.

Prop. Vito and Mary Ellen Sico   201–347–8181

Stillwater 07875

BUDD'S COUNTRY STORE ANTIQUES, Main St. (Rt. 610). Mailing address: Box 17.

Hours: By chance or phone ahead

Early to more modern furniture; iron kettles, jugs, railroad lanterns, clocks, some early tools, china and glass; general line. Nicely arranged country shop in an old general store. The building possibly dates to the 1700s.

C/A—PM. Wide range.

Prop. Charles and Nellie Budd   201–383–5610

Stockholm 07460

J–B ENTERPRISES, Rt. 23.

Hours: Wed. thru Sun. 11–6

Oak furniture, primitives; coins. Furniture refinishing. Antiques purchased.

A/C—PM. Wide range. Authentication.

Prop. Jacqueline MacDonnell, Charles M. Blakeney   201–697–4444

OLD HIGHWAY ANTIQUES, Rt. 515 (off Rt. 23 at Jorgensen Inn; ¼ mi. past Hardyston Mun. Bldg.).

Hours: Daily 10–5

Furniture and accessories.

A—PM. Wide range. Authentication.

Prop. Helen Rowett   201–697–6153

Sussex 07461

LAMP LIGHTER ANTIQUES, Rt. 23, northbound (1 mi. north of Sussex). *Also see* Repair and Restoration listing.

Hours: Mon. thru Sat. 9–6

Art glass a specialty—Steuben, Quezal, Tiffany. Glassware and primitives. Appraisals. Oil lamp repairs; brass polishing. Shop is in the rear. Organic produce fresh from the garden in summer.

A/C—PM. Affordable/Wide range. Authentication.

Prop. Cy and Loretta Lewis   201–875–6662

Swartswood 07877

GRANDPA'S ATTIC, Main St. (Rt. 521). Mailing address: P. O. Box 123.
Hours: Daily 9–6. Closed Mon.

Oak and Victorian furnishings; glass (including some Heisey and "goofs"); authentic Tobey mugs. Also reproduction pitcher and basin sets, brass, and houseplants. An attractive shop. Occasional refinishing on request.

C/A—PM. Wide range. Consignments. Authentication.

Prop. Frank and Agnes Goritski   201–383–7784

Wantage 07461

HAVENS ANTIQUES, Rt. 284 (between Sussex and Unionville, N. Y.).
Mailing address: R. D. 1.

Hours: By chance or appt.

An old carriage house filled with American primitive furniture in-the-rough. Corner cupboards, hutches, dry sinks, drop leaf tables, washstands; no upholstered pieces. Some country store items and china. Old newspapers and books, when available. In the Jersey countryside; a number of shops are within 15 minutes' driving time across the New York line.

A/C—PM. Affordable/Wide range.

Prop. Gail Havens   201–875–3814

Detail of a spindle-back Hitchcock chair, ca. 1830, showing the trademark: L. HITCHCOCK. HITCHCOCKS-VILLE. CONN. WARRANTED. Chair pictured on p. 198. *Courtesy Country Row Antiques, Inc., New Hope. Photo: George Bailey*

LEFT: French Regency carved cherry case clock. Enamelled face
marked "Vandercruysse à Baillieul"; bronze spandrels. Northern
France, ca. 1720. Ht. 106 in. RIGHT: Elegantly curved Louis XIV
walnut case clock with enamel face, bronze spandrels, and brass
"Sun King" pendulum. French, ca. 1700. Ht. 112 in. *Courtesy
Time and Tide, Point Pleasant, Pa. Photo: Christian Mattheson*

Warren County

Beattystown 07840

WHISPERING PINES ANTIQUES, Rt. 57, eastbound (Hackettstown mailing address). *Also see* Repair and Restoration listing.

Hours: Mon. thru Fri. 12–6; Sat. & Sun. 10–6; or call ahead

Primarily caned and rushed chairs at this small, congenial shop. Also china and Heisey glass. Caning and rushing to order.

A/C—PM. Affordable. Consignments. Authentication when possible.

Prop. Dianne and Henning Johansson   201–852–2587

Belvidere 07823

EASTERN SALES, 500 Greenwich St.

Hours: Mon. thru Sat. 9–5:30; call ahead suggested

Antique lighting devices, glass, brass, pewter, tin, iron. General line, including furniture, clocks, oil paintings.

A—PM. Affordable. Authentication.

Prop. Wayne Laucius   201–475–5013

EDWARD & EDWARDS ANTIQUES, Rt. 46, westbound (approx. 2 mi. west of Rts. 46–31 intersection).

Hours: 6 days 10–5. Closed Tues.

EDWARD & EDWARDS ANTIQUES *continued*

General line; "a little bit of everything." Tools, primitives, furniture, glass, china, toys, some stained glass windows, farm and country implements, some lighting. Antiques purchased. No smoking requested.

A/C—PM. Wide range. Authentication when possible.

Prop. Elsie Edwards   201–453–3232

HOMER HICKS ANTIQUES (H & H Liquidating), 427 Mansfield St. Mailing address: P. O. Box 186.

Hours: Wed., Fri., Sat. 9–5:30. Mid-June to mid Sept.: Tues. thru Sat. 9–5:30

General line; collectible furniture, china, glass. Also used furniture and household items. Furniture repair, refinishing, chair caning by arrangement.

C/A; also newer—Most prices marked. Affordable.

Prop. G. Homer Hicks   201–475–4333

THE W. P. THOMAS SHOP, Mountain Lake Rd. *Also see* Repair and Restoration listing.

Hours: Thurs. thru Sun., all day; or by appt.

Primitives and Victorian furniture a specialty. Dry sinks, drop leaf tables, chairs, candlestands; Victorian dressing tables, chests; complete walnut bedroom sets, living room sets, when available. Antiques purchased. Furniture repair, refinishing, and restoration. Mr. Thomas has been a cabinetmaker for more than thirty years.

A/C—PM. Selective/Wide range. Authentication when possible.

Prop. William P. Thomas   201–475–4818

Blairstown 07825

COTTAGE ANTIQUES, Rt. 94. Mailing address: Box 36C.

Hours: Mon. thru Sat. 10–5; Sun. & hols. by appt.

Extensive general line—small furniture, dolls, and miniature furnishings, clocks, lamps, quilts, fine china, silver, crocks, cut and pattern glass, buttons, baskets, toys, books, post cards. Old tools, kitchen utensils, iron, brass, copper, wood, tin. No reproductions. New oil, watercolor, and acrylic paintings. Home grown vegetables and berries in season. Homemade jams and jellies. Also see Country House Antiques, Great Meadows, below.

A/C; also new—PM. Wide range. Authentication when possible.

Prop. Joan Strand   201–362–8889

GRAVEL HILL WORKSHOP, Main St.

Hours: Mon. thru Sat. 10–4; winter, call ahead

Furniture, some primitives, some wicker, early tools, glass, prints, country items, some silver. The works of local artists, watercolors and prints by Susan Jo M. Hope; gifts, reproduction bottles. In a large old storefront, nicely arranged for browsing.

C/A—PM. Affordable/Wide range. Consignments.

Prop. George and Mary Jo Milne   201–362–6852

PATTEN'S ANTIQUES, at Willowbrook Farm; Millbrook Rd. Mailing address: R. D. 2, Box 196.

Hours: Mon. thru Fri. 12–6; Sat. & Sun. 10–6

What began as a midwinter barn sale expanded to an interesting selection of furniture, horse accouterments, sleighs, farm wagons, some china and glass. A 150-year-old working farm in a beautiful location. Corn, hay, and alfalfa still in the fields.

C/A—PM. Wide range. Consignments. Authentication when possible.

Prop. Bill Patten   201–362–8425

Buttzville 07829

POT-POURRI ANTIQUES, Rt. 31, southbound (⅓ mi. off Rt. 46; 1 mi. from Oxford).

Hours: Sat. & Sun. 10–5

General line; oak furniture, glassware. Antiques purchased. In an old barn.

C—PM. Wide range. Authentication.

Prop. R. J. Danhieux   201–453–2758

TRIFLES & TREASURES, Rt. 46, eastbound (close to Rt. 31 traffic light). Mailing address: Box 106.

Hours: 7 days 9:30–6 (inc. hols.); and by appt.

The proprietors are serious about their diverse specialties, and they fill seven floors in three buildings of this old farmstead on a main road to the Delaware Water Gap.

There are 2,000 to 3,000 pieces of Fiesta Ware (enough for several small hotels); '30s pottery, Depression glass. Period clothing, mint condition Victorian whites—by appt. Judy Garland and Marilyn Monroe memorabilia; collectible

TRIFLES & TREASURES *continued*

records. A considerable general line, including jewelry, some silver, furniture, pocket watches, beer steins, prints (inc. 18th- to 20th-century Japanese prints), books, dolls, toys, Japanese lusters, salts and peppers, cookie jars, crocks, lamps, old shutters and doors. Deposits held; deliveries to New York City. Mail orders on Depression glass, Fiesta Ware, and Hall pottery. Master Charge, Visa. Antiques purchased. Also to the trade. Member Pocono Mtn. Depression Glass Club.

C—PM. Wide range. Authentication.

Prop. BA Wellman, Gus Gustafson   201–453–2918

VILLAGE SHOPS, Rt. 31 (1 mi. north of Oxford, toward Delaware Water Gap).

Hours: Sat. & Sun. 10–5

Approximately ten dealers at this attractive complex of weekend shops built on the foundation of an early barn which burned in 1900. A country location, on one of the two oldest operating farms in Warren County.

Prop. JMJ Realty Corp., John G. Hall   201–453–2727

COIN MAN, Ken Coban.

American coins and paper. Old U. S. coins purchased. Coin appraisals. Member Amer. Numismatic Assoc.

A/C—PM. Affordable. Consignments. Authentication (coins).

THE COUNTRY KITCHEN, Mildred Peake.

Kitchen and dining-related items, 1920s to 1930s, occasionally older. China cannister sets, tin, woodenware, crocks, cookbooks, and booklets.

C—PM. Affordable. Consignments.

BARRY SCOTT ECKERT.

General line; china, glass, occasionally furniture. Individual pieces and estates purchased.

C—PM. Affordable. Consignments. Authentication.

JACK'S CORNER, Helen and John Siegfried. *Also see* Auctioneers listing.

Furniture, oak, pine, walnut, cherry. Auctioneer; mailing list.

C—PM. Wide range. Consignments.

VILLAGE SHOPS *continued*

PARTRIDGE HOLLOW ANTIQUES, Richard Kuehne.

General line; cut and pressed glass, some sterling, decoys, railroad items.

C—PM. Affordable. Consignments. Authentication when possible.

THE SERENDIPITY SHOP, Susan Elizabeth Hauser.

General line; glass, some furniture. Blanket chests, benches, wool winders, when available. Antiques purchased.

C—PM. Affordable. Authentication.

THE TREASURE CORNER, Carl and Jennie Rothenbeck.

Depression glass, general merchandise "with a little age." Antiques purchased, also traded.

C—PM. Affordable.

Delaware 07833

VAN'S ANTIQUES, Clinton St.

Hours: Daily 8–5 or 5:30. Closed Thurs.

Primitives and country pieces; crocks, jugs, mirrors, china, glass, mantel clocks, oak, kerosene and Art Nouveau lamps. Hand-quilted pillows by Mrs. Van Hirtum. Also to dealers and decorators.

C; also new—PM. Affordable/Wide range. Authentication when possible.

Prop. Eleanor Van Hirtum   201–475–5107

Great Meadows 07838

COUNTRY HOUSE ANTIQUES, Hope-Great Meadows Rd. (between Rt. 46 and Rt. 519). Mailing address: Box 109B, Hope Rd.

Hours: By chance or appt.

General line. Also see Cottage Antiques, Blairstown, above.

A/C—PM. Wide range. Authentication when possible.

Prop. Joan Strand   201–637–4651

Hackettstown 07840

THE SILVER THISTLE ANTIQUES, Hackettstown.
Hours: By appt.
Knowledgeable collection of early porcelains; iron, brass, wood, silver, coin silver, early blown glass, primitives; selected small, usable objects. Appraisals. Member Antiques Dealers Assoc. of Central N. J., Antique Club of N. J.
A—PM. Affordable/Selective.
Prop. Helen M. Clepper   201–852–3403

MARIE SISKO'S ANTIQUES, Hackettstown.
Hours: By appt.
Furniture, pine, walnut, oak; glass and bric-a-brac.
C—PM. Affordable.
Prop. Marie Sisko   201–852–4261

Hope 07844

GENEVIEVE RABE, Mt. Hermon Rd.
Hours: By appt.
Period furniture and accessories; early samplers. Identification of early portrait artists.
A/C—PM. Wide range. Consignments. Authentication.
Prop. Genevieve Rabe   201–459–4755

Johnsonburg 07846

DARK MOON ANTIQUES, Johnsonburg.
Hours: By appt.
American primitives. Mid- to early 19th-century furniture, some 18th-century pieces. Spinning and weaving-related items, an occasional footwarmer, kitchen utensils; well-labeled and identified. Members, Brigade of the American Revolution.
A—PM. Wide range. Authentication.
Prop. Ron and Sharon Pittenger   201–852–1052

Mansfield Twp. 07863

JIM'S JUNK ANTIQUE EMPORIUM, Rt. 57, eastbound (opp. Ralph's Motel).
Hours: 7 days 10–5

Furniture and miscellany in-the-rough and refinished to order. Stuffed birds, a ferret-like animal with small bright glass eyes, mounted horns, a thermometer "on the hoof." Also Empire pieces, a country cupboard, German baby dish, some insulators, old bottles, odd pedestals; the unusual at this congenial shop.

A/C—Some prices marked; coded. Wide range. Consignments.

Prop. James Westbrook   201–689–6528

Marksboro 07825

BRICK HOUSE ANTIQUES, Rt. 94, westbound.

Hours: Thurs., Fri., Sat. 1–5; call ahead requested

"Dignified junk and homesick furniture" in a 200-year-old one-time general store. Furniture—dry sinks, china closets, mirrored hall stands (when available); oil lamps, old bottles; general line. The proprietor was formerly a furniture buyer in New York.

C—PM. Affordable. Consignments.

Prop. Helen Martini   201–383–7988

SPIDER WEB ANTIQUES, Rt. 94, westbound.

Hours: Tues. thru Sat. 10–4:30

Mostly furniture, "whatever appeals." Victorian side chairs and sofas, Empire, Eastlake, oak; desks, drop leaf tables. Friendly shop in a beautifully decorated barn loft. Antiques scouted. Dealers welcome. Beautiful scenic view from Rt. 94 just east of this location.

C/A—PM. Wide range. Consignments.

Prop. Cathy Kassakian   201–362–8804

New Village 08886

GANG'S MANOR HOUSE ANTIQUES, Rt. 57, eastbound (at the twin city street lamps).

Hours: Wed. thru Sun. 9:30–6

SAINT PETER'S COLLEGE LIBRARY
JERSEY CITY, NEW JERSEY 07306

GANG'S MANOR HOUSE ANTIQUES *continued*

General line; country items and Victorian furniture. Inside and surrounding a 150-year-old horse barn. A ring of the bell over the "Hester Street" sign (an original), will summon the proprietor.

A/C—Most prices marked. Wide range. Authentication when possible.

Prop. Gloria Gang   201–454–9848

Phillipsburg 08865

THE FURNITURE MAN, Rt. 57, westbound (next to Lopatcong School).

Hours: Mon. thru Sat. 9–5; Sun. 12–5

Mostly oak furniture, selection of kerosene lamps, around the warmth of the corner fireplace. Shop is in the rear building.

C—PM. Affordable. Authentication.

Prop. William Reppert   201–454–4708 (bus.)
                                                                           454–1968 (res.)

REX AND LIL TOLERICO, Phillipsburg.

Hours: By appt.

Depression glass.

C—PM. Affordable. Consignments. Authentication when possible.

Prop. Rex and Lil Tolerico   201–454–4973

THE TRADING POST ANTIQUE SHOP, Still Valley Circle (near Holiday Inn).

Hours: By appt.

Signed bronzes, coins, good early American furniture, four-poster beds, Oriental Chippendale slant-top desks, grandfather clocks (from 1850, in working order); Limoges, cut glass, jewelry. Wholesale; primarily to dealers. Appraisals of antique jewelry, furniture, toys, glassware. At this location since 1949. In a stone house documented to 1690, once a stagecoach stop. Mrs. Zowarski is a third-generation dealer in antiques.

A/C—PM. Wide range. Authentication; money back guarantee.

Prop. John and Gitty Zowarski   201–454–6091

ZEHNDER'S RED BARN, 493 S. Main St.

Hours: Sat. & Sun. 10–6

ZEHNDER'S RED BARN *continued*

Early American furniture, 18th-century pieces in-the-rough; refinishing by arrangement. China, brass, copper, bric-a-brac. In business more than thirty-three years. The third oldest house in Phillipsburg, built in the early 1800s by the owners of a feed mill.

A—Prices not marked. Wide range. Authentication.

Prop. Rose Zehnder   201–454–1712

Port Murray 07865

PORT MURRAY EMPORIUM, Main St. (off Rt. 57).

Hours: Wed. thru Sat. 1 5; and by appt.

A true country antique shop, specializing in dolls (no reproductions) and related items; carriages, doll dishes, miniatures, toys. Primitives; old tools and kitchenware (mainly iron), Victorian and Empire furniture, cut and pressed glass, china, old quilts and coverlets. Doll repair; custom doll hats designed with old findings. In the Old Canal Store, beside the Morris Canal bed.

A/C—PM. Wide range. Authentication when possible.

Prop. Vivienne and Wayne Opdyke   201–689–1760

Stewartsville 08886

DENNY'S ANTIQUES, Rt. 57, eastbound. Mailing address: Box 7.

Hours: 7 days 8–6

Large collection of china, cut, pressed, Sandwich, satin, and art glass; some silver and early Oriental china in rows of oak china cabinets. Old pictures and prints; some old quilts and coverlets, when available. A venerable shop, in business thirty-seven years. Prices quoted.

A/C—Prices not marked. Wide range.

Prop. Frank F. Dennis   201–859–0789

BARBARA KLOUSER, Main St.

Hours: Weekdays by appt.; Fri. 6–8; Sat. & Sun. 10–4

Pennsylvania and New Jersey early pine and primitives; oak furniture, quilts, baskets, etc. Original black and white photographs of country scenes.

A/C—Most prices marked. Wide range. Consignments (limited).

Prop. Barbara Klouser   201–859–3660

Townsbury 07863

STONE HOUSE ANTIQUES, Rt. 46. Mailing address: Box 218, R. D.,
Oxford 07863.

Hours: By appt.

*General line; glass, china. Some small furniture, silver, lamps. Antiques shows
managed. Member Antiques Dealers Assoc. of Central N. J.*

A/C—PM. Wide range. Authentication when possible.

Prop. Joseph N. Engel   201–637–4256

Washington 07882

DOROTHEA B. HORWITZ, Mill Pond Rd. (off Rt. 57, eastbound, at Pleasant
Valley Inn; just west of Shop-Rite Supermarket).

Hours: By appt.

*A gracious shop in a beautiful setting along the Pohatcong. Primitives and
metals a specialty. Furnishings; silver, pewter, brass, iron, copper. Strap hinges.
Member Antiques Dealers Assoc. of Central N. J.*

A—PM. Wide range. Authentication.

Prop. Dorothea B. Horwitz   201–689–1941

KOCHER'S COUNTRY CORNER ANTIQUES, Rt. 57, eastbound (at Butler
Pk. Rd.).

Hours: Sat. & Sun. 10–5; weekdays by chance

*General line of country antiques nicely arranged in an attractive farmhouse
with pale yellow trim. Old and newer items, including a Hoosier cabinet, old
pine cupboard (c. 1820), spinning wheels, china cannister sets, chocolate pots,
coffee grinders, charcoal-burning sadirons, a carpet beater, old snowshoes, a
1930s radio (in playable condition), a female cigar store Indian, and advertising.
Especially pretty in spring when tulips are in bloom in the garden. Parking
at rear.*

A/C. Affordable/Wide range.

Prop. Gloria and Skip Kocher   201–689–4962

THE RED BARN, 49 Broad St.

Hours: Tues. thru Sat. 10–5; Sun. 10–5

*Newer collectibles in a small, red barn. Individual pieces and entire households
purchased.*

C—PM. Affordable.

Prop. Gloria Matthews   201–689–0209

JEANNIE STAATS, Jackson Valley Rd. (bet. Washington and Oxford; ½ mi. off Rt. 69).

Hours: By chance or appt.

China, glass; tinware, post cards, badges.

C—PM. Affordable. Authentication.

Prop. Jeannie Staats   201–689–3627

WASHINGTON'S HEADQUARTERS, 27 Belvedere Ave. *Also see* Auctioneers listing.

Hours: Wed. & Thurs. 12–5; Fri. 12–7; Sat. 11–3

American and foreign coins; Victoriana, nostalgia; wood carvings, oak, cut glass, china. Search service. Appraisals. Auctions. Member Amer. Numismatic Soc., Amer. Numismatic Assoc., Numis. Internat'l.

C/A—PM. Wide range. Consignments. Authentication.

Prop. Noël and Ralph Cannito   201–689–2025
                                                                    689–6020

Yellow Frame 07860

THE ATTIC (at Wilbur's Country Store), Rt. 94, northbound. Mailing address: R. D. 2, Box 561, Newton 07860.

Hours: Mon. thru Fri. 10:30–5:30; Sat. & Sun. 10–6. Closed Wed.

Collectible furniture, chairs, including oak. New dollhouses and miniatures. Furniture repair and restoration; hand-stripping; caning. Master Charge and layaway plan. Bright, airy shop in a small complex built around an 1847 farmhouse and barn.

C; also new—PM. Wide range. Consignments. Authentication when possible.

Prop. Steve and Helen Trimper   201–362–8880 (bus.)
                                                                    383–3946 (res.)

Advertising tins and boxes, Coca-Cola items, and breweriana in an old-time country store atmosphere. *Courtesy Big Ker's Antiques, Montclair Historical Society Antiques Market, Montclair. Photo: Kerry Rasp*

Morris County

Boonton 07005

BIRDIE'S ANTIQUES, 521 Main St.

Hours: Mon. thru Sat. 11:30–5

Large, bright shop specializing in Victorian furnishings and antique jewelry; chandeliers, fine china and glass, antique mirrors, paintings, pewter, and silver.

A/C—Prices coded. Wide range. Consignments on better pieces. Authentication when possible.

Prop. B. A. Massar   201–335–8062

BOONTON ANTIQUES, 406–408 Main St.

Hours: Mon. thru Sat. 11–5

Two adjoining shops crammed with "just about anything old." Empire and Victorian furniture, rugs, china, including Royal Worcester, Limoges, Wedgwood, Spode, Nippon; crystal, silver, paintings. Mrs. Jonnard conducts house sales and gives appraisals.

A/C—PM. Wide range. Occasional consignments. Authentication.

Prop. Rona Jonnard   201–263–6520

THE DANDYLION, 415 Main St.

Hours: Tues. thru Sat. 10–5

THE DANDYLION *continued*

Small pieces of period furniture and appropriate decorative accessories; old glass, brass and copper items, some old tools. There is an interior design service.

A/C—PM. Affordable. Authentication when possible.

Prop. Jonelle Harrison, Bettie Ratliff   201–263–5225

DISCOVERY HOUSE, 808 Main St.

Hours: Tues. thru Sat. 10–5

Antique jewelry a specialty. Some primitives, roll-top desks, corner cupboards, dry sinks, hall racks; stained glass, old cash registers. The proprietors conduct house sales and do appraisals.

A/C—PM. Affordable. Consignments. Authentication.

Prop. Jeanne Marsden, Joyce Enes   201–335–5670

LOWE'S ANTIQUES, 418 Main St.

Hours: Mon. thru Sat. 11–4

Antique and used furniture predominate; also fine china and glass, decorative accessories.

A/C—PM. Affordable. Occasional consignment.

Prop. Marianne Lowe   201–263–1078 (bus.)
    334–4866 (res.)

THE OLDE TYME MUSIC SCENE, 917 Main St. *Also see* Repair and Restoration listing.

Hours: Wed., Thurs., Sat. 10–5; Fri. 12–5; Sun. 12–4; July & Aug.: Mon. thru Sat. 10–5; Sun. 12–4

Old hand-cranked, spring-driven phonographs, cylinders, sheet music, piano rolls, out-of-print records, band charts, supplies for old phonographs. "Everything from Edison to Elvis." The owners will evaluate record collections and maintain a search service. Old phonographs repaired.

A/C—PM. Affordable. Authentication.

Prop. Lou DeCicco and Don Donahue   201–335–5040

WHITE HOUSE ANTIQUES, 215 Myrtle Ave. (Rt. 202 north). *Also see* Repair and Restoration listing.

Hours: Tues. thru Sat. 9–4; call ahead suggested

Three floors of antiques nicely displayed in a restored 1830s house. Country and period furniture and appropriate accessories are specialties. Look for decorated

WHITE HOUSE ANTIQUES *continued*

stoneware and redware, blanket chests, corner cupboards. Restoration services include replacing of splint seats, wood turning, carving, and refinishing.

A—PM. Affordable/Selective. Authentication.

Prop. Karen Kinnane   201–335–4926

WRIGHT ANTIQUES, 321 Main St.

Hours: Wed. thru Sat. 10–6

"Almost anything in advertising that's old"—tins, neon, breweriana; lots of nostalgic items, gumball machines, old cameras, 1939 World's Fair memorabilia, victrolas, sheet music, post cards, old tin toys.

C/A—PM. Affordable. Consignments.

Prop. Ron Wright   201–334–4442

Brookside 07926

JAMES LYNN KLINE, 18 Old Brookside Rd.

Hours: By appt.

American primitives, including furniture, homespun linens, coverlets, pewter, redware, stoneware, in a selective shop; also American blown and pattern glass. Appraisal service.

A—PM. Selective. Authentication.

Prop. James Lynn Kline   201–543–4072

Butler 07405

SUNNYFILL ANTIQUES, 179 Boonton Ave. (off Main St.).

Hours: Mon. thru Sat. 11–5

Early American, Victorian, and turn-of-the-century furniture are specialties; old lanterns, crockery, some china and cut glass.

A/C—PM. Affordable. Consignments. Authentication.

Prop. Sonja DelGaizo   201–838–2466

Cedar Knolls 07927

THE BEST OF THE PAST, Ridgedale Ave. (in Morris County Mall).

Hours: Tues., Sat. 11–6; Wed., Thurs., Fri. 11–9; Sun. 12–5

Attractive shop inside the mall with a nice selection of crystal, hand-painted china, silver serving pieces, antique jewelry; small pieces of antique furniture— china cabinets, secretaries, chairs. House sales conducted.

A/C—PM. Wide range. Authentication when possible.

Prop. Russ Leonard   201–267–1516

MARITA DANIELS, Ridgedale Ave. (in Morris County Mall).

Hours: Tues. thru Sat. 11–5; Thurs. 11–9

A young people's shop with nostalgic items, old telephones, old dolls, memorabilia. New gift items.

C/A—PM. Affordable. Authentication when possible.

Prop. Marita Daniels   201–539–2233 (bus.)
                                                        267–5373 (res.)

YESTERDAY ONCE MORE SHOPPE, Ridgedale Ave. (in Morris County Mall). *Also see* Repair and Restoration listing.

Hours: Tues. thru Sat. 11–5; Thurs., Fri. eves. 7–9

Antique and new clocks of all kinds—mantel, wall, grandfather. Grandfather clocks delivered and set up without charge. Antique and new clock and watch repair service. Member Nat'l. Assoc. of Watch & Clock Collectors.

A/C—PM. Wide range. Authentication.

Prop. Marilyn and Gary Lester   201–539–6449 (bus.)
                                                        992–8543 (res.)

Chatham 07928

CHACOINS, Box 563, Chatham.

Hours: By appt.

Large selection of coins and stamps; old manuscripts, guns, ivories, netsuke (Japanese decorative art). "Antiques and Collectors items." The Carvers conduct house and estate sales and do appraisals. Member Society of Philatelic Americans, the American Ordinance Assoc., the Nat'l. Rifle Assoc.

A/C—PM. Wide range. Authentication.

Prop. Natalie and Robert Carver   201–635–7083

CHATHAM GALLERIES, 34 Watchung Ave. (off River Rd.).

Hours: Tues. thru Sat. 10–4

Long-established shop in the 250-year-old Bonnel House, filled with fine old antiques. Eighteenth-century furniture, Oriental rugs, oil paintings, primitive portraits, antique frames and mirrors.

A—PM. Wide range. Authentication when possible.

Prop. Edith Ward   201–635–7709

CHATHAM SILVERSMITHS, 248 Main St. *Also see* Repair and Restoration listing.

Hours: Daily 8:30–5. Closed Thurs., Sun.

Antique, collectible, and new silver in a friendly, busy shop on the main street of town. Silver plating, polishing, repairing all done on premises.

A/C—PM. Selective. Authentication when possible.

Prop. George R. Mortat   201–635–8505

COBWEB ANTIQUES, Chatham.

Hours: By appt.

Good glass, porcelain, silver; art objects, decorative pieces, period furniture. Small line of primitives.

A/C—PM. Wide range/Selective. Authentication.

Prop. Thomas and Jane Doyle   201–635–0778

THE CRANETOWN SHOP, Box 622, Chatham.

Hours: Phone ahead

"Antiques of high quality" in a long-established shop. Early American predominates; also fine china, cut glass, jewelry, paintings, old dolls, bric-a-brac. Estates sold on commission basis; appraisals.

A—PM. Wide range. Authentication.

Prop. Isabell Elvin   201–827–9562

BARBARA GRANT'S ANTIQUE SHOP, 552 Main St. (at Garden Ave.).

Hours: Tues. thru Sat. 10:30–4

Nine rooms in a large old house crammed with antiques and collectibles. Lots of out-of-print books, prints and paintings, fine china, glass, silver and copper accessories, old kitchen collectibles; some pieces of furniture.

A/C—PM. Affordable. Authentication when possible.

Prop. Barbara Grant   201–635–2407

FRAN JAY, 24 Minton Ave.

Hours: By appt.

Depression glass a specialty; old toys, art pottery, Art Deco, kitchen primitives, advertising tins. Member of the Nat'l. Depression Glass Assoc.

C/A—PM. Affordable. Authentication.

Prop. Fran Jay   201–635–6260

MARVIN'S CRACKERS, 24 Minton Ave. *Also see* Repair and Restoration listing.

Hours: By appt.

All kinds of old toy vehicles—cars, buses, trucks, trolleys. Member of the Miniature Car Collectors Assoc. Repair and restoration of old toys.

C/A—PM. Affordable. Authentication.

Prop. Marvin Silverstein   201–635–6260

SHEPHERD'S MARKET, 331 Main St.

Hours: Tues. thru Sat. 10–4; or by appt.

Early American through Victorian furniture in several rooms of a Victorian house on the main street of town. Nice oak dining tables imported from England. Some decorative accessories. Notice the beautiful Italian marble fireplaces.

A/C—PM. Wide range. Authentication.

Prop. Rosemary Barolini, Joan Crowley   201–635–1144

Chatham Twp. 07928

CHALLENGE ACRE ANTIQUES, 641 Shunpike Rd. (in Hickory Square Arcade).

Hours: Mon. thru Sat. 10–5

Eighteenth- and 19-century formal and country furniture, mostly American, some English, nicely displayed in a tasteful shop. Brass candlesticks from the 1700s, antique clocks, old quilts. Reproduction copper Colonial lighting fixtures, weathervanes. Everything clearly identified and dated on tags—white tags for antiques, green tags for reproductions. Appraisal service.

A/C—PM. Wide range. Occasional consignment. Authentication.

Prop. Robert Daeschler   201–377–3033

TURKEYTOWNE ANTIQUES, 93 Long Hill Lane.

Hours: By appt.

Specializing in pine country furniture; tin, wooden, iron primitives; nice selection of brass and copper accessories for the country home.

A—PM. Affordable/Selective.

Prop. Eileen Kluge, Dorothy Craddock   201–635–1135

Chester 07930

BREAD BOARD COUNTRY STORE, 50 E. Main St. *Also see* Repair and Restoration listing.

Hours: Tues. thru Fri. 10–4; Sat. & Sun. 10–5

Country primitives, dry sinks, pine cupboards, buckets, benches, wood boxes, butter churns, in an old-time country store atmosphere. Unique selection of new handmade calico items and "Grandma's country curtains made to order." Furniture refinishing by Mr. Valentine.

A/C—PM. Affordable. Authentication when possible.

Prop. Barbara Valentine   201–879–7188

THE EMPORIUM, 71 Main St.

Hours: Tues. thru Sat. 11–4; Sun. 12–5

Early country furniture, refinished and redecorated buggy seats, old trunks, country store items in a charming shop c. 1868. Lots of new calico and patchwork, lampshades, new dollhouses and miniature furnishings. Member Associated Antiques Dealers of N. J.

A/C—PM. Affordable. Authentication when possible.

Prop. Joan Madsen   201–879–7751

MARY FLANAGAN, 71 Main St. (upstairs in The Emporium). *Also see* Repair and Restoration listing.

Hours: Tues. thru Sat. 11–4; Sun. 12–5

Antique dolls a specialty; some china, small pieces of furniture, silver serving pieces, bric-a-brac. Dried arrangements in antique containers by order. Complete doll repair service.

A/C—PM. Affordable. Authentication when possible.

Prop. Mary Flanagan   201–879–7751

Denville 07834

THE PIGWIDGEON'S NICHE, 26A Diamond Spring Rd. (north of Rt. 46).
Also see Repair and Restoration listing.

Hours: Tues. thru Sat. 10–5

*Antique and collectible dolls; small pieces of Victorian and oak furniture, oil
lamps, cut glass, china; new dollhouses and miniatures. Complete restoration
of antique dolls.*

A/C—PM. Affordable. Authentication when possible.

Prop. Nancy Resch   201–625–5610

Dover 07801

GRANDMA'S ATTIC, 69 W. Blackwell St. (just south of Rt. 46). *Also see*
Repair and Restoration listing.

Hours: Mon. thru Sat. 12–5

*Friendly young shop with small pieces of antique furniture, china, glass, and
decorative accessories. The owners do appraisals, and there is a caning and
refinishing service.*

A/C—PM. Affordable.

Prop. Catherine Haynes, Susan Stocknoff   201–366–8230

PEDDLER'S SHOP, 71 W. Blackwell St. (just south of Rt. 46).

Hours: Mon. thru Sat. 12–5:30

"Antiques and . . ." crowded into a busy shop. *General line of furniture,
kerosene lamps, old bottles, primitive kitchen utensils, tools, crocks, old and
new jewelry, tinware and woodenware, antique dolls, old trains. Note the
collection of watchfobs.*

A/C—PM. Affordable.

Prop. Mr. & Mrs. Earl Dennison   201–366–4147

Flanders 07836

FLANDERS BARN ANTIQUES, Rt. 206 (corner of Flanders–Netcong Rd.
and Rt. 206).

Hours: By appt.

FLANDERS BARN ANTIQUES *continued*

A two-story barn with a general line of antiques and collectibles. Early antiques on the first floor: furniture of various periods, antique jewelry, glass and china. Some "one-of-a-kind" pieces. Appraisal service.

A/C—PM. Affordable. Authentication when possible.

Prop. F. Manno, A. Vinciguerra   201–584–8079

Florham Park 07932

COUNTRY GIRL ANTIQUES AND GIFTS, 189 Ridgedale Ave. (main st. of town). *Also see* Repair and Restoration listing.

Hours: Mon. thru Sat. 10–4

Victorian furniture a specialty; nice selection of oak and wicker. General line of decorative accessories. Mrs. Riley conducts house sales and gives appraisals. Caning, rushing, splint seats replaced, refinishing.

A/C—PM. Affordable. Consignments. Authentication when possible.

Prop. Marian Riley   201–377–5440

HOUSE OF ANTIQUES, 163 Columbia Tpk. (Rt. 510, eastbound).

Hours: Wed. thru Sat. 11–4

Several rooms devoted to 18th- and 19th-century furniture; silver, glass, fine china—Meissen, R. S. Prussia, Royal Doulton, Royal Beyreuth; old and new miniatures for dollhouses. Mrs. Sossin gives informal lectures on antiques in her shop (no charge). Member Nat'l. Assoc. for Miniature Enthusiasts.

A/C—PM. Wide range. Consignments. Authentication when possible.

Prop. Henrietta Sossin   201–377–0393 (bus.)
                                                        731–2015 (res.)

PINE CREST ANTIQUES, 308 Columbia Tpk. (Rt. 510, westbound).

Hours: By appt.

Specializing in good art glass; Tiffany, cameo, cranberry glass; fine china, old dolls. Mrs. Poppele gives appraisals and is a member of the Associated Antiques Dealers of N. J.

A/C—PM. Selective. Authentication.

Prop. Sophia C. Poppele   201–377–7933

TREASURE TROVE, Florham Park. *Also see* Repair and Restoration listing.

Hours: By appt.

Selection of primitives, old trunks, quilts, jugs, and crocks; some oak furniture. Caning and furniture refinishing services.

A/C—PM. Affordable. Authentication.

Prop. Joseph and Marge Cook   201–377–6279

Gillette 07933

THE ANTIQUE NOOK, 570 Mountain Ave. (off Valley Rd.).

Hours: Mon. thru Thurs. 1–5

Tasteful collection of hand-painted china, sterling silver, antique glass; some small pieces of Victorian furniture. House sales conducted.

A/C—PM. Affordable. Authentication when possible.

Prop. Dorothy Ansari   201–647–2204

HELEN SHERMAN ANTIQUES, Gillette.

Hours: By appt.

General line of antiques and collectibles—china and glass, sterling, copper, brass, bronze decorative pieces; paintings, frames, toys, "everything old." Appraisals.

A/C—PM. Affordable. Authentication when possible.

Prop. Helen Sherman   201–647–0855
                                                                  647–5069

Hanover 07936

THE EAGLE HOUSE, 136 Mt. Pleasant Ave.

Hours: Phone call suggested

Selective shop specializing in fine china and glass, primitives, copper bed warmers, copper teakettles, early pewter, hanging lamps. The Folckes do appraisals and are members of the Associated Antiques Dealers of N. J.

A/Some collectibles—PM. Wide range. Authentication.

Prop. Richard and Mary Folcke   201–887–2317

Harding Twp. (Morristown P. O. 07960)

HAROLD B. THORPE, JR., Mt. Kemble Ave. (Rt. 202). *Also see* Repair and Restoration listing.

Hours: Mon. thru Sat. 9–5

Antique and new clocks. Restoration and repair of clocks and antique furniture.

A/C—PM. Selective. Authentication.

Prop. Harold B. Thorpe, Jr.   201–766–1334 (bus.)
                                                      267–9685 (res.)

Long Valley 07853

KAREN JOHNS, Long Valley.

Hours: By appt.

General line of early blown, flint, and pattern glass.

A/C—PM. Affordable. Authentication.

Prop. Karen Johns   201–876–3969

RUTH MARSHALL ANTIQUES, Rt. 24.

Hours: Appt. suggested

A long-established shop in a beautifully maintained 200-year-old barn displays a fine collection of Early American furnishings, a few 19th-century pieces, and a general line of early glass and china.

A—PM. Selective. Authentication.

Prop. Ruth Marshall   201–876–3258

VIRGINIA MILTIMORE, Long Valley.

Hours: By appt.

Antique dolls, old toys, and children's primitives are specialties; small pieces of early furniture, old glass and silver, some quilts. Mrs. Miltimore does appraisals and is a former president of the Antiques Dealers Assoc. of Central N. J.

A/Some collectibles—Affordable/Selective. Authentication.

Prop. Virginia Miltimore   201–852–1686

Madison 07940

ORIENT EXPRESS, 250 Main St.

Hours: Mon., Thurs., Fri., Sat. 11–6; Sun. 1–5; Tues., Wed. by appt.

ORIENT EXPRESS *continued*

Large selection of Oriental antiques, mostly from Japan, where Mrs. Sisson buys personally. Imari, Satsuma, porcelains, bronzes, ivory, floor pillows, lacquerware, old kimonos, antique obis, noh and kabuki masks; some contemporary celadon pieces and woodblock prints.

A/C—PM. Wide range. Authentication.

Prop. Christine Sisson   201–377–5544 (bus.)
                                                     539–3401 (res.)

Mendham 07945

ANTIQUE ACCENTS, 1 Hilltop Rd. (just off Main St.).

Hours: Tues. thru Sun. 10:30–4:30

Primitive and formal furniture, Heisey glass, early flint glass, fine china, sterling, and decorative accessories fill five rooms of a spacious shop.

A/C—PM. Wide range. Authentication.

Prop. Mary Simpson   201–543–7718 (bus.)
                                                     755–1573 (res.)

BULL AND BEAR ANTIQUES, 14 W. Main St.

Hours: Tues. thru Sat. 9–5; Sun. 1–5

Wide selection of fine antiques in a stately old home on the main street of town. American, English, and French furniture from the 17th, 18th, and 19th centuries; Oriental rugs, antique jewelry. Member of the New Jersey Appraisers Assoc.

A—PM. Serious collectors. Authentication.

Prop. William Whitehouse   201–543–7788

COURTYARD ANTIQUES, 5 Hilltop Rd. (off Main St.).

Hours: Wed. thru Sat. 10–5; Sun. 12–5

English antiques and collectibles are specialties. Fine china and glass, some jewelry, silver, pitcher and bowl sets, decorative objects.

A/C—PM. Wide range. Consignments.

Prop. Elly Feehan, Gloria Peralta, Vi Coffey   201–543–6377

EMANON CORNER, 1 E. Main St.

Hours: Tues. thru Sat. 10–5; Sun. 12–5; Mon. by chance or appt.

American country painted furniture, early woodenware and iron primitives, pewter, paintings, soft-paste china, nicely displayed in a bright shop.

A/C—PM. Affordable/Wide range. Consignments.

Prop. Barry and Veronica Janoff   201–543–7002

FATHER TIME, 1 E. Main St. *Also see* Repair and Restoration listing.

Hours: Mon. thru Sat. 10–6

Antique clocks of all kinds, watches, old jewelry. Mr. McDonald is an antique clock and watch repair specialist, does appraising and is a member of the Nat'l. Assoc. of Watch & Clock Collectors. Mr. Marke is a clockmaker.

A/C—PM. Wide range. Authentication when possible.

Prop. Thomas McDonald, Barry Marke   201–543–6446

THE KITCHEN DOOR, 6 Hilltop Rd. (off Main St.).

Hours: Mon. thru Sat. 10–5; Sun. 1–5

Some kitchen antiques and primitives amid a wide selection of new kitchen items.

C/A—PM. Affordable.

Prop. Joyce La Capra   201–543–2308

A. G. MASON, 1 Knollwood Dr. *Also see* Repair and Restoration listing.

Hours: By appt.

Specialist in American wall clocks from the 1800s to the early 1900s. Expert restoration and repair of wall clocks. Member of the Nat'l. Assoc. of Watch & Clock Collectors and the New Jersey Assoc. of Watch and Clock Collectors.

A/C—PM. Selective. Authentication.

Prop. A. G. Mason   201–543–2174

THE PEDDLER'S CELLAR, 6 Hilltop Rd. (off Main St.).

Hours: Tues. thru Sat. 10–5

Country furniture, antique dolls, and silver. Many new handcrafted gift items.

A/C—PM. Affordable. Consignments.

Prop. Mary Ann Ryan   201–543–2406

THORNTREE ANTIQUES, W. Main St.

Hours: By appt.

Early New England primitives a specialty; furniture, accessories, paintings, hooked rugs.

A—PM. Wide range. Authentication when possible.

Prop. Susan Pariser   201–543–2710

THE YESTERDAY SHOP, 2 Hilltop Rd. (at corner of Main St.).

                                                                           201–543–7766

Meyersville 07946

ARCHIE'S RESALE SHOP, 596 Meyersville Rd. (forks off N. Long Hill Rd.).

Hours: Sat. & Sun. 10–5

Series of outdoor sheds bulging with antiques, collectibles, odds and ends of everything. Tame deer, peacocks, horses, and other animals share the premises. Started twenty-five years ago as an area ice skate exchange, the rambling outlet now has a large collection of antique ice skates, old buggies, bicycles, sleighs, nautical items, old frames, lots of old bottles, chandeliers, bric-a-brac, books, used furniture. The Stiles' personal collection of antique toys was auctioned at Sotheby Parke Bernet in December 1976, attracting collectors from all over the country.

A/C—Some prices marked. Wide range. Authentication.

Prop. Archie Stiles   201–647–1149

TRADING POST ANTIQUES, 211 Hickory Tavern Rd. (off Long Hill Rd.).
Also see Repair and Restoration listing.

Hours: Tues. thru Sun. 10–5

Early American to Victorian furniture featured; oak tables, chests, chairs, oak china cabinets, pot belly stoves, antique clocks, in a 210-year-old restored home. Mr. Urbanski, "The Chair-Man," does all types of chair repair work— refinishing, retying springs, rewebbing, hand-caning, rushing, pressed cane, splinting; refinishing of antique furniture.

A/C—PM. Affordable/Wide range. Consignments. Authentication.

Prop. Martin D. Urbanski   201–647–1959

Millington 07946

WATTS OF MILLINGTON, 46 Sunnyslope (Division Ave., past RR Station, to Sunnyslope). *Also see* Repair and Restoration listing.

Hours: Wed. thru Fri. 12–4; Sat. 10–4; or by appt.

One of the earliest houses in the township—built as a four-room farmhouse in the 1700s, restored and enlarged in the early 1800s—is the charming background for Early American country furniture and appropriate accessories. Cupboards, tables, chairs, chests of drawers; early lamps, china, and glass. Interior design consultants, the Watts maintain a search and buying service and do appraisals. Repair and refinishing, caning, rushings, reupholstering.

A—PM. Selective. Authentication.

Prop. Mr. & Mrs. W. O. Watts   201–647–0050

Morris Plains 07950

THE MORRIS COUNTY REHABILITATION CENTER, 260 Tabor Rd.

Hours: By appt.

Antique Victorian jewelry, mostly gold, the specialty. Old pocket watches (repeaters, key wind, hunting cases) in gold and silver. The shop is staffed by volunteers. Proceeds to the Center.

A/C—PM. Affordable/Wide range. Authentication when possible.

Prop. Estelle Kanter, Member of the Board of Trustees   201–539–5636

Morristown 07960

ANTIQUES UNLIMITED OF MORRISTOWN, 17 Elm St. (off South St. by Grand Union Supermarket). *Also see* Repair and Restoration listing.

Hours: Tues. thru Sat. 10–6; Wed. 12–8

Civil War, World Wars I and II military memorabilia—sabers, uniforms, accouterments; antique clocks and watches, old coins. Repair and restoration of clocks and watches a service. Member Morristown Coin Club.

A/C—PM. Affordable. Consignments. Authentication.

Prop. Gregory Grant   201–267–0994

THE ARBOR, Mendham Rd. (opp. Burnham Park).

Hours: Daily 10–4; eves. 7–8

"Things old and new" in an old-time general store that dates to the late 1800s. Country store items—scales, old containers, collectible china and glass.

C/A—Some prices marked. Affordable.

Prop. Frances Murray   201–539–1861

THE BROWNS, 150 South St. (main east-west rd.).

Hours: Mon. thru Sat. 9:30–5

Antique Chinese porcelains, old brass fireplace equipment, antique and new lamps, general line of china, "any good old antiques."

A/C—PM. Wide range. Consignments. Authentication when possible.

Prop. Arthur I. Brown   201–538–4930

GOLDIE'S OLDIES, Peddler's Alley Mini-Mall, 33 South St. (Rt. 24).

Hours: Mon. thru Sat. 10–5:30

Clocks, watches, coins, lamps, furniture of various periods, bric-a-brac, old bottles. "We buy almost anything old or used."

C/A—PM. Affordable.

Prop. Jim Golding   201–455–9628

CORNELIA SUYDAM HERPEL, Mt. Kemble Ave. (Rt. 202, southbound).

Hours: Mon. thru Sat. 10–5

English 18th-century furniture, antique porcelains, formal lamps, decorative accessories artistically arranged in an interior designer's selective shop.

A—PM. Selective. Authentication.

Prop. Cornelia Suydam Herpel   201–766–2111

THE JEWEL BOX, 24 Park Pl. (main business st.).

Hours: Mon. thru Sat. 9:30–5; Wed., Fri. 'til 9

Fine selection of antique jewelry, rings, curios, pocket watches, clocks, in a large, full-service jewelry shop. Appraisal service.

A—PM. Wide range. Consignments. Authentication.

Prop. Seymour Cohen   201–539–0844

SCARLET PIMPERNEL ANTIQUES, Morristown.

Hours: By appt.

SCARLET PIMPERNEL ANTIQUES *continued*

Specializing in antique furniture, fine china and glass; also trunks, baskets, kitchen primitives, tins, piano rolls. The Blankenships will scout for clients and decorators.

A/C—PM. Affordable. Authentication.

Prop. Gail and Cary Blankenship   201–539–2476

Mt. Arlington 07856

ERNEST R. NORDBERG, 71 McGregor Ave. *Also see* Repair and Restoration listing.

Hours: By appt.

Nice early pieces of furniture at least 100 years old, some decorative accessories. Complete refinishing and restoration service, caning, rushing.

A/C—PM. Wide range. Authentication when possible.

Prop. Ernest R. Nordberg   201–663–3677

Newfoundland 07435

WAGON WHEEL ANTIQUES, Rt. 23, southbound (next to Newfoundland Drug Store). *Also see* Repair and Restoration listing.

Hours: Tues. thru Sat. 12–6

Large selection of clocks from the 18th century to the turn of the century— grandfather, wall, mantel; some pocket watches and jewelry; primitive to oak furniture, china, old dolls, kerosene and hanging lamps. Member of the Nat'l. Assoc. of Watch & Clock Collectors. Services include clock repair and restoration, furniture repair.

A/C—PM. Wide range. Authentication when possible.

Prop. Don and Kay Frayko   201–697–6927

Parsippany 07054

LORENE RUTH CASE, 360 E. Halsey Rd. (east of Hwy. 287 bet. Rts. 10 and 46).

Hours: By appt.

LORENE RUTH CASE *continued*

Antique furniture, with emphasis on primitive, a specialty; also nice selection of old dolls.

A/Some collectibles—PM. Affordable/Selective.

Prop. Lorene Ruth Case   201–887–0819

Pequannock 07440

IMPERIAL COINS & COLLECTIBLES, 137 Newark-Pompton Tpk.

Hours: Wed. thru Fri. 5:30–9; Sat. 10–5; Sun. 10–1

Specialists in rare coins, numismatic books and supplies; old guns; some china, glass, and silver. The Woolfs do appraisals and are members of the American Numismatic Society.

A/C—PM. Wide range. Consignments. Authentication.

Prop. Basil and Anne Woolf   201–694–1599

Pine Brook 07058

DUTCH GABLES, 58 Maple Ave. (corner Hook Mt. Rd.).

Hours: Appt. suggested

Early American furniture and accessories before 1830, attractively arranged in a fine old stone house from the early 1700s. Sandwich glass, old pewter, pottery. Many pieces tagged with identification and age.

A—PM. Selective.

Prop. Betsy Demarest, Marion Douglass   201–227–2803
                                                              227–2765

Pompton Plains 07444

ARCH GALLERIES CORP., 629 Rt. 23, northbound. *Also see* Repair and Restoration listing.

Hours: Tues. thru Sat. 10–5

Spacious shop crowded with European and Oriental furniture, French, German, and English clocks, chandeliers, fine china and porcelains. House sales

ARCH GALLERIES CORP. *continued*

conducted, appraisal service. Refinishing, repairing, reupholstering of furniture, caning and rushing.

A/Some collectibles—PM. Selective. Consignments. Authentication.

Prop. Corporation 201–835–5034

CRAZY LADIES JUNK SHOPPE, 580 Rt. 23, southbound (next to Huffman-Koos).

Hours: Mon. thru Sun. 11–6

Antique and collectible china, cut glass, clocks, some small pieces of furniture among the new gift items. "New mixed with old."

A/C—PM. Affordable. Consignments. Authentication.

Prop. Ronnie Bock 201–839–5252

THE WAYSIDE SHOP, 5 Jackson Ave. (off Newark-Pompton Tpk.).

Hours: Tues., Thurs., Sat. 1–5

Country furniture, fine china and glass in a charming two-room shop. Mrs. Jones conducts house sales and does appraising. Est. 1957.

A/C—PM. Affordable. Authentication.

Prop. Vlasta M. Jones 201–835–0993

Randolph Twp. 07081

THE HINGE ANTIQUES, 505 Rt. 10 (Center Grove Rd. and Rt. 10, eastbound).

Hours: 7 days 11–6

Wide variety of antiques and collectibles in a spacious shop shared by five dealers.

OLGA DOWNES.

Eighteenth- and 19th-century country furniture, primitives, china, early tools.

HELEN FABBOZI.

Everything in oak—tables, chairs, oak-framed mirrors; general line of china and glass.

THE HINGE ANTIQUES *continued*

GERRY and ROSS YATES.

Primitives, iron toys, trunks, china, pressed-back oak chairs, occasional tables.

IRENE YOUNG.

Old tools, toys, glassware, some primitives, linens.

LONI ZAMBETI.

Clocks of many kinds, from 18th century to Art Nouveau; schoolhouse clocks, mission oak, mantel, grandfather; pocket watches, antique jewelry, china, some turn-of-the-century furniture.

A/C—PM. Affordable/Wide range. Consignments. Authentication.

Prop. Cooperative   201–361–9819

Riverdale 07457

CENTURY HOUSE ANTIQUES & BOOK SHOP, 47 Newark-Pompton Tpk.

Hours: Mon. thru Fri. 1–5; eves. & weekends by appt.

Selective shop specializing in 18th- and 19th-century furniture, primitives, Americana, and oil paintings. Good selection of new books on antiques and related subjects in adjoining room. Appraisal service.

A—PM. Selective. Authentication.

Prop. Dorothy Hildebrant   201–835–4635

COLONIAL FARM ANTIQUES, 44 Post Lane (off Newark-Pompton Tpk.).

Hours: Tues., Wed., Fri., Sat. 11–5; Sun. 1–5

Two barns filled with antiques and collectibles—country furniture refinished and in-the-rough; brass, copper, tin accessories; fine china, old lamps, antique dolls. "General line of just about everything." Lots of old sleigh bells and hundreds of turn-of-the-century chocolate molds. Est. 1957.

A/C—PM. Wide range. Authentication.

Prop. Joan and Jim Fenstermacher   201–835–5916

Rockaway 07866

QUILT COUNTRY USA, 13 Union St. (Maple St. off Main St. to Union).

Hours: Mon. thru Sat. 9:30–5

QUILT COUNTRY USA *continued*

Devoted to quilts of all kinds, old and new, patchwork, calico, appliquéd. Lessons in quilting, supplies, large selection of material.

A/C—PM. Affordable.

Prop. Mary D'Amelio   201–625–2138

Stephensburg 07865

ROBERT GAULER, R. D. 2, Old Turnpike Rd. (off Rt. 57 at corner of Stephensburg and Old Tpk. Rd.).

Hours: Sat. & Sun 9–5:30; or by chance

A general line of old furniture, glass, blanket chests, pitcher and basin sets.

A/C—PM. Affordable.

Prop. Robert Gauler   201–852–3139

Stirling 07980

THE RESTORE, 253 Main Ave. (off Valley Rd.). *Also see* Repair and Restoration listing.

Hours: Tues. thru Sat. 9–5:30

A few pieces of antique furniture in a shop devoted to repair and restoration. Hand-stripping and hand-finishing, upholstering, rushing and caning.

A/C—PM. Affordable.

Prop. Carl W. Sundberg   201–647–0613

Towaco 07082

GAZEBO ANTIQUES, 21 Brook Valley Rd. (off Rt. 504, northbound). *Also see* Repair and Restoration listing.

Hours: Fri. thru Sun. 10–5; or by appt.

Early lamps a specialty; chandeliers, fixtures; general line of furniture, decorative accessories. New handcrafted weathervanes, lanterns, chandeliers, sconces. Services include repair and restoration of lamps, converting, electrifying; polishing of metals, silver plating.

A/C—PM. Wide range. Authentication.

Prop. A. Bertelo   201–334–0361

Black and white Wedgwood vase, "Apotheosis of Homer," ca. 1800. *Courtesy Charles B. Smith Antiques, Fairview*

Passaic County

Bloomingdale 07403

COUNTRY FAIR, 131 Main St.

Hours: Mon. thru Sat. 10–4. Closed Wed.

Two rooms filled with old tools, kitchen utensils, oak and other furniture, china, glassware; collectibles. Appraisals. Estate sales; local auctions.

A/C—PM. Affordable. Consignments. Authentication when possible.

Prop. Janet Hickman   201–838–9849

GRANDMA'S CORNER ANTIQUES & GIFTS, 62 Main St.

Hours: Thurs. thru Mon. 10–5. Closed Tues. & Wed.

Turn-of-the-century furniture, nice pieces in good condition. Depression and 1930s colored glass; new gifts. Large collection beautifully displayed.

C; also new—PM. Affordable/Wide range. Consignments.

Prop. Jim and Flo Hess   201–838–7400

Clifton 07011

CENTURY ANTIQUES, 565 Clifton Ave. *Also see* Repair and Restoration listing.

Hours: Wed. thru Sat. 11–5

CENTURY ANTIQUES *continued*

Oak furniture, mantel and wall clocks (c. 1840–1920); kerosene and other lamps. Furniture repair and restoration, hand work; free estimates. Clock repair. Caning. Supplies, "lots of free advice." Pleasant young shop. Member Appraisers' Assoc. of Amer.

C—Some prices marked. Affordable/Selective. Authentication.

Prop. Rosanne and Larry Guizio   201–365–1592

DON AND MARIE'S ANTIQUES, Clifton.

Hours: By appt.

Oak, cherry, and walnut furniture, glass, china, pottery, '20s and '30s collectibles; general line. Furniture and trunks refinished, restored.

A/C—PM. Affordable/Selective. Authentication.

Prop. Don and Marie Sutton   201–471–3689

GRANNY'S ATTIC, 1080 Main Ave.

Hours: Mon. thru Sat. 11–5

Turn-of-the-century furniture (some earlier), china, silver, jewelry, glass, clocks, pictures. General line in a very pleasant shop. Appraisals. Lectures on antiques; decorating advice. Furniture refinishing by arrangement. Mr. Lubman pens an antiques column for Seniors Today, *a northern New Jersey newspaper for senior citizens. Also see Mr. Wipple's Country Store, below.*

C/A—Most prices marked. Wide range. Consignments. Authentication.

Prop. Maury Lubman   201–772–1929

MR. WIPPLE'S COUNTRY STORE, 1076 Main Ave.

Hours: Mon. thru Sat. 11–5

Oak, walnut, and country furniture; country store items, wicker. Two floors and what is referred to as the "catacombs." Furniture refinishing by arrangement. Also see Granny's Attic, above.

C—Most prices marked. Affordable/Selective. Consignments (occasionally). Authentication.

Prop. Maury Lubman   201–772–8024

UNIQUE ANTIQUES, 430 Lexington Ave.

Hours: Mon. thru Sat. 11–6

Turn-of-the-century furniture, accessories; old jewelry. "The interesting and

UNIQUE ANTIQUES *continued*

oddball," Texas longhorns to European music boxes. Contents of homes, jewelry, old gold, sterling purchased. Wholesale/retail.

C—Prices not marked. Wide range.

Prop. Judd Berkey   201–546–5952 (bus.)
                                                          778–6345 (res.)

Passaic 07055

JAN JILL & JON, 170 Main Ave.

Hours: Mon. thru Sat. 10–6; Fri. 'til 9

Respected dealer, known for antique jewelry, sterling, bronzes, art glass, Orientalia, paintings. Also Wedgwood, fine china, porcelains, furniture, some lighting. Appraisals. Layaway plan. Member North Jersey Antique Dealers Assoc. Sales guaranteed as represented.

A/C—PM. Wide range. All sales guaranteed.

Prop. Rhoda and Seymour Zucker   201–777–4670 (bus.)
                                                          473–3375 (res.)

OLD, NEW AND IN BETWEEN, 106 Main Ave., Passaic Park.

Hours: Mon. thru Sat. 9–5. Mondays, call ahead suggested.

General line; crystal, jewelry, Fiesta Ware, Avon collectibles, lamps. Decorating advice; window decor. Flea markets and shows managed.

C/A—PM. Affordable. Consignments.

Prop. John Butler   201–473–4979

Paterson 07502

NAGLE'S, 139 Ryerson Ave.

Hours: By appt.

Trunks, furniture, kitchen implements; some copper, kerosene lamps, primitive baskets; dried flowers. Antiques purchased. Trunks refinished.

A/C; also new—PM. Affordable. Consignments.

Prop. Edward Nagle   201–278–6365

KEN ROSSER, 110 12th Ave.

Hours: after 5, anytime

Silver, stained glass, walking canes; oddities. Some repair work.

A/C—Prices not marked. Affordable.

Prop. Ken Rosser   201–525–5454

GARRY SMITH, 841 E. 29th. *Also see* Auctioneers listing.

Hours: By appt.

Primarily wholesale and varied; emphasis on paintings, Oriental art, jewelry. Estates purchased. Licensed auctioneer. Appraisals. Member N. J. Soc. of Auctioneers.

A/C—Prices not marked. Wide range. Authentication when possible.

Prop. Garry Smith   201–523–3035

Pompton Lakes 07442

DUKES CORNER SHOPPE, 4 Broad St. *Also see* Repair and Restoration listing.

Hours: Mon. thru Sat. 8–6

Collectible furniture, bric-a-brac. Specializing in furniture refinishing and antique restoration; gold leaf work, chair regluing. Caning, genuine rush, and ash splint weaving.

C/A—Most prices marked. Wide range.

Prop. Ewald Poehler, Jr.   201–839–3880

NOSTALGIC ATTIC, 322 Ringwood Ave. (opp. Ben Franklin Shopping Plaza). *Also see* Repair and Restoration listing.

Hours: Mon. thru Sat. 9–5

Furniture, glassware, small objects. Varied general line in a small, pleasant in-town shop. Furniture hand-stripping, repair, restoration, refinishing by Jim Rudi.

A/C—PM. Selective. Authentication.

Prop. Jim Rudi, Bill Antonelli   201–835–9397

Singac 07424

CURIOSITY SHOP, 159 Rt. 23, southbound.

Hours: Mon. thru Sat. 11–4. Closed Thurs.

Books, paper Americana, furniture, glass, primitives, toys, military items. Estate and garage sales conducted.

C/A—PM. Wide range. Consignments. Authentication when possible.

Prop. Doris LaRue   201–785–2341

JANE & HENRY ANTIQUES, 171 Rt. 23, southbound.

Hours: Mon. thru Sat. 11–4, or by appt; call ahead suggested. Closed Thurs. Open Aug. by appt.

General line, primarily collectibles. Jewelry, glass, post cards, furniture, books. Caning; brass burnishing.

C—PM. Affordable. Consignments. Authentication when possible.

Prop. Jane and Henry Skwirut   201–256–2296
                                                          239–0088

THEN & NOW SHOPPE, 169 Rt. 23, southbound. *Also see* **Repair** and **Restoration** listing.

Hours: Daily 11–5. Closed Thurs. & Sun.

General line; including oak chairs, (round) tables, rockers, trunks, mirrors, crystal, brass, dolls; potbelly, parlor, and cookstoves. Chair caning and rushing. New piano rolls to order. Master Charge; layaway plan. "Shoplifters will be shot."

C—PM. Affordable/Wide range. Consignments.

Prop. Terry and Jan Worden   201–256–8413 (bus.)
                                                   226–2149 (res.)

Wanaque 07465

YESTERDAY'S CHILD, 673 Ringwood Ave.

Hours: Tues. thru Sat. 10–5

Eighteenth- to mid-19th-century American primitives, oak; general line, copper, brass, pottery, bric-a-brac. Antiques purchased. Dried and silk flower arrangements, also supplies and workshops.

YESTERDAY'S CHILD *continued*

A/C; also new—PM. Wide range. Consignments. Authentication.

Prop. Mimi Sorrentino   201–839–0660 (bus.)
                                                              839–1582 (res.)

Wayne 07470

ANTIQUE ASSOCIATES, Pines Lake.

Hours: By appt.

Primarily purchase rather than sale. Fine antiques and collectibles; bronzes, art glass, sterling, jewelry, coins, quality furniture (including better oak), dolls, toys. Appraisals. Auctions arranged.

A/C—Prices not marked. Selective to serious collectors. Authentication.

Prop. Bruce Hertzberg   201–839–1212

ANTIQUES AND MEMORABILIA, Wayne.

Hours: By appt.

Large pieces of furniture, primitives. Trunks refinished and restored.

A/C—PM. Affordable. Authentication.

Prop. Lois Cummings   201–696–1249

COUNTRY PINE 'N' TIQUES, 600 Berdan Ave.

Hours: Tues. thru Sat. 11:30–4:30

Cut crystal, Depression glass, some primitives; collectibles. Handsome pine reproduction furniture a specialty, custom made by Mr. and Mrs. Verbrugge.

C; also new—PM. Wide range.

Prop. Jim and Betty Verbrugge   201–628–9358

West Milford 07480

FARM HOUSE ANTIQUES, 564 Macopin Rd.

Hours: Call ahead, or by chance

American country furniture, primitives, and accessories. Blanket chests, jam cupboards, drop leaf tables, cupboards, benches, commodes, stands, desks; country shop signs. Some pieces in-the-rough. Dried flower arrangements by Ms. Bruterri. Member Associated Antiques Dealers of N. J.

FARM HOUSE ANTIQUES *continued*

A/C—PM. Affordable. Consignments. Authentication.

Prop. Patricia Bruterri   201–838–7069

MACOPIN HOMESTEAD, 1299 Macopin Rd.

Hours: By appt.

English, French, Oriental, and American period furnishings; glass, china, clocks, lighting devices, rugs. Personal service; decorating assistance. Lectures.

A/C—Some prices marked. Selective/Wide range. Authentication when possible.

Prop. F. Vreeland, A. Stanley, J. Crawford   201–697–5616

Black and white antique Wedgwood tea set, ca. 1800. *Courtesy Charles B. Smith Antiques, Fairview*

"Die Pyramide," a 1920 poster by Walter Schnackenberg advertising a German café.
Courtesy The Exhumation, Princeton. Photo: Michael Schnessel

Bergen County

Alpine 07620

ALPINE APPRAISERS AND ANTIQUES, Closter Dock Rd. (near Rt. 9W).
Hours: Daily 1–5. Closed Mon.

Specializing in appraisals; estate liquidations. Also to the trade. Antiques purchased. Member Independent Antique Dealers of Amer., Inc., Appraisers' Assoc. of America. Est. 1940. In a 1760 blacksmith shop; good off-the-road parking.

A/C—PM. Wide range. Authentication.

Prop. Elise Hille   201–768–0026

Bergenfield 07621

CHEZ SHEA, 87 N. Washington Ave.
Hours: Tues. thru Sat. 12–5

Oriental porcelains—Japanese·(from 1830), Chinese dynasty; fine china, good prints, paintings; general line. Antiques purchased. Appraisals.

A/C—PM. Wide range. Consignments. Authentication within specialty.

Prop. Cele and Ray Shea   201–384–5510

CURIOSITY CORNER, 89 N. Washington Ave.

Hours: Mon. thru Sat. 10–5. Closed Tues.

China, glass, jewelry, furniture, silver; "antiques and elegant junque." Some dolls, toys, paintings. Estates purchased. Layaway plan.

A/C—PM. Affordable. Authentication.

Prop. Grace Toth   201–384–8033
                                                                        385–1632

THE DOOR STOP ANTIQUES, 65 N. Washington Ave.

Hours: Mon. thru Sat. 10–5

General line; primarily furniture. Wall groupings a specialty. Desks, chests, china closets, tables, armchairs, rockers, mirrors; a carved dowry chest, a pillared, carved, and mirrored Flemish hutch. Also brass, copper, Wedgwood, Haviland, sterling; quality used furniture. Decorating assistance. Very pleasant.

A/C—PM. Wide range. Selective consignments.

Prop. Lyliane Adge   201–385–6066

THE TURN-OVER SHOP, 87 N. Washington Ave.

Hours: Mon. thru Sat. 10–5

Furniture, primarily '30s and '40s; wicker, bamboo, oak tables, secretaries, desks. Depression and cut glass, stemware, pictures. House contents, estates, and individual items purchased.

C—PM. Wide range. Consignments. Authentication.

Prop. Gertrude Ansel, Evelyn Weingarten   201–384–4415
                                                                        385–6717

LARRY A. WENZEL, 79 N. Washington Ave.

Hours: Mon. thru Fri. 10:30–5

Furniture, bric-a-brac, jewelry, World's Fair and ocean liner memorabilia, general advertising; the unusual emphasized. No reproductions or contemporary items.

C—Most prices marked. Wide range. Consignments. Sales guaranteed.

Prop. Larry A. Wenzel   201–833–1427

Bogota 07603

MATTHEW'S GALLERIES, 54 W. Main St.

Hours: Tues. thru Sat. 11–6

MATTHEW'S GALLERIES *continued*

Nineteenth- and early 20th-century American paintings; some European works. Paintings from the estate of George Stimmel (1880–1964). Fine art and jewelry appraisals. Custom and antique framing. Also see Nefertiti, below.

A/C—Some prices marked. Wide range. Authentication.

Prop. Matthew W. Gerber, Nefertiti   201–343–8301

NEFERTITI, 54 W. Main St.

Hours: Tues. thru Sat. 11–6

Antique and estate jewelry; special interest in "novel" new jewelry. Victorian gold, silver, brass; cameos, stickpins, lockets, rings, paintings on porcelain; Egyptian pieces. Appraisals. Also see Matthew's Galleries, above.

A/C—PM. Wide range. Authentication.

Prop. Nefertiti, Matthew W. Gerber   201–343–8301

Cliffside Park 07010

VINTAGE YEARS ANTIQUES, 619 Palisade Ave.

Hours: Tues. thru Sat. 10–5:30; Sun. 11–4. (Closed Sun., July & Aug.)

Art Nouveau, Art Deco. Tiffany glass, Tiffany lamps, French art glass, bronzes, porcelains. Some small decorative furniture, Victorian jewelry.

C/A—Some prices marked. Wide range. Authentication.

Prop. Harry Speiser   201–945–6035

Closter 07624

THE ANTIQUE EMPORIUM, 390 Demarest Ave. (next to A & P Supermarket).

Hours: Tues. thru Sat. 10:30–5

China, glass, some furniture; general line, nicely displayed. Antiques purchased. Dealers welcome. Master Charge, Visa.

C—PM. Affordable. Authentication when possible.

Prop. Rita Cohen, Beverly Quirk, Carol Willinger   201–767–0850

HARVEY W. BREWER, Box 322.

Hours: By appt.

Antiquarian books. Specializing in art, architecture, pictorial; from the 1500s. Member Middle Atlantic Chapter, Antiquarian Booksellers' Assoc. of Amer.

A/C—Prices not marked. Wide range. Authentication.

Prop. Harvey W. Brewer   201–768–4414

Cresskill 07621

GENERAL STORE, 18 Union Ave. (just off Piermont Rd.).

Hours: Mon. thru Sat. 1–5

Collectibles in ready-to-use condition, filling the downstairs of a century-old house. New stained glass shades. Browsing welcome.

C; also new—PM. Affordable/Wide range. Consignments.

Prop. Derna Wehmann   201–568–2652

East Rutherford 07073

JEAN BARRETT, 138 Park Ave.

Hours: Tues. thru Sat. 11–4:30

General line; mostly turn-of-the-century. Silver (primarily sterling), glass, china, jewelry, prints, post cards. Leaded lamps and art glass of particular interest. Appraisals. House sales. Member Garden State Post Card Collectors Club.

A/C—PM. Affordable. Consignments. Authentication.

Prop. Jean Barrett   201–933–4771 (bus.)
                                                       759–2826 (res.)

JOAN LANG ANTIQUES, 138 Park Ave.

Hours: Tues. thru Sat. 11–4

Collectibles; glass, china, furniture. House sales. Member Nat'l. Cambridge Glass Assoc.

C—Most prices marked. Wide range. Consignments.

Prop. Joan Lang   201–933–2648 (bus.)
                                                   338–5884 (if no ans.)

Edgewater 07020

SOMETHING OLD, 1064 River Rd.

Hours: By appt.

Orientals, jewelry; porcelain, cloisonné, ivory, bronze.

A/C—PM. Wide range. Consignments. Authentication.

Prop. Norma Cybul

201–224–4102
567–3138

Elmwood Park 07407

GENE MURPHY, 18 Ackerman Ave.

Hours: By appt.

Specializing in country store items and antique toys. Old toys purchased.

A/C—PM. Affordable.

Prop. Gene Murphy

201–796–2229

Englewood 07631

THE ANTIQUE PLACE, 10 West St. *Also see* Repair and Restoration listing.

Hours: Mon. thru Sat. 12–6

General line of "this and that." Furniture stripping and refinishing. Member North Jersey Antique Dealers Assoc.

C—Prices not marked. Affordable.

Prop. Helen Fisher

201–567–9493

LEONARD BALISH, 124A Engle St.

Hours: By appt.

Knowledgeable collection of antiques and Americana. Country furniture, primitives, excellent early pottery, quilts and coverlets, folk art, paperweights, decoys, mounted weathervanes, American Indian artifacts. English pottery and porcelain. Appraisals.

A—PM. Selective to serious collectors. Authentication.

Prop. Leonard Balish

201–871–3454
568–5385 (if no ans.)

THE COLONY ANTIQUE SHOP, 1 E. Palisade Ave. (corner facing RR tracks).

Hours: Mon. thru Sat. 10:30–5:30

Antique jewelry, porcelain, china, silver, crystal, glass, bric-a-brac, furniture, some books. Consultant on interiors. Repair service. Master Charge, Visa.

A/C—PM. Wide range.

Prop. Sylvia Franklin   201–568–5357

ENGLEWOOD GALLERIES, 130 Grand Ave.

Hours: Mon. thru Sat. 12:30–5. Closed Wed.

Ornate Russian and French bronzes, French and Oriental furnishings, porcelains, Continental silver. Decorating assistance. Appraisals. Guaranteed ten-year return policy.

A—Most prices marked. Selective to serious collectors. Selective consignments. Authentication.

201–871–0073

HUNTER'S ANTIQUES, 540 Grand Ave.

Hours: Winter: Mon. thru Sat. 11–5. Summer: Tues. thru Sat. 11–5

Art Nouveau, including Gallé, Tiffany, Teplitz, paintings, bronzes, some furniture and lighting; mint condition, labeled, dated. Beautiful gallery display. Appraisals. Member Carnival Glass Assoc. of Northern N. J.

C—PM. Affordable/Wide range. Authentication.

Prop. Nick Sambogna, Asa Hoff   201–384–7647
                                                              568–4888

ROBERT A. PAULSON, 37 West St.

Hours: Mon. thru Sat. 9–5

Specializing in scarce and out-of-print books; signed volumes. Emphasis on history, biography, music, art, poetry, natural history, science. Appraisal service. Large, pleasant shop. Member Middle Atlantic Chapter, Antiquarian Booksellers' Assoc. of Amer.

C—PM. Affordable. Authentication.

Prop. Robert A. Paulson   201–871–1552

ROYAL GALLERIES, 22 Engle St.

Hours: Tues. thru Sat. 10–5

Fine 19th- to 20th-century American paintings; English and American silver,

ROYAL GALLERIES *continued*

china; 18th- and 19th-century European and American furniture. For the antiquarian and collector. Appraisals. Member Appraisers' Assoc. of Amer.

A/C (paintings)—PM. Wide range. Authentication.

Prop. Sidney Bressler   201–567–6354

TONY ART GALLERIES, 120 Grand Ave. *Also see* Auctioneers listing.

Hours: Mon. thru Sat. 1–6

Paintings, furniture, porcelain, rugs, tapestries, lighting; decorative antiques. Appraisals. Estate (tag) sales. Member N. J. Soc. of Auctioneers.

A/C—Prices not marked. Wide range. Consignments. Authentication.

Prop. Arthur Petrovic   201–568–7271

Fair Lawn 07410

ANTIQUES AT LAST, 5–02 Fair Lawn Ave. *Also see* Repair and Restoration listing.

Hours: Sat. 10–4; or by appt.

Primarily oak furniture, trunks, an occasional icebox; early kitchen items, some china, glass, crocks. Larger pieces delivered. Chairs caned. "Anything old" purchased.

C—PM. Affordable. Authentication.

Prop. Joan Last   201–278–7468

BEDLAM BRASS BEDS AND ANTIQUES, 19–21 Fair Lawn Ave.

Hours: Tues. thru Fri. 1–8; Sat. & Sun. 1–5. Closed Mon.

Original and refurbished brass, brass and iron bedsteads, c. 1890–1920. Manufacturers of new brass beds; extensive catalog of designs and parts. Custom scrollwork and bending.

Small, mostly turn-of-the-century accessory line; brass coat trees (when available), grillwork, stained glass windows, Victorian furniture, glassware, sterling, porcelain, jewelry, miniatures, bric-a-brac. Quality pieces purchased. Dealers welcome. Master Charge, Visa. Branches also in Boston, Alexandria, Va., Atlanta, Miami, New Orleans, San Antonio, San Francisco.

In the 200+-year-old Cadmus House, once part of a Dutch farm whose tranquil holdings extended over half of present-day Fair Lawn.

C—Not all prices marked. Selective. Authentication.

Prop. Dick and Marleen Grabowsky, Ron Kronenberg   201–796–7200

WHAT EVER SHOP, 28–03A Broadway.

Hours: Thurs., Fri., Sat. 10–2; or by appt.

Antiques, oddities, bric-a-brac; china, glass, stemware—an occasional mantel clock, some silver.

C. Affordable.

Prop. Mabel Kerr   201–791–6336

Fort Lee 07024

ANTIQUES & TEMPTATIONS, 134 Main St.

Hours: Mon. thru Sat. 12–5; or by appt.

Figurines, plates, some furniture, silver, prints (including Currier & Ives, Maxfield Parrish), paintings.

C/A—PM. Affordable.

Prop. Blanche Jacobson   201–944–1692

BRIDGE PLAZA ANTIQUES, 235 Main St. (in Municipal Parking Lot, across from Post Office).

Hours: 7 days 12–6

China, porcelain, glass, art glass, silver, turn-of-the-century American and European paintings, dolls, toys. Collectibles over fifty years of age. Appraisals. In the business district, with a pretty and unexpected garden.

C—Most prices marked. Affordable/Wide range. Consignments. Authentication when possible.

Prop. Mary Levy, Steven Levy   201–224–8983

Franklin Lakes 07417

FRANKLIN LAKES GALLERIES, 792 Franklin Ave. (sm. shopping plaza, diag. opp. Shell Sta.). *Also see* Repair and Restoration listing.

Hours: Tues. thru Sat. 11–5

Beyond an elegant entrance, very fine 18th-, 19th-, and early 20th-century European and American paintings. Some furnishings and decorative arts; antiques only. Restoration of paintings and frames. Household and estate appraisals. Member Amer. Assoc. of Conservators and Restorers. Galleries also in New York, London, Paris. Founded 1875. (Van Cline & Davenport, Ltd. in N.Y.)

FRANKLIN LAKES GALLERIES *continued*

A/C (paintings)—Prices coded. Selective. Consignments. Authentication.

Prop. Stephen van Cline, Michael Southeby Davenport   201–891–4588

ROWLAND E. LEWIS, 211 Mabel Ann Ave.

Hours: By appt., or call ahead

Tall case clocks a specialty; wall and shelf clocks. Antique clocks purchased, restored. Pleasant shop in the barn of a 200-year-ago Dutch farm. Member Nat'l. Assoc. of Watch & Clock Collectors, North Jersey Antique Dealers Assoc.

A/C PM. Wide range. Authentication when possible.

Prop. Rowland E. Lewis   201–891–0029

PEWTER & PINE SHOP, 233 Osage Lane.

Hours: By appt.

American primitives; painted wood, toys, animals, early birds and decoys, spongeware, redware, early candlesticks, baskets, crocks.

A—PM. Affordable. Authentication when possible.

Prop. Nancy Mulligan   201–891–3626

Garfield 07026

THE COLLECTOR, 85 Passaic.

Hours: Tues. thru Sat. 2–9

Broad general line; primarily collectibles. Jewelry, clocks, watches, pocket watches, steins, military items, trains, toys, dolls, baseball cards, wicker, Depression glass, prints, etchings. Large sellers' and finders' file, color photographs. Layaway plan. Repairs by arrangement.

C/A—Prices coded. Wide range. Consignments.

Prop. Joan Corry   201–473–1377 (bus.)
                                                         796–5908 (res.)

UNICORN ANTIQUES, 108 Harrison Ave. *Also see* Repair and Restoration listing.

Hours: By appt.

Refinished primitive, Victorian, and oak furniture; dolls, glassware, china. Appraisals. Caning; refinishing. Delivery service.

C—PM. Affordable/Wide range. Authentication.

Prop. Kay and Ken Blair   201–340–1454

Glen Rock 07452

GILBERT'S GIFT & ANTIQUE GALLERY, 356 S. Maple Ave. (several shops north of Hess Sta.).

Hours: 7 days 11–5

General line; bric-a-brac, glass, small furniture, silver; collectibles and memorabilia. Old and new comic books. Antiques purchased. Layaway plan. Browsers welcome.

C—PM. Wide range. Selective consignments. Authentication when possible.

Prop. Douglas Gilbert   201–444–9772

Hackensack 07601

ANTIQUEVILLE, 55 Linden St.

Hours: Mon. thru Sat. 10–5

Collector's items in quantity; military and aviation oddments and memorabilia, advertising, primitives, brass, copper, iron, wood. Medical and dental tools, locks, keys, mechanical antiques, a wicker fishing creel, unicycle, brass spittoon, old "No Parking" stanchion; turtle shell, minus occupant.

A/C—PM. Affordable. Authentication.

Prop. Jack Bilsky   201–489–1614

APPRAISAL AND ESTATE SERVICES, 82–84 Moore St. Mailing address: P. O. Box 871, Fort Lee 07024.

Hours: Sat. 10–5

Used furniture, household goods, antiques; "whatever comes in." House sales and liquidations. Appraisals. Member Appraisers' Assoc. of Amer.

C/A—PM. Wide range.

Prop. Perry E. Rosenblum   201–342–6682

LYDIA DELMAN, 93 Anderson St.

Hours: By appt.

Primarily refinished furniture and accessories; clocks, wicker, rugs, lamps, prints, baskets. Arranged for window browsing; also downstairs.

A/C—Most prices marked. Wide range.

Prop. Lydia Delman   201–488–8985

THE EMPORIUM, Hackensack.

Hours: By appt.

Old quilts, mostly New York State coverlets, old textiles, samplers, beaded pieces; some bric-a-brac. Especially attractive to young people, designers.

A/C—PM. Affordable. Consignments. Authentication when possible.

Prop. Eve Buttenheim   201–342–3371

THE GOLD MAN, 183 Main St.

Hours: Mon., Tues., Thurs. 10:30–4:30; Fri., Sat. 10:30–6; and by appt. Closed Wed.

Antique, estate, and out-of-pawn jewelry, watches, other objects; diamonds and color stones. Special order jewelry, personal designs. Photographs on request. Jewelry, watch repairs.

A/C—PM. Wide range. Selective consignments. Authentication.

Prop. Mr. & Mrs. George Goldman   201–342–6110

BRANDON KEENE ANTIQUES, 77 Anderson St.

Hours: Tues. thru Sat. 11–4

Pre-1940 collectibles; good used furniture, paintings, Art Deco. Antiques purchased.

C—Most prices marked. Affordable/Wide range. Consignments (occasional). Authentication on request.

Prop. Brandon Keene   201–342–4039

HELEN T. KINOIAN, GOLDEN EAGLE ANTIQUES, 57 Linden St.

Hours: By appt. Usually closed July & Aug.

Dolls, Oriental rugs, cut glass, art glass, sterling, furniture, accessories. Antiques and estates purchased; consultation for estates and individuals. Appraisals. Member, North Jersey Antique Dealers Assoc.

C—Most prices marked. Wide range. Authentication.

Prop. Helen T. Kinoian   201–487–2422

R & R ANTIQUES, 79 Anderson St.

Hours: Mon. thru Sat. 10–5

Nice selection of wicker; oak, mahogany, and walnut furniture; jewelry, silver, Deco-era apparel, bric-a-brac, old children's toys.

R & R ANTIQUES *continued*

A/C—Most prices marked. Wide range. Consignments. Authentication when possible.

Prop. Roslyn Gradinger, Joan Oberman   201–489–8040

ROADRUNNER ANTIQUES, 837 Main St. (Also in Cape May.)

Hours: Weekdays, by appt. or chance

Oak furnishings a specialty; general line of furniture, collectibles. Delivery service.

C/A—Most prices marked. Wide range.

Prop. Carol Gomm   201–342–3281

SHELLEY'S, 102 Anderson St.

Hours: Mon. thru Sat. 11–4

Attractive shop with a sign advising that "The time to buy it is when you see it!" China, glass, collectibles; unusual things. Appraisals. Member North Jersey Antique Dealers Assoc.

A/C—PM. Affordable/Wide range.

Prop. Shelley Allen   201–343–2639

STONEMILL ANTIQUES & STAINED GLASS ART SHOP, 75½ Anderson St.

Hours: Saturdays; and by appt.

Stained glass windows and doors, framed and unframed; Americana, Victoriana, glassware. Some silver, china, art pottery, furniture. Special order reproduction Tiffany shades at wholesale prices; selection by photograph. Stained glass repair.

C/A—Most prices marked. Wide range. Consignments. Authentication on request.

Prop. Barry Hanulak, R. Kurtz   201–489–7155
                                                                         343–4820

Hasbrouck Heights 07604

COLLECTOR'S GALLERY, Hasbrouck Heights. Mailing address: Box 162.

Hours: By appt.

Continental, American, and Oriental porcelains. Chinese export porcelain and Staffordshire pottery specialties. Eighteenth- and early 19th-century American

COLLECTOR'S GALLERY *continued*

furniture, American primitive paintings, Japanese wood block prints, early ivories. Five-year exchange plan. Appraisals. Mrs. Gross teaches adult school classes in antiques. Prices are firm.

A—PM. Selective to serious collectors. Authentication.

Prop. Mr. & Mrs. Louis Gross   201–763–5851

HABITAT ANTIQUES, 286 Terrace Ave. *Also see* Repair and Restoration listing.

Hours: Mon. thru Sat. 10–6

Refinished oak and wicker furniture. Restoration and refinishing; caning, wicker reweaving.

C—Most prices marked. Selective. Consignments. Authentication.

Prop. Ed Zipfel   201–288–4180

Haworth 07641

ANTIQUITIES & "UNCOMMON COLLECTIBLES," Haworth.

Hours: By appt.

General line of "early things and uncommon collectibles." Early lighting, covered animal dishes, early baskets, motto prints. The proprietor teaches adult education courses, lectures, and is registered with the N. J. Women's Club Speakers Bureau. House sales conducted.

C/A. Affordable. Consignments. Authentication when possible.

Prop. Helen M. Hartjc   201–384–6277

SAMIDE, Haworth.

Hours: By appt.

General line; old and new. Furniture, kitchenware, bric-a-brac, baskets. Gift wrapping. Free local deliveries.

A/C—PM. Affordable. Consignments. Authentication when possible.

Prop. Mary A. Feliciotti   201–384–4766

Leonia 07605

TRASH & TREASURE ANTIQUES, 41 Hawthorne Terr.

Hours: By appt.

TRASH & TREASURE ANTIQUES *continued*
Furniture, primitives, and accessories.
A/C—PM. Wide range.
Prop. Judy Zied   201–944–4787

Little Ferry 07643

J-P TIQUES, 27 Williams St.
Hours: By appt.
Depression and Art Deco glass; kitchen implements.
C—PM. Affordable.
Prop. Judy DeAngelis, Pat Mahoney   201–641–4664
                                                            935–1942

Lodi 07644

N. RICHMAN & ASSOCIATES, 509 Westminster Pl.
Hours: Sat. 9–5 ("no early callers"). Merchandise pickup: following Fri.
10–8, Sat. 9–5.
Large establishment; vast amount of home furnishings, some antiques—
furniture, glassware, bric-a-brac, lighting. Prices firm. Delivery service available.
Complete contents of homes purchased. Parking across street.
C/A—PM. Wide range.
Prop. Nancy Richman   201–772–9027

Lyndhurst 07071

PAUL MANGANARO'S PLAYER PIANOS, 121 Valley Brook Ave. *Also see*
Repair and Restoration listing.
Hours: By appt.
Player pianos and rolls (1915–1930), reproducing pianos, nickelodeons; some
music boxes. Automatic musical instruments purchased; also repaired and
restored. Member Music Box Soc.
A—PM. Serious collectors. Consignments.
Prop. Paul Manganero   201–438–0399

Mahwah 07430

ROBERT G. SIMPSON ANTIQUES, Rt. 17, northbound (in Traffic Safety Bldg.).
Hours: Tues. thru Fri. 10–4:30; Sat., Sun., & eves. by appt.
Selective American primitives; early painted furniture, blanket chests, cupboards, crocks, baskets; accessories.
A—PM. Wide range.
Prop. Robert G. Simpson   201–327–6050
                                                914–357–8735 (if no ans.)

TOP OF THE STAIRS, 3 Miller Rd.
Hours: Mon. thru Sat. 2:30–dark; Sat. & Sun. by appt.
Furniture (including china closets); glass.
A/C. Affordable.
Prop. Anne Lyons   201–529–3996

Midland Park 07432

JULIE ANDERSON, 100 Glen Ave.
Hours: By appt.
Primitives, Victorian furniture, glass, and china. Pieces authenticated or sold at lower price. Proprietor has decorating background.
A/C—PM. Affordable/Wide range. Authentication.
Prop. Julie Anderson   201–447–3126

BROWNSTONE MILL, 11 Paterson Ave. (off Goffle Rd.).
Hours: Mon. thru Sat.; days and hours vary with shop
Rambling arrangement of congenial and attractive antique shops in an 1826 grist mill on Wagaraw Brook, a mill site since the 1700s.
Mgr. Jerry Krawitz   201–796–4362

    THE ANTIQUE COLLECTOR.
    Hours: Mon. thru Sat. 12–5
    Well-chosen, unusual old store fixtures, counters, cash registers, oak furniture; scales, tools, advertising chromos. Descriptive labels. Estates purchased; house sales arranged.

BROWNSTONE MILL *continued*

A/C—PM. Affordable. Consignments. Authentication.

Prop. Richard Payne   201–742–3429

BANBURY CROSS ANTIQUES.

Hours: Mon. thru Sat. 11–5; Fri. 'til 8. Closed Tues.

China a specialty. Pine cupboards, primitives, cut glass, etchings;
"anything old and pretty." Reproductions noted.

A/C—PM. Affordable/Wide range. Consignments. Authentication when
possible.

Prop. Julie Anderson, Jackie Weisman, assoc.   201–447–3126

COUNTRY COLLECTOR.

Hours: Sat. 12–5; Fri. eve. 6–8; other eves. by appt.

Country furniture and primitives; rope, sleigh, and spool beds, stenciled
cottage furniture (when available); old farm implements, tools, hardware;
pottery, glass, kitchenware. Caning, rushing; furniture repair.

C/A—PM. Affordable/Wide range. Authentication when possible.

Prop. Lenore H. Coomber   201–652–6435 (after 5)

DEN OF ANTIQUITY.

Hours: Wed. thru Sat. 10:30–4:30

Quilts, pattern glass, china, pottery, small sterling items, furniture.
Lectures. Appraisals. Estate liquidation.

A/C—PM. Affordable. Authentication (selective).

Prop. Maureen C. Kovach   201–445–6173

DOROTHEA'S BYE GONES.

Hours: Wed. thru Sat. 10–5

"Past to almost present"; antique and Art Deco furniture; linens, toys,
some kitchenware. Advice on furniture purchase.

C/A—PM; also coded. Wide range.

Prop. Dorothy Van Der Horn   201–444–2104

NEXT TO NEW SHOPPE.

Hours: Mon. thru Sat. 10:30–5. Closed Tues. (Closed Mon. & Tues.
in summer.)

BROWNSTONE MILL *continued*

Silver, glass, furniture, tools, brass; general line, primarily on consignment.

C/A—PM. Affordable. Consignments.

Prop. Roberta Collins 201–445–8688

PRO ANTIQUES. *Also see* Repair and Restoration listing.

Hours: Fri. 5–7; Sat. 10:30–5

Radios, victrolas, cameras, old fishing tackle, and the proprietors' enthusiasm. Extensive collection of old records and cylinders. Repair of wind-up phonographs and old radios.

C—Some prices marked. Wide range. Consignments. Authentication within specialty.

Prop. "Tony Provenzano, Vic Trola" 201–652–7453 (bus.)
445–7898 (res.)

FLORENCE DANIEL INTERIORS, INC., 621 Godwin Ave. (opp. Shell Sta.). *Also see* Repair and Restoration listing.

Hours: Mon. thru Sat. 10–5; or by appt.

Interior design, antiques as accents. Fine porcelains, objets d'art, furniture, accessories. Also reproductions, decorative new pieces. Specializing in upholstery and restoration of antique furniture; upholstery workroom on premises. Custom draperies, slipcovers; shop-at-home service. Visa, Master Charge, Yes Plus card (United Jersey Bank).

A/C; also new—PM. Wide range. Consignments.

Prop. Florence Daniel 201–445–2828

TIGERS', 247 Godwin Ave.

Hours: Mon. thru Fri. 12–5; Sat. by appt.

Good, old glass; general line of "incoming" antiques. Novices and collectors welcome. Lectures on antiques.

C/A—PM. Affordable. Authentication when possible.

Prop. Mrs. William Tiger 201–447–2477

Montvale 07645

KNOCK ON WOOD, 33 S. Kinderkamack Rd. *Also see* Repair and Restoration listing.

KNOCK ON WOOD *continued*

Hours: Wed., Thurs., Fri., Sun. 11–5; Sat. 11–4. Mon. & Tues. by appt. (Closed Sun. July & Aug.)

Attractive, substantial pieces; mid- to late 19th-century oak and walnut. Dining tables, hall stands, side-by-sides, desks, bookcases, armoires, dressers. Furniture hand-stripping, repair, custom refinishing, upholstering. Caning and rushing. Antique clocks repaired, restored.

C—PM. Wide range.

Prop. Billie and Dave Marshall   201–391–1414

MONTVALE ANTIQUE MALL, 30 Chestnut Ridge Rd. (Grand Union Shopping Center; exit 172, Garden State Pkwy.).

Hours: Thurs. thru Mon. 11–5:30; Sat. 'til 9:30. Closed Tues. & Wed.

Approximately thirty antique shops downstairs at the suburban Montvale Mall. Relaxed and attractive; climate controlled, ample parking.

Mgr. John Sayers   201–391–3940

ALL THAT GLITTERS. . . .

Gold and silver jewelry, sterling holloware; lamps. Custom stained glass lampshades. Jewelry and stained glass lamp repair. Metal polishing.

C—PM. Wide range.

Prop. Barbara Ann Bergman, Lorraine Bergman   201–568–3561

THE BOOK NOOK.

First editions, old magazines (pre-1900 and later), children's books, old playbills, post cards, stereo cards, sheet music. Howard Chandler Christy illustrated volumes; poetry, medicine, law, novels. Search service. No reproductions.

A/C—PM. Wide range. Authentication.

Prop. Mildred Marowitz   201–573–1525

THE COUNTRY PARLOUR.

Completely refurbished American oak; china, glass, bric-a-brac, old prints, mirrors. General line in a pleasant shop.

C/A—PM. Selective. Authentication when possible.

Prop. Polly Hogan, Betty McCourt   201–391–0881

MONTVALE ANTIQUE MALL *continued*

COUNTRY ROADS.

Country furniture and kitchen collectibles; trunks, telephones, hanging scales, creative plant containers.

C—PM. Affordable.

Prop. Linda Ciofalo   201–573–9797

DISCOVERY ANTIQUES.

English, French, and American furniture (c. 1840–1900s), decorative accessories; eclectic selection in a tastefully arranged small shop. Decorating assistance. Estates purchased.

A/C—PM. Wide range. Authentication.

Prop. Edith Klein   No phone

O. C. FASS.

Primarily 18th- and 19th-century silver, porcelain, vases, music boxes. Furniture, 18th- to 20th-century table, mantel, and grandfather clocks; general line. Quality antiques and collectibles in a small, elegant shop.

A/C—PM. Selective to serious collectors. Consignments. Authentication.

Prop. Estelle Fass   201–391–3484

GREENFIELD ANTIQUES.

Orientals; bronzes, ivory.

A—PM. Selective to serious collectors. Consignments. Authentication.

Prop. Lila Greenfield   No phone

THELMA LASUS ANTIQUES GALLERY.

Jewelry, fine porcelain; small furniture, silver, lamps, bric-a-brac, attractively displayed. Interiors. Layaway plan. Estate sales; appraisals.

A/C—PM. Wide range. Consignments.

Prop. Thelma Lasus   201–573–9843

MARIANNE LAURANCE.

Fine European antiques and furniture; Oriental pieces. Porcelain, art glass, silver, mirrors, chandeliers, prints, paintings, decorative miniatures. Estates and individual pieces purchased. Member Nyack Antiques Soc.

A—PM. Wide range. Consignments. Authentication.

Prop. Marianne Laurance   201–391–8323

MONTVALE ANTIQUE MALL *continued*

LOST & FOUND ANTIQUES (also Tocks n' Things).

Convivial shop, clocks and large furniture specialties. Primarily Victorian oak and walnut dining and bedroom sets, hall racks, washstands; Victorian accessories. Tiffany-style lamps, some attractive hanging fixtures; jewelry. Antique clocks purchased and repaired. Custom floral arrangements. Mr. Sapounas is a member of the Nat'l. Assoc. of Watch & Clock Collectors.

A/C—PM. Wide range. Consignments. Authentication when possible.

Prop. Terris Strauss, Carol Sapounas   201–391–0060

FLORENCE McCOY.

Sterling, porcelain, bronzes, chandeliers, clocks, oak and Victorian furniture. Antiques purchased.

C/A—PM. Affordable.

Prop. Florence McCoy   No phone

THE MUSEUM SHOP.

Depression glass, Nippon, Japanese china. Custom beaded flower arrangements.

C—PM. Affordable.

Prop. Laura Laskin   914–356–2019

ONCE UPON A TIME.

Antiques, collectibles, curios, better bric-a-brac, antique jewelry. Jewelry for men: rings, fobs on gold chains, match safes, cigarette cases, watch chains, neck chain ornaments, stickpins, large cuff links. Antiques purchased. Appraisals.

C/A—PM. Affordable/Wide range. Authentication.

Prop. Genie and Vern Cowell   201–391–2028 (bus.)
                                                          743–1260 (res.)

THE PLATE LADY, LTD.

Mid-18th- to mid-20th-century English, French, German, Austrian, and Italian china and porcelain. Early Staffordshire. Metal holders for plates, pictures, and bowls. Layaway plan. Porcelain and glass repair by arrangement.

A/C—PM. Wide range. Authentication.

Prop. Mildred Marowitz   201–573–1525

MONTVALE ANTIQUE MALL *continued*

REMEMBER ME ANTIQUES.

Emphasis on antique jewelry, up to the '30s; silver, porcelain, glass, bronzes (for advanced collectors), old Hummels. Antiques purchased. Bright and down-to-earth; the proprietor is listed in Who's Who of American Women *as a specialist in antique jewelry.*

A/C—PM. Wide range. Authentication.

Prop. Norma Coley

201–391–6180
797–5948

R.S.C. COINS, INC.

Coins, currency, campaign and sports buttons, old pennants, baseball cards, old and new stamps. Coins, silver, Franklin Mint issues purchased. Numismatic supplies. Member Amer. Numismatic Assoc.

C. Wide range. Authentication.

Prop. Bob Cantor

201–573–1111

TREASURE CHEST ANTIQUES. *Also see* Repair and Restoration listing.

General line; furniture, lighting fixtures, sterling, bric-a-brac in a double-tiered shop with railed balcony. Emphasis on Victorian. Furniture, lamps, and chandeliers repaired, restored, refinished; lamps and chandeliers rewired.

C/A—PM. Affordable/Wide range. Authentication when possible.

Prop. L. Cohen

914–354–4205 (res.)

THE WAY WE WERE.

Antiques, nostalgia, collectibles; wicker, porcelain, Wedgwood, Nippon, glass, old prints. Ms. Bring is a member of the Wedgwood Collectors Soc.

C—PM. Affordable. Consignments.

Prop. Barbara Bring, Roberta Goldstein

201–391–2233

YESTERDAY FOREVER.

Early American walnut, cherry, and mahogany furniture; desks, dining room tables, side tables, washstands. Also mirrors, inexpensive old prints, bric-a-brac.

A/C—PM. Wide range. Consignments.

Prop. Jean and Chuck Jann

201–652–4750

New Milford 07646

CAROLE K. SOSSLAU, ANTIQUES, 351 Madison Ave.

Hours: By appt.

Cut glass and china. Appraisals of cut glass.

A/C—Not all prices marked. Wide range. Consignments. Authentication.

Prop. Carole K. Sosslau   201–261–0328

Oakland 07436

AHLERS ANTIQUES, 11 Long Hill Rd.

Hours: Mon. thru Fri. 9–5; or by appt.

Affordable primitives and collectibles; antique toys, tools, furniture, bronzes, paintings, clocks, china, glass, pottery, fireplace accessories. Wholesale and retail. Est. 1940.

A/C—PM. Affordable/Wide range. Authentication when possible.

Prop. Robert Ahlers   201-337-5577
                                       337–8490, 337–7560 (if no ans.)

ROEDER SMITH ASSOCIATES, 409 Ramapo Valley Rd. *Also see* Repair and Restoration and Auctioneers listings.

Hours: Mon. thru Sat. 9–5

Primitives, oak and other furniture, clocks, china, glass, bric-a-brac. Appraisals. Furniture repair and restoration. Auctions at least once a month; mailing list. Member Nat'l. Soc. of Auctioneers, N. J. Soc. of Auctioneers. Pleasant shop in an Edwardian-era house.

A/C—Most prices marked. Affordable/Wide range. Consignments. Authentication.

Prop. Eileen M. Smith, Charles B. Roeder   201–337–4500 (bus.)
                                                         337–0458 (res.)

Old Tappan 07675

OAKWOOD ANTIQUES, 1079 Washington Ave. *Also see* Repair and Restoration listing.

Hours: By appt.

OAKWOOD ANTIQUES *continued*
Oak furnishings; bedroom and dining room sets, most with original hardware and glass. Antiques purchased. Oak furniture refinished. Caning.
C—PM. Selective. Authentication.
Prop. Dennis Grace 201–666–3535

Oradell 07649

CUBBYHOLE ANTIQUES, 200 Kinderkamack Rd.
Hours: By appt.
Primitives, glass, crocks, some furniture and jewelry.
A/C—PM. Affordable. Authentication when possible.
Prop. Winifred Robertson 201–262–1896

Paramus 07652

JOAN L. OSTROWSKI, 281 Homestead Rd.
Hours: By appt.
Antiques and nostalgia. Small furniture, including oak; printer's trays, primitives.
C—PM. Affordable.
Prop. Joan L. Ostrowski 201–262–8623

CAROL RIESTER, 334 Sherwood Dr.
Hours: By appt.
Old, new, and handmade. Miniatures, patchwork, some small furniture, old type trays. Advice and instruction. Especially nice for children.
C; also new—Some prices marked. Affordable. Consignments. Authentication.
Prop. Carol Riester 201–261–0247

THE SPORTS CORNER, Garden State Plaza. Rts. 4 and 17.
Hours: Mon. thru Sat. 10–9
Sports cards, magazines, books, old comics, political buttons, oddities. No reproductions.
C—PM. Affordable/Wide range. Authentication.
Prop. Rick Barudin, Bud Kurzweil 201–843–3170

VILLAGE SQUARE, Bergen Mall. Rt. 4.

Hours: Tues. thru Sat. 11–5:30; Thurs., Fri. 'til 9:30. Closed Sun. & Mon.

An escalator ride below the bustle of the Bergen Mall Shopping Center is Village Square, a lower mall municipality of more than fifty antique, gift, and specialty shops ringed by town walls and an entry gate.

Inside, quaint storefronts with picture book architecture look out on carpeted streets named for the Founding Fathers. Bright-light sunny and browsable, the necessities sold are the ones that give pleasure.

Prop. Lawrence Garfield   201–843–1776

COLLECTORS COMIC SHOP.

Old and new comic books; related items. Search service. Reproductions noted.

C; also new—PM. Affordable/Wide range. Consignments. Authentication.

Prop. Frank Grembowiel   201–368–9890

THE COLLECTOR'S GALLERY.

Emphasis on Impressionist and post-Impressionist art; contemporary and older paintings. Original signed prints, drawings, watercolors, pastels; usually below market price. Works by major artists accepted on consignment. Investment counseling; advice on portfolios; finders' service. Beginning collectors encouraged. Authentication accompanied by written appraisal. In New York: Allan S. Park Gallery, 698 Madison Ave.

VILLAGE SQUARE *continued*

A/C—PM. Selective to serious collectors. Consignments (selective). Authentication.

Prop. Allan S. Park   201–843–6750

FROHMANS ANTIQUE JEWELRY. *Also see* Repair and Restoration listing.

Jewelry (antique thru Art Deco); Art Nouveau and Art Deco objets d'art and collectibles. Gift wrapping. Old jewelry purchased. Repair of antique jewelry a specialty. Visa, American Express.

C/A—PM. Wide range. Authentication.

Prop. Al and Fran Frohman   201–843–3113

LUCILLE GREGORY.

Cut glass, Nippon, Victorian furniture, sterling, and jewelry in a pleasant shop. Appraisals.

C—PM. Wide range. Authentication.

Prop. Lucille Krikorian   No phone

THE JEWEL TABLE.

Jewelry, china, glass, lamps, paintings. China and jewelry repair for customers. Member N. J. Antique Club. In business more than twenty years.

C—PM. Affordable. Consignments. Authentication.

Prop. Edith McGarry, Marilyn McGarry   201–843–4555

MEMORIES LANE.

Oak furniture, including tables, chairs, dressers, desks. Also clocks, mirrors, bric-a-brac. Large, open shop inviting browsing.

C/A—PM. Wide range. Consignments. Authentication.

Prop. Dorothy Krug, Muriel Stableford   201–843–1776

OBJECT D'ART ANTIQUES.

Russian bronzes, cloisonné, palace pieces, Meissen, K.P.M. porcelains; and reproductions. Appraisals.

A/C—Most prices marked. Wide range. Authentication.

Prop. Norman Lanchart   201–368–9888

VILLAGE SQUARE *continued*

OCEANTIQUES

Marine antiques and collectibles; some new reproductions. Appraisals. Pieces researched. Visa.

C/A—PM. Wide range. Authentication when possible.

Prop. Bruce M. Matheson   No phone

PHILLYS DILLYS. *Also see* Repair and Restoration listing.

Antique jewelry, cameo brooches, rings; collectibles and furniture. Watch, clock, and jewelry repairs. Antiques purchased.

C—PM. Affordable. Consignments. Sales guaranteed.

Prop. Philip Bader   201–843–0466

THROUGH THE LOOKING GLASS.

Country pieces, older collectibles and new; no oak. Commodes, washstands, decoys, bowls, pitchers, glassware, bric-a-brac. Beautiful selection of new dollhouses and miniatures.

A/C; also new—PM. Affordable. Authentication when possible.

Prop. Janet M. Cory   201–843–3335

Ramsey 07446

MILK HOUSE ANTIQUES, 78 Elbert St.

Hours: By appt.

Depression era glass, advertising items, sewing-related collectibles, post cards and paper ephemera. "Old things" purchased. Lectures on Depression glass. Member North Jersey Depression Glass Collectors Club, Hudson Valley (N. Y.) and Del Marva Depression Glass Clubs.

C—PM. Affordable.

Prop. Ann and Harry Rutten   201–327–7197

Ridgefield Park 07660

FAIRMOUNT ARTISANS, 432 Teaneck Rd. (corner Preston St.).

Hours: Daily 2–5. Closed Mon.

Broad general line; antiques, collectibles, curios. Antiques purchased. Member North Jersey Antique Dealers Assoc.

A/C—PM.   201–440–0909

Ridgewood 07450

A & A ANTIQUES, Ridgewood.

Hours: By appt.

American and some European wall and mantel clocks, 1760 to turn-of-the-century. Member Nat'l. Assoc. of Watch & Clock Collectors.

A/C—PM. Wide range. Authentication.

Prop. A. M. Luce   201–447–2928

BARRETT JEWELERS, 185 E. Ridgewood Ave. *Also see* Repair and Restoration listing.

Hours: Mon. thru Sat. 10:30–5:30; or call ahead

Primarily antique and estate jewelry. Large selection of pocket and pendant watches; silver "smalls"—sewing and chatelaine items; cameos, stickpins; cut glass, Wedgwood, old quilts. Anything old or of value purchased; watches purchased in any condition. "Expert watch and jewelry repairs." Member Art and Antique Dealers Assoc. of the Nyacks. (Also Barrett Antiques, 78 S. Broadway, Nyack, N. Y. 10960; 914 358 6010.)

A/C PM. Wide range. Consignments.

Prop. Burt Stern   201–445–3060

CACHEPOT, Ridgewood.

Hours: By appt.

Eighteenth- and 19th-century furniture, some 20th-century reproductions; 18th- and 19th-century Oriental porcelains and collectibles; brass, silver.

A/C—PM. Wide range.

Prop. June Chinigo   201–444–2373

HORSE FEATHERS—WEST, 185 E. Ridgewood Ave.

Hours: Mon. thru Sat. 10:30–5:30; Thurs. 'til 9

General line; furniture, primitives. Gold, silver, jewelry, antique watches purchased. Antique watches repaired. Visa, Master Charge.

A/C—PM. Affordable. Consignments. Authentication.

Prop. Joyce and Lester Solney   201–444–6633

MIMBY, 373 Shelbourne Terrace.

Hours: By appt.

Paintings, 19th-century furniture, odd pieces and collectibles.

A/C—PM. Affordable.

Prop. Miriam Belsky   201–444–9898

RAYMOND POLLENZ, INC., 11 S. Broad St.

Hours: Tues. thru Sat. 9:30–5:30

English and European antiques; silver, porcelain, clocks, glass, pewter, and brass in a small, well-filled shop. Reproductions in the gifts section. Antiques purchased. Appraisals for insurance, estates, etc. Silver plating and repair; free estimates. Member Appraisers' Assoc. of Amer., North Jersey Antique Dealers Assoc.; consultant, Antiques Dealer magazine.

A—PM. Wide range. Authentication.

Prop. Raymond and Anna Grace Pollenz   201–652–2411

River Edge 07661

THE ANTIQUE CARAVAN, 832 Kinderkamack Rd.

Hours: Tues. thru Sat. 10:30–5; Thurs. 1–5; or call ahead.

Antiques and gifts; emphasis on jewelry. Older gold and silver jewelry; collectible costume jewelry, American Indian turquoise.

A/C—PM. Wide range. Authentication.

Prop. Paul Walter   201–265–2545
                                                             345–9357 (eves.)

MEDLEY ANTIQUES, 192 Wayne Ave.

Hours: By appt.

General line. Also see Memories Lane, Village Square (Bergen Mall), Paramus.

C—PM. Affordable. Authentication on request.

Prop. Muriel Stableford   201–261–4798

Rutherford 07070

AMERICANA ANTIQUE & COIN GALLERY, 13 Sylvan St.

Hours: Mon. thru Sat. 10:30–6

AMERICANA ANTIQUE & COIN GALLERY *continued*

Coins, paper currency, paper advertising, documents; small general line of collectibles. Coin appraisals. Antiques purchased.

C—PM. Affordable/Wide range. Consignments.

Prop. Clay Hermansky   201–933–8855

STUDIO I, 6 Highland Cross (the Holman Bldg.). *Also see* Repair and Restoration listing.

Hours: Tues. thru Fri. 1–5

Very fine selection of antique laces, textiles, trims; old beads. Antique clothing, tapestries, and hangings restored. Beads restrung. Member Internat'l. Old Lacers.

C—PM. Affordable. Consignments. Authentication.

Prop. Marguerite Morgan   201–939–7222

Saddle River 07458

RICHARD C. KYLLOS, 210 W. Saddle River Rd.

Hours: Thurs., Fri., Sat. 1–4:30

Good early American furniture and accessories. Eighteenth- and 19th-century pine and cherry corner, wall, and Hackensack cupboards, highboys, chests, desks, tables; some pieces with original paint. No Victorian or oak. Also Bennington pottery, Pennsylvania slipware, brass, lanterns, baskets. Furniture repair. And to the trade.

A—PM. Wide range. Authentication when possible.

Prop. Richard C. Kyllos   201–327–7343

PAST IN PRESENT, Barnstable Court., E. Allendale Ave. *Also see* Repair and Restoration listing.

Hours: Tues. thru Sat. 10:30–5:30

Primarily American antiques in an 1800s hay barn. General line; art and cut glass, furniture, mantel and tall clocks, dolls, china. Oil paintings cleaned and restored (by Lorene Slater Steinberg). Clock and doll repairs by Robert Slater. Member North Jersey Antique Dealers Assoc.

A/C—PM. Affordable. Authentication.

Prop. Mary and Robert Slater   201–327–0229

SAMP MILL FARM ANTIQUES, 70 E. Allendale Ave. Mailing address: 109 W. Saddle River Rd.

Hours: Wed. thru Fri. 1–4:30; Sat. 10–5; or by appt.

Picturesque and pretty; approached by footbridge and up a flight of wooden steps. American formal and country furnishings and accessories; furniture, tole and woodenware, early iron, quilts, coverlets, unusual folk art. Splint baskets a specialty. Estate appraisals. Member Saddle River Valley Antique Dealers Assoc.

A/C—PM. Wide range. Consignments. Authentication.

Prop. Susan Stagg, Kathie James   201–327–6252

STABLE ANTIQUES, 116 E. Saddle River Rd. *Also see* Repair and Restoration listing.

Hours: By appt.

Late 19th- and early 20th-century oak bedroom and dining room pieces. Turn-of-the-century furniture hand-stripped and refinished.

C—PM. Affordable. Authentication.

Prop. Henry Muller   201–327–0646

Teaneck 07666

ADVENTURINE ANTIQUES SHOP, 401 Cedar Lane.

Hours: Mon. thru Sat. 10–5

General line; china, glass (including cut glass and art glass), paintings, country furniture, primitives.

C/A—PM. Wide range. Consignments. Authentication.

Prop. Jeanne V. Vigna   201–836–9211

CEDAR LANE ANTIQUE SHOP, 394 Cedar Lane.

Hours: Mon. thru Sat. 11–5

General line; including furniture, china, glass, wicker, lighting, advertising items; Americana. Antiques purchased. Nicely displayed for browsing.

A/C—Most prices marked (and coded). Wide range. Consignments.

Prop. Faye Greenspan, Mildred Larsson   201–836–5288

THE DON JUAN SHOP, 924 Garrison Ave.

Hours: By appt.

THE DON JUAN SHOP *continued*
China, glass; paper collectibles.
C—PM. Affordable. Authentication when possible.
Prop. Don Madden, Juan Yanes   201–836–1073

THE HOLLIDAYS, 308 Van Buren Ave.
Hours: By appt.
Pine country furniture; miniatures. Furniture refinishing.
A/C—PM. Wide range. Consignments.
Prop. Elizabeth W. Holliday   201–836–5171

MORRIS WALDSTEIN, 586 Ramapo Rd.
Hours: By appt.
*Antiquarian books and fine bindings. Out-of-print nonfiction, art folios,
children's books; sheet music. Interest in New Jersey history. Books purchased.*
A/C—Some prices marked. Wide range.
Prop. Morris Waldstein   201–836–8585
                                       836–0755

Tenafly 07670

FRAMES 'N' THINGS, 35–37 Highwood Ave.
Hours: Mon. thru Sat. 10–5:30
*European and Oriental accessories, clocks, lamps, jewelry; reproductions and
new. Custom framing; silk flowers and arrangements; original art, prints.*
C/A; also new—Most prices marked.
Prop. Florence Moffatt   201–871–1110

JUDI STERN INTERIORS, 17 Wight Pl.
Hours: By appt.
*Decorative accessories, old and new. American and English antiques; small
furniture, mirrors, some silver, crocks, curios; Oriental rugs. Emphasis on
interior design and "an individual look."*
A/C—PM. Wide range. Authentication.
Prop. Judi Stern   201–569–9449

SWEET YESTERDAY ANTIQUES, 17 S. Summit St.

Hours: Tues. thru Sat. 11–5; and by appt. Closed July 1 thru Labor Day.

Antiques, Americana, and nostalgia. Country and Victorian furniture, art, accessories; lamps, mirrors, candlesticks, vases, pressed glass, early advertising, paper goods, political items. Search service for dealers and decorators. Also to the trade. Several rooms downstairs, well-displayed for browsing. Parking at rear. Visitors are advised with a note on the beveled glass front door that "Bare feet are acceptable, food and drink are not. Little children are welcome" [if reasonably behaved], and that "Same rules apply to adults." Umbrellas are left on the front porch.

A/C—PM. Wide range. Occasional consignments. Authentication when possible.

Prop. Pearl Grayson   201–567–3660

WELLINGTON JEWELERS, 63 Oak Ave.

Hours: By appt.

Hand-strung beaded jewelry, combining old and new findings. Preference for Oriental designs and a sophisticated, natural look. Adult education courses in jewelry making.

A/C—Prices not marked. Affordable/Selective. Consignments. Authentication.

Prop. Norma Wellington   201–567–7554

Upper Saddle River 07458

MIKE & MARY TACKACH, 30 Sunrise Lane.

Hours: By appt.

Primitives, furniture, paintings, china, glass, toys; Orientals. Money back guarantee. Antiques purchased. Member Rush Light Club.

A/C—PM. Wide range. Purchases guaranteed.

Prop. Mike and Mary Tackach   201–327–5332

Waldwick 07463

HAROLD NESTLER, Waldwick.

Hours: By appt.

Antiquarian books, maps, manuscripts, pamphlets, autographs, correspondence related to New Jersey, New York, New England, and the Delaware Valley.

HAROLD NESTLER *continued*

Books and materials on the French and Indian War, the Revolution, the War of 1812; also concerning the Shakers and early American industry. Member Middle Atlantic Chapter, Antiquarian Booksellers' Assoc. of Amer.

A/C—PM. Wide range.

Prop. Harold Nestler   201–444–7413

Westwood 07675

THE ART & FRAME SHOP, INC., 561 Broadway.

Hours: Mon. thru Sat. 10–5:30. Closed Wed.

Original graphic art, antique prints, old posters. Custom framing.

A/C—PM. Wide range. Authentication.

Prop. Gerald Geltman   201–664–1132

CINDER WENCH ANTIQUES.

Hours: By appt.

General line; Empire, some 18th-century furniture; china and glass. Antiques and estates purchased.

A/C—PM. Affordable/Selective. Authentication.

Prop. Kathy and Tony Frasco   201–666–8198

GARDNER'S II, 349 Broadway.

Hours: Mon. thru Sat. 10–6

Large selection; in a complex of adjoining specialty shops. Furniture, china, glass, prints, paintings, books; general line. Two annual sales, on Super Bowl Sunday and coinciding with the Westwood sidewalk sale in July. Appraisals (with Julie Kruger). Also to dealers and decorators. Member N. J. Soc. of Auctioneers and Appraisers, Nat'l. Assoc. of Dealers in Antiques. No smoking requested.

C/A—PM. Wide range. Authentication when possible.

Prop. Walter and Gertrude Gardner   201–664–0612

HERITAGE ANTIQUES.

Hours: By appt.

Sterling (from George III); Gallé, Steuben, and Tiffany art glass; American paintings, porcelain figurines, steins, bisque doll heads, dolls, early American and European furniture. Appraisals.

HERITAGE ANTIQUES *continued*

A/C—PM. Affordable/Selective. Consignments. Authentication when possible.

Prop. Andrew and Alta Levesque   201–664–0670

ROYAL FIREPLACE STORES, 224 Fairview Ave.

Hours: Mon. thru Sat. 9–6

Small, selective collection of unusual andirons; copper pots. Extensive selection of new fireplace equipment. Congenial shop; established 1927.

A/C; also new. Wide range.

Prop. Spencer Rosenberg   201–664–0167

STRIP 'N BROWZE, 591 Broadway. *Also see* Repair and Restoration listing.

Hours: Tues. thru Sat. 8:30–5

Oak and other furniture; china, bric-a-brac. Primarily furniture repair and restoration. Hand- and vat-stripping, veneer repair, hand-finishing; touch-ups, polishing. Pickup and delivery available.

A/C—PM. Affordable/Selective. Consignments.

Prop. The Stocknoffs   201–666–3218

THRU THE YEARS, 441 Broadway (exit 168, Garden State Pkwy.).

Hours: Mon. thru Sat. 10:30–5; Fri. 'til 11

Sports, advertising, political, and movie star memorabilia. Wide selection, including advertising clocks, posters, buttons, trays, glasses, baseball cards, old and new movie star glossies. Also older and reproduction bubble gum machines. Related items purchased.

C; also new—PM. Affordable/Wide range. Consignments. Authentication.

Prop. Eli Golden   201–664–3336

Woodcliff Lake 07675

SANDY BEE'S COUNTRY STORE & ANTIQUES, 400 & 430 Chestnut Ridge Rd. (across from Tice's Farm).

Hours: 7 days 10–5 (at 400 address); Wed. thru Sun. 10–5 (at 430 location).

More formal 19th- and some 18th-century furniture; lamps; general line. A country store. Member North Jersey Antique Dealers Assoc.

A/C—PM. Affordable. Consignments. Authentication when possible.

Prop. Sandra Besser   201–391–7826

Wyckoff 07481

EVELYN ANDRITO, Wyckoff.

Hours: By appt.

Country furnishings and accessories. Kitchen items an enthusiastic specialty. Early cookware, stoneware, tins, iron implements; lighting, samplers, quilts, baskets; folk art. Member North Jersey Antique Dealers Assoc., Antiques Club of N. J.

A—PM. Affordable. Consignments. Authentication.

Prop. Evelyn Andrito   201–891–2997

COUNTRY LAMPS & ANTIQUES, 290 Godwin Ave. (behind Dairy Queen). *Also see* Repair and Restoration listing.

Hours: Tues. thru Sat. 10–5:30

Small, pleasant shop specializing in Victorian-era lamps, 1860–1910. Authentic hanging gas fixtures; student, gone-with-the-wind, piano, and country store lamps; kerosene post lamps. Also glass, china, prints. Quality antiques purchased. All types of lamps repaired and restored. Custom early American shades; new replacement parts.

A/C—PM. Wide range. Authentication.

Prop. R. and M. Polla   201–891–0044
                                                             337–4310 (cves.)

HERITAGE ANTIQUES, 362 Main St.

Hours: Tues. thru Sat. 11–5

General line, more formal pieces. Some furniture, china, glass, porcelain, silver, mirrors, pictures. Usually a roll-top desk or two on hand. Member North Jersey Antique Dealers Assoc.

A/C—PM. Wide range.

Prop. Mary Olson   201–891–1159

L'ÉGLISE, 630 Wyckoff Ave.

Hours: Mon. thru Sat. 10–6

Interior design specialists, commercial and residential. Selection of quality European and American antiques and decorative accessories. Lamps, cachepots, mirrors, candlesticks, plates, inkwells, a few furniture pieces. Custom flower arrangements and fine giftware.

A; also new—PM. Selective/Wide range. Authentication when possible.

Prop. Joseph Villano, John Giovatto   201–891–3622

Selection of art glass blown at Victor Durand's Flint Glass Works between 1924 and 1931. From left, clockwise: green and pink vase with coiled decoration, opal vase with blue and gold hearts and gold spiderwebbing, 16-in. King Tut vase in gold and green, ruby overlay cut to crystal vase with pulled feather decoration, blue overlay dessert plate cut to crystal with pulled feather decoration, Venetian lace bowl in topaz with opal threads. *Courtesy The Wheaton Historical Association, Millville*

Hudson County

Bayonne 07002

TRADING POST ANTIQUES, 1207 Kennedy Blvd. (corner W. 54th St.).
Hours: Mon. thru Sat. 6 a.m.–9 p.m.
Furniture, trunks, bric-a-brac, antique jewelry, primitive tools, weaponry; some imports. Trunks restored. Delivery service. House and estate sales.
C/A—Prices coded. Affordable/Wide range. Consignments. Authentication on request.
Prop. Jack Koval, Jr. 201–858–3333

Guttenberg 07093

GÉS FINE METAL FINISHING, 7013 Park. *Also see* Repair and Restoration listing.
Hours: Mon. thru Fri. 8–5:30
General line, including turn-of-the-century European bronzes. Metal repair and restoration; patinas a specialty.
C—Some prices marked. Selective. Authentication.
Prop. Dave Ciocher 201–869–0033

Hoboken 07030

KENNETH C. SCHULTZ, Hoboken. Mailing address: Box M 753.

Hours: By appt.

*Specializing in ocean liner, World's Fair, exposition, royalty, presidential,
campaign, and Disney memorabilia. Books, pennants, recordings, mugs, figurines,
photos, etc. Related items purchased. Member World's Fair Society.*

C—PM. Affordable. Consignments. Authentication.

Prop. Kenneth C. Schultz   201–656–0966
                                                               659–6565

WINDOW ANTIQUE SHOP, 636 Washington St.

Hours: Mon. thru Sat. 10–6; or by appt.

*Antiques, collectibles, memorabilia, "anything old in good condition."
Victoriana—furniture, bronzes, bric-a-brac. Pre-Revolutionary Chinese ceramics
and works of art (nothing under forty years of age). Furniture appraisals.
Repair and restoration by arrangement.*

A/C—PM. Affordable/Wide range. Consignments. Authentication when
possible.

Prop. Terry Halloran   201–420–1225

Jersey City 07304

ANTIQUES BY CANARIS, 60 Harrison Ave. *Also see* Repair and Restoration
listing.

Hours: By appt.

*General line; furniture, silver, glass, dolls, jewelry, post cards. Coins, foreign
and domestic paper currency. Furniture restoration and repair. Appraisals.*

A/C—PM. Wide range. Consignments. Authentication.

Prop. Peter Canaris   201–333–2840
                                                               332–0252

FREDERICK CHARLES ANTIQUES, 580 Summit Ave. (opp. red brick First
Baptist Church).

Hours: Mon. thru Fri. 11–4; Sat. by chance

FREDERICK CHARLES ANTIQUES *continued*
General line, primarily turn-of-the-century, in an interesting old shop. Antiques, coins, books, collector's items and estates purchased. Appraisals.
C/A—PM. Affordable. Authentication on request.
Prop. Frederick Charles   201–656–4150

MICHAEL HULINGS, 3524 Kennedy Blvd. *Also see* Repair and Restoration listing.
Hours: Mon. thru Fri. 1–6; Sat. 11–6
Oak and pine furniture. Individual pieces and estates purchased. Furniture repair and restoration.
C—Most prices marked. Wide range. Consignments. Authentication when possible.
Prop. Michael Huling   201–659–6863

TRUDY SELIGMAN ANTIQUE ARTS, 507 Summit Ave. (adj. to Burger King; 1 bl. from Journal Sq.); zip code 07306.
Hours: Mon., Fri., Sat. 12–6; or by appt.
Ethnographic and tribal jewelry, textiles, and artifacts. Including Tibetan jewelry, Iket weavings, Coptic textiles, Indian silk, African and Pacific tribal masks, early Persian pottery; Victoriana. An established shop, formerly in Greenwich Village.
A/C—Most prices marked. Wide range. Authentication.
Prop. Trudy Seligman   201–433–4441 (bus.)
                                                          659–1829 (res.)

Union City 07093

BOOKS ON FILE, Guttenberg. Mailing address: Box 195, Union City.
Hours: Primarily mail order.
Mail-order search service for out-of-print books. Specific titles, details required. Member Middle Atlantic Chapter, Antiquarian Booksellers' Assoc. of Amer.; Amer. Booksellers Assoc.; Antiquarian Bookmens' Assoc. of Amer.
Prop. Mary Snyder   201–869–8786

Portrait of American Revolution naval officer Alexander Gillon attributed to Gilbert Stuart by the Frick Museum. *Courtesy Catherine Blair Antiques, Summit. Photo: Ann Ross*

Essex County

Caldwell 07006

ANTIQUES 'N THINGS, 3 Smull Ave. (off Bloomfield Ave.).

Hours: Mon. thru Sat. 10–5:30

Antiques, imports, and fine arts classes in a bright shop. General line of fine china and glass, decorative accessories, bric-a-brac, new imported gift items. Appraisal service; house sales conducted.

A/C—PM. Affordable. Consignments. Authentication.

Prop. Dorothy Brockel

201–226–1060 (bus.)
226–2914 (res.)

THE ROCKING HORSE ANTIQUES, 25 Roseland Ave. (off Bloomfield Ave.).

Hours: Wed. thru Sat. 11–4

"A little bit of everything"—furniture, wicker, glass, fine china, dolls of various ages, old crocks, bric-a-brac. House sales conducted.

C/A—Most prices marked. Affordable. Consignments.

Prop. Maria Lordi, Elaine Stout

201–226–8437

Cedar Grove 07009

THE LITTLE GALLERY, 479 Pompton Ave. (Rt. 23).

Hours: Tues. thru Sat. 1–5

THE LITTLE GALLERY *continued*

Tastefully arranged formal French furniture, porcelains, Oriental teakwood, paintings, crystal, quality china in a selective shop. Appraisal service; house sales conducted.

A—Most prices marked. Selective. Consignments. Authentication.

Prop. Marion Korby   201–239–6789

THE MULBERRY BUSH, 496 Pompton Ave. (Rt. 23).

Hours: Mon., Tues., Thurs., Sat. 12:30–4:30

A charming old house that was once the Cedar Grove Post Office is now filled with antiques, "accessories that go with antiques," and collectibles. Oak and pine furniture in the barn to the rear of the house. Everything is on consignment. Appraisal service; house sales conducted.

A/C—PM. Affordable. Consignments. Authentication.

Prop. Margaret Meding, Irma Keiran   201–239–9357 (bus.)
                                                      228–2582 (res.)

East Orange 07017

LOUIS MARDER STUDIO, 564 William St.

Hours: By appt.

Quality antiques in a selective shop. Large collection of antique silver, English, French, and German china; porcelains, some formal furniture (all periods). Mr. Marder is a former president of the Appraisers' Assoc. of America and does appraisals for individuals, museums, and banks. Est. 1922.

A—PM. Selective. Authentication.

Prop. Louis Marder   201–673–1050

Fairfield 07006

THE OLD SMUGGLER, 592 Rt. 46, eastbound (immed. before Passaic Ave. overpass). *Also see* Repair and Restoration listing.

Hours: Tues. thru Sat. 12–6; Wed., Fri. 'til 9

Stained glass a specialty, including old and new Tiffany-type lamps and hand-crafted windows. Oak and turn-of-the-century furniture, decorative pieces,

THE OLD SMUGGLER *continued*

copper, brass, jugs. Nice selection of antique beds. Furniture stripping and refinishing.

A/C—PM. Wide range. Authentication when possible.

Prop. Sam Mercer 201–227–6665 (bus.)
785–0087 (res.)

Glen Ridge 07028

BAGGAGE ROOM ANTIQUES, 224 Ridgewood Ave. (Erie Lackawanna Station).

Hours: Tues. & Fri. 11–4

Nice shop in an old railroad station features 18th- and 19th-century furniture, antique dolls, paintings, silver, fine china, and glassware. Appraisal service, house sales conducted.

A/C—PM. Wide range. Authentication.

Prop. Lois Schenck 201–743–9260 (bus.)
743–8569 (res.)

Irvington 07111

COLONIAL ANTIQUE GALLERIES, 1021 Clinton Ave. (bisects Springfield Ave., main st. thru town).

Hours: By appt.

Old fireplace equipment, some paintings, and a general line of china and glass. Est. 1926.

A/C—Some prices marked. Affordable.

Porp. Irma Greenstone 201–372–8830

WILLIAM D. GROSS ANTIQUES, 1286 Springfield Ave. (main business st.).
Also see Repair and Restoration listing.

Hours: Mon. thru Sat. 10–11:30; 2:30–7

Well-chosen line of French furniture, porcelains, chandeliers, decorative accessories, in a roomy shop. Mr. Gross has been a dealer for thirty-five years, gives appraisals on a general line and also on musical instruments. Repair and restoration services.

WILLIAM D. GROSS ANTIQUES *continued*
A/C—PM. Wide range. Authentication.
Prop. William D. Gross   201–373–1753 (bus.)
                                                         762–5802 (res.)

HOUSE OF 7 WONDERS, 759 Springfield Ave. (main business st.). *Also see* Repair and Restoration listing.
Hours: Mon. thru Sat. 10–5:30

Mixture of antiques and collectibles from the 1850s on. Furniture, bric-a-brac, Oriental rugs, on two floors. Estates bought and sold, appraising. Services are china restoration, furniture refinishing and restoring, caning.

A/C—PM. Affordable. Authentication.
Prop. John and Lucy Arakelian   201–373–5618 (bus.)
                                                         763–0954 (res.)

Livingston 07039

THE COUNTRY STORE ANTIQUES & SUNDRIES, 60 E. Mt. Pleasant Ave. (Rt. 10).
Hours: Tues. thru Sat. 11–5

Primitive Americana, country store items, including old gumball and peanut machines, and antique advertising in an old-time atmosphere. Mrs. Fertig lectures on antiques and is a member of the Tin Container Collectors Assoc. and the National Assoc. of Breweriana.

A/C—PM (and dealer coded). Wide range. Authentication.
Prop. F. and H. Fertig   201–994–9066

FOXEE ANTIQUES, 72 W. Northfield Rd.
Hours: By appt.
A general line of antiques and collectibles, decorative pieces, some furniture, and personal floral arrangements.
C/A—PM. Affordable. Authentication.
Prop. Paula Fox   201–992–4048

LENI HELLER ANTIQUES, 24 E. Mt. Pleasant Ave. (Rt. 10).
Hours: Mon. thru Sat., except Wed., 10–5. Closed July & Aug.

LENI HELLER ANTIQUES *continued*

Tasteful selection of French, English, Oriental furniture, chandeliers, decorative accessories, in an interior designer's shop. Also antique jewelry, mirrors, paintings, leather-bound books.

A/C—PM. Wide range. Authentication.

Prop. Lenore Heller   201–992–1488

THE RED ROOSTER, Livingston.

Hours: By appt.

Interesting selection of small primitive accessories and collectible china, glass, bric-a-brac. Member Associated Antiques Dealers of N. J.

A/C—PM. Affordable. Authentication.

Prop. Fran Rominski   201–994–2875

REVIVAL HOUSE ANTIQUES & DECORATIVES, Livingston.

Hours: By appt.

Victorian furniture, old parlor stoves, hall stands, desks, antique wall hangings in a selective shop.

A—PM. Selective. Authentication when possible.

Prop. Robert Dalton   201–992–2950

Maplewood 07040

BEN JOSEPH ORIENTAL RUGS & ANTIQUES, LTD., 530 Valley St.
Also see Repair and Restoration listing.

Hours: Mon. thru Sat. 10–6; eves. by appt.

Antique, semiantique, and new Persian and Oriental rugs a specialty; European furniture, French porcelain, tapestries, objets d'art, Persian antiquities. Appraisals and estate sales. Oriental rug repairing and cleaning specialists.

A/Some collectibles. Selective. Authentication.

Prop. Ben Joseph Setareh   201–762–2087

SARA FIVERSON ANTIQUE INTERIORS, 509 Valley St.

Hours: Mon. thru Sat. 1–5

Nineteenth-century French and English furniture, chandeliers, fine china, and decorative pieces in a tasteful designer setting. The Fiversons are direct importers of European antiques and spend three months of each year personally buying in

SARA FIVERSON ANTIQUE INTERIORS *continued*

Europe. Antiques with a "utilitarian" quality are emphasized. "Items that can be used and enjoyed in a home, not just looked at." Longtime dealers, the Fiversons provide knowledgeable assistance and are registered with the New York Board of Trade. Interior design service.

A—PM. Selective. Authentication.

Prop. Sara and Harold Fiverson   201–762–9155

Millburn 07041

JEAN BARTLEY'S, 2 Taylor St. (off Main St., in center of town).

Hours: Mon. thru Sat. 11–5

"Antiques, collectibles 'n bric-a-brac" in a very large shop. General line of china, cut glass, some furniture, wicker, and lots of collectibles.

A/C—PM. Affordable. Authentication.

Prop. Jean Bartley   201–379–5970 (bus.)
                                                            964–7045 (res.)

GLENN GABRIEL, INC., 63 Main St. *Also see* Repair and Restoration listing.

Hours: Mon. thru Fri. 10–4:30

Quality antiques and "relativia" nicely displayed in a shop that has many interior design customers. French, Italian, English furniture and Oriental accessories. Antique restoration, lamp mountings, opaque shades, and painted finishes.

A/Some collectibles—PM. Selective.

Prop. Glenn Gabriel   201–379–7292

THE GOLDEN PINEAPPLE, 14–16 Main St.

Hours: Mon. thru Sat. 9–5; or by appt.

Large shop with attractively displayed furniture—chests, highboys, breakfronts, corner cupboards, both formal and country. Spode, old Lenox, pewter, crystal, brass accessories. Contemporary pieces include hand-decoupaged lamps from early prints. Mr. Chapman maintains a search service, conducts house sales, gives appraisals.

A/C—PM. Wide range. Consignments. Authentication.

Prop. Richard H. Chapman   201–379–6968

THE LENNARDS, 358 Millburn Ave. (main business st.).

Hours: Mon. thru Sat. 9:30–5:30

Specializing in quality antique jewelry and some reproductions. Antique clocks, fine china, silver serving pieces, and some small pieces of formal furniture. Appraisals; jewelry repairing.

A/C—PM. Wide range. Consignments. Authentication when possible.

Prop. Alvin and Selma Schlossberg   201–376–7274

JOHN A. MENDELSON, 2½ Taylor St. (off Main St., in center of town).

Hours: Mon. thru Sat. 1–5

A good-sized shop crowded with antiques, collector's items, Americana. General line of furniture, fine selection of cut glass, decorative pieces.

A/C—PM. Affordable. Authentication.

Prop. John A. Mendelson   201–379–4121

RONNIE'S ANTIQUES, 358 Millburn Ave. (main business st.).

Hours: Tues. thru Fri. 10–3; Sat. 10–5; Thurs. eve. 7–9:30

Well-chosen line of golden oak, some Victorian furniture, chandeliers, elderly lamps, accessories, in an inviting shop. A few reproduction baker's racks and chandeliers.

A/C—PM. Wide range. Consignments.

Prop. Ronnie Varadi   201–376–9498

Montclair 07042

ABBEY ANTIQUES, 217 Glen Ridge Ave. (off Bloomfield Ave., main business st.).

Hours: Mon. thru Sat., ex. Wed., 11–5; closed Sat. in summer

Charming old home converted to a sizable shop that carries a general line of fine china, cut glass, silver, porcelains, some Orientalia. Member Antique Dealers at Montclair.

A/C—PM. Affordable.

Prop. Mildred and Harry Berg   201–744–4432

ALADDIN ANTIQUES, 444 Bloomfield Ave. (main business st.).

Hours: Mon. thru Sat. 10–4

ALADDIN ANTIQUES *continued*

"Everything fine that's old" in a gracious shop. Art glass, porcelains, paintings, china, some formal furniture. "Antiques and decorations bought and sold," house sales conducted, appraisal service. Mrs. Bielitz is a member of the Associated Antique Dealers of N. J. and Antique Dealers at Montclair.

A/C—PM. Wide range. Authentication when possible.

Prop. Mabel A. Bielitz   201–746–1324 (bus.)
                                                             338–9066 (res.)

ANTIQUE ALLEY, 411 Bloomfield Ave. (main business st.).

Hours: Mon. thru Sat. 11–5

"Odd pieces of antique furniture," paintings, silver, jewelry, bric-a-brac. Member Antique Dealers at Montclair.

A/C—Prices not marked. Affordable. Consignments. Authentication.

Prop. Peter Galante   201–783–6161

ANTIQUE STAR, 627 Bloomfield Ave. (main business st.).

Hours: Mon. thru Sat. 10:30–5

Antique French and American clocks a specialty; brass and marble candelabra, some formal furniture, old trunks. Member Antique Dealers at Montclair.

A/C—PM. Wide range. Consignments.

Prop. V. Nicolaisen   201–746–0070

AUTOGRAPHS, COLLECTIBLES, AMERICANA, 346 Bloomfield Ave. (main business st.).

Hours: Sat. & Sun. 10:30–4:30; or by appt.

All kinds of "collectible paper"—autographs, original comic art from the 1930s to the 1970s, signed books, political Americana. Appraisals. Member Antique Dealers at Montclair.

C/A—PM. Affordable. Consignments. Authentication.

Prop. Paul Hartunian, Steve Koschal   201–746–9132

BROVACO GALLERY, 436 Bloomfield Ave. (main business st.). *Also see* Repair and Restoration listing.

Hours: Mon. thru Sat. 9–4

Selected American 19th-century paintings, Currier & Ives, Audubon prints, in a shop that also specializes in expert cleaning and restoration of paintings.

BROVACO GALLERY *continued*

A/C—Prices not marked. Selective. Authentication.

Prop. Robert E. Brovaco   201–744–3111

BROWNELL & CO., 460 Bloomfield Ave. (main business st.).

Hours: Tues. thru Sat. 11–5

Specialists in rare coins; some cut glass, silver, and collectibles in an extremely large corner building. Mr. Brownell does appraisals and is a life member of the American Numismatist Assoc.

A/C—Most prices marked. Wide range. Consignments. Authentication.

Prop. Marvin Brownell   201–746–9199

BROWSER'S NOOK, 322 Orange Rd. (off Bloomfield Ave.).

Hours: Tues. thru Sat. 10–4

Formal period furniture, appropriate accessories and decorative items, fine china, copper and brass pieces. House sales conducted.

A/C—PM. Affordable.

Prop. Loretta Brownlee   201–744–1619

THE CALICO CAT, 6 Midland Ave. (off Bloomfield Ave.).

Hours: Mon. thru Sat. 11–4

A friendly invitation to "come and browse" in a pleasant shop carrying a general line of furniture, crystal, porcelains, glassware. The Kellers conduct house sales, give appraisals, and are members of Antique Dealers at Montclair.

A/C—PM. Affordable. Consignments. Authentication.

Prop. Robert and Mary Keller   201–744–1244 (bus.)
                                                          748–4466 (res.)

CLAIRMONT LTD., 51 Church St. (off Valley Rd.; 1 block above Bloomfield Ave.).

Hours: Mon. thru Sat. 10–5:30

A wide range of antiques and collectibles—jewelry, silver, dolls, fine china, cut glass, paintings, Oriental objects, rugs, American and foreign coins. Appraisals available. The mounting of lamps and custom-made shades are services. Member Antique Dealers at Montclair.

A/C—PM. Wide range. Authentication.

Prop. Phil Schwartz   201–746–3641

JEAN ELKIN ANTIQUES, 334 Bloomfield Ave. (main business st.).

Hours: Mon., Tues., Thurs., Sat. 12–5; or by appt.

Browsable shop carrying a general line of china and glassware, lamps, silver, antique jewelry, paintings, hand-carved wood. Member Antique Dealers at Montclair.

A/C—PM. Affordable. Consignments. Authentication.

Prop. Jean Elkin   201–783–4440 (bus.)
                                     667–1317 (res.)

F & S ANTIQUES, 32-A Church St. (off Valley Rd.). *Also see* Repair and Restoration listing.

Hours: Mon. thru Sat. 11–5:30

Just about everything in a diversified shop—Oriental art, bronzes, wood carvings, antique jewelry, watches, clocks, paintings on porcelains, art glass, crystal, chandeliers, china, silver, objets d'art. "Thirty years' experience serving the trade." Repair and restoration of antique jewelry, watches, clocks, silver, paintings, and lamps. Member Antique Dealers at Montclair.

A/C—Most prices marked. Wide range. Authentication.

Prop. S. J. Smith, S. H. Feingold   201–744–2622

FRIENDLY SHOPPERS ANTIQUE MART, 406 Bloomfield Ave. (main business st.).

Hours: Mon. thru Sat. 11–4

Nice line of cut glass, fine china, Oriental porcelains, sterling silver, and decorative items. Appraisal service; house sales conducted. Member Antique Dealers at Montclair.

A/C—PM. Wide range. Consignments. Authentication.

Prop. Elinor Garelick   201–744–9140 (bus.)
                                          467–9143 (res.)

THE HAMLET, 340 Bloomfield Ave. (main business st.).

Hours: By chance or appt.

Large shop crowded with furniture of various periods, "early pieces, elegant pieces," Oriental rugs, china, lamps, paintings, clocks, silver, art objects. Member Antique Dealers at Montclair.

A/C—Prices not marked. Wide range.

Prop. Brian Gage   201–746–1775 (bus.)
                                     744–1553 (res.)

HODGE PODGE SHOP, 209 Glen Ridge Ave. (off Bloomfield Ave.).

Hours: Mon. thru Sat. 11–4; or by appt.

A little bit of everything—antique and used furniture, bric-a-brac, linens, silver, jewelry, household and miscellaneous items. Estate and house sales conducted.

A/C—PM. Affordable.

Prop. Frances V. Barnham   201–783–4422 (bus.)
                                                                                  667–3157 (res.)

WALTER HULL ANTIQUES, 410 Bloomfield Ave. (main business st.).

Hours: Mon. thru Sat. 12–4

Quality antiques in a selective shop—paintings, antique lamps, fine china, brass candlesticks, sconces, sterling, nice selection of andirons. Member Antique Dealers at Montclair.

A—PM. Selective. Authentication when possible.

Prop. Walter Hull   201–744–1335 (bus.)
                                                                                  731–9093 (res.)

JACK HUNTER'S ANTIQUES, 24 S. Fullerton Ave. (off Bloomfield Ave.).

Hours: Mon. thru Sat. 12–5, except Wed. 12–3; or by appt.

General line of furniture of all periods, silver, china, jewelry, bric-a-brac, in a large shop. Member Antique Dealers at Montclair.

A/C—Some prices marked. Wide range. Authentication.

Prop. Jack Hunter   201–226–4041

THE IVORY BIRD, 555 Bloomfield Ave. (main business st.).

Hours: Mon. thru Sat. 10–5

Attractively displayed Oriental pieces—Korean chests, Imari, Japanese cloisonné, ivories, fine porcelains, early Ming and Sung; some American furniture. Appraisals available. Member Antique Dealers at Montclair.

A/C—PM. Selective. Occasional consignment. Authentication.

Prop. Meredith Burke, Mary Heyman, Gene Sullivan, Roseanne Zanowski
                                                                                  201–744–5225

LILLIAN'S ANTIQUES, 404 Bloomfield Ave. (main business st.).

Hours: Mon. thru Sat. 9–4

Well-chosen collection of fine continental porcelains, Meissen, Sèvres, Old Paris, Royal Worcester; general line of furniture; Orientalia, antique jewelry, paintings, art glass. Member Antique Dealers at Montclair.

LILLIAN'S ANTIQUES *continued*

A/C—PM. Wide range. Authentication when possible.

Prop. Lillian Rabinowitz   201–746–2006 (bus.)
                                                                            673–2603 (res.)

MILT'S ANTIQUES, 662 Bloomfield Ave. (main business st.).

Hours: Mon. thru Sat. 11–5

Sizable shop crammed with a general line of furniture, stained glass windows, china, glass, jewelry, books. Appraisals available. "We buy and sell from one item to complete households." Member Antique Dealers at Montclair.

A/C—Most prices marked. Affordable. Authentication.

Prop. Milt Braneck   201–746–4445 (bus.)
                                                                            778–7044 (res.)

MONTCLAIR HISTORICAL SOCIETY ANTIQUES MARKET, Lackawanna RR Station, Lackawanna Plaza (at Grove St. and Bloomfield Ave., main business st.).

Hours: Tues. thru Fri. 10:30–3:30; Sat. 10–5

When the Erie-Lackawanna station in Montclair was abandoned by the railroad in 1974, the Montclair Historical Society leased the station, which is listed in the State and the National Register of Historic Places, and made it a year-round fund-raising antiques market. The Historical Society staffs and maintains a consignment shop in the big baggage room downstairs, while associated dealers in antiques share the enormous waiting room.

Proceeds from dealer rentals and from the Society's consignment shop go to the preservation of the historic Israel Crane House, built originally in 1796 and added to in 1830. Open to the public on Sunday afternoons, the Crane House is furnished with appropriate antiques of the period and welcomes group tours by appointment. Call 201–744–1796.

MONTCLAIR HISTORICAL SOCIETY CONSIGNMENT SHOP.

The nonprofit shop sells used merchandise of all kinds: furniture, china, collectibles, bric-a-brac. Donated items are tax deductible. House sales conducted; appraisal service.

BIG KERR'S FUTURE ANTIQUES, Kerry Rasp.

Nostalgia, advertising tins, breweriana, Coca-Cola collectibles.

THE CABOOSE, Barbara Churchfield.

General line of china and glass, lamps, decorative accessories.

MONTCLAIR HISTORICAL SOCIETY ANTIQUES MARKET *continued*

CATTAIL CURIOS, Pat Peykar and Helen Taylor.

Crystal, porcelains, pottery, small pieces of furniture, primitives.

ENCORE, Mina Mandelbaum and Shirley Shaller.

Jewelry, china, lamps, small pieces of furniture.

EXOTIC ANTIQUES, Alvida Collins.

Old jewelry, china and glass, dolls.

FRED'S ANTIQUES, Fred Bright.

"Items particularly appealing to men" : old tools, brass, copper, wood carvings, maps, pewter, curios.

THE SPIDER'S WEB, Rose Ann Keinis.

Predominantly furniture—Empire, Victorian, some Early American.

THE WOODEN DUCK, Helen Kirrer.

Prints, etchings, old documents, post cards, miscellaneous collectibles.

A/C—PM. Wide range. Consignments. Authentication.

Prop. Montclair Historical Society, Suzanne Fischer, Mgr.   201–746–9337

POOR RICHARD'S FURNITURE CO., 69 N. Willow St. (off Bloomfield Ave.). *Also see* Repair and Restoration listing.

Hours: Tues. 9:30–8; Thurs. thru Sat. 9:30–5:30

Old and new brass beds are specialties in a shop that provides many repair and restoration services—furniture refinishing and repair, wrought iron and wicker refinished, caning, rushing, reupholstering. Member Antique Dealers at Montclair.

A/C—PM. Affordable.

Prop. Rick Mordwin   201–783–5333

RANDALL HOUSE ANTIQUES, 221 Glen Ridge Ave. (off Bloomfield Ave.).

Hours: Mon. thru Sat. 10–5

Oriental and domestic rugs, English, French, and some Dutch furniture, old paintings, predominate in this very large shop. General line of decorative accessories. Appraisal service.

A/C—PM. Wide range. Authentication.

Prop. Harry Feldman   201–783–6246

EARL ROBERTS, 17 S. Fullerton Ave. (off Bloomfield Ave.).

Hours: Tues. thru Sat. 11:30–5:30

Three rooms filled with formal furniture, paintings, porcelains, Oriental objets d'art, crystal, chandeliers, bronzes, silver accessories. An old stone firehouse to the rear of the main shop has a selection of country furniture in-the-rough. Appraisals available; house sales conducted. Member Antique Dealers at Montclair.

A—PM. Selective. Consignments. Authentication.

Prop. Earl Roberts   201–744–2232

WILLIAM A. SABLON, 411 Bloomfield Ave. (main business st.).

Hours: Mon. thru Sat. 9:30–5:30

A big old Victorian building crammed with furniture of various periods, paintings, china, decorative accessories. "Complete purchase and removal of estates." Appraisal service. Member Antique Dealers at Montclair.

A/C—PM. Wide range. Consignments. Authentication.

Prop. William A. Sablon   201–746–4397 (bus.)
                                                                 228–2634 (res.)

PATTERSON SMITH, 23 Prospect Terrace.

Hours: By appt.

Rare and out-of-print books on criminology, social, technical, and business history. Mr. Smith maintains a search service and is a member of the Antiquarian Booksellers' Assoc. of America, Middle Atlantic Chapter.

A/C—PM. Wide range. Authentication.

Prop. Patterson Smith   201–744–3291

TRENT ANTIQUES, 494 Bloomfield Ave. (main business st.).

Hours: Mon. thru Sat. 11–5

General line of furniture, predominantly Victorian. Abundance of fine china, cut glass, crystal; paintings, Oriental rugs. Mr. Trent also buys and sells musical instruments, music boxes, old Victrolas. Appraisals; house sales conducted. Member Antique Dealers at Montclair.

A/Some collectibles—Most prices marked. Wide range. Occasional consignment. Authentication.

Prop. Ed Trent   201–783–4676

TWO WORLDS BAZAAR, 225 Glen Ridge Ave. (off Bloomfield Ave.).

Hours: Mon. thru Sat. 11–5

Selection of formal furniture, cut glass, china, old quilts, chandeliers, bric-a-brac. "Best of two worlds—old and new." Member Antique Dealers at Montclair.

A/C—PM. Affordable. Consignments.

Prop. Pearl Gambino   201–744–5557 (bus.)
                                               744–7749 (res.)

VICTOR E. WANGNER, 9 Midland Ave. (off Bloomfield Ave.).

Hours: Mon. thru Sat. 10–5

Antiquarian books, first editions, authors' manuscripts, old prints, along with a selection of carnival glass, Limoges china, crystal, steins. Hand-engraving of old and new pewter, gold and silver. Appraisals available.

A/C—PM. Wide range. Consignments. Authentication.

Prop. Victor E. Wangner   201–783–6961

WEATHERVANE ANTIQUES, 6 Midland Ave. (off Bloomfield Ave.).

Hours: Mon. thru Sat. 11–4

Good old country antiques, a general line of fine china and glass, old dolls. Appraisal service; house sales conducted. Member Antique Dealers at Montclair.

A/C—PM. Affordable. Consignments. Authentication.

Prop. Hil Alexander   201–744–1244

ENID WEISS ANTIQUES & COLLECTIBLES, Montclair.

Hours: By appt.

Antiques and collector's items—glass, porcelains, Royal Doulton, Staffordshire, Limoges, decorative accessories; some small pieces of period furniture. Mrs. Weiss will search for individual pieces of furniture at customer's request.

A/C—PM. Affordable. Authentication when possible.

Prop. Enid Weiss   201–744–7870

RUTH WENGER ANTIQUES, 410 Bloomfield Ave. (main business st.).

Hours: Mon. thru Sat. 12–4:30; or by appt.

Thousands of antique post cards, all categorized, a unique specialty; also fine china and glass, antique dolls. Mrs. Wenger is a member of the Garden State

RUTH WENGER ANTIQUES *continued*

Post Card Club, the Associated Antiques Dealers of N. J., and Antique Dealers at Montclair.

A/C—PM. Affordable. Authentication.

Prop. Ruth Wenger   201–744–8336 (bus.)
                                                                             239–0730 (res.)

Upper Montclair 07043

THE FINDER'S KEEP, The Mews, 894 Valley Rd. (main business st.).

Hours: Mon., Tues., Thurs., Fri. 10:30–4; Sat. 10:30–5

Victorian and 1920s clothing, some Victorian furniture, stained glass, old jewelry, china, glass, downstairs in a quiet little enclave of commercial shops off busy Valley Rd.

A/C—PM. Affordable. Occasional consignment.

Prop. Maria Cleary, Tony Meramo   201–744–5513

LEONARDS ANTIQUES & COLLECTIBLES, 229 Bellevue Ave. (off Valley Rd.).

Hours: Mon., Tues., Thurs., Sat. 10–4

Selection of oak furniture, old lamps, prints, clocks, bric-a-brac, attractively arranged in the upstairs area of a large corner building. Member Antique Dealers at Montclair.

A/C—PM. Affordable. Consignments. Authentication when possible.

Prop. Barbara Artale, Betty Iannarone   201–746–8110

MONTCLAIR WOMEN'S EXCHANGE, 197 Bellevue Ave. (off Valley Rd.).

Hours: Mon. thru Sat. 11–4

Everything on consignment—antique jewelry, china, silver, bric-a-brac, small pieces of furniture, lots of collectibles. Appraisals; house sales conducted. Member Antique Dealers at Montclair.

A/C—PM. Affordable. Authentication.

Prop. Ausma Grimes   201–746–3754

GEORGE RHEN, 212 Bellevue Ave. (off Valley Rd.).

Hours: Tues. thru Sat. 10–3, 6–9

GEORGE RHEN *continued*

American country and primitive furniture, collectibles, in a big old turn-of-the-century house that also has a dining area for lunches and dinners.

A/C—PM. Affordable. Occasional consignment. Authentication.

Prop. Edith Vulpi, George Rhen   201–744–7125

THE SIDE DOOR, The Mews, 594 Valley Rd. (main business st.).

Hours: Mon, thru Sat. 9–3

Pleasant shop in a charming mews right off the main business street shows Oriental artifacts—Chinese temple carvings, temple jars, Oriental curio cabinets, porcelains, bronzes, paintings and prints. Member Antique Dealers at Montclair.

A/Some collectibles—PM. Selective. Occasional consignment. Authentication.

Prop. Queenie Davidson   201–783–4334

WOMEN'S WORK SALESROOMS AND CONSIGNMENT SHOP, 545 Valley Rd. (main business st.).

Hours: Mon. thru Sat. 11–4

Antiques and collectibles on consignment. China, glass, bric-a-brac, jewelry, some furniture.

A/C—PM. Affordable. Consignments. Authentication when possible.

Prop. Zoyla Hausner   201–746–8231

Newark 07102

GEORGE SCHEINER & SON ANTIQUES, 429 Broad St.

Hours: Mon. thru Fri. 12–5

Quality antiques in a shop that has been in business since 1897. American antiques predominate in furniture, paintings, silver, porcelain, glass. Past sales have included those to museums. Mr. Scheiner is a member of the Appraisers Assoc. of America.

A—Prices not marked. Serious collectors. Authentication.

Prop. Augustus Scheiner   201–621–8311

Orange 07050

A TOUCH OF OAK, 618 Freeman St. (bet. Valley and Scotland Rds.).
Also see Repair and Restoration listing.
Hours: Mon., Tues. 1:30–6; Thurs. thru Sat. 1:30–6
Nicely finished pieces of oak furniture in a shop that specializes in repair and refinishing of antiques, caning, Victorian wicker weaving where damaged, polishing of metals. Appraisal service.
A/C—PM. Affordable. Authentication.
Prop. J. Rosser   201–673–1551

LESLIE GOULD, 391 Tremont Pl. *Also see* Repair and Restoration listing.
Hours: By appt.
Mechanical musical instruments, including old phonographs, music boxes, a specialty in a shop that repairs and restores player pianos and other musical instruments. Member Automated Musical Instrument Collectors Assoc.
A/C—PM. Wide range. Authentication when possible.
Prop. Susan and Leslie Gould   201–672–4060

ORANGE JEWELERS, 217 Main St.
Hours: Mon., Tues., Thurs., Sat. 10–5:30; Fri. 10–7:30
Nice pieces of antique jewelry in a modern jewelry shop. Appraisal service.
A—PM. Wide range.
Prop. Elaine and Robert Goldman   201–677–3179

Roseland 07068

VIRGINIA B. CANNON ANTIQUES, 178 Eagle Rock Ave. (at rear of Roseland Plaza).
Hours: Sat. 11–4:30; or by appt.
Early American glass, early furniture, paintings, coin silver, and a general line of china in a selective shop. Appraisals; house sales conducted. Member Associated Antiques Dealers of N. J. and the Antiques Dealers Assoc. of Central N. J.
A—PM. Wide range. Authentication.
Prop. Virginia B. Cannon   201–226–2812

South Orange 07079

ANTIQUE EVELYN, 132 South Orange Ave. (main business st.).

Hours: Mon. thru Sat. 10–4

"Everything Old"—china, glass, furniture, brass, copper, bronze, jewelry, dolls, clocks, toys, paintings, chandeliers. Appraisals available.

A/C—PM. Wide range. Authentication.

Prop. Evelyn Malekoff   201–762–7700 (bus.)
                                                                762–4928 (res.)

ANTIQUES, LTD., 108 W. South Orange Ave. (main business st.).

Hours: Tues. thru Sat. 11–4; closed Sat. June 15–Sept. 15

Large collection of china, glass, and antique jewelry. Some small pieces of formal furniture and chandeliers.

A/C—PM. Affordable.

Prop. Doris Lewczuk   201–762–6160

CARRIE TOPF ANTIQUES, 50 W. South Orange Ave. (main business st.).

Hours: Tues. thru Sat. 11–4

Formal French furniture, chandeliers, Haviland, Dresden, and other fine china; art glass, good decorative accessories in a long-established shop.

A/C—PM. Selective. Consignments. Authentication when possible.

Prop. Carrie Topf   201–762–8773 (bus.)
                                                        762–9475 (res.)

ROBERTA WILLNER, 112 W. South Orange Ave. (main business st.).

Hours: Tues. thru Sat. 11–4

Small pieces of French and Chinese furniture, china and porcelains, along with a large selection of American Indian jewelry, new and old, that Mrs. Willner personally selects at reservations in the West.

A/C—PM. Affordable. Consignments. Authentication when possible.

Prop. Roberta Willner   201–762–8844

Upper Montclair 07043

See listings following MONTCLAIR.

Verona 07044

AGELESS NOSTALGIA ANTIQUES, 30 Pompton Ave. (Rt. 23).

Hours: Tues. thru Sat. 12–5:30

Mixture of antiques and collectibles in a good-sized shop. General line of china, silver, clocks, jewelry, lamps, some furniture, bric-a-brac. "We buy one item or complete estates." Appraisals; house sales conducted.

A/C—Prices not marked. Affordable. Authentication.

Prop. Bernice Nanni   201–857–1306

ALEX'S CLOCK SHOP, 133 Bloomfield Ave. (main business st.). *Also see* Repair and Restoration listing.

Hours: Wed. thru Sat. 12–5

Antique clocks a specialty, with emphasis on American clocks; selection of antique pocket watches; also mechanical phonographs, small pieces of furniture, kerosene lamps. Appraisals on clocks; repair of antique clocks and watches. Mr. Karr is a member of the Nat'l. Assoc. of Watch & Clock Collectors.

A/C—PM. Wide range. Authentication on clocks.

Prop. Alex Karr   201–239–5025 (bus.)
                                                                  226–7784 (res.)

GLOBETROTTER ANTIQUES, 25 Pompton Ave. (Rt. 23).

Hours: Mon. thru Sat. 9–4:30

An enormous shop crowded with antique and used furniture, carvings, objets d'art, china, cut crystal, old gold, jewelry, bric-a-brac. Note the extensive collection of primitive kitchen utensils, early farm implements, woodworking tools. Estate appraisals.

A/C—Most prices marked. Wide range. Authentication.

Prop. Larry Murray; Larry Grimes, Mgr.   201–746–3253

NOEL'S PLACE, 133 Bloomfield Ave. (main business st.).

Hours: Thurs. thru Sun. 1–5

Lots of collectibles, some antiques, in a genial shop. China and glass, jewelry, crystal, Art Deco, a bit of furniture. Appraisals available.

C/A—PM. Affordable. Authentication.

Prop. Noel Brogan   201–857–1061

West Orange 07052

JAMES ROSE UPHOLSTERING, 72 Harrison Ave. *Also see* Repair and Restoration listing.

Hours: Mon. thru Sat. 9–4:30

Primarily specialists in repairing, restoring, reupholstering of antiques; some pieces of upholstered antique furniture for sale.

A/C—PM. Affordable. Authentication when possible.

Prop. James Rose   201–325–3364

WHAT NOT SHOP, 606 Eagle Rock Ave.

Hours: Tues., Thurs., Fri., Sat. 11:30–3:30

Good selection of antique porcelains, a general line of furniture, collectibles, decorative accessories. Mrs. Fischer will search out and match pieces of silver services for customers. Appraisals.

A/C—PM. Wide range. Consignments. Authentication when possible.

Prop. Claire Fischer   201–731–4949

Bejeweled and boldly carved carousel horse in the Coney Island style by Charles Carmel, ca. 1912. Carmel often decorated his horses with figures—in this case, a realistically carved head emerging from under the saddle. *From the Charlotte Dinger Collection. Courtesy The Brandywine River Museum. Photo: Edward Cliney*

In the Hills and Beyond
The Central Counties

A child's pierced wood chair made in 1872 at the Glen Gardner factory in rural Hunterdon County. More than 300 people were employed here until the factory was severely damaged by flood in the 1880s. Church pews and railroad seats were also made. *Courtesy Shop of Unusual Things, Hampton. Photo: Andrew Jacobs*

Hunterdon County

Annandale 08801

BUTTONWOOD FORGE ANTIQUES, 83 Beaver Ave. *Also see* Repair and Restoration listing.

Hours: Sat. & Sun. 9–5; or by appt.

Primitives and early iron—strap hinges, latches, locks, fireplace irons (including cranes and trammels); pine and cherry furniture, early advertising tin. Design; restoration of early iron. In an old barn that was once a blacksmith shop.

A/C. Wide range. Authentication when possible.

Prop. Bernard Francfort   201–735–5235

DECORATOR'S WORKSHOP, Beaver Ave. (Adjacent to I78 and Rt. 22. Shop bldg. is at rear; ample parking.)

Hours: Mon. thru Fri. 10–2 (call ahead suggested); and by appt.

Antiques and decorating service "for the total home." Specializing in decorative accessories, furniture, some china and glass. American and English grandfather clocks (some new); Tiffany-style and other lamps. Also benches, chairs, tables, rockers. Full line of decorator fabrics, flooring, wallcoverings; custom draperies. Visa. Gift wrapping.

A/C—PM; also new. Wide range. Authentication when possible.

Prop. Bonnie McIntyre, Mairzy Leciston   201–735–7475 (bus.)
                                             782–8034 (res.)

Bloomsbury 08804

HOLLY HILL, R. D. Box 275-C.

Hours: By appt.

Silver, English royal commemoratives; glass, china, and pottery. Shopping and mailing service.

A—PM. Affordable/Selective. All pieces guaranteed.

Prop. Diane Adam   No phone

Califon 07830

BLUE SPRUCE ANTIQUES SHOP, Hoffman's Crossing Rd.

Hours: 7 days 9–5; check for Jan. & Feb. closing

Early American pressed glass and fine china. Pressed goblets, pitchers, creamers, plates. China, including Limoges; demitasse teacups and saucers.

C—PM. Affordable. Authentication when possible.

Prop. Gladys V. Farley   201–832–2270

Centerville 08853

THE RED SLEIGH, Rt. 202, southbound (midway between New York and Phila.). Mailing address: Neshanic Station 08853.

Hours: 7 days; "If I'm here, I'm open."

Picture frames, lamps, "anything and everything." Antiques purchased. Dealers welcome.

C. Affordable. Authentication when possible.

Prop. Ann Demjanow   No phone

Clinton 08809

ART'S RESALE, 250 Rt. 31 north (2 mi. north of Rt. 78; adjacent to Spruce Run Reservoir).

Hours: Mon. 3–6; Tues. thru Sun. 9–6

A roadside warehouse with merchandise enough to boast "We've got it all." Victorian, carved, and oak furniture; tin, brass, oil lamps; crocks, jugs, stoves,

ART'S RESALE *continued*

fireplace equipment, telephones, cash registers, old musical instruments, etc. "Antiques of tomorrow," finished and in-the-rough; accent on the unusual. Advice is "Don't let price come between us." Also to "Ask, maybe we can do better." Contents of homes, estates, and individual pieces purchased. Dealers welcome.

C/A—PM. Affordable/Wide range.

Prop. Art and Virginia Napolitano   201–735–4442

THE ATTIC, 27 Center St. (corner Halstead St.).

Hours: Tues. thru Sat. 11–5

General line, proprietors' preference for "antiques and nice old things." Primitives, good used furniture, trunks, antique clothing, crocks, jugs, bric-a-brac.

C—PM. Affordable. Consignments. Authentication.

Prop. Gloria Barrett, Gloria Dempsey   201–735–8150

CRAFT HOUSE ANTIQUES, 38 Center St. (facing Halstead St.).

Hours: Fall & winter: Tues. thru Fri. 10–3; Sat. & Sun. 12–5. Spring & summer: daily 12–5. Closed Mon.

Quilts, kerosene and oil lamps, pottery, advertising tins, crocks and jugs; general line. Caning, rushing, and splint work. A Federal-style residence dating to 1847, remodeled in 1880.

C/A—PM. Wide range. Authentication.

Prop. Dominic Yacobucci   201–735–4382

LONG HOUSE ANTIQUES, 16 W. Main (next to Silversmith Shop). *Also see* Repair and Restoration listing.

Hours: Tues. thru Sun. 11–5; Fri. 'til 9. Closed Mon.

Oil lamps, lanterns, tools, old keys, pocket watches. Also blanket chests, trunks, some old cameras, books, stoves, iceboxes, crocks, jugs, old bottles. Furniture repair and refinishing. Interesting shop with handsome old barber's cabinets built into the wall to house displays.

C—PM. Affordable/Wide range (furniture higher). Consignments. Authentication when possible.

Prop. Ronald Gyuro   201–735–4838 (bus.)
                                                             735–7994 (res.)

THE PADDY-WAK, 19½ Old Rt. 22.

Hours: Tues. thru Sat. 10:30–5; Sun. by chance or appt.

Diverse general line at an attractive in-town shop. Furniture, oil paintings, fine china. Appraisals.

A/C—PM. Wide range.

Prop. Elaine and Dwayne Gonzalez, Jean Brogley   201–735–9770

SILVERSMITH SHOP, 14 W. Main.

Hours: Tues. thru Sun. 11–5; Fri. 'til 9. Closed Mon.

Handwrought sterling and gold jewelry in a beautifully appointed shop. Small selection of antique jewelry complements Mr. Bray's work. Also necklaces from the Middle East, Persia, India, Afghanistan; some rings, small boxes, cigarette cases and holders. Repair and restoration of jewelry, holloware, and other metal objects. Member American Craftsman's Council.

The 1790s building was originally the residence of Nehemiah Dunham, a cattleman who owned 600 acres west of the South Branch of the Raritan River. During the Revolution, Dunham supplied meat to the Continental Army.

A/C—PM. Affordable/Selective. Consignments. Authentication when possible.

Prop. Kenneth R. Bray   201–735–4838

Everittstown 08867

THE YANKEE PEDDLERS ANTIQUES, corner Rts. 513 and 519.

Hours: By chance or appt. Closed Jan., Feb., March.

Primitives, early American furniture, decoys, old kitchen utensils; general line. Antiques from Maine. The proprietors refinish their pieces, hand-mix stains. Member Associated Antiques Dealers of N. J.

A—PM. Selective. Authentication when possible.

Prop. Ellen and Franklin Appel   201–996–4682

Fairmount 07830

REGENCY ANTIQUES GALLERY, Fox Hill Rd.

Hours: Sat. & Sun. 10–6; and by appt.

Nineteenth-century American paintings, bronzes, objets d'art. Early furniture, Orientals, Wedgwood, glass, and guns. In an 1811 stone barn.

A/C—PM. Wide range. Consignments. Authentication when possible.

Prop. Margaret Price   201–832–2036

Flemington 08822

A & S ANTIQUES, 163 Main St. *Also see* Repair and Restoration listing.

Hours: Mon. thru Fri. 11–4; Sat. & Sun. 11–5

*Oriental objects, oak tables; china, glass, silver, brass (including inkwells),
fireplace accessories; a "general store of antiques." Cactus and succulents provide
pleasant greenery and are for sale. Furniture repair and restoration; hand-
stripping. No smoking requested.*

C/A—PM. Affordable/Wide range. Authentication.

Prop. Anne and Stephen Soodul   201–782–5270

COUNTRY ACRES ANTIQUES, Rockafellow Mills Rd. Mailing address:
R. D. 3, Box 632.

Hours: By appt. or chance

*General line, mostly antiques. Primitives, furniture, glass, crocks, kitchenware,
toys. An interesting shop in the barn. One of the original farms in the area,
the property dates back more than 200 years; presently a 90-acre beef farm.*

A/C—PM. Affordable/Wide range. Authentication when possible.

Prop. Ken and Alice Williams   201–782–8474

CURTIS ANTIQUES, 91 Main St. (opp. Hunterdon County Nat'l. Bank).

Hours: Mon. thru Sat. 1–4. Closed Sun.

*General line. Some oak, Victorian, and small furniture; Depression glass.
Good large pieces, sofas and dining room sets; also purchased.*

C—Most prices marked. Affordable/Wide range.

Prop. Carolyn Curtis   201–782–8979

GREAT THINGS, Turntable Junction.

Hours: 7 days 10:30–5:30

*Antiques, collectibles, decorative accessories; no primitives. Furniture, china,
hanging fixtures, trunks. Unusual fireplace equipment, fireplace screens,
beveled glass inkwells, butler's stands, Meissen; pieces from England, France,
Germany. "Our collectibles, tomorrow's antiques."*

A/C—PM. Wide range. Authentication when possible.

Prop. Cheryl Kozikowski   201–782–8855

THE HUNTERDON EXCHANGE, 155 Main St. (adj. to Turntable Junction).
Hours: Mon. thru Sat. 10–5; Sun. 1–5

*Selective all-consignment shop staffed by volunteers. Profits benefit the
Hunterdon Medical Center. Large general line; china, glass, pottery, small
furniture. Some tin, silver, metalware, clocks, jugs and crocks, insulators;
Rockingham. Also handcrafts, a room devoted to nearly new things, candies;
some older books and maps just inside the entrance.*

C/A; also new—PM. Affordable. All consignment.

Prop. Volunteer Board of Officers   201–782–6229

IORIO GLASS SHOP, S. Main St. Mailing address: Box 304. *Also see* Repair
and Restoration listing.

Hours: Mon. thru Sat. 11–5:30; Sun. 12–5

*Primarily early American blown glass, American and European art glass,
American cut glass of the "brilliant" period (1880–1925). Paperweights; some
antique lighting. Contemporary art glass. Custom glass cutting, engraving, glass
blowing. Repair and restoration of blown glass and china. Lamp repairs,
restoration, and parts. Member Early Amer. Glass Collector's Club, Amer.
Paperweight Assoc.*

*A third-generation artisan, Mr. Iorio's craftsmanship spans nearly a half-
century. He is represented in Europe by galleries in Frankfurt and Berne. Iorio
glass is in the permanent collections of the Corning Museum of Glass, the
Bergstrom Art Center and Museum (Neenah, Wis.), and the Wheaton Museum
(Millville, N. J.). A magnificent punch-bowl set by Mr. Iorio's father (c. 1905)
is in the exhibit room at the Flemington studio, as is more recent work by
Iorio sons.*

A/C; and contemporary—PM. Wide range. Authentication.

Prop. William and Eleanor Iorio   201–782–5311

RAGGEDY ANN DOLL HOSPITAL & MUSEUM, 171 Main St. *Also see*
Repair and Restoration listing.

Hours: Tues. thru Sun. 10–5:30. (Holiday weeks, open Mon., closed Tues.)
Closed Jan. & Feb.; call ahead during March.

*Extensive collection of antique and collector's dolls and cast-iron toys on museum
display. Dolls and toys also fill a separate sales room. Old dolls and doll parts,
cast-iron, tin, and wood toys purchased. Hospital for dolls of "reasonably good
quality"; new doll clothes made of older fabric. Lectures. Member United Fed.
of Doll Clubs, N.Y.C. Doll and Toy Collectors Club, patron Nat'l. Institute of*

RAGGEDY ANN DOLL HOSPITAL & MUSEUM *continued*

Amer. Doll Artists. Museum admission 50¢ for children ages 5–12; 75¢ for adults. Groups by arrangement.

A/C—Some prices marked; coded. Wide range/Selective to serious collectors. Authentication when possible.

Prop. Robert and Jean Bach   201–782–1243

WEB CABINET SHOP, 160 Main St. *Also see* Repair and Restoration listing.

Hours: Daily 9–6 or 7. Closed Mon.

Victorian furniture. Antiques purchased. Furniture repair, refinishing, restoration; carving, inlay, and custom work. Clock repairs.

A/C—Some prices marked. Wide range. Authentication when possible.

Prop. William E. and Katherine S. Bieg   No phone

Frenchtown 08825

FRENCHTOWN HOUSE OF ANTIQUES, 8 Bridge St.

Hours: Sat. & Sun. 12–6

Eighteenth-century American country and formal furniture; spatterware a specialty. Early glass, china, and slipware; primarily 19th-century American paintings; mirrors, clocks, candlesticks, copper, tinware; blanket chests. Interior design. Appraisals. Restoration of paintings by arrangement. In an 1864 haberdashery with lofty ceilings 16 feet high and in the small 1860s depot beside the Penn Central tracks.

A/Some collectibles—PM. Wide range. Authentication; money back guarantee.

Prop. Val Tyler, Walter Laughlin   201–996–2482

Glen Gardner 08826

HUNT HOUSE ANTIQUES, Rt. 31, corner Hunt Pl.

Hours: Sat. & Sun. 9–6

American primitives; Victorian furniture, bric-a-brac displayed with care and taste. Silver, coin silver, chairs, tables, cupboards, kitchenware, early pottery, flint glass. Appraisals. Entry is through the age-mellowed and charming 1700s core of the house; the main section was built in 1853.

A/C—PM. Affordable/Wide range. Consignments.

Prop. James Barnette, Michael Landino   201–537–4760

Hampton 08827

SHOP OF UNUSUAL THINGS, off Rt. 31 on Hampton-Changewater Rd.
(6 mi. north of Clinton, 3 mi. south of Washington; opp. New Hampton
General Store).
Hours: Wed. thru Sat. 11–5; Sun. 12–6
*Primarily gift and gourmet. Nice collection of country primitives and early
painted furniture. Also pewter, crocks, baskets. A 1785 stone house, the site of
the Prall Furniture Factory which flourished from the early 1800s to the turn
of the century.*
A/C—PM. Wide range. Consignments. Authentication.
Prop. Walter Lundquist   201–537–4737

High Bridge 08829

MONROE AND BEVERLY HOFFMAN, 51 E. Main St. *Also see* Repair and
Restoration listing.
Hours: Mon. thru Sat. 9–5; or by appt. Closed Sun. April thru end Oct.
*Primitives and country furniture. Furniture refinishing. Flea market Sundays
8–6 on Rt. 31, Glen Gardner; antiques, general merchandise, fruits and
vegetables.*
A/C—PM. Affordable.
Prop. Monroe and Beverly Hoffman   201–638–6466

THE RED FOX, W. Main St.
Hours: Sat. & Sun. 12–5
Early to mid-18th-century primitives; furniture, lamps.
A/C—PM. Selective. Consignments.
Prop. James W. Fox, Al Castro   201–638–8480

Lambertville 08530

ARCHANGEL & CO., 77 Bridge St. (corner Main St.).
Hours: Mon. thru Fri. 10:30–2:30; Sat. & Sun. 11–5
Russian items of special interest; military accouterments from the Civil War and

ARCHANGEL & CO. *continued*

earlier. General line; glass, china, silver, jewelry. "Anything Russian" purchased; also old guns and swords.

C—PM. Affordable. Authentication.

Prop. Joseph Cavallaro, Charles Buttaci 609–397–3655 (bus.)
883–1078 (eves.)

BONNET AND TOPPER ANTIQUES, 25 Ferry St.

Hours: Daily except Thurs. 1–9; Thurs. 4–9; and by appt.

China and glass; emphasis on pressed pattern glass. Antiques and collectibles purchased. The house dates to 1850.

C—PM. Affordable. Authentication when possible.

Prop. Frank Mazzacco, Jr., Laura Hopwood 609–397–2864

CASABLANCA, 63 Bridge St.

Hours: Mon. thru Fri. 11–5; Sat. & Sun. 10–7

Art Deco and Art Nouveau displayed with style; Tiffany glass a specialty. Austrian porcelains, stained glass, lighting, Oriental kimonos and shawls, juke boxes, French silk-screened prints. Quezal and Tiffany shades matched.

C—PM. Selective to serious collectors. Consignments. Authentication.

Prop. Al Castillo 609–397–1858

GOVERNOR'S ANTIQUE MARKET, Rt. 179 (1½ mi. north of Lambertville).

Hours: Sat. & Sun. 8–5. Summer outdoor market: Wed., Sat., Sun. 8–5

A vast display of antiques and collectibles exhibited in several dozen booths within the capacious interior of a former bowling alley. Heated, air-conditioned, a breakfast and lunch counter with Italian specialties; ample parking. In better weather, up to 200 dealers outdoors. No admission charge.

C/A—Prices generally marked.

Prop. Estelle Cad 609–397–2010

GREENBRANCH ANTIQUES, 3 Lambert Lane (just before New Hope-Lambertville Bridge).

Hours: 7 days 10 or 11–4 or 4:30; call ahead suggested

Wicker, "unusual, eye-catching" decorative pieces; oak, antique wire furniture,

GREENBRANCH ANTIQUES *continued*

including tables, chairs, plant stands. Local deliveries. A late 1700s stone riverfront house just east of the bridge.

C—PM. Affordable. Consignments. Authentication.

Prop. Bill Bunce   609–397–1225 (bus.)
                                                    201–782–6650 (res.)

ROSEMARY JONES ANTIQUES, 3 N. Union St.

Hours: Mon. thru Sat. 12–5; Sun. by appt.

Painted country furniture and folk art in a small, discriminating shop. Iron, baskets, pottery, decoys, small rugs, quilts, coverlets. Member Antiques Dealers Assoc. of Central N. J.

A—PM. Affordable/Selective. Authentication when possible.

Prop. Rosemary Jones   609–397–0999 (bus.)
                                                    215–862–2195 (res.)

LAMBERTVILLE ANTIQUE MARKET, Rt. 29.

Hours: Sat. & Sun. 8–5

Nicely arranged permanent shops in booths indoors, dozens of dealers in fair weather outside. Open year 'round. A few miles south of Lambertville beside a scenic, unspoiled stretch of the Delaware.

Prop. Ed and Florence Cook   609–397–0456
Mgr. Beverly Errhalt

> CRAFTIQUES, Rene Lentini.
>
> *Signed art glass and lamps; art pottery. Stained glass windows, when available. Art Nouveau shades. No reproductions. Appraisals of good art glass.*
>
> C—PM. Wide range. Consignments. Authentication.
>
> 201–782–6005 (res.)
>
> FRAN'S ANTIQUES, Fran Boschen.
>
> *Antique jewelry, Nippon; general line.*
>
> C/A—PM. Affordable. Consignments. Authentication.
>
> GIBSONS' ANTIQUES, Michael and Rosann Gibson.
>
> *American art pottery; primarily 20th-century dolls, bisque to hard plastic. Mission furniture, when available. General line of collectibles. Doll repairs; caning.*
>
> C—PM. Affordable. Consignments. Authentication.
>
> 215–489–7116 (res.)

LAMBERTVILLE ANTIQUE MARKET *continued*

HERMAN'S ANTIQUES & COLLECTIBLES, Herman and Florence Lotstein.

Mechanical objects a specialty; trains, clocks, music boxes. Railroad memorabilia, military items, Coca-Cola advertising, old sheet music; general line. Trains repaired. Collector's list for railroad items. Antiques purchased. New books within specialty. Member Delaware Valley Antique Dealers Assoc.

C—PM. Affordable/Wide range. Consignments. Authentication.

NOSTALGIA, Yolanda Holmak.

Turn-of-the-century oak and mahogany; Depression glass, china, Nippon. Beer trays, knickknacks, dolls, silver, jewelry. Some new books on antiques. Caning.

C—PM. Affordable. Authentication.

MARIE'S ANTIQUES, Marie Daunton.

Early American pottery, Depression glass; some furniture and lighting. General line.

C/A—PM. Affordable/Wide range. Authentication.

NELLIE'S ANTIQUES, Nellie Engel.

Old cut glass, sterling, Lenox, Limoges, and other china; prints, candlesticks, ornate lighting.

A/C—Most prices marked. Wide range. Authentication when possible.

NIDDY-NODDY ANTIQUES & COLLECTIBLES, Hilda and Pete Shuhala.

General line; antiques and older collectibles. Antiques purchased. All pieces backed by the proprietors and researched.

C/A—PM. Affordable. Authentication.   201–254–5902 (res.)

MAYFAIR HOUSE, INC., 15 Bridge St.

Hours: Mon. thru Sat. 10–5. Closed Sun.

Selective shop. Formal American and English 18th-century furniture beautifully displayed and identified. Known for more than twenty-five years. Appraisals.
A—Most prices marked. Selective to serious collectors. Consignments. Authentication.

Prop. Joseph Franklin   609–397–3059

NORTH COUNTRY ANTIQUES, 10 N. Union St. *Also see* Repair and Restoration listing.

Hours: Mon. thru Sat. 12–4:30; or by appt.

Country furniture; redware, old quilts, crocks and jugs, primitives, prints, silver. Interior decorating. Refinishing and restoration assisted by Mr. Raywood's sister, Beatrice Raywood.

A—PM. Wide range. Consignments. Authentication.

Prop. Paul F. Raywood   609–397–2177

PANDORA'S BOX, 22 Bridge St.

Hours: Tues. thru Sat. 11–4

Antiques entirely. American country furniture; glass, china, tin, wood, iron. Gaudy ironstone, pottery, crocks, redware. Appraisals. Interior design. Dried arrangements to order.

A—PM. Selective. Consignments. Authentication.

Prop. Dorothy Kirk   609–397–1126

VARTANIAN'S ANTIQUES, 8 Bridge St.

Hours: 7 days 10:30–5:30

Nineteenth-century English and American furniture. Crystal and art glass; clocks, oil paintings. Antique, semiantique, and new Oriental rugs. Oriental rug repair and cleaning by arrangement. A century-old private residence close to the Delaware River.

A/C—PM. Wide range. Consignments. Authentication.

Prop. Andrew and Pat Vartanian   609–397–1667

Lebanon 08833

THE DOLLHOUSE FACTORY, 157 Main St. Mailing address: Box 456. *Also see* Repair and Restoration listing.

Hours: Wed. thru Sat. 11–6; Sun. 11–3

> *"Do not be dismayed by our DUST. . . . If you look closely, you will see it is 1" to 1' scale!!!"*

Old and new comfortably blended. Emphasis on custom-made dollhouses and contemporary furnishings; small but nice selection of early Victorian and

THE DOLLHOUSE FACTORY *continued*

collectible dollhouses, some period miniatures. Consultation on dollhouse construction. Repair and restoration service.

Mr. Dankanics writes the "Ask Mr. Dollhouse" and "A Gallery of Old Friends" columns for Doll Castle News, *published bimonthly by Castle Press Publications, Inc., Washington, N. J. Dolls from this shop have appeared on the "Kojak" television series and in commercial advertising. The proprietors welcome a "well-supervised child"; handcuffs available for the "bad guys." Member The Antique Trail.*

A/C; also new—PM. Wide range. Consignments. Authentication.

Prop. Robert Dankanics   201–236–6404

JACK LEWIS LTD., R. D. 1, Rt. 31. *Also see* Repair and Restoration listing.

Hours: Mon. thru Sat. 8–7

Antique restoration and custom cabinetmaking by a craftsman. Hand-stripping, furniture repair, and fine veneer work. Mr. Lewis trained in Great Britain, works with apprentices. Limited amount of antique furniture for sale.

A/C—PM. Selective. Authentication.

Prop. Jack Lewis   201–735–7444

ONE SUTTON PLACE, Main St. and Sutton Pl. *Also see* Repair and Restoration listing.

Hours: Mon., Tues., Fri. thru Sun. 11–5. Closed Wed. & Thurs.

Specializing in early telephones, c. 1880–1925. Golden oak; some early furniture, china and glass, Hummel figures. Telephone restoration. Member The Antique Trail.

A/C—PM. Affordable/Wide range. Authentication.

Prop. Margaret Mary Wilson   201–236–6200

POOR MAN'S ANTIQUES, 81 Main St.

Hours: By chance or appt.

Antiques, curios, collectibles, and primitives on the porch of an 1820s merchant's residence. General line; copper, brass, glass, furniture, blanket chests, fireplace equipment, lamps, baskets. Member The Antique Trail.

A/C—PM. Affordable. Consignments.

Prop. Pat and Chuck Hampton   201–236–6754

WHAT-DA-YA-WANT?, 152 Main St. (downstairs at The Old Mill).
Also see Repair and Restoration listing.

Hours: Mon. thru Sat. 10–5; Sun. 12–5

Older and more recent decoys (original and repainted), most from New Jersey.
Old tools, pine and oak; prints, maps. Furniture stripping and refinishing. New
deerskin products.

C; also new—PM. Affordable.

Prop. Dale Dalrymple   201–236–2849

YE OLDE LAMP SHOP, 55 Main St. *Also see* Repair and Restoration listing.

Hours: Mon. thru Sat. 10–12, 3–5. Closed Sun.

Specializing in lamps; brass, copper. "Lamps out of anything"—electrified,
repaired, restored; mountings. Parking on street; entrance at rear door. Member
The Antique Trail.

A/C—PM. Wide range.

Prop. Carl H. Dilts   201–236–2345

Mountainville 08833

THE KITCHEN CABOODLE. Mailing address: R. D. 2, Lebanon 08833.

Hours: Tues. thru Sat. 10:30–4:30; Sun. 1–5. Closed Mon.

The kitchen-related antiques not only contribute to the wonderful atmosphere
of this country shop, they're all for sale. Gourmet cookware, frozen delicacies,
and fresh herbs are the specialités du maison. *Catering and cooking classes*
in the large studio kitchen. Box lunches to enjoy surrounded by the antiques and
greenery, or to take along. The bread, of course, is homemade. Member
The Antique Trail.

A/C; also new—PM. Wide range. Consignments. Authentication when possible.

Prop. Elizabeth Cameron, Elizabeth Wroth   201–832–7218 (bus.)
                                                          832–7445 (res.)

POTTER'S OLD MOUNTAINVILLE HOTEL ANTIQUES, Main St. (5 mi.
north of Rt. 22, Lebanon; 5 mi. northwest of Oldwick).

Hours: Daily 10:30–4:30. Closed Mon.

Furniture, refinished and in-the-rough. Quilts, china, bottles; general line.
New calico, patchwork pillows; crafts. The large white frame building is a local
landmark. Built in 1825, it was known as the Mountainville Tavern House.

POTTER'S OLD MOUNTAINVILLE HOTEL ANTIQUES *continued*
Rechristened the Mountainville Hotel, it was highly regarded in another era
for its applejack whiskey. Mrs. Potter is the fifth generation here.
A/C; also new—Most prices marked. Affordable/Selective (furniture).
Consignments. Authentication of known pieces.
Prop. Meta Potter   201–832–7240

THE SHED BOUTIQUE AT MAIL POUCH FARM, Main St. Mailing
address: R. D. 2, Lebanon 08833.
Hours: Tues. thru Sat. 10–5; Sun. 1–5. Closed Mon.
Antiques, collectibles, and country crafts; "the things I like." Farm primitives,
country store items, a good supply of old kitchen gadgets. Old and new quilts,
including a splendid heirloom patchwork and a number of old quilts from Ohio.
Tools, benches, crocks and jugs of all sizes; wood, iron, china, and glass.
A large old red barn with stone foundation, built in 1857, warmly heated
in winter. Member The Antique Trail.
A/C—PM. Affordable.
Prop. Eleene C. McCann   201–832–7194

Mt. Airy 08530

THE BACK PORCH, Rt. 179, southbound (halfway between Ringoes and
Lambertville). Mailing address: R. D. 2, Box 110A, Lambertville 08530.
Hours: Mon., Wed. 10–5; Sat. & Sun. 9–5
Collectibles; pine furniture. Reproductions marked. Also at Tomato Factory,
Hopewell (Mercer County).
C—PM. Affordable. Authentication.
Prop. Virginia Van Doren   609–397–3684

Oldwick 08858

ANTIQUES ETCETERA, Main St.
Hours: Wed., Thurs., Sat. 10–3; Sun. 12:30–3:30. And by chance.
Early American primitives, some furniture, and accessories. Well-selected
country store items, Shaker pieces, baskets, and old toys. Some new calico
handcrafts and hand-dipped candles. A pleasant, inviting shop.
A/C; also new—PM. Affordable/Wide range.
Prop. Winette Dawdy   No phone

CREEK HOUSE, Rockaway Rd. (bet. Oldwick and Mountainville). Mailing address: Box 76.

Hours: Sun. 1–5; and by appt.

Primitives and accessories, antique toys, prints, signs, trunks, redware. Beautifully displayed in a low stone 18th-century blacksmith's shop on a country road opposite Rockaway Creek. Decorating consultation with Ms. Madigan; fabric selection. Member The Antique Trail.

A/C—PM. Affordable/Wide range.

Prop. Carol Madigan, Nancy Gilbert   201–236–2420

THE MAGIC SHOP, Main St. (Old Tpk. Rd., next to Zion Lutheran Church).
Hours: Mon. thru Sat. 10–1, 2–5. Closed for lunch 1–2 P.M.

Profits benefit the Bonnie Brae Farm for Boys in nearby Millington. A small, knowledgeable collection of American and English antiques displayed in two of the old low-ceilinged rooms; including country and period furniture, decorative pieces, fireplace accessories, and mirrors.

Long known for well-selected new toys, dollhouses, and engaging room-size boutiques devoted to children's and women's clothing and gifts. Holiday events are scheduled to delight youngsters: an old-fashioned slide down the "Rabbit Hole" at Easter, a visit with Santa at Christmas, horse rides in other seasons. Reservations required.

Partially destroyed by fire and rebuilt not long ago, the venerable 1700s house is actually two that have been joined.

A—PM. Selective. Consignments. Authentication when possible.

Staff: Mrs. John Watts, Mrs. Reeve Schley, Jr., Mrs. Robert Pulleyn
                                                                     201–439–2330

MELODY COTTAGE ANTIQUES, Rts. 517 and 523, at the crossroad.
Hours: Tues. thru Sat. 10–5; Sun. 1–5

Art glass; furniture from the 1830s to 1900s (prior to 1900 preferred); quilts. Chair caning.

A/C—PM. Affordable.

Prop. Edith and L. D. Cregar   201–439–2519 (eves.)

SAN ANTONIO ANTIQUES, Main St. (corner James St.).
Hours: 7 days 9–6

General line of furniture; refinished trunks, kitchen cupboards, armoires. A charming Victorian home in the center of Oldwick.

A—PM. Selective. Consignments. Authentication.

Prop. Mary San Antonio   201–439–2952

TEWKSBURY ANTIQUES, at the crossroads.

Hours: Tues. thru Sun. 10–5

Eighteenth- and 19th-century furniture, primitives, and accessories. Painted American country furniture, folk art, old quilts, signed homespun, baskets; good antique and "semiantique" Oriental rugs. Early andirons. All pieces identified and dated. Appraisals.

A—PM. Selective to serious collectors. Occasional consignments. Authentication.

Prop. Audrey and Doug Wiss   201–439–2221

TOM & ETHEL WARD ANTIQUES, opp. Tewksbury Inn.

Hours: Mon., Wed., Thurs., Sat. 10–5

Country antiques, primitive furniture, collectibles, "nostalgic items of general interest"; wood, iron, tin, copper, brass. Weathervanes, butter molds, fireplace equipment, old wooden farm implements, crocks. Member The Antique Trail.

A/C—PM. Affordable.

Prop. Tom and Ethel Ward   201–234–0176

WEATHERCOCK FARM, Rt. 523 (close to I78).

Hours: Shops open Mon. thru Sat. 10:30–4:30. Closed Sun. Restaurant hours: luncheon, Tues. thru Fri. 11–4; luncheon and dinner, Sat. & Sun. 11–9

Time here is leisurely. Luncheon and dinner are served in the 250-year-old manor house, a stately Colonial with bright yellow awnings whose approach is distinguished by an avenue of cedar trees. A number of interesting, browsable antique and gift shops are in the large two-story barn and adjoining outbuilding. Member The Antique Trail.

A/C; also new—PM. Wide range. Consignments. Authentication when possible.

Prop. Eleanora Genito   201–439–3006

Pittstown 08867

ANDJAC ANTIQUES, R. D. 1, Box 42. *Also see* Repair and Restoration listing.

Hours: By appt.

Oak and primitives. Oak chairs, round oak tables; decorated stoneware, oil lamps, washstands, china closets, rockers. Natural chair caning, splint weaving. Custom refinishing, also taught at adult school courses.

A/C—PM. Wide range. Authentication.

Prop. Andy and Jackie Burachynski   201–735–7569

ROBERT & KENNETH APGAR ANTIQUES, Main St. (2 doors from Post Office). Mailing address: Box 4.

Hours: By appt.

Specializing in 18th- and 19th-century furniture, country things, and collectors items, finished and in-the-rough. Cupboards, tables, Windsor chairs, dark blue historical china, Rockingham, redware, woodenware, iron, tin, early lighting, and baskets. Attractive early 19th-century pierced tin footwarmers. In an old stone house. Est. 1950. Member Antiques Dealers Assoc. of Central N. J.

A—PM. Selective to serious collectors.

Prop. Robert and Kenneth Apgar   201–735–8659

Quakertown 08868

THE OLD VILLAGE STORE, Main St. (Rt. 579). Also at Tomato Factory, Hopewell (Mercer County).

Hours: Sat. & Sun. 12–5 (call ahead); and by appt.

General line of primitives and country pieces, including country store items and advertising. Brass, copper, tin, molds, some furniture. Antiques purchased. Member Antiques Dealers Assoc. of Central N. J., Pa. Antique Dealers Assoc., Tin Container Collectors Assoc.

A/C—PM. Affordable. All pieces guaranteed.

Prop. George Miller   201–735–8043

Ringoes 08551

POPKORN, Rt. 202, southbound (immed. south of Country Club Rd. light). Mailing address: R. D. 1, Box 218.

Hours: Sat. & Sun. 11–6; and by appt.

Young, enthusiastic shop with newer specialties. Hall and Fiesta china, Depression glass in quantity, "household" Art Deco, railroad memorabilia— hand and switch lanterns, books, keys, locks. Old cameras and photographs, beer and whiskey advertising, tin and agate ware, country store items, some post cards. Free Depression glass identification; identification also of Cambridge, Heisey, Fostoria.

C—PM. Affordable. Authentication.

Prop. Bob Perzel   201–782–9631

TOBERMORY ANTIQUES. Mailing address: R. D. 1. *Also see* Repair and
Restoration listing.

Hours: By appt.

*Primitives, quilts, country furniture, miniature lead soldiers. Interesting selection
of quimper. Antiques shows managed. The proprietor also does tole restoration.*

A—PM. Selective. Authentication.

Prop. Joan Darling   201–782–5610

Rosemont 08556

RALEIGH ANTIQUES. Mailing address: P. O. Box 48.

Hours: By appt.

*Formal furniture, porcelains; selected fine antiques. Member Antiques Dealers
Assoc. of Central N. J., North Jersey Antique Dealers Assoc.*

A—PM. Selective. Authentication.

Prop. Lee Kolarsey   609–397–2700

Sergeantsville 08557

LEE DAVIS ANTIQUES, Rt. 523 (at the blinker).

Hours: 7 days 10–5

*Fine 17th- to 19th-century lacquer and Chinoiserie furniture; Oriental porcelain
and furniture. Prices as quoted. Appraisals of earlier porcelain, lacquer
furniture; works of the early Japanese potters a specialty.*

A—PM. Selective to serious collectors. Authentication.

Prop. Lee Davis   609–397–3102
                                                  215–297–5602 (if no ans.)

GINNY HOOK, Rosemont-Ringoes Rd. (next to Post Office). Mailing address:
Box 93.

Hours: Wed. thru Sat. 10–5; Sun. 12–5. Call ahead suggested.

*American primitives and the antiques of childhood in an attractive country shop.
Including furniture, butter churns, tinware, cradles, youth chairs, rocking
horses. Caning and furniture refinishing by arrangement. The proprietor's
paintings of wildlife on old wood are exhibited.*

C—PM. Affordable; furniture higher. Consignments. Authentication when
possible.

Prop. Ginny Hook   609–397–0553

JINGLESTONE ANTIQUES, Sergeantsville-Ringoes Rd. (at the blinker).
Hours: Wed. thru Sat. 10–5; Sun. 1–5

Quality 18th- to early 19th-century American country and period furniture and accessories. Early to mid-19th-century paintings (primarily American), "unusual, one-of-a-kind" porcelains; sponge and spatterware, some lithographs. Full descriptive notations. Estate appraisals. Member Nat'l. Trust for Historic Preservation.

A/C (paintings)—PM. Wide range. Consignments. Authentication.

Prop. H. Robert Griffiths   609–397–0077

Stanton Station 08822

FURSTOVER ANTIQUES, Rt. 31 and Stanton Sta. Rd. Mailing address: R. D. 5, Box 79.

Hours: Fri., Sat., Sun., Mon. 1–5; other times call ahead

"Old and not so old" affordable collectibles and antiques in a country barn dating to 1830. General line of furniture—tables, chairs, cabinets, chests; lighting, including 1940s floor lamps. Some paintings, mirrors, fireplace equipment, old iron, and shutters. Small replacement inventory of chimneys and globes, old strap hinges, glass pulls (including an occasional piece of Sandwich).

C/A—PM. Affordable.

Prop. Robert Clark   201–782–3513

THE SIGN OF THE MERMAID, Lilac Dr. (rt. turn just before RR tracks; house immed. past Mobil Sta.). Mailing address: R. D. 5, Box 86A, Flemington 08822.

Hours: By chance or appt.

Well-researched and labeled glass and china. Mostly 19th-century English ceramics, Staffordshire, porcelain; Steuben, art glass, flint pattern glass, early blown glass. Small selection of reasonably priced children's gifts (everything under $5) in the "Little Mermaid's Corner," presided over by the proprietor's daughter, Carolinn. Shop is downstairs; the building housed the Stanton Grange, 1905 to 1948. Member The Antique Trail.

A/C—PM. Affordable/Wide range. Authentication.

Prop. Pat Pocher   201–782–7725

Stockton 08559

CARRIAGE HOUSE ANTIQUES, Main St.

Hours: Mon. thru Fri. 9–5:30; Sat. & Sun. 10:30–6. Call ahead suggested.

Primitives and country furniture; ironware, tools, pottery. Furniture restoration and refinishing. Also to the trade.

A—PM. Affordable/Serious collectors. Consignments.

Prop. Robert J. Lutz   609–397–3398

HAWTHORN & GRAY, the depot.

Hours: Wed. thru Sun. 10–6

Interior design studio with much that's new and attractive. Unusual older decorative pieces emphasized; small furniture, selected wicker, silver, and crystal. A sophisticated shop in the old train depot in the center of Stockton. Member A.S.I.D.

A/C; also new—PM; well labeled. Selective. Consignments. Authentication; documentation when possible.

Prop. James W. Gray   609–397–2359

PALINURUS, R. D. 1, Box 257.

Hours: By appt.

Antiquarian books, generally dating between 1750 and 1940; some 16th-century works. Specializing in literature, art reference, science, philosophy. Appraisals. Catalog on request. Individual volumes, libraries, and collections purchased.

A/C—PM. Selective. (Selective) consignments.

Prop. John Hellebrand   609–397–1831

SIGN OF THE BLACK DUCK, Rt. 29. Mailing address: Box 13.

Hours: Wed. thru Sun. 10–5; or by appt.

Antique miniatures and dolls, early glass and china; furniture. Doll repair. Member Antiques Dealers Assoc. of Central N. J. In a stone house dating to 1730.

A/C—PM. Affordable/Selective. Authentication.

Prop. Jeanne Karsan   609–397–2440

Whitehouse 08888

HUNTERDON ANTIQUES 'N THINGS, Rt. 22, westbound.

Hours: 7 days 10–5; call ahead suggested

General line; primitive and period furniture, art glass, cut and pattern glass, lamps, lighting, china, porcelain, brass, copper. Mint condition; individually selected. Nicely arranged for browsing. Member The Antique Trail.

A/C—PM. Wide range. Authentication when possible.

Prop. Edith Schiffman   201–534–4819

WHITEHOUSE MANOR ANTIQUE CENTER, Rt. 22, westbound (opp. A & P Supermarket; just before Whitehouse turnoff).

Hours: Mon. thru Sat. 10–5; Sun. 12–5

Once part of a 400-acre farm and later a tavern, Whitehouse Manor has recently been refurbished and transformed into an attractive antiques center. Built in 1820, the structure retains much of its original exterior grace. The upstairs rooms, less touched by time and modernization, are especially serene and pretty. There are several shops offering a wide general line, interesting specialties. Ample parking.

Mgr. Carol Vlearbone   201–534–9904

APPLEWOOD ANTIQUES, Jacqueline Liebermann.

Early American pattern glass a specialty; jewelry, primarily early 19th-century furniture. Appraisals of pattern glass. Member The Antique Trail.

A/C—PM. Affordable. Authentication on request.

BEAR NECESSITIES, Pauline Skibra, Joseph Truitt.

European and American porcelain, American glass, crystal (1830 to contemporary); trains, railroad memorabilia, toys, military and Civil War items, paper documents. European porcelains, trains accepted on consignment.

C/A—PM. Affordable/Wide range. Consignments. Authentication.

INDIAN ARTIFACTS, Charles and Pat Kaufmann.

Old silver Indian jewelry, signed, one-of-a-kind. Antiques, primitives; much that's new.

A/C; also new—PM. Wide range. Authentication.

WHITEHOUSE MANOR ANTIQUE CENTER *continued*

MYRTLE KOFORD.

Glass, china, and decorative objects. Old inkwells, Orientals, bisque; old chairs. Also in Middlesex (Middlesex County).

C—PM. Wide range. Consignments.

'MOST EVERYTHING SHOPPE, Emily and Gladys.

Emphasis on furniture, decorative pieces, and quilts. Washstands, Lincoln rockers, overstuffed rockers, small furniture, especially chairs. Old pictures and prints; some china and glass, including cut glass. New quilts and quilted pillows. Upholstering by arrangement.

C/A; also new—PM. Affordable. Authentication.

THE QUAINT SHOP, Mary Atman.

Antique clothing, Civil War items, books (primarily devoted to the Civil War); collectibles. Authentic uniforms and uniform buttons; no reproductions.

A/C—PM. Wide range/Serious collectors (uniforms). Authentication.

RED ROOSTER ANTIQUES, Carol Vlearbone.

Primitives; iron, tin (including advertising tins), woodenware; fireplace equipment.

A/C—PM. Wide range. Authentication.

THE TIMEPIECE SHOP, Thomas J. Stratford.

Antique clocks a specialty; furniture, hanging and table lamps, fine china, brass, old iron, pewter. Clocks purchased. Member Nat'l. Assoc. of Watch & Clock Collectors. Also in Bound Brook (Somerset County).

A/C—PM. Wide range. Authentication.

TIMPSON'S ANTIQUES, Wayne and Sue Timpson. *Also see* Repair and Restoration listing.

Victorian and earlier furniture, refinished. Nice selection, cherry and pine preferred. Furniture repair and restoration; caning, rushing.

A/C—PM. Selective. Authentication when possible.

An 1840 Pennsylvania pieced quilt with Rose of Sharon appliqué; measuring approximately 86 in. × 98 in. Red, pink, orange, and green Rose of Sharon buds and running vine border. *Courtesy The Pink House, New Hope. Photo: George Bailey*

Somerset County

Basking Ridge 07920

THE ACORN SHOP, 31 S. Finley Ave. *Also see* Repair and Restoration listing.
Hours: Wed. thru Sat. 10–5; Tues. by appt.
Bustling shop specializing in old and new lamps, lamp chimneys, parts, repairs and conversions. Also antique and new china, decorative accessories, and gifts.
A/C—PM. Affordable. Authentication when possible.
Prop. Elizabeth Richards   201–766–5776

CHARLES HOCKENBURY, JR., ANTIQUES, 376 Mt. Airy Rd. (bet. Liberty Corner and Bernardsville, 3/10 mi. toward Liberty Corner from the Mt. Airy Rd. exit of Rt. 287).
Hours: Sat. & Sun. 12:30–5; appt. advisable weekdays
"Antiques to live with" crowded into a pre-Revolutionary farmhouse and outbuilding. Pine, cherry, and maple country furniture, accessories and beds, refinished and in-the-rough. Antique beds adapted to modern needs. General line of jugs, crocks, bottles, tinware, glass, and lamps. Antiques bought and sold; nothing later than 1860 or '70, and "no oak!"
A—PM. Wide range. Authentication
Prop. Charles Hockenbury, Jr.   201–766–2956

LANTERN HOUSE ANTIQUES, 135 S. Finley Ave.

Hours: Wed., Thurs., Sat. 10–5; or by appt.

A fine collection of American period furniture, decorative accessories, collector's items, Oriental pieces, clocks and lamps graciously displayed in a 200-year-old home. Mrs. Boehlert will appraise furniture for insurance purposes.

A/C—PM. Selective. Authentication when possible.

Prop. Marion Boehlert   201–766–2084

STAGECOACH ANTIQUES, P. O. Box 23.

Hours: By appt.

General line of period furniture, Oriental export porcelain, Oriental rugs, bronzes, early silver. Appraisal service; house sales and liquidations.

A—PM. Selective. Authentication when possible.

Prop. Ann and Dick Clinedinst   201–766–3786

WHITE'S, Basking Ridge.

Hours: By appt.

Fine American and English furniture; silver, china, glass.

A/C—PM. Affordable. Authentication.

Prop. Doreen White   201–647–6266

Bedminster 07921

THE BIG DIPPER, Rt. 206 (next to Cumberland Farms, just before Lamington Crossroads light). *Also see* Repair and Restoration listing.

Hours: Tues. thru Fri. 9:30–7; Sat. & Sun. 9–5. Closed Mon.

Antique and collectible furniture, refinished and in-the-rough. Specializing in furniture stripping and refinishing, including wicker. Caning and repairs. Mr. McCleary also builds and sells grandfather clocks.

A/C—PM. Affordable. Occasional consignment. Authentication when possible.

Prop. Greg McCleary   201–234–2511

FIRESIDE ANTIQUES, Lamington Rd.

Hours: Mon. thru Fri. 9–5; weekends, appt. suggested

American pewter, early iron cooking utensils, 18th-century lighting devices and

FIRESIDE ANTIQUES *continued*

fireplace equipment. Known for early American furniture and accessories. Appraisal service.

A—Prices 75 percent marked. Serious collectors. Authentication.

Prop. Lisa and Joseph Millard   201–234–1472

Belle Mead 08502

BELL POST ANTIQUES, R. D. 2, Dutchtown Rd. (next to Harlingen Church). *Also see* Repair and Restoration listing.

Hours: 7 days 10–6

Selected general line; tinware, quilts, primitives, oil lamps, toys; some Victorian furniture, pressed-back oak chairs, rugs. Also to dealers. Extensive repair and restoration service: furniture refinishing, lamp conversions, chandeliers rewired, brass polished; casting, trivets mended; lamp parts. Pleasant shop in a former carriage house. The gold-painted residence once served the community as #2 school.

A/C—PM. Wide range. Authentication when possible.

Prop. Vern Spence   201–359–6730

THE CARRIAGE HOUSE, R. D. 2, Bridgeport Rd. (off Rt. 206, northbound).

Hours: 7 days 8–5

Charming shop to the rear of the main house specializes in country furniture, clocks, porcelains, copper, brass; general line of lamps, china, crystal. Also a large red hay barn filled with furniture, refinished or in-the-rough.

A/C—PM. Wide range. Authentication when possible.

Prop. Edith S. Drake   201–359–5959

MURRAY FARM, Dutchtown Rd.

Hours: By appt.

Glass, china, advertising tins, beer collectibles. An interest in books on the American Indian and Western lore.

C—PM. Affordable. Consignments. Authentication.

Prop. Barbara and Steve Tucker   201–359–6595

RED BARN ANTIQUES, Rt. 202 (on right-hand side going south).

Hours: Tues. thru Sun. 10:30–5:30

An old red carriage house, c. 1771, filled with antiques. Shop is poorly marked on busy road. Avoid parking to rear of barn in wet weather.

A/C—PM. Affordable. Authentication when possible.

Prop. Theresa Stoveken   201–359–6418

Bernardsville 07924

ANTIQUE CORNER, 41 Olcott Sq. (corner Mt. Airy Rd. and Rt. 202).

Hours: Wed. thru Sat. 10–4

Furniture, mirrors, lamps, and a general line of antiques and collectibles. The owners also stock lamp parts and will arrange for factory polishing of copper and brass. Appraisals given.

A/C—PM. Wide range.

Prop. Claryse Doerr, Dolores Sheppard   201–766–3915
                                                                    757–1869

THE CONNOISSEUR, 20 Claremont Rd. *Also see* Repair and Restoration listing.

Hours: Tues. thru Sat. 9:30–5:30

Antique art, old and new prints, and Oriental rugs. Specializing in scientific restoration and conservation of paintings and custom framing. American paintings bought and sold.

A/C—Prices coded and cataloged. Serious collectors. Consignments. Authentication.

Prop. Phillip Fico   201–755–1139

GEORGE AND MARTHA, 127 Claremont Rd.

Hours: Tues. thru Sat. 10–4

General line of antiques and collectibles in a genial shop. Advice on interior design. Mrs. Palty buys entire estates.

A/C—PM. Wide range. Consignments. Authentication.

Prop. Martha Palty   201–766–6124

NOTHING NEW, 25 Morristown Rd. (Rt. 202 north).

Hours: Mon. thru Sat. 10–4

Some antiques; mostly collectibles and decorative accessories. House sales conducted.

C/A—PM. Wide range.

Prop. Susan Scharfenberg, Ellie Howland, Sally Kemper   201–766–9707

SOMERSET ANTIQUES, 29 Olcott Sq. (Rt. 202 south).

Hours: Tues. thru Sat. 10–4

Small, bright shop for old and new quilts, some small furniture, and a general line of merchandise. Will buy antique and collectible furniture, silver, china, quilts, jewelry, and glass. Appraisals.

A/C—PM. Wide range.

Prop. Betty M. Saddington   201–766–2027

Bound Brook 08805

THE TIMEPIECE SHOP, 132 W. Franklin St. Also at Whitehouse Manor Antiques Center, Whitehouse (Hunterdon County).

Hours: By appt.

Specializing in old clocks and imported brass. Member Nat'l. Assoc. of Watch & Clock Collectors and the Pennsylvania Antique Dealers Assoc.

A—PM. Selective.

Prop. Thomas J. Stratford   201–356–6920

Branchburg 08876

BRANCHBURG ANTIQUE CENTER, Rt. 202, northbound (a few minutes west of Somerville), painted dark barn red. Mailing address: Box 156, Neshanic Station 08853.

Hours: Daily 11–5. Closed Wed.

An unprepossessing 1900s auto barn has been transformed by Mrs. Rosenthal and her associates into the Branchburg Antique Center, a mall-in-miniature of ten interesting and browsable antique shops open six days a week and run as a

BRANCHBURG ANTIQUE CENTER *continued*

cooperative. Wide range of antiques and collectibles: country and formal furniture, glass, fine china, pewter, silver, prints and paintings, old books, primitives.

A/C—PM. Wide range.

Prop. Janet Rosenthal   201–369–6811

East Millstone 08873

THE SPOT, Amwell Rd. (Rt. 518, on the Delaware and Raritan Canal).

Hours: Wed., Thurs., Fri. 11–4; Sat. & Sun. 10–6

General Burgoyne never got to see the totem in the yard, and the kitchen utensils were in cupboards, not on the rafters, but the old Franklin Inn probably hasn't changed much since the Revolution, or since 1734 when it began as a stagecoach stop. A general line of just about everything fills several rooms upstairs and down, including furniture, electric, oil and kerosene lamps, pictures, prints, frames and books. Large collection of glass, metalwork, jewelry, wearable items. Younger collectors can browse through the post cards, dolls, records—and baseball cards. Mr. and Mrs. Rusher buy complete contents of homes and do appraisals.

A/C—PM. Affordable/Wide range. Authentication.

Prop. Mr. & Mrs. Wallace L. Rusher   201–844–7074
                                                                          359–5040

The nearby East Millstone Canal House, built in 1834, is being restored and refurbished as a museum through the efforts of the Rushers and others who have formed the East Millstone Canal House Assoc. The historic structure will contain period furnishings and will be open to visitors weekends during the shop hours of 10–6, weekdays on request.

Far Hills 07931

BROWNSTONE BARN ANTIQUES, R. D. 1, Box 129

Hours: By appt.

Seventeenth- and 18th-century furniture, including oak, walnut, mahogany, fill two large barns. Select collection of early English oak. Interior design service.

A—PM. Selective. Authentication.

Prop. Mrs. Bertalon de Nèmethy   201–234–2340

COLLINS CORNER, Dumont Rd. (opp. bank). *Also see* Auctioneers listing.
Hours: Wed. thru Sun. 9:30–6

A friendly invitation to "come in and look around" at this large, open shop specializing in antique and collectible glass, porcelain, Staffordshire, silver, brass, and copper. Also a general line of predominantly formal furniture and "modern," dating to the early 1900s. Mr. Collins is also an auctioneer.

A/C—PM. Wide range. Authentication when possible.

Prop. Betty and Bill Collins   201–234–0995 (bus.)
                                                            234–2269 (res.)

Green Brook 08812

SCARINCI BROTHERS, Rt. 22, eastbound at Washington Ave. *Also see* Repair and Restoration listing.

Hours: Mon. thru Sat. 9–5

Furniture and family deacquisitions predominate. Oak, primitives, and chairs vie for space with heavy carved Oriental tables and chests imported directly from the factory on Taiwan. The brass beds, always on hand, are machine buffed with jeweler's rouge and simonized. "Seven generations of craftsmanship" are applied to the furniture stripping and refinishing, chair caning and rushing, and general refurbishing services. Antiques bought and sold.

A/C—PM. Selective. Consignments. Authentication.

Prop. Albert Scarinci   201–968–7270

Kingston 08528

AGNES SHEEHAN, 64 Main St. (Rt. 27 south).

Hours: 7 days 10:30–5

Sophisticated setting for antique and collectible dolls, toys, miniatures, china, glass, small furniture, tables, and chairs. Some Americana.

A/C—PM. Wide range. Authentication when possible.

Prop. Agnes Sheehan   201–924–1286

Martinsville 08836

GRANDMOTHER'S TRUNK, 1236 Washington Valley Rd. (in the center of town).

Hours: Wed. thru Sat. 11–4

Country antiques and collectibles—small pieces of furniture, wall cabinets, chairs, kerosene lamps, kitchen utensils, and primitives. Interiors planned. Deposit and hold service.

A/C—PM. Affordable. Authentication when possible.

Prop. Diane Zepp, Effie Amon   201–469–0430

THE MOUNTAIN HOUSE, Martinsville. *Also see* Repair and Restoration listing.

Hours: By appt.

Decorator's and collector's selection of Oriental porcelains, art glass, 18th-, 19th-, and early 20th-century wall and shelf clocks, limited edition Kauba bronzes (reproduction). "Things for people who really appreciate what they are." Owners welcome designers, maintain a search service, and provide expert clock restoration. Member Nat'l. Assoc. of Watch & Clock Collectors, American Watchmakers Institute, listed under clock restoration in Interior Design *magazine. All clocks are delivered, set up, and guaranteed. A mail-order brochure and schedule of special open house events are available. The owners prefer known customers.*

A/C—Some prices coded. Selective. Authentication when possible.

Prop. Carl and Jane Tonero   201–469–2195

PEG OZZARD'S CONVERSATION PIECE, Washington Valley Rd. (corner of Chimney Rock Rd.).

Hours: Wed. thru Sat. 10–5; or by appt.

Though primarily a gift, card, and craft shop, a section of this remodeled colonial farmhouse is devoted to antique and collectible glass, china, some furniture. Miss Ozzard is a member of the Antique Appraisal Assoc. of America.

A/C—PM. Affordable/Wide range. Occasional consignment. Authentication when possible.

Prop. Peg Ozzard   201–356–4456

Middlebush 08873

TUCKER'S TREASURE TROVE, Colonial Village, Amwell Rd. (next to Villagers Barn Theatre).

Hours: Tues. thru Sun. 11–4; or by appt.

Selective early collectibles, 1890 to 1920, small furniture—tables, chairs, bookcases, plant tables; china, glassware. Some Art Nouveau and Art Deco collector's items, including lamps. Appraisals; house sales conducted. The 1940s general store, built in colonial style with four bow windows and wide-plank floor from an old barn in Cranbury, is part of the much older Voorhees farm and historic property which dates from 1760.

C—PM. Affordable/Wide range.

Prop. Marge and Joan Tucker   201–873–3804

This is also the attractive rural setting of the Villagers Barn Theatre, O'Connor's Colonial Farms Restaurant (a branch of the Watchung establishment), a bakery, gift and plant shop. The Artists' and Craftsmen's Guild workshop and gallery displays stained glass, weaving, macramé, wood sculpture, pottery, oils, water colors, and photography. Theater hours: Seasonal productions spring and summer. Restaurant hours: Luncheon, Mon. thru Sat., 11:30–2:30. Dinner, Mon. thru Sat., 5–10:30; Sun. 1–9:30.

Millstone 08849

The historic North River Street area of Millstone, alongside the Millstone River, has been revived by a complex of friendly, browsable shops. The old blacksmith's forge, used from 1693 to 1959, has been designated a state landmark and is open weekends from 1 to 4 p.m. as a museum.

GRANDPA'S ATTIC, N. River St.

Hours: Fri. thru Sun. 10–5

Wide assortment of affordable antiques, collectibles, and selected old things, plus spillover from River House next door, which Mrs. Clarkson runs.

A/C—PM. Affordable.

Prop. George Clarkson   201–359–4451 (River House)

LAUVINS ANTIQUES, Main St. (northbound, past N. River St.).
Hours: Tues. thru Sat. 10–5
Iron and glass antiques and collectibles, some furniture, gathered downstairs in an early country home. Everything tagged.
A/C—PM. Affordable. Authentication when possible.
Prop. Laurene and Vincent Faso   201–359–5039

RIVER HOUSE, 33 N. River St.
Hours: Fri. thru Sun. 10–5; or by appt.
Nice 18th-century to early 1920s furniture, engravings, etchings, prints, and Americana graciously displayed in a remodeled wheelwright's shop, c. 1710. Mrs. Clarkson specializes in antiques (Mr. Clarkson runs Grandpa's Attic next door) and does appraisals.
A—PM. Selective. Authentication if history is known.
Prop. Anne and George Clarkson   201–359–4451

Mt. Bethel 07060

KING GEORGE ANTIQUES, MARIE'S ANTIQUES: See listings under WARREN.

Neshanic 08853

SPINNING WHEEL ANTIQUES, Neshanic.
Hours: By appt.
Furniture, primarily oak; tinware.
C—PM. Affordable. Authentication when possible.
Prop. Roger and Virginia Stranzenbach   201–369–4946

Neshanic Station 08853

WILLOWBROOK, Box 334, R. D. 2.
Hours: By appt.
Pre-1850 pewter, primitive furniture, tole; general line, in a 1745 farmhouse. Pewter searched. Member Antiques Dealers Assoc. of Central N. J.
A—PM. Selective. Authentication when possible.
Prop. Joan Brown   201–782–4583

North Branch 08876

LITTLE HOUSE ANTIQUES, Rt. 22, eastbound. Mailing address: 3355 Rt. 22, Somerville 08876. *Also see* Repair and Restoration listing.

Hours: Sat. thru Wed. 12–5

Small, cheery shop specializing in brass beds, country furniture, and oak. Selection of primitives, china and glass, lighting fixtures and lanterns. Antiques and collectibles. Owners provide brass and copper burnishing service. Member The Antique Trail.

A/C—PM. Affordable. Authentication.

Prop. Charles and Kay Halsted   201–526–0243

RIVER EDGE FARM, Rt. 28 (Rt. 22 west to Rt. 28 exit; 1/4 mi. west, yellow house on right). Mailing address: Rt. 28, R. D. 3, Somerville 08876.

Hours: Generally open weekends; or by chance or appt.

Dealers and browsers welcome at this long-established shop specializing in country furniture, primitives, and baskets. Also, well-chosen line of pewter, iron fireplace and cooking utensils, early wood, painted furniture, and early lighting. Members The Antique Trail.

A/Some collectibles—PM. Affordable/Wide range. Authentication.

Prop. Mary and Stan Lawrence   201–722–3554

SMOKE HOUSE ANTIQUES, Rt. 28 (next to market in North Branch Village). Mailing address: R. D. 3, Box 37F, Somerville 08876.

Hours: Afternoons and weekends; or phone ahead

General line of antiques and collectibles.

A/C—PM. Affordable.

Prop. Madelaine Grafton   201–722–3578

YESTERDAY'S BARN ANTIQUES, corner Rt. 28 and Milltown Rd. (Rt. 22 West to Milltown Rd. exit, red barn on right).

Hours: Sat. & Sun. 10–5; or by appt. or chance

Friendly shop in an old red barn. An abundance of primitives and pressed glass. General line of lamps, clocks, and country furniture—Rayo lamps, lamp chimneys, lanterns, blanket chests, corner cupboards, oak, crocks, and prints. Member The Antique Trail.

A/C—PM. Affordable.

Prop. Bob and Lillian Sanders   201–725–7089

North Plainfield 07060

P. CHERUBINO UPHOLSTERY, 339 Somerset St. *Also see* Repair and Restoration listing.

Hours: Mon. thru Fri. 9–6; Sat. 9–3

Upholstery of antique furniture. Some antiques for sale, mostly chairs ready to be finished.

A—Prices not marked. Wide range.

Prop. Joseph Cherubino   201–756–4950

COLLECTOR'S CORNER, 326 Somerset St. *Also see* Repair and Restoration listing.

Hours: Mon. thru Sat. 10–5

Dealer in coins and antique jewelry. Clock and watch repair on premises. Appraisals. Member Nat'l. Assoc. of Watch & Clock Collectors.

A/C—PM. Wide range. Consignments.

Prop. Richard C. Schwartz   201–753–2650

GARY HOOK REFINISHING, 79 Wilson Ave. (off Rt. 22, westbound, behind Fabric Land). *Also see* Repair and Restoration listing.

Hours: Mon. thru Sat. 9–5

Primarily refinishing and restoration. Brass beds polished. Victorian and some Empire furniture for sale; will scout pieces in the Caribbean.

A/C—PM. Affordable.

Prop. Gary Hook   201–753–6166

LOOKING BACK, 93 Somerset St. *Also see* Repair and Restoration listing.

Hours: Mon. thru Sat. 9:30–5:30

General line; selected collectibles. Primarily furniture, some glass, bric-a-brac. Repair and restoration; no upholstery.

C—PM. Affordable.

Prop. Gary Johnson   201–753–1020

ANNA OLENSKY, 30 Grove St.

Hours: By appt.

Extensive selection of antiques and collectibles—china, bric-a-brac, art and cut

ANNA OLENSKY *continued*

glass, collector's items, lamps, oddities, and campaign buttons. Dealers welcome. Mrs. Osborn will buy "a plate to an estate."

A/C—Most prices marked. Affordable. Authentication.

Prop. Anna Olensky Osborn 201–755–6744

SIGN OF THE HARLEQUIN ANTIQUES, North Plainfield.

Hours: By appt.

Specializing in flow blue china, art glass, silver. Some primitives, cut and pressed pattern glass. Mint condition; no repairs or touch-ups. Instructor, adult education classes on antiques.

A/C—PM. Wide range. Consignments (better pieces). Authentication when possible.

Prop. Victor R. Saginario 201–754–0253

Peapack 07977

CRAB APPLE CORNER, 88 Main St. (Rt. 512).

Hours: Tues. thru Sat. 10–5

Country and Victorian furniture a specialty. General line of accessories, hooked rugs, paintings, and china. Also, "new and unusual gifts and housewares."

A/C—PM. Selective. Authentication when possible.

Prop. Joe and Bobbi Cox 201–234–2040

Pluckemin 07978

BEA'S TREASURES AND TRINKETS, Rt. 202.

Hours: Tues. thru Thurs. 6–9; Sat. & Sun. 10–6; Mon & Fri. chancey, call ahead

Collection of old paperbacks, sheet music, china, and glass; small amount of clothing.

C—PM. Affordable.

Prop. Bea H. McKiernan 201–658–3023

COUNTRY ANTIQUE SHOP, Rt. 202 (1 block north of shopping center).

Hours: Wed. thru Sat. 9–6; eves. by appt.; Sun. 10–6

Large two-story barn filled with modestly priced and carefully marked antique

COUNTRY ANTIQUE SHOP *continued*

country furniture. Antiques also purchased. A wryly humorous sign behind Mrs. Haines observes that "Prices are firm. We are not emotionally equipped to haggle."

A—PM. Affordable. Authentication.

Prop. Eleanor and Bob Haines   201–658–3759

Pottersville 07979

THE WOODEN BARROW, Rt. 512.

Hours: Tues. thru Fri. 10–4; Sat. 10–5; Sun. 1–5

A delightful gift and craft shop tucked away in the Somerset Hills. Some antiques, more collectibles. Antique dollhouses a specialty, occasionally taken on consignment. Complete new dollhouse accessories and furnishings in stock. Amish quilts, calico and patchwork gift items; antique banks, some pieces of primitive furniture.

C/A—PM. Affordable. Authentication when possible.

Prop. Audrey Teed   201–439–2707

Raritan 08869

TOWNE ANTIQUE AUCTION, INC., 56 W. Somerset St. *Also see* Auctioneers listing.

Hours: Phone ahead

Primarily an auction service. Member New Jersey Auctioneers Assoc. Shop specializes in "most anything"—small bronze statues, music boxes, clocks, cut glass, Mettlach steins, some oil paintings. Also George Washington Americana, paintings, buttons, etc. Auction mailing list.

A/C—Prices not marked. Selective. Authentication when possible.

Prop. John Torlish   201–722–2280

Rocky Hill 08553

JOSEPH'S COAT, Rt. 27 south, Little Rocky Hill (5 mi. north of Princeton).

Hours: 7 days 10:30–5

Country furniture, early pottery, basketry, china, some lamps, Victorian

JOSEPH'S COAT *continued*

candlesticks, and bird cages. Antiques only, no reproductions. Gift certificates available.

A—PM. Selective.

Prop. Helen Schumacher   609–821–9447

Somerville 08876

ALTEG POLY MARBLE, 73 Second St. *Also see* Repair and Restoration listing.
Hours: Mon. thru Fri. 8–5:30; Sat. 10–1

Up-to-date vintage bath fixtures; footed tubs, porcelain, vitreous china. Specializing in tub and tile resurfacing. Manufacturer, cultured marble; authorized Lectroglaz dealer.

C—PM. Selective.

Prop. Alan and Louise Glenn   201–526–2777

BITS AND PIECES ANTIQUES, 92 E. Main St.
Hours: Mon. thru Thurs. 9:30–9; Fri., Sat. 9:30–10; Sun. 10–9

A small youthful shop specializing in oak furniture and varied collectibles, including old sheet music. Informal browsing encouraged; note the credo on the wall, "Come in—we can be very friendly." Owners buy, sell, trade, and offer free appraisals.

C—PM. Affordable. Authentication when possible.

Prop. Keith, LaVerne, and Paul   No phone

EDITH BREUER ANTIQUES—COLLECTIBLES, 509 Stony Brook Dr.
Hours: By appt.

Small silver and antique jewelry, and a general line of popular antiques at affordable prices. Mail-order service with a five-day return privilege.

A/C—PM. Affordable.

Prop. Edith Breuer   201–722–6574

OLDIES BUT GOODIES, 137 E. Main St. Also at Packard's Farmer's Market,
Rt. 206 south, Wed. & Fri. noon–10.
Hours: Mon. thru Fri. 11–9

Brightly redone antique stoves, some cut glass, much new brass and copper.

C/A—PM. Affordable.

Prop. Steve Woody   201–722–7677

TONY'S DISCOUNT CENTER, 135 Rt. 206 south (in front of Packard's Market).

Hours: Wed. & Fri. 10–10

Collection of castoffs and collectibles in the shed and outside.

C—PM. Affordable.

Prop. Tony   201–526–1424

WINDSOR ANTIQUES, 1011 Rt. 202, eastbound.

Hours: 7 days 9–5

A veritable supermarket of antiques and collectibles, filling all wall and floor space. What isn't visible is very likely downstairs, waiting. Clocks, lanterns, and Americana are specialties; also clock repair. Genially presided over by the Lorings, who also find time to teach an adult education course on antiques and do appraisals.

A/C—PM. Wide range. Authentication.

Prop. Abe and Regina Loring   201–722–3618

South Branch 08881

ANTIQUE CUT GLASS, Box 12.

Hours: By appt.

Specializing in American cut glass collectibles. Also exquisitely arranged pressed flowers by Mrs. Carr, reasonably priced.

C/A—PM. Affordable/Selective.

Prop. Helen and Edward Carr   201–369–6021

Warren 07060

KING GEORGE ANTIQUES, 184 Mt. Bethel Rd., Mt. Bethel (Warren); opp. King George Inn.

Hours: Fri., Sat., Sun. 1–4:30; or by appt.

A selective shop specializing in 17th- and 18th-century American furniture in cherry, pine, maple, and mahogany. No oak. Chests of drawers, Windsor chairs, primitive paintings, marine paintings, old prints, some decorative accessories.

KING GEORGE ANTIQUES *continued*

Appraisals. Member Antiques Dealers Assoc. of Central N. J. and the Appraisers Assoc. of America.

A—PM. Selective. Authentication.

Prop. Madeline Nies   201–647–3832 (bus.)
                                                       762–8042 (res.)

MARIE'S ANTIQUES, 152 Mt. Bethel Rd., Mt. Bethel (Warren).

Hours: By appt.

Select collection of fine crystal, china, porcelains, bronzes, pewter. American pieces as well as English, French, German, Polish, Czechoslovakian, Russian, and Italian. Some small formal furniture and antique stained glass. "Antiques and collectiques of charm and distinction."

A/C—PM. Selective. Authentication.

Prop. Marie R. Siwiec   201–647–1492

WILLIAM F. WITTREICH. 14 Reinman Rd. (shop entrance is downstairs, in rear).

Hours: Thurs., Fri. 1–5; Sat. & Sun. 11 5; or by appt.

Quality formal and country furniture, paintings (some new), prints, lamps, rugs, china, silver, attractively displayed. Mr. Wittreich is an antiques consultant and does appraising.

A—PM. Selective. Authentication.

Prop. William F. Wittreich   201–469–3464

Watchung 07060

THE PAST ERA ANTIQUES, Watchung.

Hours: By appt.

English silver, Wedgwood, cloisonné; selected decorative accessories. In England at 59/61/63 High St., Berkhamsted, Herts. W. Lawson, prop.

A/C—PM. Selective. Authentication.

Prop. Alan and Jean Driver   201–755 7482

BOTTOM: Rare stoneware salt-glazed punchbowl inscribed *Elizabeth Crane, May 22, 1811, C Crane*. Flowering vine and scalloped coggle-wheel rim decoration incised in cobalt blue. Probably New Jersey. Ht. 7¾ in., diam. 15½ in. TOP: Interior of the punchbowl with incised cobalt blue fish. *Courtesy Sotheby Parke Bernet Inc., New York*

Union County

Berkeley Heights 07922

McDONOUGH STUDIO, 500 Springfield Ave.

Hours: Mon. thru Sat. 10–5

General line of antiques and collectibles. Paintings by Mr. McDonough.

A/C—PM. Affordable. Consignments. Authentication on request.

Prop. John and Virginia McDonough   201–464–0260 (studio)
                                                                             464–1900 (res.)

Cranford 07016

CARRIE ANN ANTIQUES, 10 North Ave. E. *Also see* Auctioneers listing.

Hours: Mon. thru Sat. 9–5

Oak, marble tops, brass beds; general line. If requested, Mr. Kiamie "can dig it up." Antiques purchased, traded, appraised. Children welcome. Also in Earlville, N. Y. (outside Hamilton) and Williamsport, Pa.

C—Prices not marked. Affordable.

Prop. Edmond Kiamie   No phone

163

GOOD FAIRY DOLL HOSPITAL & MUSEUM, 205 Walnut Ave. *Also see* Repair and Restoration listing.

Hours: Wed. 11–7; or by chance

Primarily a doll hospital and museum. Tours and charitable exhibits; duplicates only sold. Emphasis on portrait and comic sheet dolls. Dolls purchased. An unusual display, life-size wax heads of the Dionne quintuplets as little girls. Recent changes in the wax, eerily suggesting sadness in the impassive faces, have been noted by Mrs. Connors. Member Keepsake Doll Club, Fanwood.

A/C; new and reproductions—Prices not marked. Authentication.

Prop. Elizabeth and Jim Connors   201–276–3815

ARTHUR MAYNARD, 8 Riverside Dr.

Hours: By appt.

Fine English antiques; furniture, china, silver, glass. Interior design and consultation.

A—PM. Serious collectors.

Prop. Arthur Maynard   201–276–3434

NANCY'S ANTIQUES & 2ND HAND FURNITURE, 108 Walnut Ave.

Hours: Mon. thru Sat. 9:30–5

Congenial shop for Victorian furniture, early American primitives, glass, china, some old quilts, baskets, stoneware, picture frames; "no junk." Appraisals, estate sales, and to the trade.

A/C—PM. Affordable. Authentication when possible.

Prop. Nancy Slaff   201–272–5056
                                                                     233–8157

GERALDINE ROBERTSON, 302 Central Ave.

Hours: By appt.

Primitives, boxes, advertising tins; Victorian furniture. Interiors and accessorizing. Also at Hopewell Antiques Center (Tomato Factory).

A/C—PM. Selective. Authentication.

Prop. Geraldine Robertson   201–272–4360

WISH I HAD ANTIQUES, 105 Miln St.

Hours: Tues., Wed. 1–5; Thurs. 1–9; Fri. & Sat. 9:30–5. Closed Sun. & Mon.

General line, including china, glass, some furniture, lamps, mirrors. Metal

WISH I HAD ANTIQUES *continued*

plating and polishing, caning, refinishing by arrangement. Exchange privilege.
A/C—PM. Affordable. Authentication when possible.
Prop. Ross K. Miller   201–245–2583

Elizabeth 07208

CHARLES & ANN BAUMANN, Elizabeth.
Hours: By appt.

A quest may well end here with a choice. Eighteenth-century English, Oriental, and Continental porcelains; 18th- and 19th-century furniture, paintings, elaborate grandfather (and other) clocks, in working condition. Extensive collection of English cottages, 18th- and early 19th-century Meissen, Sèvres, Worcester, Derby, Chelsea, Spode, Samson, Delft; Staffordshire animals, porcelain figurines. Silver and copper luster, teapots, mugs; Chinese export, Rose Medallion, Ming pieces. Selection of shaving mirrors, pre-1830 samplers, prints. Appraisals. Member Nat'l. Assoc. of Watch & Clock Collectors.

A—Prices not marked. Selective to serious collectors. Authentication.
Prop. Charles and Ann Baumann   201–354–0535

SAM'S ANTIQUES, 555 Westminster Ave.
Hours: Tues. thru Sat. 10–7

Jewelry, crystal, some silver, glass, paintings; also purchased. Emphasis on newer items.

C—Not all prices marked. Selective. Consignments.
Prop. Samuel Schwartz   201–965–0222

TONY'S ANTIQUES, 1 Prince St. (cor. N. Broad).
Hours: Mon. thru Fri. 11–2; Sat. 11–4

General line, including glass, china, dolls, some furniture, Chinese soapstone, red amber, old costume jewelry, bric-a-brac.

C/A—Prices not marked. Affordable.
Prop. Anthony Carbone   201–289–2892

Fanwood 07023

THE DOLL'S CORNER, 115 Martine Ave. *Also see* Repair and Restoration listing.

Hours: Tues., Thurs., Sat. 1–6; or by appt.

Dolls purchased, appraised, and sold. Complete hospital service. Lecture and slide programs. Member United Federation of Doll Clubs, Keepsake Doll Club of N. J. Mrs. Paardecamp is a Doll Hospital School graduate.

A/C—PM. Selective to serious collectors.

Prop. Yvonne Miller, Lee Paardecamp   201–388–1869
                                                        322–1774

T. D. SCHOFIELD, ANTIQUES, 240 Herbert Ave.

Hours: By appt.

Pine and country furniture, tin, oil lamps. Dealers welcome.

A—PM. Affordable/Wide range.

Prop. T. D. Schofield   201–889–5771

Linden 07036

LENNY & LEE SMOLENSKY'S ANTIQUES & MORE, Linden.

Hours: By appt.

Crystal, ivory, jewelry, miniatures, saltcellars, sterling, tinware, Heisey, and gifts. "Estates managed with sincerity and sensitivity." Pleasant shop.

A/C—PM. Affordable/Wide range. Consignments. Authentication when possible.

Prop. Lenny and Lee Smolensky   201–486–5815

Mountainside 07092

DUTCH OVEN ANTIQUES, 1260 Rt. 22, westbound.

Hours: By appt. or chance. Closed Wed.

A Rt. 22 landmark for more than forty years. Collector's choice of good American country furniture; benches, painted mirrors, fireplace cranes and

DUTCH OVEN ANTIQUES *continued*

accouterments, pewter, tole trays, crocks, decoys, shelf clocks, and an occasional grandfather clock. In the Fitz-Randolph farmhouse, dating to 1755.

A—PM. Selective. Authentication "on my word."

Prop. Walda Rosencrantz 201–233–1567

DON MAXWELL, 885 Mountain Ave. *Also see* Repair and Restoration listing.

Hours: Mon. thru Fri. 8–5; Sat. 9–3. Closed Sat. during June, July, & Aug.

General line; furniture, some glass. Refinishing, restoration, and upholstering a specialty; extensive repair shop. Furniture appraisals for insurance purposes. At this location since 1926.

A/C—PM. Affordable. Authentication.

Prop. Don Maxwell 201–232–0226

HISTORIC MURRAY HILL SQUARE

Murray Hill 07974

MURRAY HILL SQUARE, Floral Ave. (off South St., New Providence).

Hours: Mon. thru Sat. 9:30–5:30; Thurs. 'til 9. Some shops open Sun. 12–4:30

At the hospitable sign of the pineapple, a beautifully reproduced Colonial community of more than fifty fine shops. Cultural events scheduled throughout the year.

Prop. Nat Conti 201–464–5097

MURRAY HILL SQUARE *continued*

AVIARY ANTIQUES, 75 Floral Ave. *Also see* Repair and Restoration listing.

An attractive shop. Emphasis on early furniture; American, formal and country French, and Pennsylvania Dutch. Including Welsh cupboards, lowboys, highboys, kas', chests, Jenny Lind beds. Selected wicker, pewter, unusual aviaries. Repair and restoration of antique furniture; hand work. Visa, Master Charge, American Express. Open Sun. 12–4:30.

A/C (some)—PM. Wide range. Authentication when possible (conservative estimates).

Prop. Rosemary and John DeLuca   201–464–8422

HOBBIT SHOP, 66 Floral Ave.

Youthful shop for antiquarian books, first editions, leather bindings, color-plate volumes, autographs, and prints. Appraisals, "correct framing" of old prints, bookbinding and repair. Mailing list. Open Sun. 12–4:30.

A/C—PM. Wide range. Authentication.

Prop. Arby Rolband   201–464–1336

PLUMQUIN LTD., 72 Floral Ave.

Distinctive antique accessories and furniture, and a wide selection of gifts at this sophisticated shop combining old and new. Interior decorating. Furniture refinishing by Wm. H. Plummer (203 Meyersville Rd., Chatham Twp., Morris County). Open Sun. 12:30–4.

A/C; also new—PM. Wide range. Consignments. Authentication.

Prop. Mrs. William H. Plummer   201–464–3131

Plainfield 07060

THE BIRD CAGE ANTIQUES, 146 North Ave.

Hours: Mon. thru Sat. 10–4:30. Closed Sat. during July & Aug.

Large selection of china and glass. Limoges, Parian ware, Satsuma, Nippon, Rose Medallion, Picard, Heisey. Some bronzes, ivory, sterling, turn-of-the-century furniture, toys, and cast-iron banks. Antiques purchased; traded. Estates appraised; liquidated.

A/C—PM. Wide range. Authentication.

Prop. James J. Bird   201–753–7762
                                                           756–8761 (if no ans.)

CAMEO ANTIQUES, Plainfield.

Hours: By appt.

CAMEO ANTIQUES *continued*
Chinese export, early 18th- and 19th-century English and European porcelains; cut glass. All pieces identified and dated. Appraisals.
A—PM. Serious collectors. Authentication.

Prop. David P. Willis   201–757–2923
                                                           757–0102

P. M. BOOK SHOP, 321 Park Ave.

Hours: Mon. thru Sat. 9:30–5

Large selection of used, scarce, out-of-print books; scholarly, reference, special interest, children's, and series. Well-organized regional Americana; magazines and periodicals. Libraries and individual volumes purchased. Well-known downtown shop.

C/A—PM. Affordable. Authentication when possible.

Prop. Sidney Pinn   201–754–3900

SHIR-NORM ANTIQUES, 1308 E. Front St. *Also see* Repair and Restoration listing.

Hours: Sat. 10–5

General line, the "odd and unusual." Including antique clothing and accessories, some old dolls, furniture, baskets, old musical instruments, china, glass, bric-a-brac. House sales; appraisals. Delivery service. Furniture repair and refinishing.

A/C—PM. Affordable/Wide range. Consignments. Authentication.

Prop. Shirley Nichols   201–561–3640

Rahway 07065

THE CANDLEWYCK GIFT SHOP, 85 E. Cherry St.

Hours: Mon. thru Sat. 10–5; Thurs. 'til 9

Decorative collectibles in an attractive corner setting and nicely interspersed among the cards and gifts. Handsomely refurbished trunks.

C; also new. Selective.

Prop. Bernadette Pirone   201–381–7717

THE COUNTRY CORNER ANTIQUES, 107 Monroe St.

Hours: Wed. thru Fri. 11:30–5:30; Sat. by appt. Closed Mon. & Tues.

Eighteenth- to early 20th-century furniture, some silver, jewelry; general line. Interiors purchased. Scouting list. "No children, please."

THE COUNTRY CORNER ANTIQUES *continued*

A/C—PM. Wide range. Consignments. Authentication.

Prop. Sally Gassaway   201–382–1616
                                                                 388–7112

THE ODDS & ENDS SHOP, Rahway. *Also see* Repair and Restoration listing.

Hours: By appt.

Antique clocks, cut glass, china, some silver. Antiques purchased. Complete clock repairs and restoration. Member Nat'l. Assoc. of Watch & Clock Collectors.

A/C (some)—PM. Affordable/Wide range. Authentication.

Prop. Ethel and Robert Wiley   201–382–1145

OLD SERENDIPITY ANTIQUES, 690 W. Grand Ave.

Hours: Wed. thru Sat. 1–4

China, glass, wall clocks; decorative accessories, wall arrangements, and miniatures tastefully displayed in two rooms. Also some paintings, old lanterns, hanging fixtures, primitives. Appraisals; household liquidations. Off-street parking at rear.

A/C—PM. Affordable. Authentication.

Prop. John McLaughlin   201–388–4393
                                                           388–1265 (if no ans.)

Scotch Plains 07076

BELL RINGER ANTIQUES, 1707 E. 2nd St.

Hours: Tues. thru Sat. 11:30–4

Primitives, small furniture. Some silver, glassware, insulators, books; general line. Estates purchased. House sales, decorating assistance, and to the trade. Informal free appraisals. Blue Willow and silverplate registries; requests on card file.

C/A—PM. Affordable.

Prop. Jean Kroeger   201–322–9119
                                                                 376–5980

HEINEMEYER'S FLORIST & ANTIQUES, 1380 Terrill Rd.

Hours: Mon. thru Sat. 9–6; Sun. 9–3 (call ahead suggested)

Greenery and flowers complemented by a small general line of china, cut glass, "unique and unusual antiques." Antiques purchased.

A/C—PM. Affordable/Wide range. Authentication when possible.

Prop. Ilse Heinemeyer   201–756–2838

HERMETIC TREASURES, 2228 Newark Ave.

Hours: Mon. 9–4; and by appt.

Some silver, jewelry (including costume jewelry), small boxes, Sabbath candlesticks, collectible oddities. The proprietor "loves to bargain"; never the ticket price.

C; also new—PM. Affordable. Consignments. Authentication when possible.

Prop. Lorraine M. Goldstein   201–233–7552

McGINN'S ANTIQUES, 1913 Westfield Ave.

Hours: Mon. thru Sat. 10–5. Closed Wed.

General line; well-selected cut and pressed glass, art glass, paperweights, some antique furniture, sterling, paintings, prints, bronzes, dolls, lamps, objets d'art exhibited with care and courtesy. Wholesale/retail. Antiques from Vermont and Prince Edward Island.

A/C—PM. Wide range. Consignments.

Prop. Bertha McGinn   201–322–7275

SECOND LOOK ANTIQUES, 1701 E. 2nd St.

Hours: Mon. thru Sat. 9–5; Sun. by appt.

Good selection of oak tables and chairs. Pictures, clocks, old magazines, glass, bottles, primitives, nostalgic items. An idea of what you're looking for and wish to spend might be helpful.

C—Prices not marked. Affordable. Authentication "sometimes."

Prop. Seymour Eisen   201–322–8120

STAGE HOUSE VILLAGE, Park & Front Sts.

Hours: Mon. thru Sat. 10–5. (The Inn also open Sundays 10–2 and 4–9.)

Clustered around the historic Stage House Inn, built in 1737, are nearly a dozen shops in early buildings that have been relocated and reconstructed near the site of the Battle of Scotch Plains. Outdoor events and exhibits during warmer weather.

Prop. Charles H. Detwiller, Jr.   201–322–4224 (the Inn)

AD'S ANTIQUES, 366 Park Ave.

Hours: Mon. thru Sat. 10:30–5. Earlier opening and closing during summer months.

Specializing in house and estate sales. General line; old iron stoves, old diplomas, Oriental and early American items, Victorian furniture, porcelains, paintings, rugs, wicker, odd lamps, some jewelry, filling the

STAGE HOUSE VILLAGE *continued*

cozy main rooms of a 1683 farmhouse. Once located on Terrill Rd.,
the structure was moved to its present location in 1961. Appraisals.

A/C—PM. Affordable. Consignments. Authentication when possible.

Prop. Adelyn Struening   201–322–4540
                                                          322–7044 (eves.)

CENTENNIAL ANTIQUES, 1833 Front St.

Hours: Mon. thru Sat. 10–5

Less usual selection of china, silver, furniture, prints, jewelry, and art
forms. A young man, Mr. DeFreitas has been a collector since the age of
sixteen, gained experience as a runner for other dealers, and now welcomes
them among his "best customers."

A/C—PM. Affordable. Authentication.

Prop. Douglas DeFreitas   201–753–9171

STERLING SILVERSMITHS, Front St. *Also see* Repair and Restoration
listing.

Hours: Mon. thru Sat. 8–5

Mr. Bruno has been "selling art more than silver" for more than forty
years. A craftsman known for fine repair, restoration, and plating. Good
English and American silver purchased.

A/C—PM. Wide range. Authentication.

Prop. Anthony Bruno   201–322–5854

Summit 07901

A CENTER OF ANTIQUES, 488 Springfield Ave. (at Kent Pl. Blvd.).

Hours: Tues. thru Sat. 11:30–5

Antiques and decoratives; emphasis on "beauty and craftsmanship." Furniture, accessories, wicker, fine porcelains, Ravca dolls, and giftables. Mrs. Weill will assist with wall arrangements and decorating.

A/C—PM. Selective. Authentication when possible.

Prop. Sophie Weill   201–273–0307
                                                              687–4863 (if no ans.)

CATHERINE BLAIR ANTIQUES, 350 Springfield Ave.

Hours: Mon. thru Sat. 11–5; or by appt.

Fine 18th- and 19th-century American and English furniture and accessories.

A—PM. Selective to serious collectors. Authentication.

Prop. Catherine Blair   201–273–5771

THE BRASS LANTERN, Summit.

Hours: By appt.

Clocks, Oriental porcelains, boxes, brass, iron, scrimshaw, and decorative objects selected with a discerning eye. Clock repair. Member Rush Light Society, Nat'l. Assoc. of Watch & Clock Collectors.

A—PM. Selective. Authentication when possible.

Prop. Jess and Phyl Prather   201–273–3436

EDITH O. ELIGUR—ANTIQUES, 506 Morris Ave. (near CIBA-Geigy).

Hours: Mon. thru Sat. 10–5:30

Oriental objects and rugs, furniture, paintings, jewelry, decorative accessories, elderly items, and "interesting junk." Antiques purchased. Estate appraisals; household sales. Prices coded, on file. Dealers welcome.

A/C—Prices coded. Wide range. Consignments.

Prop. Edith O. Eligur   201–277–0077

GALLERY ANTIQUES, 39 Maple St.

Hours: Mon. thru Fri. 10–5; Sat. 10–5:30

Warning!
Antique Pox
Very Contagious To Adults
No Known Cure
To be buying is relaxing—VISIT

GALLERY ANTIQUES *continued*

—a signed invitation to this friendly shop. Cut glass and jewelry a specialty. Nice old prints, china, pattern glass, Heisey, thimbles, small collectibles; some dollhouse miniatures, wicker, tin, old quilts. Antiques purchased. Appraisals; house sales. Old and new collector's plates at prices usually less than issue. Selection of new books on antiques. Master Charge, Visa.

A/C—PM. Affordable/Wide range. Consignments. Authentication when possible.

Prop. Marian Burros, Frank Kane   201–277–4242

889–5055 (if no ans.)

GARRISON HOUSE ANTIQUES, 16 Colt Rd.

Hours: By appt.

Tools, primitives, collection of sewing accessories—thimbles, needle cases, pincushions, sewing birds, small sewing baskets and boxes.

A—PM. Affordable. Authentication when possible.

Prop. Florence and Max Richardson   201–273–7709

GEORGE'S AUCTION ROOMS, 83 Summit Ave. *Also see* Auctioneers listing.

Hours: Mon. thru Sat. 7–3

Dealers in antiques and Oriental objets d'art for more than forty years. Primarily to the trade; retail sales not encouraged. Auctions on premises; mailing list. Insurance appraisals. Member Appraisers' Assoc. of America.

Prop. George's Auction Rooms, Inc.   201–277–0996

GLASS-SMITH SHOP, 7 Bank St.

Hours: Mon. thru Sat. 8:30–5:30

Glass-cutting shop. Some old glass sold. Grinding, polishing; old mirrors resilvered.

Prop. Elliot Saunders   201–277–0411

ERNEST HICKOK, 382 Springfield Ave.

Hours: By appt.

Sporting books, prints, paintings a specialty, some etchings; including the works of Frank Benson, Roland Clark, A. B. Frost, William Schaldach. Member

ERNEST HICKOK *continued*

Middle Atlantic and Nat'l. Chapters, Antiquarian Booksellers' Assoc. of America.

C—Most prices marked. Wide range/Selective. Authentication when possible.

Prop. Ernest Hickok   201–277–1427 (bus.)

LAMP CLINIC, INC., 513 Morris Ave. (1 block from CIBA-Geigy). *Also see Repair and Restoration listing.*

Hours: Mon. thru Fri. 10–5. Closed Wed.

Quality antique lighting; decorative accessories. Custom lampshades; lamp wiring, refinishing, and mountings.

A/C—PM. Selective.

Prop. Bob Royer   201–273–1323

MURIAL'S ANTIQUE GALLERY LTD., 451 Springfield Ave. (next to Strand Theatre).

Hours: Mon. thru Sat. 11–5. Closed Wed.

General line. Oriental porcelains, antique and Art Deco jewelry. Estate sales; appraisals. Member N. Y. Appraisers' Assoc.

A/C—PM. Affordable/Selective. Consignments. Authentication.

Prop. Muriel Goldberg   201–277–0959
                                       277–3761 (if no ans.)

THE SECOND HAND, 519 Morris Ave. (½ block from CIBA-Geigy).

Hours: Mon. thru Sat. 10–6

Chairs and small furniture outside; more inside, including oak. An assortment of old canning jars, china, glass, silver, replacement chimneys, advertising tins, bottles, Oriental pieces, prints. The wooden cream cheese boxes still make fine planters for marigolds.

C—Most prices marked. Affordable. Authentication when possible.

Prop. Jim Lant   201–273–6021

SUMMIT AUCTION ROOMS, 47 Summit Ave.

Hours: Mon. thru Sat. 7:45–4:30; Sat. 'til 4

Ample room to wander through several rooms of English and American furniture. Large stock; 99 percent dealer trade. Adjoining shop sells new fireplace equipment at discount. Estates purchased. Appraisals. Member N. J. Appraisers' Assoc.

SUMMIT AUCTION ROOMS *continued*

A—Prices coded. Wide range. Authentication.

Prop. Irving Silverstein   201–273–2118

SUMMIT GLASS SHOWCASE, 465 Springfield Ave.

Hours: Mon. thru Sat. 9–5:30; Thurs. 'til 9.

Primarily an art gallery, frame, and glass shop. Some decorative antiques; fireplace accouterments, curio cabinets, end tables, an occasional grandfather clock. Art restoration by arrangement.

A/C—PM. Wide range. Consignments. Authentication.

201–277–0365

JOSEPH ZICHICHI & SONS, INC., 474 Morris Ave. Workshop address: 513 Morris Ave. *Also see* Repair and Restoration listing.

Hours: Mon. thru Sat. 10–4:30. Workshop: Mon. thru Sat. 6–5

American antique and country furniture bought and sold. Furniture repair, restoration, refinishing. Appraisals.

A/C. Wide range.

Prop. Joseph Zichichi   201–277–1402

Union 07083

COLONIAL ARMS ANTIQUES, Union. *Also see* Repair and Restoration listing.

Hours: By appt.

Specializing in antique clocks and watches. Also firearms, oil lamps, mostly Victorian furniture. Clock repair and restoration. Appraisals. Member Nat'l. Assoc. of Watch & Clock Collectors.

A/C—PM. Wide range. Consignments. Authentication.

Prop. Lawrence Young   201–688–3932

SHIRLEY'S ANTIQUES, 2385 Rt. 22 (on the island).

Hours: Daily 10–9; Wed., Sat. 10–6. Closed Sun.

European antiques; some reproductions—the old, new, decorative, ornate, unusual. Furniture, emphasis on Victorian and turn-of-the-century; large selection of converted gas fixtures, chandeliers (no crystal), wall and grandfather

SHIRLEY'S ANTIQUES *continued*

*clocks, decorative objects. Mirrored pier armoires, reproduction parquet dining
tables, spoon racks, copper molds, carved dressers, chairs, chests. Large
establishment. Also in Brooklyn, N. Y. at 6216 Ave. U.*

A/C; reproductions—PM. Wide range. Authentication.

Prop. Shirley Green's Antiques, Ltd.; H. Greenberg   201–964–4022

HILDA SUCHOW, Union.

Hours: By appt.

*Fine country English furniture and accessories. Late 18th- and early 19th-century
pieces, including china. Bed warmers a specialty. Delivery service.*

A—PM. Selective. Authentication when possible.

Prop. Hilda Suchow   201–686–1459 (day & eves.)

THE UNION EXCHANGE, 1001 Vaux Hall Rd.

Hours: Wed. thru Sat. 10–6

*Miscellany; including old furniture, china, glass, some lighting, insulators,
typeboxes, old medicine cabinets, cameras. Antiques, collectibles, used furniture
purchased. Estate sales.*

C—PM (90 percent). Affordable. Consignments.

Prop. Carol Menza, Jane Carno   201–687–8984

Westfield 07090

THE ATTIC, 415 Westfield Ave.

Hours: Mon. thru Sat. 9:30–5:30

*From basement to. . . . A full general line of antiques and old things.
Fedoras, furniture, china, silver, glass; new, handmade doll furniture. Upstairs,
chairs and a grandmother's selection of hard-to-find baby equipment for little
visitors. The proprietors maintain a reference library, care about their antiques,
and enjoy children. Appraisals; estate sales.*

A/C—PM. Affordable/Wide range. Consignments. Authentication when
possible.

Prop. Vena Sharer   201–233–1954

KAY BELLA ANTIQUES—GIFTS, 519 South Ave. W. (at the circle).

Hours: Tues. thru Sat. 11–5

KAY BELLA ANTIQUES—GIFTS *continued*

Glass, art glass, lamps, clocks, paintings, jewelry, small furniture. Quality collectibles purchased. Also at Black Angus Antique Market, Adamstown, Pa. (near Lancaster), Sundays.

C—PM. Wide range. Consignments. Authentication.

Prop. Kay Bellezza   201–232–7172

BARBARA BURKE, 400 W. Broad St.

Hours: Mon. thru Sat. 10–5. Closed Wed.

Stained glass, oak furniture; general line. Furniture refinishing, hand-rubbed.

C/A—Some prices marked.

Prop. Barbara Burke   No phone

CURIOSITY SHOP, 324 South Ave. E. (obliquely opp. Firestone Car Service).

Hours: Thurs., Fri., Sat. 11–5

General line; interesting items moderately priced. Clocks, Orientals, better costume jewelry and old beads, china, glass, iron, linens, silverplate, some books. Generally no reproductions.

A/C—PM. Affordable. Authentication (selective).

Prop. Sonia Reagan   201–654–3622

LILLIAN DEWITT, 517 South Ave.

Hours: Mon. thru Sat. 11–5

Antique jewelry, furniture, clocks, watches. Also china, cut glass, Orientals, cloisonné, some paintings, copper, crocks, primitives, books, old cameras. Rummage room. Antiques purchased. Appraisals.

A/C—PM. Affordable/Selective.

Prop. Lillian Dewitt   201–272–6915
                                                                     654–4222

EILEEN'S ANTIQUES, 27 E. Broad St. (rear section, White Elephant Shop).

Hours: Tues., Sat. 9:30–5; or inquire at White Elephant Shop

China, glass, collectibles; small selection of old prints. Some appraisals. Call list maintained with White Elephant Shop. Note: parking at meters in front of

EILEEN'S ANTIQUES *continued*

shop prohibited 4:30–6:30 p.m., Mon. through Sat. Public parking in Elm St. lot.

C—PM. Affordable.

Prop. Eileen Nott 201–232–2281

GILBERT & RUTH FOSTER, 635 Glen Ave. (off North Ave. at Edgewood). *Also see* Repair and Restoration listing.

Hours: By appt.

Pine, cherry, and walnut primitives and country furniture "restored, refinished, ready to be used." Washstands a specialty. Also dry sinks, jam and corner cupboards, chests of drawers, tool and blanket chests, whiffletrees, old chairs, crocks, jugs. Decoys, iron tools always on hand. Antiques purchased. Appraisals. Hand-stripping; old wood employed in restorations.

A—PM. Affordable/Selective.

Prop. Gilbert E. and Ruth C. Foster 201–232–2577

K & R HANDLER ANTIQUES, 1272 Central Ave.

Hours: By appt.

Specializing in Wedgwood. Jasperware, china, bone china; some new limited edition pieces. Member Wedgwood Collectors Soc.; the Buten Museum of Wedgwood (Merion, Pa.).

A/C. Wide range. Authentication.

Prop. Roberta Handler 201–233–6060

JANTIQUES, 305 South Ave. W.

Hours: Tues. thru Sat. 11–4:30

Turn-of-the-century furniture, decorative accessories. Oak, wicker, mirrors, lamps, pictures. Baskets and country pieces upstairs in an attractive open gallery.

C—PM. Affordable/Selective. Consignments.

Prop. Janice Illion 201–654–4046

OLD THINGS, 115 New St. (cor. South and Central, behind Nat'l. State Bank; opp. Texaco Sta.). Shop is upstairs.

Hours: Tues. thru Sat. 9:30–5

"An overabundance of things" led to the opening of this friendly shop. Small

TOP: Cabbage leaf dish with Meissen-inspired polychrome bouquets; "Dr. Wall" Worcester, first period. L. 11¾ in., the largest size made. English, 1765–1770. BOTTOM: Caughley tea set with gilt and blue enamel decoration; including rare original teapot stand, spoon tray, and sandwich plate. English, 1790. *Courtesy The Pink House, New Hope. Photos: George Bailey*

OLD THINGS *continued*

general line; including usable furniture, some toys. In the corner, an heroic old Abercrombie croquet set, perfect for puttering around the estate.

C—PM. Affordable.

Prop. Geraldine Berenson   No phone

PARAGON ANTIQUES & GIFTS, 115 New St. (cor. South and Central, behind Nat'l. State Bank; opp. Texaco Sta.).

Hours: Tues. thru Sat. 11–5; call ahead suggested

General line, emphasis on glass, porcelain, china; some furniture, bronzes, vases.

C/A—Most prices marked. Affordable/Wide range. Consignments (selective). Authentication when possible.

Prop. Janet Papandrea   201–232–3835

THE WHIPPLETREE, 522 Central Ave. (cor. Park).

Hours: Mon. thru Sat. 10–5:30; Thurs. 'til 9

Emphasis on furniture and collectibles. Fireplace equipment, lamps and parts, hardware, glass, china, silver, old magazines, post cards, advertising items, prints, old farm tools. Appraisals; estate sales.

A/C—PM. Affordable. Consignments.

Prop. Joyce and Dick Smythe   201–233–6644

WHITE ELEPHANT SHOP, 27 E. Broad St.

Hours: Mon. thru Sat. 9:30–5

Consignment service specializing in jewelry, silver, glass, china, and small furniture. Est. 1928. Note parking prohibition 4:30–6:30 p.m. Mon. through Sat. Convenient public lot around the corner on Elm St. Shares premises with Eileen's Antiques.

C—PM. Affordable/Wide range. All-consignment. Authentication.

Prop. Ruth Smalley   201–232–2281

An 1895 poster by Edward Penfield advertising *Harper's* magazine. *Courtesy The Exhumation, Princeton. Photo: Michael Schnessel*

Middlesex County

Avenel 07001

VILLAGE COMMONS, 1490 Rahway Ave. (opp. Rahway prison).

Hours: Tues. thru Fri. 12–4; Sat. 10–5. Summer Hours: Wed. 10–4; Fri. 12–6:30; Sat. 10–5; and by appt.

A number of shops in a rambling carriage house built c. 1879. Facilities also for twenty-two flea market dealers in a pleasant grove. The flea market primarily bric-a-brac, collectibles; general merchandise. Flea market open Wed. 10–4; Sat. 10–5; May until fall, weather permitting.

Prop. Dorothy M. Magyarits   201–574–8599

THE ANTIQUE LOFT, Bernadette Pirone.

Furniture, china; general line. Upstairs also.

A/C—PM. Affordable/Wide range.

THE GAZEBO, Marge Sankner.

General line; glass, some linens in an upstairs aerie. Handmade pillows to order.

C—PM. Affordable/Wide range.

DOROTHY M. MAGYARITS, ANTIQUES.

General line; primitives, oak, small turn-of-the-century furniture, china, porcelain, some dolls, old linens.

C/A (some)—Most prices marked. Affordable. Authentication when possible.

VILLAGE COMMONS *continued*

THE UPSTAIRS CELLAR, Bea Boiko.

Primitives; small furniture, cupboard items, kitchenware, insulators. Emphasis on glass and old painted china—Davenport, Ridgeway, Haviland, Chelsea.

A/C—PM. Affordable/Wide range.

RESURRECTED RECOLLECTIONS, 1903 Village Dr. *Also see* Repair and Restoration listing.

Hours: By appt.

Specializing in 18th- and 19th-century timepieces; tall case clocks, carriage clocks, complicated watches. Music boxes from the early 19th century to the 1900s. Appraisals. Complete restoration service. Member Nat'l. Assoc. of Watch & Clock Collectors, Music Box Soc. of Gt. Brit., Amer. Music Box Soc.

A/C—PM. Wide range. Consignments within specialty. Authentication.

Prop. Gary Cleveland, Bentley Terrace   201–574–9281

Cheesequake 08879

THE ANTIQUE MART, Rt. 34, northbound (2 mi. north of Matawan).

Mailing address: Box 180A, Matawan 07747.

Hours: Mon. thru Sat. 12–5; Sun. 12–6

Antiques and collectibles attractively displayed in seven rooms. Browsers welcome.

Prop. Julia Lazarski   201–566–9870

MARGE AHLEMEYER ANTIQUES & COLLECTIBLES.

Primitives, oak, and Victorian furniture; china, some brass, lamps. Occasional pieces taken on consignment.

C—PM. Affordable/Wide range.

RAY GANNON.

"Smattering of everything"; art glass and antique jewelry preferred. Victorian furniture, sterling, cut glass.

A/C—PM. Wide range. Authentication when possible.

JULIA LAZARSKI.

General line; furniture, primitives, "eclectic collectibles." Antiques purchased annually in Ireland. Appraisals. In business more than twenty-five years.

A/C—PM. Wide range. Authentication; documentation.

THE ANTIQUE MART *continued*

GAIL PEARLMAN.

Victorian furniture, hall racks, desks; jewelry and accessories. Interior design consultation.

A/C—PM. Affordable. Authentication.

Colonia 07067

STONEWALL ANTIQUES, 35 Gaywood Ave.

Hours: Sat. 11–7; and by appt.

Glass, porcelain; general line. Design services by C. H. Laughery; diploma, N. Y. School of Interior Design. Member Atlantic Seaboard Antique Dealers Assoc., Nat'l. Early American Glass Club.

A/Some collectibles—PM; dated when possible. Selective. Authentication.

Prop. C. H. Laughery, J. S. Hallowell   201–381–6084

Cranbury 08512

FIELD ANTIQUES, 61 N. Main St.

Hours: Tues. thru Sat. 10–5; Sun. 1–5

Selected 18th- and 19th-century furniture. Chinese porcelains, glass, lamps, decorative accessories tastefully arranged. New pierced lampshades. Estates and partial estates purchased. Appraisals.

A—PM. Wide range. Authentication.

Prop. Thornton S. Field, Jr., Wendy K. Field   609–655–0310

THE LANTERN ANTIQUES, S. Main St. (next to Hagerty florist).

Hours: Call ahead

Country furniture, accessories, primitives; collectibles, good selection of pressed glass. Copper and brass cleaned. Some antiques in the house, built in 1849; most in the small red barn at rear. Informal.

A/C—PM. Affordable.

Prop. Dorothy S. Titzel   609–395–0762

JEAN M. MUIZNIEKS. Mailing address: 13 Channing Way, R. D. 1.

Hours: By appt.

Early American folk art, 18th- and early 19th-century furniture and accessories.

JEAN M. MUIZNIEKS *continued*

Painted furniture, quilts, boxes, baskets, early woodenware, copper, tin. Including an unusual butter scale, maple sugar mold; old cookie cutters. Selection for beginners and advanced collectors. Member Antiques Dealers Assoc. of Central N. J.

A/Some collectibles—PM. Wide range. Authentication.

Prop. Jean M. Muiznieks   609–799–1793

NOW 'N THEN SHOP, 63 N. Main St.

Hours: Tues. thru Sat. 11–5; Sun. 1–5

General line; primitives, accessories, old pressed glass; dollhouses and miniatures, mostly new. Changing selection of new handcrafts. Hand-painting on porcelain, stenciling; rushing, caning. Old clocks repaired. Appraisals.

A/C; also new—PM. Affordable/Selective. Consignments. Authentication.

Prop. Barb Flanner   609–395–1685

Dunellen 08812

TULLY'S COINS & ANTIQUES, 383 North Ave.

Hours: Mon. thru Sat. 10–5

Coins and paper currency, furniture; small general line. Coins and antiques purchased, appraised.

A/C—Some prices marked. Wide range. Authentication when possible.

Prop. William and Anna Tully   201–968–2060

East Brunswick 08816

ANTIQUES AND UNIQUES BY JANICE, East Brunswick.

Hours: By appt.

Jewelry, silverplate, sterling, cut and pressed glass; general line. No Depression glass.

C/A—PM. Wide range. Consignments. Authentication.

Prop. Janice Morganstein   201–257–9160

THE GOLDEN COACH ANTIQUES, 18 N. Woodland Ave.

Hours: By appt.

THE GOLDEN COACH ANTIQUES *continued*

China, silver, cut glass. Appraisals.

C/A—PM. Selective. Authentication.

Prop. Theresa and George Dixon   201–545–1610

THE GRAND EMBLEM ANTIQUES, 42 Colburn Rd.

Hours: Sat. & Sun. 9–5; and by appt.

Specializing in Currier & Ives; prints, maps, pre-1870 city views. Some period country furniture, quilts, ceramics (art pottery and country stoneware); an occasional Oriental rug. Old prints, maps, ephemera mailed on approval; return privilege.

A/Some collectibles—PM. Selective. Consignments. Authentication.

Prop. Gordon and Judy Kunz   201–249–3675

SHOWCASE ANTIQUES. Mailing address: P. O. Box 532.

Hours: By appt.

Victorian era European porcelains; jewelry, sterling, bronzes, brass. General line. Appraisals.

C/A—PM. Affordable. Authentication.

Prop. Gerard and Fran Magliocca   201 251 5117

MARION THOMAS, 9 Rt. 18, eastbound.

Hours: By chance

Long-established dealer. Emphasis on Orientals, large collection of antique gas, alcohol, and charcoal sadirons; general line. "Head to toe" selection of antique clothing and accessories. Nothing later than turn-of-the-century. Appraisals. Extensive schedule of Board of Education-sponsored courses in antiques at Mrs. Thomas' 150-year-old home. Member N. J. and N. Y. Appraisers' Assocs.

A/C—Prices not marked. Wide range. Authentication.

Prop. Marion Thomas   201–249–8552

Edison 08817

BYERLEE'S ANTIQUES, 812 Grove Ave.

Hours: By appt.

Mantel and shelf clocks, rocking chairs, jugs, crocks; general line.

A/C—PM. Affordable/Wide range. Consignments. Authentication.

Prop. Ron and Meg Byerlee   201–549–0536

BEATRICE & EDWARD KASNER, 18 Stephenville Pkwy.

Hours: By appt.

China, glass, silver.

A/C—PM. Wide range.

Prop. Beatrice and Edward Kasner   201–548–8107

Highland Park 08904

THE BEADED BUTTERFLY, 100 N. Second Ave.

Hours: Sun. thru Thurs. 11–5

General line, including furniture, glass, china; Wedgwood, Christmas plates. Consulting; moving sales, estates.

C—Most prices marked. Affordable. Consignments.

Prop. Lois Lebbing   201–828–4445

THE HOUSE OF REMEMBRANCE, 35 Cleveland Ave.

Hours: By appt.

Well-researched general line. Victorian antiques, fine cut and engraved glass; good china, bisque, old luster. Also to dealers. Appraisals.

A/C—PM. Affordable.

Prop. George Willgus   201–247–3351

KARWENS ANTIQUES, 68 Raritan Ave.

Hours: Tues. thru Sat. 11–4:30

Primarily turn-of-the-century oak, walnut, and mahogany furniture; prints, pastels, lithographs; silver, glass, china, lamps. Layaway plan. Visa, Master Charge. General line, nicely arranged for browsing.

C—PM. Affordable. Authentication when possible.

Prop. Freda Werther   201–828–5575

RUTGERS GUN AND BOAT CENTER, 127 Raritan Ave.

Hours: Mon., Tues. 10–6; Thurs., Fri. 10–9; Sat. 9–5. Closed Wed. & Sun.

Antique guns (1830–1875); extensive selection of arms literature. New Jersey gunsmiths a specialty. Modern guns; wholesale, retail. Dealership for boats, campers, trailers, outboard motors, and accessories. Master Charge. Member Ohio Gun Collectors Assoc., Pa. Antique Gun Collectors Assoc., Arms and

RUTGERS GUN AND BOAT CENTER *continued*

Armour Soc. of London, Forks of the Delaware (Pa.), Amer. Soc. of Arms Collectors. Located in a 1918 automobile showroom, one of the first in the area.
A—PM. Selective to serious collectors. Consignments. Authentication.
Prop. Mark Aziz   201–545–4344

Kingston 08528
(additional listings under Somerset County)

THE CALICO CAT, 55 Main St.
Hours: Wed. thru Sat. 10:30–4:30; and by appt.
Americana. Country furniture, wicker, chests, coverlets, quilts, early iron, fireplace equipment; dollhouses and furnishings to scale.
A/C—PM. Wide range.
Prop. Clara Kennedy, Tita Vivian, Gerry Busse   609–924–8765

OWEN'S ANTIQUES, 77 Main St. *Also see* Owen's Barn, below.
Hours: Tues. thru Sun. 11–5
A special interest in Victorian jewelry, French furniture, and primitives. Appraisals. Small, pretty complex with a red and white gatehouse. The 150-year-old residence has an earlier section at the rear. Built prior to 1730, it was once a stagecoach stop known as "Beehive Inn."
A/C—PM. Wide range. Authentication when possible.
Mgrs. Joan Shuss, Tania Midney, Dorothy Oppenheim   609–921–7164

OWEN'S BARN, 77 Main St.
Hours: Tues. thru Sun. 11–5
General line of American antiques; glass, silver, furniture in-the-rough. Appraisals. In the century-old barn. Also see Owen's Antiques, above.
A/Early collectibles—PM. Affordable. Authentication when possible.
Prop. Mary Etta Owen   609–921–7164

LOUIS SINCAK, SR., 65 Main St.
Hours: Wed., Thurs., Fri. 9–5; Sat. 9–3
Old pocket watches; old clocks, occasionally. Watches repaired. Member Amer. Watchmakers Institute, Watchmakers Assoc. of N. J.
A/C—PM. Wide range.
Prop. Louis Sincak   609–921–6048

Metuchen 08840

BORO ART CENTER, 505 Middlesex Ave. *Also see* Repair and Restoration listing.

Hours: Tues. thru Sat. 11–5

Late 19th- to early 20th-century American and European paintings and clocks; general line. Clock repair, restoration, cleaning. Search service for old clocks. Member Nat'l. Assoc. of Watch & Clock Collectors. The atmospheric old building with patterned tin upper walls and ceiling formerly housed Washington Hose Co. No. 1, organized 1897.

A/C—PM. Wide range. Occasional consignments. Clocks guaranteed as sold.

Prop. Ann Geschlecht   201–549–7878

BRASS LANTERN ANTIQUES, 327 Main St. *Also see* Repair and Restoration listing.

Hours: Mon. thru Sat. 10:30–5:30; Sun. 1–5:30

A crowded country store on Main St. Some early and later furniture, advertising items, kitchenware, sterling serving pieces, old sheet music, vintage apparel, old crochet, samplers. Also candles, cards, new gifts. Gift certificates, wrapping; merchandise club. Hand-stripping; repair and restoration.

C/A; new gifts—PM. Wide range. Consignments. Authentication when possible.

Prop. Lois Mazza   201–548–5442

MERRY GO ROUND ANTIQUES, 9 Calvin Pl. (opp. Post Office).

Hours: Wed. thru Sat. 12–4

Depression glass, pressed and carnival glass, china, bric-a-brac, old bottles, canning jars, small furniture, pictures. Member Hudson Valley Depression Glass Club.

A/C—PM. Affordable. Occasional consignments. Authentication when possible, within specialty.

Prop. Carolyn Urich   201–872–1182

Middlesex 08846

BROWSE AROUND ANTIQUES, 563 Bound Brook Rd. *Also see* Repair and Restoration listing.

Hours: Mon. thru Sat. 12–8

BROWSE AROUND ANTIQUES *continued*

Clocks a specialty, including regulators, gingerbread, school; furniture, glass. Antiques purchased. Antique clocks repaired.

C—PM. Affordable; clocks higher.

Prop. Constance Bolton   201–968–7220

MYRTLE KOFORD, Middlesex. *Also see* Whitehouse, Hunterdon County.

Hours: By appt.

Glass, china, and decorative objects. Old inkwells, Orientals, bisque; old chairs.

C—PM. Wide range. Consignments.

Prop. Myrtle Koford   201–356–3020

Milltown 08850

GARAGE SALE CORNER, 60 N. Main St. (corner W. Church St.).

Hours: Tues., Thurs. 10–4; Wed. 12–4; Fri., Sat. 11–4. Closed Sun. & Mon.

China, glassware, salt cellars, Depression glass, some furnishings, mantel clocks, in a tidy corner shop. Antiques purchased. Furniture refinishing by arrangement.

C/A—PM. Affordable. Authentication.

Prop. Irene Pardun   201–846–8181

NAN'S ANTIQUES AND GIFT SHOP, 87 Washington Ave.

Hours: Tues. thru Sat. 10–5; Thurs. eves. 7–9. Open Mon. Oct. thru Christmas

General line; glass, furniture. Gifts. Master Charge, Visa. At "Country Crossing," a small, charming center with shops specializing in plants, dollhouses, clothes, and shoes.

C/Also new—PM. Affordable. Authentication.

Prop. John Anderson, Jr.   201–828–2306 (bus.)
                                                       247–0712 (res.)

THE SILVER PORRINGER, 314 Brook Dr.

Hours: By appt.

Coin silver, sterling flatware and holloware; china, glass.

A/C—PM. Wide range. Authentication when possible.

Prop. William and Marilynn Catchings   201–249–1927

New Brunswick 08901

AARON AARDVARK & SON, 119 French St.

Hours: Mon. thru Sat. 9:30–6

General line; lamps, antique apparel, furniture. Appraisals.

C—PM. Affordable; furniture higher.

Prop. Susan Dods, Arthur Milgrom   201–246–1720

GEORGE BAHASH, 101 Easton Ave.

Hours: Eves., Mon. thru Sat. 6:30–8:30

General line; old bric-a-brac, glass, some antique and used furniture. The high-stooped residence is pre-Civil War.

C—PM. Affordable. Consignments.

Prop. George Bahash   201–247–4436

BILL'S TRADING POST, 10 Dennis St.

Hours: Mon. thru Sat. 9–5

Enormous amount of general merchandise; collectibles, turn-of-the-century pieces, used items. Appraisals. Auctions. Less disorder than amplitude; Mr. Weber threads the maze to the obscure with assurance. The sturdy brick structure was the 1884 Municipal Hall, later a firehouse, in more recent conversion a moving picture theater.

C—Most prices marked. Wide range. Consignments. Authentication.

Prop. William Weber   201–247–4406

BORROWED TIME, 159 French St.

Hours: Tues. thru Sat. 10–5

Nostalgia. Antique clothing and linens, lace tablecloths; some foreign coins. Used and out-of-print recordings; new and used records purchased. Visa.

C—PM. Affordable. Consignments.

Prop. Charles Ewen, Ruth Weeks   201–846–1720

GASLIGHT ANTIQUES RELIGIOUS & GIFT SHOP, 53 French St. (corner Brown St.).

Hours: Mon. thru Sat. 9:30–6

General line; clocks, old trunks, glassware, lamps, Staffordshire, Chinese export. New Jersey coin silver spoons, almanacs, crocks, etc. Selection of religious

GASLIGHT ANTIQUES RELIGIOUS & GIFT SHOP *continued*

articles and giftware. Repair of antique and modern clocks, watches, jewelry. Member American Watchmakers Institute.

A/C—Prices not marked. Wide range. Consignments. Authentication.

Prop. William Kazar   201–247–8341

U. S. #1 FLEA MARKET. Rt. 1, southbound.

Hours: Weekends: Fri. 12–9; Sat. 10–9; Sun. 10–7:30

Several-score dealers occupying the vast indoor acreage of a former discount emporium. Predominantly general merchandise, apparel, plants, food and grocery items, cleaning agents, novelties. Varying number of booths devoted to antiques and collectibles, expected to increase.

Mgr. Ray Travis   201–846–0900

THE ANTIQUE SHOPPE, Patrick Palumbo.

General line. Antiques auctioned Friday nights. Also at 1 De Baun Ave., West Caldwell, Essex County.

C/A—PM. Affordable/Wide range. Consignments. Authentication.

THE SHOPPE OF AGES, Madeline Baker, Jeanne Baker.

Glass, bric-a-brac; some costume jewelry. Mailing address: Box 1337, Edison 08817.

C—Most prices marked. Affordable.

North Brunswick 08902

LAWRENCE LANE, 1187 Dakota Rd.

Hours: By appt.

Old maps (extensive collection, 1600–1900), prints, books, fine Civil War and Revolutionary paper goods, costumes. Americana; no reproductions. Search service. Mail order; catalogs. Appraisals.

A/C—Most prices marked. Wide range/Serious collectors. Authentication when possible.

Prop. Florence and Larry Lane   201–246–0248

Old Bridge 08857

TRASH OR TREASURE SHOP, Old Bridge-Englishtown Rd. *Also see* Repair and Restoration listing.

Hours: Weekends: Sat. 10–5; Sun. 12–5

Victorian, Empire, pine, and turn-of-the-century furniture, restored and in-the-rough; lighting fixtures, porcelain, china, glass, Oriental throw rugs. Appraisals. Fine furniture repair and restoration by Mr. Nielsen; all hand work. No smoking requested.

A/C—Some prices marked. Affordable. Authentication; repairs noted.

Prop. Brent and Florence Nielsen   201–446–6572

Perth Amboy 08861

THE CRYSTAL SHOPPE, 289 High St. (1 block from the site of the old Colonial Market Square).

Hours: Mon. thru Sat. 10–5. Closed Wed. (Open Wed. Nov. & Dec. only).

Selected antiques and gifts. American pewter, old and new Delft, complete collection Royal Copenhagen Christmas plates, from 1908 first issue; cut crystal, silver, porcelain, Orientals, Chinese cloisonné. Also art glass, Bristol, early American stoneware; pine, oak. Miscellany in the "flea market" room, rear. Antiques purchased. Appraisals. Member Independent Antique Dealers of Amer., Inc. At this location since 1940.

A/C; new gifts—PM. Wide range. Consignments. Authentication.

Prop. Lena Ginsberg   201–442–2704

YE BYGONE YEARS ANTIQUES, 462 Amboy Ave. *Also see* Repair and Restoration listing.

Hours: Mon. thru Sat. 11–6; Sun. 11–3

Primarily furniture, heavy late Victorian pieces, turn-of-the-century, imported. General line, some china, glass, desk stands, bric-a-brac, brass; some reproductions, new pieces. Reference library. Antiques purchased. Furniture stripping, repair, refinishing by Bob Kubiak.

A/C; also new—Most prices marked. Wide range. Authentication when possible.

Prop. A. Salerno   201–826–2628

Piscataway 08854

COUNTRY ANTIQUES, 1023 River Rd.
Hours: By chance or appt.
Early country antiques, some furniture, small chests and boxes, decorative accessories; glass, china.
A—PM. Affordable.
Prop. Elisabeth Stuart   201–463–9359

NANNY'S NICK NAXS, 213 2nd Ave.
Hours: By appt.
General line. Antiques purchased.
A/C—PM. Affordable/Selective. Consignments.
Prop. R. and J. Stone   201–356–6929

South Plainfield 07080

ANTOINETTE'S ANTIQUES, 102 Caffrey Terr.
Hours: By appt.
Silver flatware, holloware, N. J. pottery; some scrimshaw, paintings, bronzes, glass. Appraisals.
A/C—PM. Affordable/Selective (paintings). Authentication when possible, on request.
Prop. Antoinette DeMeo   201–754–6398

South River 08882

HOBBY HOUSE, 230 Main St.
Hours: Tues. thru Sat. 10–4:30, by appt.
Primitives; woodenware, iron, tinware, kitchen items, pressed glass; some furniture, china. New apple dolls.
A/C—PM. Affordable. Authentication when possible.
Prop. Clara DeVoe   201–254–7817

Art Nouveau style silver brooch, brush, and tray made by Unger Brothers, Newark, after 1903. *From a private collection. Courtesy The Newark Museum. Photo: Armen Photographers*

MAGIC TOUCH REFINISHERS, 4 Klausers Lane (off Water St., opp. Sunoco Sta.).

Hours: Tues. thru Fri. 9:30–4:30; Sat. 9:30–1:30

Furniture, carnival and Depression glass, toys. General furniture repair and restoration; cabinetry by Dennis Humphrey at The Wood Knot, this location.

C—PM. Affordable. Authentication when possible.

Prop. Jack and Rose Humphrey   201–238–3032

Woodbridge 07095

ADRIENNE'S ANTIQUES & GIFTS, 739 St. George's Ave. (on the low side of the triangle where Amboy Ave. meets St. George's; opp. Woodbridge H.S.).

Hours: Tues. thru Sat. 1–5; call ahead suggested

General line of collectibles; furniture, art glass, fixtures, copper, brass, steins. Antiques, estates purchased.

C/Some antiques—PM. Wide range. Authentication when possible.

Prop. Adrienne Jafferian   201–636–1727

Highly collectible Meissen pastoral figurine. German, ca. 1820. *Courtesy Red Gate Antiques, New Hope. Photo: George Bailey*

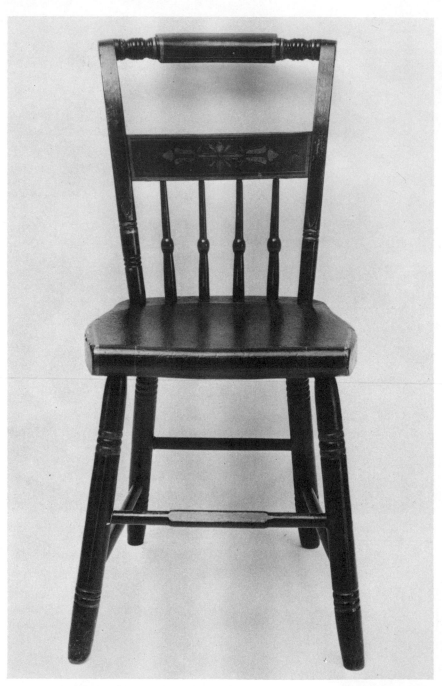

One of a rare set of 6 spindle-back Hitchcock chairs with plank seat and original stenciling, ca. 1830. Ht. 34 in. See trademark detail pictured on p. 13. *Courtesy Country Row Antiques, Inc., New Hope. Photo: George Bailey*

Monmouth County

Adelphia 07710

BLUE BALL EMPORIUM, Rt. 524 (Adelphia-Farmingdale Rd.).
Hours: Tues. eve. 8–10; Thurs., Fri. 6–10; Sat. 12–5; and by appt.
Glass, china, bottles, brass, cameos, prints. Artist's materials; custom framing, restoration.
C/A—PM. Affordable. Consignments.
Prop. Bruce F. Fallender   201–462–7675

MARY ANNE MARINACCIO, Rt. 524 (Adelphia Rd.).
Hours: Wed. thru Sun. 12–5
General line; furniture, printer's type drawers, collectibles. Large selection reproduction Colonial and Victorian dollhouse furniture, handcrafted accessories; dollhouses, dollhouse patterns. Friendly country shop.
C/A—PM. Affordable/Wide range. Consignments within specialty. Authentication when possible.
Prop. Mary Anne Marinaccio   201–431–2942

Allentown 08501

THE BARN ANTIQUES, USED ITEMS, 24 S. Main St. (in the original Allentown *Messenger* bldg.).
Hours: Mon. thru Sat. 9–5

THE BARN ANTIQUES *continued*

"Just a few things" in a congenial shop. An occasional primitive or piece of art pottery; items of known provenance.

C—PM. Affordable.

Prop. Ellis F. Hull   609–259–7997

BUSHMILL'S ANTIQUES, 9 S. Main St.

Hours: Mon. thru Fri. 5–9; Sat. & Sun. 10–5

Country primitives, Victorian. Furniture restoration. Also restoration of old dwellings.

A/C (some)—PM. Wide range. Authentication; bonded, insured.

Prop. Kathryn E. Marley   609–259–9266

Allenwood 08720

JEAN JOHNSON'S MINIATURES, the Allenwood General Store, Allenwood-Lakewood Rd. (north end).

Hours: Mon. thru Sat. 7–6; Sun. 10–5

Old and new dollhouses and miniatures. Pleasant, affordable for children.

C; also new—PM. Affordable/Wide range.

Prop. Jean Johnson   201–223–4747

Ardena 07728

ARDENA ANTIQUES, Rt. 524.

Hours: By appt.

Eighteenth- and 19th-century American antiques; kerosene, whale oil lighting. Early Victorian, pre-Industrial Revolution pieces; nothing later than Art Nouveau. Antiques purchased, appraised. Courses taught at home, the main portion of which dates to 1825. Member Amer. Inst. of Antiques.

A—PM. Wide range. Authentication.

Prop. Secilie Greenley Bean   201–431–1681

Asbury Park 07712

GIFTS BY TINA, 509 Cookman Ave. Also located on Boardwalk, Ocean Grove.
Hours: Mon. thru Sat. 11–5:30
Hummel figurines (U. S. zone mark), Tiffany vases and accessory pieces, Quezal glass, Meissen; collector's plates. Old jewelry purchased. Mending by arrangement. Member Goebel Collectors' Club, Retail Jewelers of Amer., Inc.
A/C—PM. Wide range. Authentication.
Prop. Tina Skokos   201–774–0457

McLAIN STUDIOS ODD'IIQUES, 503 Cookman Ave.
Hours: Mon. thru Sat. 10–4:30
General line, including new items. Oak, glassware, art pottery, sterling serving pieces, lamps, metalware, prints, some paintings; decorative accessories. Artists, fashion and interior designers welcome. Wanted to purchase: antique clocks; pre-1940 nude and seminude prints and posters; Maxfield Parrish original prints; turn-of-the-century oak and wicker; French and Oriental furniture; unusual pottery.
A/C; also new—PM. Wide range. Authentication.
Prop. Lois McLain   201–774–5552

WHITE'S GALLERIES, INC., 607 Lake Ave. (near Press Plaza).
Hours: Mon. thru Sat. 10–5
Old and new books for collectors and researchers. Libraries, estates, and collections purchased. Appraisals. Mail-order service. Mr. White is an author and translator. Literate selection in a friendly, helpful shop.
C—PM. Wide range. Authentication.
Prop. Alex Sandri and Evelyn White   201–774–9300 (bus.)
                                                                      531–4535 (if no ans.)

Atlantic Highlands 07716

ADAMS' REFINISHING, 142 Memorial Pkwy. *Also see* Repair and Restoration listing.
Hours: Mon. thru Sat. 8–5
Specializing in repair, refinishing, restoration of antiques, furniture. Some lamps, jewelry, "odds and ends."
C/A—PM. Selective. Consignments. Authentication when possible.
Prop. Bob Adams   201–872–0656

EAST HOUSE ANTIQUES, Rt. 36, westbound (at Sears Ave.).

Hours: Call ahead or by chance

General line; mainly china and glass, old bottles.

A/C—PM. Affordable.

Prop. Jacqueline and Michael Arentoft   201–291–2147

Belford 07718

TOM'S MIDDLETOWN JEWELERS, 82 Leonardville Rd.

Hours: Daily 10–6; Mon., Fri. eves. 7–8:30. Closed Wed. & Sun. (1 P.M. closing in summer; open 7–8:30)

Old, new, and estate jewelry. Silver (mostly sterling), fancy flatware, serving pieces. Jewelry, clock, and watch repairs. Dealers welcome.

C; also new—Most prices marked. Affordable.

Prop. Thomas Keigher, Mildred Henschel   201–671–0750

Belmar 07719

CHRISTINE'S 1890s, 1110 F St. (opp. Belmar Elem. School).

Hours: Mon. thru Sat. 10–5

"The new antiques"; dishes, bric-a-brac, used furniture, trunks. Used furniture purchased.

C—PM. Affordable. Authentication when possible.

Prop. Daphne and Hank Fox   201–681–3097

LINK TO THE PAST ANTIQUES, 1822 H St. (Rt. 71, West Belmar).

Hours: Mon. thru Fri. 9:30–4:30; Sat. 9:30–4

Large varied collection. Glass, china, art glass, Tiffany bronze desk sets, mantel clocks, copper, kerosene lamps, some pocket watches, silver; small decorative collectibles. Excellent reference library. Antiques and scrap silver purchased. Dealers welcome. Est. 1936.

C—PM; some coded. Affordable/Wide range.

Prop. Wall Auto Wreckers, Inc.   201–681–2476

Bradley Beach 07720

LOU'S THRIFT SHOP, 716 Main St. *Also see* Repair and Restoration listing.

Hours: Mon. thru Sat. 10–6

Usually some older pieces; oak, Victorian, Empire. A number of comfortable old porch rockers. Primarily used furniture, plants, small handmade novelties. Rockers repaired; restored to usable condition. Hand-stripping, reupholstering of old pieces. Moving service.

C; also newer—Prices not marked. Affordable. Authentication.

Prop. Lou Neevers-Scholte   201–776–9080

Brielle 08730

ANTIQUES AN'NON, 400 Higgins Ave. *Also see* Repair and Restoration listing.

Hours: Wed. thru Sun. 12–4

Furniture (some 18th century, to 1920s), china, glass, prints, bric-a-brac; small collection of pocket watches. Also to dealers. Hand and pressed caning; rushing.

C/A—PM. Wide range. Authentication.

Prop. Marian Olson   201–528–5943

Deal 07723

LAWRENCE GALLERIES, 272 Norwood Plaza (entrance at shop directory sign; shop and parking at rear).

Hours: Eves. by appt.

Antiques and fine arts. Bronzes, art glass, jewelry, Oriental rugs; antique and used furniture, silver. Individual items and estates purchased. Estate liquidation. Personal and commercial appraisals. Visa. Affiliated with William Doyle Galleries, New York.

A/C—PM. Wide range. Selective consignments.

Prop. John E. Lawrence   201–531–2848

Eatontown Village 07724

THE GOLDEN GOOSE, 27 Main St.

Hours: Mon. thru Sat. 1–5 (the hardware store is open 8:30–5)

Railroad, marine, coach, and signal lanterns, paperweights, woodworking planes and tools, pressed glass; chocolate, cigar, metal, and lead molds, apothecary pestles; servant's bells, school, sleigh, and shaftbells. Also decoys, insulators; mostly Victorian occasional furniture. House contents purchased. An interesting, concentrated selection occupying the windowfront corner of B. D. Wolcott's Sons Paints & Hardware, at this location since 1891. A commercial building, pre-1850 vintage.

A/C—PM. Affordable. Consignments.

Prop. Phyllis Bulmer, Nancy Wolcott   201–542–0054

Elberon 07740

THE RARE BIRD (ANTIQUES), Elberon.

Hours: By appt.

Victorian jewelry, paperweights, small silver and enamel boxes, silver serving pieces, some china; framed and unframed prints. Guarantee with return policy. Appraisals. House sales priced.

A/C—PM. Affordable/Selective. Consignments. All sales guaranteed.

Prop. Annette B. Sacks   201–229–0338

Englishtown 07726

NIDDY NODDY ANTIQUES, Englishtown Antiques Center. (Englishtown-Old Bridge Rd., ¾ mi. north of Englishtown Flea Market).

Hours: Sat. 9–6; Sun. 10–6

General line; glass, china, jewelry, furniture.

C—PM. Affordable. Authentication when possible.

Prop. Hilda and Pete Shuhala   201–446–9834

Fair Haven 07701

BLUE STOVE ANTIQUES, 769 River Rd. (diag. opp. Amoco Sta.).

Hours: Tues. thru Sat. 11–5

Clocks, watches, oak and turn-of-the-century furniture, porcelain, glass, silver, jewelry, prints, frames, hanging fixtures. Repair and restoration of clocks and watches by arrangement. An eclectic collection upstairs in a 19th-century residence converted into a number of attractive shops.

A/C—PM. Wide range. Consignments. Authentication: clocks, watches.

Prop. Myra Burstein, Sally Flaxman   201–747–6777

BURIED TREASURE ANTIQUES, 775 River Rd.

Hours: Tues. thru Sat. 10–5; or by appt.

Early to mid-19th-century furniture, fine china, silver, some coin silver, fans, paintings. Also at Antiques Center of Red Bank, Bldg. II (Annex).

A/C—PM. Wide range. Selective consignments. Authentication.

Prop. Robert F. Gunkel, Jr.   201–741–5231

THE COLLECTOR'S EYE, 795 River Rd.

Hours: Tues. thru Sat. 11–4

Tasteful selection of pine and mahogany furniture, china, paintings, rugs, glass, jewelry, silver. Appraisals. House sales conducted. Also at Antiques Center of Red Bank, Bldg. II (Annex).

A/C—PM. Wide range. Occasional consignments. Authentication when possible.

Prop. Carter de Holl, Janet Vogt   201–842–9878

JEAN LUDEMAN ANTIQUES & GIFTS, 560 River Rd. (rear, Fair Haven Shopping Center-Acme Supermarket).

Hours: Mon. thru Sat. 10:30–5; Sun. by appt.

Broad general line, some new gifts. Furniture, porcelain, glass, cut glass, silver, lamps, miniature oil lamps, Oriental rugs. "Modest amount" of primitives, including an occasional corner cupboard. Christmas and contemporary collector's plates to order. Search file. Gift wrapping. Appraisals.

A/C; also new. Affordable/Wide range. Consignments. Authentication when possible.

Prop. Jean Ludeman   201–747–2855 (bus.)
                                                          747–5920 (res.)

DON PONS, JEWELERS, 799 River Rd. *Also see* Repair and Restoration listing.
Hours: Tues. thru Sat. 10–5

Antique jewelry, mantel clocks, some grandfather clocks. Jewelry designed, remodeled, repaired. Antique clocks repaired; grandfather clocks serviced. Member Nat'l. Assoc. of Watch & Clock Collectors.

C—PM. Wide range. Consignments. Authentication.

Prop. Don Pons   201–842–6257

Farmingdale 07727

FITZGERALD'S ANTIQUES, 44 Academy. *Also see* Repair and Restoration listing. Workshop at Squankum-Yellow Brook Rd., Howell Twp.
Hours: Sat. & Sun. 11–5; weekdays by appt.

General line, primarily Victorian and turn-of-the-century oak and walnut furniture, cherry when available; some small collectibles. Antiques purchased. Furniture repair and restoration; hand-stripping, gluing, veneer work, spoke and spindle replacement. Pleasant shop.

C—PM. Wide range. Authentication.

Prop. Jane and Robert Fitzgerald   201–938–5591

Freehold 07728

ANDY'S PLAZA, Rt. 9, southbound (4 mi. south of racetrack). *Also see* Auctioneers listing.
Hours: Sat. 7 A.M.–9 P.M.; Sun. 8 A.M.–6 P.M. Mon. thru Fri. by chance. Auction every Sat. eve., 7:30

Weekly consignment auctions. Estate sales. Appraisals. Some of "anything and everything" for floor sale. Used furniture purchased.

A/C; also newer. Wide range. Consignments. Authentication.

Prop. Jim Anderson   201–431–3212

LLOYD'S BOOK SHOP & GALLERY, 30 E. Main St.
Hours: Wed., Thurs., Fri. 11:30–2:30; Sat. 9:30–5:30

Books, American history, English literature; fine prints, old maps. Appraisals. Framing; matting. Member Amer. Historical Print Collectors Soc.

A/C—PM. Wide range. Consignments. Authentication.

Prop. Charles C. Lloyd   201–462–8334

B. J. WOOLFORD & SON, Freehold. Also at Manasquan Antiques Center.

Hours: By appt.

Country furniture and tools.

A/C—PM. Affordable. Qualified appraisals by arrangement.

Prop. B. J. Woolford & Son   201–462–2194

Howell Twp. 07731

HOMESTEAD ANTIQUES, Rt. 524 (Ardena Rd., opp. police station).

Hours: By appt.

Fine collection of well-researched light blue transfer; Enoch Wood, Thomas Mayer, Ridgeway, Staffordshire, Phillips, Adams. Victorian china, small furniture and prints; glass, decorative pieces, Oriental porcelain. Small, lovely shop occupying part of an 1828 house.

A/C—PM. Affordable/Selective. Authentication; researched, written.

Prop. Bill and Ida Fellenberg   201–938–2746

Keyport 07735

GALLERY 35, Rt. 35, northbound.

Hours: Tues. thru Sun. 12:30–6

Primarily used furniture; turn-of-the-century carpenter's tools, paintings, etc. Bright and unassuming. Painting and furniture repairs. Oil painting restoration.

C—PM. Affordable. Authentication.

Prop. John J. Ventura   201–739–0978

THE ROCKING CHAIR ANTIQUES, Rt. 35, northbound (near the blue water tower).

Hours: Tues. thru Sun. 1–5

General line, country things in-the-rough; pressed glass, lamps, reproduction dolls.

In a rambling, late 1700s building that has been more peripatetic than permanent. The structure began as a farmhouse, a stable, and a store, all separate until joined on the present site. Now in its fourth haven, and an unerring indicator

THE ROCKING CHAIR ANTIQUES *continued*

of urban progress, the store was built in Red Bank, moved to the eventual path of Rt. 36, and relocated again to what became the location of the Garden State Parkway.

C/A—PM. Affordable. Consignments. Authentication when possible.

Prop. Flora Scherling   201–264–6617

Leonardo 07737

GATEWAY ANTIQUES, Rt. 36 and Homestead Ave.

Hours: Daily 11–4. Closed Mon.

General line; primarily collectibles. Appraisals.

C/A—PM. Affordable. Selective consignments.

Prop. Philip Goldstein   201–291–5250

Little Silver 07739

THE ANTIQUES GALLERY, 333 Silverside Ave. (off Oceanport Ave.). At J. Turk Antiques.

Hours: Tues. thru Sat. 10–5

Primarily 19th-century French and English accessories; lamps, fireplace equipment, vases, boxes; some furniture. Advice on the decorative use of antiques.

A—PM. Selective. Consignments. Authentication.

Prop. Julia Graziano   201–842–7600

RUSCIL'S SYCAMORE GREENS ANTIQUES, 36 Sycamore Ave. *Also see* Ruscil's Furniture & Art Galleries, 25 E. Front St., Red Bank.

Hours: Mon. thru Sat. 9–5

Large, modern showcase. Silver, china, glassware, paintings, prints, Continental furniture; general line. Also reproduction and new furniture. Complete contents of homes and estates purchased. Appraisals. Decorating assistance. "Exceptional pieces" taken on consignment. At this location more than a decade; in Red Bank nearly forty years.

A/C; also new—PM. Wide range. Consignments ("exceptional pieces"). Authentication.

Prop. Andrew E. Ruscil, Frank Ruscil   201–741–8506

J. TURK ANTIQUES, 333 Silverside Ave. (off Oceanport Ave. at Gulf Sta.; across RR tracks). *Also see* The Antiques Gallery, above.

Hours: Tues. thru Sat. 10–5

Gallery of superb 18th- and 19th-century Oriental fine art and furnishings imported from China, Japan, Korea, Thailand. Chests, tables, boxes, screens, stands, carved and inlaid wall hangings, wood block prints, paintings, scrolls, sculptures, ivory carvings, tiles, rugs, embroideries, garment panels, porcelains, jardinières, lacquer dishes, cinnabar. No reproductions. Lacquer restoration by arrangement. Mailing list; photographs sent on serious inquiry. Member Asia Soc.

A—PM. Selective to serious collectors. Authentication when possible.

Prop. C. Brice de Ganahl   201–842–7600

Locust 07760

LOCUST ANTIQUES, 69 Locust Point Rd.

Hours: Tues. thru Sat. 1–5; or by appt.

General line of furniture and decorative items; brass, china, lamps, andirons and fireplace equipment. Lamp rejuvenation. A c. 1840 general store on a country road; the unexpectedly formal cast-iron-front building still has the early corrugated tin ceilings.

A/C—PM. Affordable/Wide range. Consignments. Authentication.

Prop. A. Stephen Anderson   201–291–4575

Long Branch 07740

COURTSIDE ANTIQUES, Long Branch. *Also see* Woods Edge Antiques listing, Shrewsbury.

Hours: By appt.

Well-researched silver, glass, and china. Adult education courses on antiques.

A/C—PM. Affordable.

Prop. Mr. & Mrs. Wayne M. Stevenson   201–229–0083

DOWN EAST ANTIQUES, 298 Branchport Ave.

Hours: Mon. thru Sat. 8–4

DOWN EAST ANTIQUES *continued*

General miscellany, and an enjoyable stop. Perhaps a darning knee, single badminton racquet, milk glass bowl, Canadian commemorative china. Appraisals.

C—PM. Affordable. Authentication.

Prop. Edward H. Emmons, Dwight E. Mahar   201–870–3233

TOYBOX ANTIQUES, 295 Norwood Ave.

Hours: By appt.

Toys, china, books, primitives; Americana a specialty.

A/C—PM. Wide range. Authentication when possible.

Prop. Lillian Abramson   201–222–6995

Manasquan 08736

WILLIAM & PATRICIA HORR, Manasquan Antiques Center, Rt. 71.

Hours: Tues. thru Fri. 11–4:30; Sat. 10–5

Ancient and Greek coins and artifacts, antique weapons, military items; books, prints, 18th-century furniture. Consignments accepted within specialty areas. Adult education courses, lectures, articles; cataloging for auctions. Appraisals. Member Amer. Numismatic Assoc., Amer. Numismatic Soc., Soc. for Ancient Numismatics, Numismatics Internat'l. By appt. in Sea Girt, 609–449–9285.

A/C—PM. Wide range. Consignments within specialty. Authentication.

Prop. William and Patricia Horr   201–223–1439

LAMPS UNIQUE, Manasquan.

Hours: By appt.

Decorative antiques and collectibles fashioned into custom lamps. Selection from the proprietors' collection or personal objects. Nicely priced.

Affordable.

Prop. Tom Waltsak, Andy Spagnolia   201–449–3773 (T. W.)
                                                   449–2624 (A. S.)

MANASQUAN ANTIQUES CENTER, Rt. 71 (½ mi. north of Main St. intersection).

Hours: Tues. thru Fri. 11–4:30; Sat. 10–5

Well-diversified general line displayed by a dozen dealers within the amplitude of two large storefronts. Early nautical shadow boxes, other nautical items,

MANASQUAN ANTIQUES CENTER *continued*

country furniture, trunks, silver, prints, paintings, early tools, weapons, decoys, old bottles and books; collectibles predominate. Antiques purchased.

C/A—PM. Affordable.

Prop. John Mayberry   201–223–1439

> B. J. WOOLFORD & SON, Manasquan Antiques Center, Rt. 71.
>
> Hours: Tues. thru Fri. 11–4:30; Sat. 10–5
>
> *Country furniture and tools. Also see Freehold listing.*
>
> A/C—PM. Affordable. Qualified appraisals by arrangement.
>
> Prop. B. J. Woolford & Son   201–223–1439

Marlboro 07746

THE ANTIQUE TOOL SHED, 6 Girard St.

Hours: By appt.

Specializing in 17th- to 19th-century primitive tools; special craft tools, hand-forged iron work, broad-axes. Member Early Amer. Industries Assoc.

A/C—PM. Affordable/Wide range.

Prop. Elliot Matlin   201–536–4032

GRANDMA'S TREASURES ANTIQUES AND COUNTRY STORE, Rt. 79, southbound (3 mi. north of Freehold).

Hours: Daily 12–5; Sun. 1–5. Closed Wed.

General line. Furniture, china, glass, bric-a-brac, crocks, jugs, costume jewelry, some lighting, old bottles, advertising; Oriental figures (turn-of-the-century and earlier). Appraisals. In the small building at rear.

C. Affordable. Authentication when possible.

Prop. Jack and Alida Hendrickson   201–462–2381

Matawan 07747

THE COLLECTORS, 83 Main St. *Also see* Auctioneers listing.

Hours: Mon. thru Sat. 12–5; Sun. "by appt. or accident"

Antiques, collectibles, and newer things in a blue and white picturebook

THE COLLECTORS *continued*

Victorian, c. 1840. Furniture, china, glass, cut glass, silver, lamps, prints, pictures, frames, some jewelry, quilts. Dolls, dollhouses, doll furniture, old and new miniatures in an upstairs hideaway. Also kitchenware, crocks, jugs, tools, Depression glass, bottles. Estates purchased. Auctions; mailing list. Appraisals. Member N. J. State Soc. of Auctioneers, Inc.

A/C; also new—PM. Wide range. Consignments. Authentication when possible.

Prop. Edward R. and Doris Kibble   201–583–3222

THRU THE YEARS, 277 Main St. (west of Rt. 34).

Hours: Mon., Tues., Fri., Sat. 9–5; Wed. & Thurs. by appt.

Selected general line in an established shop. Railroad plates, Royal Copenhagen, figurines, art and cut glass, Orientals, some silver, jewelry, prints, andirons, fireplace equipment. At this location nearly thirty years.

In a century-old farmhouse, once a restaurant, at another time a butcher shop; the tin walls and ceiling of an early modernization are still evident. Children requested to remain outside.

C/A—PM. Selective.

Prop. Elizabeth Welstead   201–566–2173

Navesink 07752

CONRAD PAULUS, Box 163.

Hours: By appt.

General line; china, pictures, glass, furniture, books; some Oriental rugs.

A/C—PM. Affordable/Wide range. Selective consignments. Authentication when possible.

Prop. Conrad Paulus   201–291–4306

New Monmouth 07748

CHERRY TREE FARM ANTIQUES, New Monmouth.

Hours: By appt.

Painted country furniture, folk art, primitives; stoneware, redware. Search

CHERRY TREE FARM ANTIQUES *continued*

service. Authentic pieces within specialty areas taken on consignment. Member Jersey Shore Bottle Club.

A—PM. Wide range. Consignments within specialty. Authentication when possible.

Prop. Yvonne Cinkala 201–671–9695

Oakhurst 07755

COPPER KETTLE ANTIQUES, 251 Monmouth Rd.

Hours: Mon. thru Sat. 9–5

Substantial collection of "antiques to decorate with." Two well-filled floors in a turn-of-the-century riding stable. Furniture, blanket chests, brass beds, coat racks, stripped oak, wicker, trunks, lighting fixtures, chandeliers, stained glass windows, pictures, wall hangings, Belgian porcelain stoves, wood stoves, copperware, fireplace accessories, nautical items, easels; wall, table, and mantel clocks, Art Nouveau, Art Deco. Custom bakers' racks and butcher tables. Also to decorators and restaurants. Brass and metal polishing; antique lighting fixtures rewired; furniture refinishing. Insurance and estate appraisals. There is fenced-in yard space with a swing set for youngsters. Member Appraisers' Assoc. of Amer.

A/C—PM. Wide range. Authentication.

Prop. Fred and Thelma Teicher 201–531–1699

Ocean Grove 07756

GIFTS BY TINA, #1-North End Boardwalk. *Also see* Asbury Park listing.

Hours: July & Aug. (until Labor Day): Mon. thru Sat. 11–10

Hummels, figurines, collector's plates, gold and silver jewelry.

A/C—PM. Wide range. Authentication.

Prop. Tina Skokos 201–774–0457

THE HOUR GLASS, 50 Pitman Ave. (at Pilgrim Pathway).

Hours: May 1–Sept. 15: Mon. thru Sat. 10–5

Primarily collectibles (c. 1900–1950); selected clocks, European collectibles, coins, limited amount of furniture. Also cards, gifts, animal supplies. Minor clock repair and adjustments. Visa, Master Charge.

C; also new—PM. Affordable. Consignments.

Prop. Gary and Fran Heiser 201–774–1151

Red Bank 07701

THE ANTIQUES CENTER OF RED BANK, W. Front St. (exit 109, Garden
State Pkwy.). Four buildings.

Hours: Daily 11–5; Sun. 1–5

*The antiques and collections of more than 100 dealers abundantly displayed in
four large buildings within browsing distance of each other. Individual booths
range from counter and backdrop space to the area of a small shop. Most
proprietors on-site weekends; less crowded weekdays. Long-established. Parking.*

Prop. Nan Johnson   201–842–3393

> BLDG. I, 217 W. Front St.   201–741–5331
>
> *General line; andirons, fireplace fenders, mantels, early advertising, china,
> glass, bric-a-brac, lamps, lamp parts, a few chandeliers, furniture, silver,
> Art Deco, Art Nouveau, prints, some old books. At random, a palatial
> bed, matching dressing table and chaise longue, carved eagle, old sled, and
> barber pole.*
>
> Mgrs. Pat and Leon McNamara
>
>> BEHIND THE TIMES, Pat and Leon McNamara.
>>
>> *Period 18th- and 19th-century furniture; Orientals, early porcelains,
>> table, floor, and some miniature lamps. Estates purchased. Appraisals.
>> Assistance with interiors; scouting. Moving sale management.
>> Custom-designed lamp finials.*
>>
>> A/C—PM. Wide range. Consignments. Authentication.
>>
>> ALICE H. CASEY.
>>
>> *Jewelry, decorator items; theatrical masks. Search and purchase
>> service.*
>>
>> C/A—PM. Affordable. Authentication when possible.
>>
>> KEITH LIBRARY & GALLERY, Quentin and Sylvia Keith.
>>
>> *Books; old, rare, limited editions, signed copies; fine leather
>> bindings, sets and odd volumes. Prints, including local prints;
>> old maps. At this location over ten years.*
>>
>> A/C—PM. Wide range. Authentication.

> BLDG. II (ANNEX), 195 W. Front St.   201–842–3393
> Mgr. Phyllis Leary (Hour Way Antiques)

THE ANTIQUES CENTER OF RED BANK *continued*

MARGE AHLEMEYER.

General line.

C/A (a few)—PM. Wide range. Authentication.

ALADDIN ANTIQUES, Celeste Aladdin.

General line.

C—PM. Affordable.

ANTIQUES N' THINGS, Betty Rugg.

General line. Also at 5 Wharf Ave., Red Bank.

C—PM. Affordable. Consignments.

ARCHERS TWO ANTIQUES, Joel and Lois Scheckner.

Oak, some Victorian furniture; stained glass.

C/A—PM. Selective. Authentication.

BUD BAHR & DOROTHY WILDE.

Nautical items, mantels, some paintings, and furniture; large seashells. Commercial window display by Ms. Wilde, a professional decorator.

A/C—PM. Wide range. Authentication.

WENDY BEY.

Minerals, gems, gold and silver jewelry. New Indian jewelry.

C; also new—PM. Affordable. Authentication.

BURIED TREASURE ANTIQUES, Robert F. Gunkel, Jr.

General line; china, pictures, 19th- and 20th-century Victorian and oak furniture. Also see Fair Haven listing.

C/A—PM. Wide range. Consignments. Authentication.

THE COLLECTOR'S EYE, Janet Vogt and Carter de Holl.

Early 19th-century furniture; general line. New Butterfield shadow boxes (individual rooms detailed in miniature; for serious collectors). Appraisals; hourly fee. Also see Fair Haven listing.

A; also new—PM. Wide range. Consignments. Authentication.

DAHLROSE ANTIQUES, Phil May, Herb Bachmann. *Also see* Repair and Restoration listing.

THE ANTIQUES CENTER OF RED BANK *continued*

Antique dolls; miniatures, mostly antique. Doll hospital. Lectures. Member Nat'l. Doll Fed.

A/C—PM. Wide range. Consignments. Authentication.

PHYLLIS DANZIG.

General line; lap desks, boxes; interesting and functional pieces.

A/C (some)—PM. Wide range. Authentication.

DAVIS ASSOCIATES, Rod Davis. (600 Bowne Rd., Wayside; 201–922–1299). *Also see* Auctioneers listing.

Oriental rugs; boxes, blanket chests. Appraisals. Auctions. Member Nat'l. Assoc. of Auctioneers, N. J. Soc. of Auctioneers.

A/C—PM. Wide range. Authentication.

THE DEN OF ANTIQUITY, Pam Carroll, Linda Selick Anagnostakes.

Antique furniture, rugs.

A/C—PM. Wide range/Selective. Authentication.

BOOTH #58, Hazel Does.

Small pieces of furniture, older collectibles, boxes, primitives; general line.

A/C—PM. Affordable. Consignments. Authentication when possible.

EAGLE'S AERIE, Floyd De Nicola.

Nineteenth- and 20th-century furniture; country pieces.

C/A (a few)—PM. Wide range. Authentication.

ELEGANT PACK RAT, Barney and Barbara Silkworth.

Pine, primitives, tins, crocks, and jugs.

A/C—PM. Wide range. Consignments. Authentication.

EL'S ANTIQUE CORNER, Eldred Stenzel.

Selected furniture, paintings; some china. All pieces identified.

A/C—PM. Wide range/Selective. Authentication.

FLORA-DORA GIRL, Flora de Stefano.

Small decorative pieces, silver, pewter; dresser sets.

C—PM. Affordable. Authentication when possible.

THE ANTIQUES CENTER OF RED BANK *continued*

ALMA FOLMSBEE.

General line; prints, glass.

C—PM. Affordable. Authentication.

HOUR WAY ANTIQUES, Art and Phyllis Leary.

Victorian jewelry, kitchen items, beautifully pressed baby and children's clothes (c. 1890–1930). New miniatures and miniatures handmade by the Learys. Jewelry identified, guaranteed; appraised.

C; also new—PM. Wide range. Authentication.

ALICE JACOBI.

Currency and coins; some jewelry, Carlsbad plates, chocolate sets; old clothes and personal linens, including pantaloons.

C—PM. Wide range. Consignments. Authentication.

NAN JOHNSON.

"Just everything." Brass polishing, silver plating, caning, refinishing, by arrangement. Appraisals. Ms. Johnson is proprietor of the Center, est. 1963.

A/C—PM. Wide range. Authentication.

GEORGE VLADIMIR KEDROWSKY. *Also see* Auctioneers listing.

Art bronzes, cut glass, silver; decorative accessories. Antiques warehoused, also available through associates. Oriental rugs, bronze and metal statues purchased. "Significant antiques and fine arts" accepted on consignment. Consultation, research on acquisition, authentication, and disposition of art objects and antiques. Appraisals for insurance, estate settlement, liquidations. Complete auctioneer services. Member Amer. Philatelic Soc.

A/C—PM. Selective. Selective consignments. Authentication.

BOB & PEG LASKY.

Oak furniture, some wicker; flow blue, Rookwood china, paintings.

C—PM. Affordable/Wide range. Authentication.

MARIE'S ANTIQUES & FLORAL DESIGNS, Marie Foti.

Attractive corner boutique; 1920s reproduction Hepplewhite and Duncan Phyfe; complementary accessories. Silk flower arrangements.

C; also new—PM. Selective.

THE ANTIQUES CENTER OF RED BANK *continued*

JACK OSHINSKI.

Art Deco, collectibles, decorative accessories.

C—PM. Selective. Authentication.

OWL ANTIQUES, Jill and Mike Oltz.

Country pieces and primitives; original painted furniture. Also in South Amboy, by appt.; 201–721–2607.

A/C—PM. Wide range. Consignments. Authentication.

VINCE & LESLEY PACE.

Early 20th-century metalware; silverplate, brass, some copper.

C—PM. Affordable.

DORIS PRICE.

Dolls; general line. Member Nat'l. Doll Fed. Also in Bldg. III.

A/C—PM. Wide range. Consignments. Authentication.

REVIVAL HOUSE, Robert Dalton.

Antiques, decoratives. Victorian furniture, oak, hall mirrors; stoves.

C—PM. Wide range. Authentication.

ARTHUR & JOYCE ROBERTS.

Orientals.

A/C—PM. Wide range. Authentication.

ROSLYN SCHULMAN.

Art Deco, wrought iron, stained glass; in a small separate room.

C—PM. Wide range. Authentication.

THE SHAFERS, Jim and Helen Shafer.

Primitive furniture, table linens, glass, bric-a-brac. Toys; French, German, American, and papier-mâché dolls. Member Antiques Dealers Assoc. of Central N. J.

A/C—PM. Wide range.

TINTON FALLS ANTIQUES, Alice Ober.

China, glass, crocks, primitives. General line, displayed with care.

A/C—PM. Wide range. Authentication.

THE ANTIQUES CENTER OF RED BANK *continued*

TRADER "31", Dot and Irv Eggert.

Collectibles, early 20th-century furniture; general line.

C—PM. Wide range. Authentication.

THE TROTTERS, Donald and Arlene Trotter.

Antiques and interiors; primitives, country furniture.

A/C—PM. Wide range. Authentication when possible.

GORDON WATSON.

Kitchen items, pots; boxes, mirrors.

C—PM. Affordable. Authentication.

BLDG. III, 226 W. Front St.   201–842–4336

"BOOTH 101," Lee Wargotz and Bob Wayman.

Beautifully arranged silver (primarily sterling), sterling souvenir spoons, fine porcelain; Art Nouveau, Art Deco. Antiques purchased. Appraisals.

C—PM. Affordable. Authentication when possible.

ANN BOWDEN.

Primitives, coin silver; some old dollhouse furnishings, small blanket chests, early farm tools and baskets, door locks and keys. Decorating assistance.

A/C—PM. Wide range. Authentication.

B. DURIK.

Handsome new tavern, shop, and inn signs. Traditional, classic quarterboards and sternboards, hand-carved with chisel and mallet. Muted "Old Sturbridge" colors; 23k gold leaf and/or ornamentation. A difficult-to-find specialty.

New (specialty service). Selective.

GEORGE HOWER. *Also see* Repair and Restoration listing.

Authentic, interesting old tools a specialty. Repair and restoration. Also at 35 N. Bridge Ave., Red Bank.

A/C—PM. Affordable. Authentication when possible.

THE ANTIQUES CENTER OF RED BANK *continued*
    EDWARD JENOVE.
    Turn-of-the-century and earlier paintings, watercolors, prints,
    pastels. Descriptive notations.
    A/C—PM. Wide range. Authentication.

    KINGFISHER GALLERIES, Barbara Ross.
    General line; new collector's conservation prints. Adult school
    lectures on antiques. 201–741–7921.
    C—PM. Affordable.

    JOANNE LEONARD.
    Architectural finds; windows, frames, arches, bathroom equipment.
    Solid wood paneled doors available.
    A/C—PM. Affordable. Authentication.

    HAROLD MORRISON.
    Books, furniture, stained glass windows, baskets.
    C—PM. Affordable. Consignments.

    CHRIS MYER & ROB RANDOLPH.
    Old bottles (local); jugs, crocks, insulators, some old books, prints,
    advertising items. Stoneware, old bottles, Monmouth and Ocean
    County items; collections purchased. Bottle appraisals.
    A/C—PM. Wide range. Authentication.

    JOHN NEUBER. Also in Port Jervis, N. Y.
    Advertising posters and signs; furniture, old cupboards, bottles.
    Knowledgeable dealer. Reference library at Port Jervis location.
    C—PM. Wide range. Authentication.

    GARY NIELSEN. *Also see* Repair and Restoration listing.
    Handmade country furniture, old and new. Restoration, refinishing;
    hand-carving.
    A/C; also new—PM. Selective. Authentication.

    REMEMBER WHEN, Carol Dickstein.
    Country and oak furniture, baskets, cream cheese boxes; pieces
    refinished prior to sale. Antiques purchased.
    C—PM. Wide range. Authentication.

BLDG. IV, corner Shrewsbury Ave. and Catherine St.   201–842–1449
A newer addition. Furniture, primarily early 20th century and more recent.

ANTIQUES N' THINGS, 5–7 Wharf Ave.

Hours: Mon. thru Sat. 11–5; Sun. browsing

General line; furniture, china, glass, prints, some paintings, nautical items, when available. Shares premises with Ivins Antiques, see below. Also at Antiques Center of Red Bank (Annex).

A/C—PM. Wide range. Consignments. Authentication.

Prop. Betty Rugg   201–842–9639

GAS LIGHT ANTIQUES, 216 W. Front St.

Hours: By appt. or chance

Good sterling, crystal, Limoges, Spode; Victorian, Sheraton, Queen Anne, c. Louis XV furniture; candelabrum. Specializing in complete estates handled "one at a time." Estate antiques purchased privately.

A/C—PM. Wide range. Authentication.

Prop. Evelyn McCabe   201–741–7323 (day & eve.)

HOWER'S ANTIQUES, 35 N. Bridge Ave. *Also see* Repair and Restoration listing.

Hours: By appt.

Early 18th- to mid-20th-century carpenter and blacksmith tools, hand-forged ironware, lighting devices; primitives. Furniture repair. Also see listing Antiques Center of Red Bank, Bldg. III.

A/C—PM. Affordable.

Prop. George Hower   201–747–5499

IVINS ANTIQUES, 5–7 Wharf Ave.

Hours: Mon. thru Sat. 11–5

Early and more recent furniture a specialty; silver, some china. Insurance appraisals. Estate liquidations. Antiques n' Things also at this location.

A/C—PM. Wide range. Consignments. Authentication.

Prop. Ed and Linda Ivins   201–842–9639
                                                           842–4064 (if no ans.)

"R" BARN, 640 W. Front St. *Also see* Repair and Restoration listing.

Hours: Tues. thru Sat. 10–5; and by appt.

Well-selected primitives, Victorian and oak furniture, early household tools, matchsafes, baskets, old bottles, paperweights. In a warm and inviting paneled

"R" BARN *continued*

barn, built in 1852. "Victorian parlor" furnishings in a newer extension.
Prices firm. Refinishing; caning.

A/C—PM. Wide range. Consignments. Authentication.

Prop. Mary and Christine Vanderbilt   201–747–9226

RUSCIL'S FURNITURE & ART GALLERIES, 25 E. Front St.

Hours: Mon. thru Sat. 9–5:30; Fri. 'til 8

Vast, friendly shop in which the proprietors "buy and sell anything." Additional
merchandise behind the closed rear doors and upstairs. Complete contents of
homes and estates purchased. Appraisals. In Red Bank more than forty years.
Antiques emphasized at the Little Silver location, 36 Sycamore Ave.

C; also new/A—PM. Wide range. Authentication.

Prop. Andrew E. Ruscil, Frank Ruscil   201–741–1693

Rumson 07760

MARY-JANE ROOSEVELT, 109 E. River Rd. (corner Black Pt. Rd.).

Hours: Sat. all day; afternoons 1–5

European and French antiques, bronzes; cameo glass, "feminine" pieces of
furniture, silver. Appraisals. Repair and restoration. Member Appraisers' Assoc.
of Amer.

A/C—PM. Wide range/Selective. Authentication on request.

Prop. Mary-Jane Roosevelt   201–842–3159

Shrewsbury 07701

THE COUNTRY KITTEN ANTIQUES, 26 Thomas Ave. (rt. turn off Rt. 35,
southbound at Sunoco Sta. light). *Also see* Repair and Restoration listing.

Hours: Summer: Tues. thru Fri. 12–4. Winter: Tues. thru Sat. 12–4

Several shops within a shop, six rooms in an old two-story barn. General line;
primitives, glass, furniture, kitchen items, some interesting old clothes,
miscellany. A "Sweet Sue" character doll and hand-fashioned couture wardrobe
wrapped in tissue in a large old apparel box from Saks, a little girl's dream
(barely touched). Caning and lessons by Mary Ellen Thompson.

A/C. Affordable/Wide range. Authentication when possible.

Prop. Edna Aklus   201–747–1286

THE HUDSON SHOP, INC., 511 Broad St.

Hours: Wed. thru Sat. 10–5

Fine American country and formal furniture and accessories. Appraisals. Cabinet work by arrangement. Member Appraisers' Assoc. of Amer. Art and Antique Dealers League of Amer.; consultant, Smithsonian Assoc.; trustee, Monmouth County Hist. Assoc.

A—PM. Wide range. Authentication.

Prop. C. Alan Hudson   201–747–2003

INTERNATIONAL GALLERIES, 159 Newman Springs Rd. (Garden State Pkwy., exit 109).

Hours: Mon. thru Sat. 10–5

Extensive selection 16th- thru 19th-century American, English, and Continental furniture and paintings. Orientals, carpets, mantel and hall clocks, fine china, porcelain, cut glass, art glass, lamps, chandeliers, girandoles; jewelry, antique watches, flatware, holloware. Also coach lamps, lanterns, fireplace accessories, copper, brass, steins. Examples of pre-Columbian art; Etruscan artifacts. Antiques purchased. Courtesy interior design service. Appraisals. Member Appraisers' Assoc. of Amer.

A/C—Prices cataloged (available to customers). Consignments. Authentication.

Prop. Frank Martelli   201–747–6200

THE SERGEANTS, Shrewsbury.

Hours: By appt.

Period and country furniture; oil paintings, decoys. Also wholesale and to the trade. Extensive reference library.

A/C. Selective to serious collectors. Authentication when possible.

Prop. Gary and Susy Sergeant   201–842–1407

WOODS EDGE SHOPPES, 655 Broad St.

Hours: Mon. thru Sat. 10–5:30

Several fine antiques dealers in a serene, attractively landscaped complex of six showrooms. Some gifts and crafts.

Prop. Dick and Carol Lackman   201–842–9219

COURTSIDE ANTIQUES, Mr. & Mrs. Wayne M. Stevenson.

Silver, china, glass. Antiques purchased. Adult school courses on antiques. Also see Long Branch listing (by appt.).

A/C—PM. Wide range. Authentication.

WOODS EDGE SHOPPES *continued*

DOELGER ANTIQUES, Richard J. Doelger, Jr.

Formal and informal period and early American furniture.

A—PM. Selective. Authentication.

WILLIAM & PATRICIA HORR.

Ancient artifacts a specialty. Appraisals.

A/C—PM. Selective. Authentication.

ED LUZZI. *Also see* Repair and Restoration listing.

Kerosene and oil lamps; candlesticks. Lamp wiring, polishing, lacquering, repair.

A/C—PM. Wide range. Authentication.

WOODS EDGE ANTIQUES, Dick and Carol Lackman. *Also see* Repair and Restoration listing.

Primitives and period furniture. Appraisals. Antique restoration. Also gifts and crafts.

A—PM. Wide range. Authentication.

Squankum 07731

THE 1807 HOUSE, Farmingdale-Lakewood Rd. (Rt. 547).

Hours: 7 days; knock at door

Excellent collection of decoys, shore birds, and waterfowl. A. B. Frost and other sporting prints, Pennsylvania furniture, blanket chests; kerosene lamps, some electrified. Reference library.

Fine antiques in a gracious old house reflecting the influence of the Southern gentleman who had it built in 1807. (The kitchen wing is of an earlier date.) A lovely setting; ample parking at rear. Mr. Davies is a 1919 graduate of Rutgers. The Lamp Post shares premises, see below.

A/C—PM. Selective. Authentication when possible.

Prop. Ray Davies   201–938–5544

Richly detailed Federal carved pine mantel. Rayed sunbursts, urns, and fluted tapering columns. Ht. 5 ft. 1 in., w. 7 ft. 4½ in., opening 40 in. × 59 in. *Courtesy Sotheby Parke Bernet Inc., New York*

THE LAMP POST, Farmingdale-Lakewood Rd. (Rt. 547).

Hours: Daily

> "Please
> Do not assume that we don't know
>   what we are doing.
> All items are misplaced exactly
>   where we can find them.
> Everything is in a well regulated
> and systematic state of confusion."

Selected collection of antique tools, meticulously displayed—planes, including a fine rounding plane, rules, hewing axes, coopers' and forming tools, wheelrights' instruments, a screw box. Also wood and iron, horse accouterments; an occasional washstand, pitcher and bowl sets. All tools well cleaned, explained with congenial patience. Shared with The 1807 House, see above.

A/C—PM. Affordable.

Prop. Jim Dufford   201–938–5544

Wall 07719

PIER STREET ANTIQUES, P. O. Box 1143.

Hours: By appt.

Silver, scrimshaw, marine-related items, 18th- and 19th-century American furniture; early metalware—copper, brass, pewter. Antiques purchased from private sources. Appraisals. Lectures and courses. Member Appraisers' Assoc. of Amer.

A—PM. Wide range/Selective to serious collectors. Authentication.

Prop. Patricia S. Pierce   201–681–2227

West End 07740

BIJOU JEWELERS, 665 Second Ave.

Hours: Mon. thru Sat. 10:30–4:30

Antique, collectible, and contemporary jewelry. One-of-a-kind rings, pendants, earrings, slides, bracelets, lockets, cameos; gold pencils. Men's jewelry. Layaway

BIJOU JEWELERS *continued*

plan. Repair service. Sophisticated shop specializing in beautiful design and workmanship.

A/C; contemporary—PM. Wide range. Purchases guaranteed.

Prop. Rita L. Epstein   201–229–8111

MOTHER, 61 Brighton Ave.

Hours: 7 days 10–6

Young, incense-filled shop with large selection of American art pottery, Art Nouveau, Art Deco; old clothes, turn-of-the-century fringed lighting. Art Deco, Art Nouveau, and new jewelry; cigarette cases, vases, jardinières, prints, an occasional ceiling fan. Antiques purchased. Jewelry repair. Pottery and porcelain repair and restoration.

C—PM. Wide range. Authentication.

Prop. Anthony Wreiole   201–222–6469

Graceful Art Deco nude. A large, softly colored table piece. French, ca. 1925. *Courtesy The Golden Griffins*

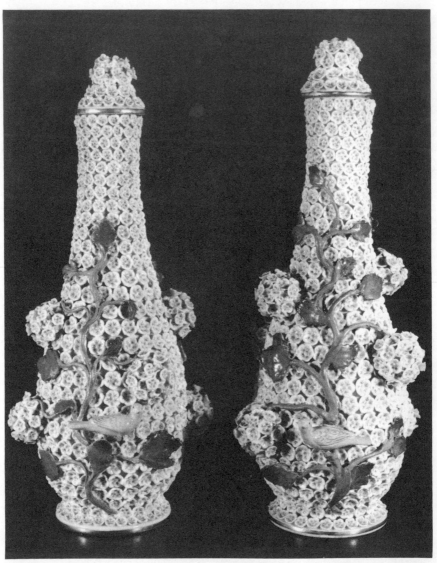

A pair of Meissen-inspired vases by Helena Wolfson with reproduction 18th century Augustus Rex mark. German, ca. 1860. *Courtesy Red Gate Antiques, New Hope. Photo: George Bailey*

Mercer County

East Windsor 08520

EAGLE'S NEST, 346 Franklin St. (Rt. 33 at exit 8 N. J. Tpk.).

Hours: Mon. thru Sat. 10–5; Sun. 11–3

Three floors of antiques and collectibles arranged in homelike settings in a warm shop. Country and Victorian furniture, some oak; lots of old bottles; primitives in the basement. "Things for the house—old, new, in-between."

A/C—PM. Affordable.

Prop. Ruth and Mer Ivins   609–448–2200

Hamilton Square 08690

JAMES HALL'S ASSOCIATED JEWELRY & COLLECTIBLES, 3640–44 Nottingham Way (north of Hwy. 33, 5 mi. east of Trenton).

Hours: Tues. thru Sat. 10:30–7; or by appt. *Also see* Repair and Restoration and Auctioneers listings.

An old former church, replete with stained glass windows, is now crammed with antique and collectible furniture, antique jewelry, glass, china, bric-a-brac, everything from estate sales. Appraisal service. Mr. and Mrs. Hall are auctioneers and conduct auctions twice a month. Repair, restoration, refinishing of furniture.

A/C—Some prices marked. Wide range. Consignments. Authentication.

Prop. James Hall   609–890–0926

Hamilton Twp. 08620

GREENWOOD ANTIQUES, 1918 Greenwood Ave. (Rt. 33).
Hours: Mon. thru Sat. 11–5; phone call suggested
American and European paintings are specialties. Paintings are guaranteed, and there is a return privilege. Small pieces of oak and walnut furniture, china, porcelain, glassware. Mr. Coyle will refinish furniture if requested.
A/C—PM. Affordable. Consignments. Authentication.
Prop. Bob Coyle   609–586–6887 (bus.)
                                                                                   587–8439 (res.)

Hightstown 08520

KATHLEEN CHRISTIANSEN, 145 Ward St. *Also see* Repair and Restoration listing.
Hours: By appt.
Specializing in 18th- and 19th-century country furniture and primitives, painted country furniture, early treen—carved woodenware ladles mostly from Ohio and western Pennsylvania; pottery, baskets, selection of old and new quilts and coverlets. Refinishing and restoration of furniture. Member Princeton Weaver's Guild.
A/C—PM. Wide range/Selective. Authentication.
Prop. Kathleen Christiansen   609–443–4508

THE COLLECTIQUE, 153 S. Main St.
Hours: Mon. thru Fri. 10–5:30; Sat. 10–5
Bright shop featuring antiques, collectibles, and new gift items. Home decorative accessories, china, glass, silver, lamps, prints, some furniture. Gift items include Williamsburg reproductions, Delft, International pewter, brass, iron, wood accessories.
A/C—PM. Affordable. Consignments. Authentication when possible.
Prop. Ruth and Howard Birdsall, Jeannette and Bill Rue   609–443–5801

HANKIN'S ANTIQUES, 169 Mercer St.
Hours: Tues. thru Sat. 11–4:30; or by appt.
Large corner shop on the main business street carries a general line of antiques

HANKIN'S ANTIQUES *continued*

in all price ranges. Period furniture, china, glass, silver, cut glass, antique jewelry, paintings.

A/Some collectibles—PM. Wide range. Authentication.

Prop. Aileen and Harold Hankin   609–443–4102

SMITH'S ANTIQUES, Box 428, Hwy. 33 (bet. Hightstown and Freehold).

Hours: Mon. thru Sat. 9–5

Primitives, a general line of furniture and glassware fill one spacious room in a private home and spill over into a barn in back. Mrs. Smith calls her shop "a rooting shop," where customers are welcome to come in and "root around."

A/C—PM. Affordable. Authentication.

Prop. Mrs. Anna Smith   609–443–1220

Hopewell 08525

ANJAC ANTIQUES, Rts. 31 and 518.

Hours: Sat. & Sun. 10–5

General line of "oldies and oddities": clocks, cut glass, art glass, lamps, some baskets and small pieces of furniture.

A/C—PM. Wide range. Authentication.

Prop. Anne and Jack Byrne   609–466–3493

AT THE SIGN OF THE BLACK KETTLE, 47 W. Broad St. (Rt. 518).

Hours: Tues. thru Sat. 10–5

Lots of room in this shop on the main street for a large collection of kerosene lamps; also glass, china, iron, copper, and brass items, some small pieces of country and period furniture. Good stock of lamp parts and accessories, including Rayo shades.

A/C—PM. Affordable. Authentication when possible.

Prop. Spencer Moore   609–466–0222

COX'S COBWEB ANTIQUES, 21 E. Broad St. (Rt. 518).

Hours: Fri. thru Sun. 11–4; or by appt.

Specializing in country furniture and appropriate accessories; large collection of stoneware jugs, brass, old china, glass. The Coxes give local appraisals.

A/C—PM. Affordable/Selective. Authentication when possible.

Prop. Ruth and Raymond Cox   609–466–1614

THE HIGH BUTTON SHOE, 2 Bank Place (just off Broad St.).

Hours: Mon. thru Sat. 11–5; Sun. 12–5

A rambling red-clapboard colonial building is shared by five dealers showing a varied selection of antiques and collectibles.

ANDY ANDERSON.

Early decorative accessories, lamps, brass, copper pieces.

LEWIS DEVLIN.

Lots of steins, iron dogs, other iron and metal items.

FLORENCE DOWNER.

Victorian furniture, celadon ware, Staffordshire, American paintings, old samplers.

BOB AND GINNY HOLCOMBE.

Country furniture, early quilts, old tools, primitives.

CLARA KENNEDY.

Charming antique dollhouses, dollhouse miniatures, antique plant stands, general line of furniture and china.

A/C—PM. Wide range. Authentication.

Prop. Cooperative   No phone

THE STAINED GLASS STUDIO OF HOPEWELL, 25–29 Railroad Pl. *Also see* Repair and Restoration listing.

Hours: Tues. thru Sat. 10–5

A design studio dealing in "anything that has to do with stained glass." A large stock of American and European leaded glass, including turn-of-the-century pieces, antique doors and windows, ceiling panels, lamps. The owners design new pieces and restore the old, either in the shop or on site.

A/C—Prices not marked. Wide range. Authentication when possible.

Prop. Brooke Baumann, Daurelle Golden   609–466–3747

THE TOMATO FACTORY ANTIQUES (Hopewell Antiques Center), Hamilton Ave. (2 blocks off the main street).

Hours: Mon. thru Sun. 10:30–5

A roomy, two-story tomato cannery c. mid-1800s has been completely refurbished (though you can still see the drains in the floor for the juice to run off) and

THE TOMATO FACTORY ANTIQUES *continued*

turned into an antiques center for fifteen browsable shops. The owners, Mr. and Mrs. Maurice Browning, provide complete decorating services, with a fine selection of wallpaper, fabrics, imported Italian, French, and Portuguese tiles; upholstering and slip covering, too.

MADELEINE BOUDAT.

Spanish provincial antiques, some South American and Philippine pieces; new tin lighting devices in the Spanish style, imported Spanish rugs.

NONDAS CASE.

Formal period furniture, handsome mirrors, old Irish glass, porcelains.

NINA COSENTINO.

Fine glass, centennial furniture, small pieces of silver, paintings.

JOHN HALLOWELL, CHARLES LAUGHERY.

Specializing in British porcelain, American art glass.

ROSE AND PAUL JAMIESON.

China, blown and pattern glass, country furniture, primitives.

MARIAN KATZ.

Hand-finished oak furniture, old trunks and sea chests.

GEORGE MILLER.

Old-time store items, some cupboards, small tables, tin lighting devices; new brass and copper accessories.

HELEN PENELLI.

Antique and collectible dolls, pewter, Imari pieces.

SARA SCULLY.

Wicker and informal furniture are specialties.

DONALD THOMAS.

English china, memorabilia, including a large collection of old post cards.

LIZ-ANN VAN DOREN.

Mixture of "oldies" and nostalgia—small pine pieces, posters, even gumball machines.

THE TOMATO FACTORY ANTIQUES *continued*

VIRGINIA VAN DOREN.

Country furniture, old tinware, brass accessories.

TITA VIVIAN.

Good selection of old quilts, country furniture, crocks, baskets, variety of country accessories.

JOAN WEINSTOCK.

Prints, old and new; posters, paintings, some small furniture.

CAROL AND DUDLEY WOODBRIDGE.

General line of country antiques, mostly furniture; baskets and jugs.

A/C—PM. Wide range. Authentication when possible.

Prop. Maurice Browning   609–466–2990

ELISABETH WOODBURN, Booknoll Farm.

Hours: By appt.

Rare and out-of-print books on horticulture, early agriculture, landscaping, beverages. Mrs. Woodburn maintains a search service and is a member of the Antiquarian Booksellers Assoc. of America, Middle Atlantic Chapter.

A/C—PM. Wide range. Authentication.

Prop. Elisabeth Woodburn   609–466–0522

North Crosswicks 08515

ANTIQUES AND STUFF, Church St.

Hours: By appt.

Spacious 1832 home that was used as an Underground Railroad station during the Civil War now houses a large and varied collection of antiques and collectibles. Early Victorian, late Victorian, Empire furniture, old Victrolas, over 3,000 pieces of Indian artifacts, china, cut and pressed glass, antique iron toys, a nice collection of old sleigh bells, and good duck decoys. Appraisal service.

A/C—PM. Wide range. Occasional consignment.

Prop. Alfred and Dorothy Newbold   609–298–0575

Pennington 08534

MAIN STREET ANTIQUES, 10 N. Main St.

Hours: Mon. thru Sat. 10:30–5

Specializing in Victorian and Empire furniture and appropriate accessories; china, glass, mirrors, prints, paintings.

A/C—PM. Affordable. Authentication when possible.

Prop. Joan Schwarzwalder   609–737–1396

JOAN PUSECKER ANTIQUES, 219 Ingleside Ave.

Hours: By appt.

Country primitive and painted furniture, redware, duck decoys, old quilts, iron and tin items in a selective shop.

A—PM. Selective. Consignments. Authentication when possible.

Prop. Joan Pusecker   609–737–0665

Princeton 08540

ASSEMBLÉE GALLERY, 4 Spring St. (1 block south of Nassau St.).

Hours: Tues. thru Sat. 11–4:30

Art Nouveau and Art Deco a specialty; Oriental art, bronzes, antique jewelry, good collection of old quilts. Mrs. Murphy gives appraisals only on quilts.

A/C—PM. Wide range. Occasional consignment. Authentication.

Prop. Dimitria Murphy   609–924–2841

THE EXHUMATION, P. O. Box 2057.

Hours: By appt.

Quality posters and original graphics from the late 1800s to 1940. Paintings, drawings, and etchings, Art Deco, porcelains, figurines. Appraisals on artwork, books, prints, and posters. Catalogue of posters available ($2); mail-order service.

C/A—PM. Affordable. Authentication.

Prop. Dominick Procaccino, Michael Schnessel   609–921–2339

EYE FOR ART, INC., 6 Spring St. (1 block south of Nassau St.).

Hours: Tues. thru Sat. 10–5

Extensive collection of prints from the 18th through the early 20th centuries;

EYE FOR ART, INC. *continued*

Winslow Homers, mid-1800s shell and flower prints, plenty of Beardsleys and Art Nouveau. Framing of all kinds, with emphasis on conservation-type framing to preserve rare prints.

A/C—PM. Affordable/Wide range. Consignments. Authentication.

Prop. Helen Benedict   609–924–5277

HOUSE OF TREASURES, Rt. 1, southbound (at Princeton Traffic Circle). *Also see* Repair and Restoration listing.

Hours: Tues. thru Sat. 11–5

Seven rooms of antiques and collectibles. Victorian furniture, general line of china, silver, crystal, some Orientalia, pitcher and bowl sets, trunks, old clocks and watches, antique jewelry, baskets and linens. Appraisals available. Services include furniture repair, watch and jewelry repair.

A/C—PM. Wide range. Authentication when possible.

Prop. Liz Benedik   609–452–1234

LEIGH ANTIQUES, INC., 192 Nassau St.

Hours: Sat. 10–4; or by appt.

Exceptional collection of American 18th-century formal furniture, Queen Anne, Hepplewhite, Chippendale, beautifully displayed in a spacious shop. Early paintings. "Antiques for pleasure and investment" for advanced collectors or those who wish to build a good collection. A longtime and knowledgeable dealer, Mr. Leigh sells all over the country and is a member of the Art and Antique Dealers League of America.

A—Prices not marked. Serious collectors. Authentication.

Prop. Ardis Leigh   609–924–9310

MILHOLLAND & OLSON, INC., 8 Stockton St. (facing Rt. 206 at Nassau St.). *Also see* Repair and Restoration listing.

Hours: Mon. thru Fri. 9–5

Primarily devoted to residential and commercial interior design, this shop in a beautiful old home in the heart of Princeton shows furniture, rugs, and paintings of all periods from antique to contemporary. Complete and total care and restoration of furnishings.

A/C—PM. Selective/Serious. Authentication through own sources.

Prop. Milholland & Olson, Inc.   609–924–2175

Estate auction preview display, including (right) a set of Oriental chain-mail armor. Epaulets and apron draped over a small chest, body suit, face mask on the floor. *Courtesy Elwood Heller, Lebanon. Photo: Ed Schuetz*

ON CONSIGNMENT, 4 Chambers St. (off Nassau St.).

Hours: Mon. thru Sat. 10–6; Fri. eve. 'til 9

Mixture of old and used furniture, bric-a-brac, crafts, "anything except clothing," in a total consignment shop. A few antiques amid the newer items.

C/A—PM. Affordable. Consignments.

Prop. Van and Deb Blakeman   609–924–1989

Trenton

BEVERLY ANTIQUES, 2516 Pennington Rd. 08638 (Rt. 31, southbound, just past Pennington Circle).

Hours: Tues. thru Sat. 10–4; eves. by appt.

A "shop in the house" featuring a general line of china and glass, selection of iron dogs, steins, Toby mugs, cut glass; some paintings, clocks, small pieces of furniture.

A/C—PM. Affordable. Authentication.

Prop. Harry and Sarah McKim   609–737–0073

CASTAWAYS, Trenton 08618. *Also see* Repair and Restoration listing.

Hours: By appt.

Specializing in Victorian and oak furniture. New handmade quilts always available. Hand-stripping of furniture, caning, turnings, mirror resilvering, brass polishing.

A/C—PM. Affordable. Authentication when possible.

Prop. Clarence J. Haney   609–393–6103

THE CLOCKWATCHER, Trenton 08618.

Hours: By appt.

Antique clocks and watches of all types. "Buy, sell, trade." Member Nat'l. Assoc. of Watch & Clock Collectors.

A—PM. Wide range. Authentication.

Prop. Carl Pletenyik   609–883–3099
                                                                883–3080

PENNY'S MILITARY, 1755 W. McGalliard St. 08610.

Hours: By appt.

PENNY'S MILITARY *continued*

Antique and collectible military memorabilia—firearms, swords, uniforms, leather accouterments. Mrs. Holloway appraises guns.

A/C—PM. Wide range. Authentication.

Prop. Penny Holloway   609–888–1274

S. & S. COLLECTIBLES, 1520 Princeton Ave. at N. Olden Ave. 08638

(Alt. Rt. 1, southbound). *Also see* Repair and Restoration listing.

Hours: Phone call suggested

Large shop crammed with "antiques of all types." General line of furniture, oil lamps, "Gone with the Wind" lamps, clocks, bric-a-brac. Mr. Sredinski sells wholesale and retail and provides furniture and lamp repairing.

A/C—Prices not marked. Wide range. Authentication.

Prop. Stanley J. Sredinski   609–599–1520 (bus.)
                                                       883–0742 (res.)

Yardville 08620

THE CELLAR SHELF, 4217 S. Broad St. (Rt. 206, southbound).

Hours: Tues. thru Sun. 1–4

Warm shop to the rear of main house has country maple furniture, Early American oil lamps, pressed glass, old Lenox, primitive kitchen utensils, decorative accessories. New lamp chimneys and lamp parts. Appraisals available.

A/C—PM. Affordable. Consignments. Authentication.

Prop. Gena D. Hawthorne   609–585–6778

From the Pine Barrens to the Shore
The Southern Counties

A superb Chippendale mahogany desk and bookcase of uncommonly small size. Philadelphia, ca. 1770. Ht. 8 ft. 5 in., w. 40 in., depth 22 in., writing level 29 in. *Courtesy H. & R. Sandor, Inc. Photo: Helga Photo Studio, Inc.*

Burlington County

Bordentown 08505

AMERICAN BELLEEK SHOP, 173 Second St.

Hours: By appt.

Specialists in antique American belleek porcelain, including Ott and Brewer, Willetts, the Ceramic Art Company, Lenox. Member Burlington County Antique Dealers Assoc.

A—PM. Selective. Authentication.

Prop. Erma and Harry Brown   609–298–1974

VINCE AMICO ANTIQUES, 340 Farnsworth Ave.

Hours: By appt.

Nice selection of nautical ivory, scrimshaw; also antique guns and old cameras.

A/C—PM. Affordable. Consignments.

Prop. Vince Amico   609–298–5370

Burlington 08016

BURLINGTON ANTIQUES, 229 High St.

Hours: By appt.

Steins of all kinds—porcelain, pewter, regimental, stoneware, and salt glaze.

BURLINGTON ANTIQUES *continued*

Formal Victorian furniture, walnut and oak; general line of china, glass, antique jewelry. Appraisals for insurance purposes. Member Burlington County Antique Dealers Assoc.

A/Some collectibles—PM. Selective. Authentication.

Prop. Ted Heilman   609–386–6732
                                                          386–2537

Centerton 08054

CROWN AND FEATHER ANTIQUES, 163 E. Moorestown-Centerton Rd.

Hours: Tues. thru Sun. 12–5; eves. by appt.

Selected country furniture and accessories, paintings, fine china, and a "comprehensive stock of Early American pressed glass always," nicely displayed in an early home c. 1752 that was once a stagecoach stop between Camden and Burlington. Mrs. Wright writes a weekly column on antiques for several newspapers and is a member of the Nat'l. Antique Dealers Assoc. and former president of the Burlington County Antique Dealers Assoc.

A/Some collectibles—PM. Wide range. Consignments. Authentication.

Prop. May E. Wright   609–234–0432

Cinnaminson 08077

HELEN E. SCHOLL ANTIQUES, 1600 Riverton Rd.

Hours: Better to phone ahead

General line of early furniture, some primitives, china and glass. Member Burlington County Antique Dealers Assoc.

A/C—PM. Wide range. Authentication.

Prop. Helen E. Scholl   609–829–1105

Crosswicks 08515

JACK AND MARY'S, Main St. *Also see* Repair and Restoration listing.

Hours: Mon. thru Fri. 9–5

Large collection of antique dolls in a small shop adjoining a charming old home

JACK AND MARY'S *continued*

that still retains a portion built in 1690. General line of furniture shown by appointment. Services include refinishing, stripping, caning, rushing.

A/C—PM. Affordable. Authentication.

Prop. Jack Cooney, Mary Waite   609–298–2035

Hainsport 08036

GREENBRIAR ANTIQUES, Fostertown Rd. (500 feet southeast of Rt. 38).

Hours: By chance or appt.

Early primitives, including tinware and woodenware, along with a general line of furniture, mostly small pieces that are billed as "antiques to delight you." Member Delaware Valley Antique Dealers Assoc.

A/C—PM. Affordable. Authentication.

Prop. Larry and Ella Corn   609–267–7388

J. R. IANNI ANTIQUES, Rt. 38, eastbound.

Hours: Tues. thru Sat. 10–5; Sun. 12–5; Wed., Fri. eves. 7–9

Antique furniture from the late 1700s through the early 1900s. Four spacious rooms show Queen Anne, Chippendale as well as Victorian and turn-of-the-century oak; decorative accessories, chandeliers, lamps, clocks, paintings.

A/C—PM. Wide range. Authentication.

Prop. J. R. Ianni   609–267–8555

Lower Bank 08215

THE DUCK BLIND ANTIQUES, Main Rd. *Also see* Repair and Restoration listing.

Hours: Mon. thru Sat. 10–6

Country pieces in a country setting—primitives, furniture, art glass, pottery. The antiques are combined with a small selection of new cooking items, tinware, and dried flowers. Lamp repair and restoration.

A/C—PM. Affordable. Consignments. Authentication.

Prop. Ursula L. Holman   609–965–2902

Lumberton 08048

TONY & JUNE WELLS ANTIQUES, Lumberton. *Also see* Repair and
Restoration listing.

Hours: By appt. only

*Mainly repair and restoration, including caning, rushing, reeding, wicker repair,
Shaker tape, willow and sea grass. The Wells have some old furniture, a large
selection of side chairs and benches. They do furniture appraisals and are
members of the Burlington County Antique Dealers Assoc.*

A/C—PM. Affordable. Authentication.

Prop. Tony and June Wells   609–261–2922

Marlton 08053

COUNTRY KITCHEN ANTIQUES, Marlton.

Hours: By appt.

*Good old kitchen items, both antique and collectible. Essentially primitives.
The Carletons are also located in Spruce Head, Maine, and are members of the
Delaware Valley Antique Dealers Assoc. and the Burlington County Antique
Dealers Assoc.*

A/C—PM. Affordable. Authentication when possible.

Prop. Jean and Paul Carleton   609–983–4637

PAULA'S PLACE, Corner of Main St. and Maple Ave.

Hours: Mon. thru Sat. 10–5; Sun. 12–4

*Antiques share a spacious corner shop with arts and crafts and classes in
macramé, pottery, batik, and weaving. Large pieces of period furniture, hall
stands, clothes trees, old picture frames, some glass and china.*

A/C—PM. Affordable. Consignments. Authentication when possible.

Prop. Paula Vallen   609–983–6880

YESTERYEARS SHOPPE, INC., and THE NOOK, 16 N. Maple Ave.
(off Main St.).

Hours: Tues. thru Sat. 10–5

Two shops share the same address on a main street of town. "Antiques, uniques,

YESTERYEARS SHOPPE, INC. *continued*

*and collectibles" in both: Depression glass, old prints, advertising tins, some
furniture, decorative accessories. Estates purchased.*

A/C—PM. Affordable. Consignments.

Prop. Lee Sabich (Yesteryears), Isabel Sirolly (The Nook)   609–983–1414

Medford 08055

LA FERME, Hartford Rd. (north of Rt. 70).

Hours: Mon. thru Sat. 9:30–5; Sun. by chance or appt.

*A charming shop to the rear of a 200-year-old home has a nice selection of old
and new quilts, early furniture, oak and turn-of-the-century, refinished and
in-the-rough; large collection of rockers, chairs, and frames; kerosene lamps.
New accessories include handmade patchwork from Tennessee. Member
Burlington County Antique Dealers Assoc.*

A/C—PM. Affordable. Consignments. Authentication.

Prop. France and Marcel Baloche   609–654–2915

POTPOURRI, 301 Stokes Rd. *Also see* Repair and Restoration listing.

Hours: Thurs. thru Sun. 12–5

*Select country and Victorian furniture in a tasteful shop. Kerosene and Tiffany-
type lamps, old guns, clocks, and a nice collection of stained glass. Repair
service for old and new stained glass. Appraisals.*

A/C—PM. Selective. Authentication.

Prop. Miriam Armstrong   609–654–7011

PRECIOUS PIECES, Old Marlton Pike and Hartford Rd. (1 block off Rt. 70).
Also see Repair and Restoration listing.

Hours: Tues. thru Fri. 11–5; Sat. 11–6; Sun. 12–4

*Spacious corner shop filled with primitive and country furniture, some oak and
Victorian, wicker, cupboards, roll-top desks, oak china cabinets, old tools, and
crocks. Reproduction brass beds, copper accessories, Tiffany-type lamps. Services
include stripping, refinishing, repairing furniture, polishing of copper and brass,
mirror resilvering.*

A/C—PM. Wide range. Authentication.

Prop. Ken Bittner, Peter Clarke   609–654–8555

ROCKY AND HIS FRIENDS, 18 S. Main St. *Also see* Repair and Restoration listing.

Hours: Mon. thru Sat. 10–5:30

Old and new dolls and their accessories, dollhouses and miniatures. Large collection of Depression glass, small pieces of furniture, china. Doll repair and dressing. The Gambacortas are members of the Nat'l. Depression Glass Assoc. and the Burlington County Antique Dealers Assoc.

A/C—PM. Affordable. Consignments. Authentication.

Prop. Rocky and Nance Gambacorta   609–654–8558

SPIRIT OF '76, 5 Union St. (off Main St.).

Hours: Mon. thru Sat. 11–5; Fri. eve. 'til 8

Warm little shop with a selection of Victorian and oak furniture, some primitives, and a general line of china.

A/C—PM. Affordable.

Prop. Paul and Ginny DeMarco   609–654–2850 (bus.)
                                                             654–5420 (res.)

THE TOLL HOUSE, Medford-Mt. Holly Rd. (Rt. 541).

Hours: Daily 11–4

Country antiques and American primitives in an 1830 toll house on the main line from Medford to Mt. Holly. Several rooms of tinware, tools, china, glass, silver, pottery, old kerosene lamps, new brass beds. Anything that is new is marked. Notice the calico.

A/C—PM. Wide range. Authentication.

Prop. Richard T. Brocksbank   609–654–5300

Medford Lakes 08055

GRANNY'S DOLL SHOP AND HOSPITAL, Stokes Rd. (Medford Lakes Shopping Center). *Also see* Repair and Restoration listing.

Hours: Mon. thru Sat. 10:30–5

Antique dolls bought and sold, doll accessories, new dollhouses and miniature furnishings of all kinds. Also a doll hospital for complete repair.

A/C—PM. Affordable. Authentication when possible.

Prop. Mary Bittner   609–654–4727

LAKESIDE ANTIQUES, 149 Chippewa Trail. *Also see* Repair and Restoration listing.

Hours: By appt.

Antique furniture of various periods, fine china and glass. The DeFuscos do caning, rushing, upholstering, stripping, brass polishing, and lacquering. Member Burlington County Antique Dealers Assoc.

A/Some collectibles. Wide range. Authentication when possible.

Prop. Helen and Tom DeFusco   609–654–5194

YESTERDAY & TODAY, Stokes Rd. (Medford Lakes Shopping Center). *Also see* Repair and Restoration listing.

Hours: Mon. thru Sat. 10:30–5

Old clocks a specialty, and a general line of furniture, some china, nicely arranged in a plant-filled shop. Clock repairs.

A/C—PM. Affordable. Authentication when possible.

Prop. Randi and Robert Gomel   609–654–7786

Moorsetown 08057

AULD LANG SYNE, 111 E. Main St.

Hours: Tues. thru Sat. 11–4

Tasteful shop specializing in early paintings; selected porcelains, some country and period furniture, Staffordshire, decorative accessories. Appraisals. Member Burlington County Antique Dealers Assoc.

A—PM. Selective. Authentication when possible.

Prop. Janet Uzzell   609–234–5014

ELDERLY THINGS, Camden Ave.

Hours: By appt.

Antique lamps and early Victorian furniture are specialties. Nice collection of pattern glass and old quilts. Member Burlington County Antique Dealers Assoc.

A/C—PM. Affordable. Authentication when possible.

Prop. Edith H. Whitney   609–235–1747

THE FOXES, 21 E. Main St.

Hours: Mon. thru Sat. 9–5

Some antiques and many new imported quality gift items in a combination gift

THE FOXES *continued*

and antiques shop. Collectible china and glass. The Foxes have been in business thirty-five years and are members of the Burlington County Antique Dealers Assoc. Appraisals.

C/A—PM. Affordable. Authentication.

Prop. Firm Fox   609–235–3266

GRAND JUNCTION ANTIQUES, 101 Chester Ave. (corner Main St.).

Hours: Tues. thru Thurs., Sat. 11–4; or by appt.

Three spacious rooms displaying period furniture before 1900, country pieces, porcelains, mirrors, old frames; good selection of antique jewelry, decorative accessories, "the unusual." Appraisal service. Mrs. Rosenthal is a member of the Burlington County Antique Dealers Assoc. and the Delaware Valley Antique Dealers Assoc.

A/Some collectibles—PM. Wide range. Consignments. Authentication.

Prop. Muriel Rosenthal   609–235–5282 (bus.)
                                                                 795–4399 (res.)

KINGSWAY ANTIQUES, 527 E. Main St.

Hours: By chance or appt.

General line of furniture of various periods, glass, fine china, crystal, old books. Mrs. Hagarty is a member of the Burlington County Antique Dealers Assoc.

A/C—PM. Affordable. Consignments.

Prop. Kate Hagarty   609–235–0789

RAIN BARREL ANTIQUES, 55 E. Main St.

Hours: Mon. thru Sat. 11–5

Unusual collection of very old infant feeders and a general line ranging from a 1600s blanket chest to present-day collectibles. Cut glass, fine china, coin silver. Appraisals. Member Burlington County Antique Dealers Assoc., Delaware Valley Antique Dealers Assoc., and American Collectors of Infant Feeders.

A/C—PM. Wide range. Authentication.

Prop. Bess Bay   609–234–3944

WELSH JEWELERS AND ANTIQUES, 115 S. Church St. *Also see* Repair and Restoration listing.

Hours: Mon. thru Sat. 9:30–5:30

Wide selection of furniture from primitive through Victorian, fine china and

WELSH JEWELERS AND ANTIQUES *continued*

glass in the downstairs area of a full-service jewelry shop. Clock and watch repairs, brass polishing, silver plating are services. Member Burlington County Antique Dealers Assoc.

A/Some collectibles—PM. Wide range. Authentication.

Prop. Mary and Jack Welsh   609–234–2445

Mount Holly 08060

THE BROWSE AROUND SHOP, INC., Rt. 38 (7 mi. east of Moorestown Mall). *Also see* Repair and Restoration listing.

Hours: Wed., Thurs. 10–5; Fri. 10–8; Sat. 10–5; Sun. 12–5

A "one stop shopping center for antiques" in an enormous shop with three spacious rooms of Victorian furniture, some primitive, some mission. A large selection of glass and china, lamps and lamp parts. New brass beds and Tiffany-type chandeliers. A special clock department and clock repair service. Interesting new collectibles are paperweights by Ray Banford, South Jersey glass artist. The Johnsons sell wholesale and retail. Refinishing, restoring of furniture, mirrors resilvered, lacquering of metals. Repair supplies for dealers and "do-it-yourselfers." New books on antiques. Member Burlington County Antique Dealers Assoc.

A/C—PM. Wide range. Authentication.

Prop. Chuck and Charlie Johnson   609–261–0274

THE WOODEN NICKEL, 86 High St.

Hours: Mon. thru Sat. 11–4

Charming shop on the main street of town carrying a general line of furniture, decorative accessories, paper items—old deeds, letters, elderly post cards; fine china and glass. Member Burlington County Antique Dealers Assoc.

A/C—PM. Affordable. Authentication.

Prop. Joan O. Washer   609–267–2932

Pemberton 08068

CANDLELIGHT ON PINE, 28 Hanover St.

Hours: By appt.

CANDLELIGHT ON PINE *continued*

Specializing in country primitive furniture, completely refinished and restored by Mr. Wack. Some handmade reproduction gift items.

A—PM. Affordable/Selective. Authentication.

Prop. Leon and Helen Wack   609–894–9165

STONE HEARTH ANTIQUES, Wynwood Dr. (Juliustown Rd. east off Rt. 206, 2 mi. to Arney's Mount-Pemberton Rd., right toward Pemberton to Wynwood Dr.). *Also see* Repair and Restoration listing.

Hours: Tues. thru Sun. 11–5

A sprawling shop filled with antique furniture from early country to 1900. Country primitives, tin, iron, crockery, lots of china and glass in their own sections of the building. A Whistlestop Country Store and snack shop in an old Birmingham railroad station adjoins. For the children, a charming little house furnished with child-size furniture in the colonial tradition. Appraisals. Refinishing and restoring of furniture, lamp repair, burnishing, refurbishing pewter. Member Nat'l. Assoc. of Dealers in Antiques, Inc., Burlington County Antique Dealers Assoc., Pennsylvania Appraisers Assoc.

A/C—PM. Wide range. Authentication.

Prop. Ruth Isgro   609–267–6919

YE OLD PEMBERTON ANTIQUES, 30 Hanover St.

Hours: Mon. thru Fri. 10–8; Sat. & Sun. 10–5

Victorian furniture a specialty; antique clocks, kerosene lamps, decorative accessories.

A/C—PM. Wide range. Occasional consignment. Authentication.

Prop. Charles and Beverly Kelly   609–894–8940

Rancocas 08073

HOMESTEAD ANTIQUES, 3 Main St.

Hours: By chance or appt.

Friendly "shop in the house" carrying a general line of fine china, old glass, pewter, silver, and antique jewelry. Some pieces of early furniture. The Wilkins are members of the Burlington County Antique Dealers Assoc.

A/C—PM. Affordable. Authentication.

Prop. Bob and Kathryn Wilkins   609–267–6959

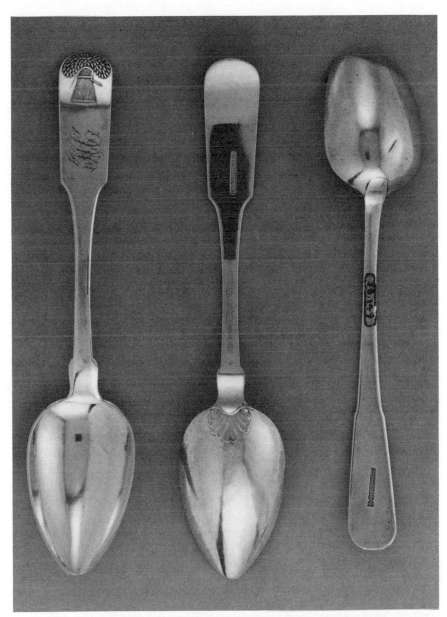

American silver tablespoons: (Left) fiddleback spoon with die stamp wheat sheaf design, monogram "ICC"; (middle) fiddleback porridge spoon with rounded drop on back, monogram "UPD", stamped "B. Cleveland"; (bottom) Cleveland porridge spoon made in Newark, ca. 1820. Lengths 10 in. *Courtesy The Newark Museum. Photo: Armen Photographers*

Rancocas Woods 08073

THE CARPETBAGGERS, Creek Rd. *Also see* Repair and Restoration listing.

Hours: Tues. thru Sun. 11–5

In the heart of a picturesque community of impressive log cabin homes is the Rancocas Woods Village of Shops. The Carpetbaggers is downstairs in a main log cabin called "The Emporium." Specialties are antique dolls, antique doll furniture, old and new dollhouses and their petite accessories. Nice handmade quilts (new). Mrs. Greenwood repairs and restores antique dolls.

A/C—PM. Affordable. Consignments. Authentication.

Prop. Virginia Greenwood   609–234–5095

Vincentown 08008

BARTHOLDS' ANTIQUES, 166 Main St.

Hours: Daily 9–6

Nice selection of antique furniture, mostly Victorian, in a friendly shop. General line of fine china, glass, silver; antique dolls and old linens. Est. 1945.

A/C—PM. Affordable. Consignments. Authentication when possible.

Prop. H. Barthold   609–859–3339

CASSIDY'S CORNER, Junction of Rts. 38 and 206. *Also see* Repair and Restoration listing.

Hours: Mon., Tues. 10–5; Wed. thru Sun. 9–5; Fri. 'til 8

Antique and collectible furniture from the 1800s to the 1930s and appropriate decorative accessories. Mr. Bohn wholesales to dealers and is a member of the Burlington County Antique Dealers Assoc. Resilvering of mirrors a service.

A/C—PM. Affordable.

Prop. Gene Bohn   609–261–2230

CREEKSIDE ANTIQUES, Rt. 206 at Retreat Rd.

Hours: Thurs., Fri., Sat. 11–4

Two rooms filled with a general line of glass, china, decorative accessories, small pieces of furniture, some primitives. Member Burlington County Antique Dealers Assoc.

A/C—PM. Affordable.

Prop. Sheila McMillan   No phone

MOORE'S PLACE ANTIQUES, Rt. 206, northbound.

Hours: Mon. thru Fri. 9–9; Sat. 9–6; Sun. 9–5

Country and oak furniture, kerosene lamps, pitchers and bowls, washstands, clocks, and old rockers in a busy modern-day general store. The Moores are members of the Burlington County Antique Dealers Assoc.

A/C—PM. Affordable.

Prop. William and Ann Moore   609–859–2662

PUMP HOUSE ANTIQUES, Newbold Rd.

Hours: Mon. thru Sat. 9–5

Early American glass a specialty in this wholesale shop; general line of fine china, country furniture, duck decoys. The Gager family has long been associated with glass, forefather Lester Gager having been one of the founders of the Tansboro Glass Works, started about 1848. Josephine Gager is a charter member of the Burlington County Antique Dealers Assoc. and does estate appraisals.

A/C—Prices not marked. Wide range. Authentication.

Prop. Josephine Gager   609–463–3120

SIMONS ANTIQUES, Hilliard Bridge Rd.

Hours: Sat. & Sun. 11–5; or by appt.

Large collection of Heisey glass and "all around antiques," including oak furniture, art glass, Depression glass, carnival glass. Member Burlington County Antique Dealers Assoc. and Delaware Valley Antique Dealers Assoc.

A/C—PM. Affordable. Authentication.

Prop. Paul C. Simons   609–463–3360

Chinese export porcelain displayed on the butterfly shelves of an early built-in corner cupboard with cathedral doors. At an estate "open house" prior to auction. *Courtesy Elwood Heller, Lebanon. Photo: Ed Schuetz*

Ocean County

Barnegat 08005

HERITAGE HOUSE ANTIQUES, 409 Main St. (Rt. 9). *Also see* Repair and Restoration listing.

Hours: Sat. & Sun. 11–5

Victorian and oak furniture, some primitives, "odd pieces," bric-a-brac, in a big old carriage house. Furniture repaired and restored.

A/C—PM. Affordable. Authentication.

Prop. Henry Tawyea   No phone

WHITE ELEPHANT SHOP, P. O. Box 231, Rt. 9.

Hours: Mon. thru Sat. 10–5

Two rooms of a 200-year-old house devoted to small pieces of furniture, china, glass, some silver, brass, picture frames, "a little bit of everything."

A/C—PM. Affordable.

Prop. George Petersen, Jr.   609–698–3136

YELLOW BIRD, Rt. 9.

Hours: Sat. & Sun. 10–5; or by appt.

Specializing in Victorian furniture; some primitives, decorative accessories, glass, and lamps. Member Antique Dealers Assoc. of Ocean County.

A/C—PM. Affordable.

Prop. Pat Kuryllo   609–698–3501

Barnegat Light 08006

BEACON ANTIQUES, 8th St. at Central (main st.).

Hours: May 31–June 16: Sat. & Sun. 12–9; June 17–Sept. 15: 7 days 10–10

Fine Oriental and European porcelains, oil paintings, Oriental silks, and American period furniture are featured in a selective shop. Associated with the Calvert Gallery, Washington, D.C. Appraisals.

A—PM. Wide range. Consignments. Authentication.

Prop. Peter Colasante, Jesse Plumley   609–494–7288

LIGHTHOUSE ANTIQUES, 5th St. and Broadway (forks off Central).

Hours: Summer season (June–Sept.): Daily 10–10; off-season: Sat. & Sun. 10–4, except Jan., Feb., Mar.

Original old period prints, maps and engravings from England are a unique specialty (Mr. Connolly is exclusive representative in this country for an English family). Selective English and American formal furniture, fine English porcelains, Oriental accessories, rugs, antique silver. Appraisals. Member American Historical Print Soc.

A—PM. Selective/Serious. Consignments. Authentication.

Prop. Arthur Connolly   609–494–3954

THE RUDDER, 7th and Broadway (forks off Central).

Hours: Summer season (July 4–Labor Day): Daily 10–9; off-season: Sat. 10–5; Sun. 10–3; closed in winter

Early American furniture, trunks, and a general line of fine china and glass. Many new gift items in "The Gift Shop of Discriminating Originals."

A/C—PM. Affordable. Authentication.

Prop. A. M. Dolan   609–494–6462

THE SAMPLER OF BARNEGAT LIGHT, 709 Broadway (forks off Central). *Also see* Repair and Restoration listing.

Hours: Summer season (June–Sept.): Tues. thru Sun. 10–10; off-season: Sat. & Sun. 10–4

A combination gift and antique shop with some primitive and Victorian furniture, chandeliers, and old glass. Lots of calico by the yard and an unusual collection of handcrafted designer pillows. Furniture repair, refinishing, and restoring.

A/C—PM. Affordable. Authentication.

Prop. Stanley and Marilyn Wasilewski   609–494–3493

SEAMAN'S LANDING, 4th and Broadway (forks off Central).

Hours: Summer season (June–Sept.): Daily 10–10; off-season: Sat. & Sun. 10–5; closed in winter

Specializing in early 1900s English and American washstands, oak dressers; general line of china and glass. Many new handcrafted gift items and a gourmet gallery.

A/C—PM. Affordable. Authentication when possible.

Prop. Anne S. Higgins   609–494–1247

Bay Head 08742

THE BAREFOOT PEDDLER, 512 Main Ave. (Rt. 35).

Hours: By appt.

Nice selection of Early American country furniture, some Victorian pieces, early lamps and accessories.

A/Some collectibles—PM. Affordable.

Prop. Anne G. Schenck   201–899–8458 (bus.)
                                                    892–0557 (res.)

EARLY ATTIC, 414 Lake Ave. (off Rt. 35).

Hours: Summer season (June-Sept.): Daily except Tues. 10–5; or by appt.

A charming shop overlooking Twilight Lake has three rooms of country and Victorian furniture, lamps, silver, china and glass, paintings and prints. House sales conducted.

A/C—PM. Affordable. Consignments. Authentication.

Prop. Greta Morgan   201–892–7018

MARIE LISTER ANTIQUES, 509 Main Ave. (Rt. 35).

Hours: Daily 10–4; or by appt.

Select collection of American beleek, early Lenox, antique silver, fine glassware, some Victorian furniture. Appraisal service. Member Atlantic Seaboard Dealers Assoc. and Delaware Valley Antique Dealers Assoc.

A/Some collectibles—PM. Wide range. Authentication.

Prop. Marie Lister   201–295–4032

MEMORY SHOPPE, 72 Bridge Ave.

Hours: Daily 11–4

Small pieces of period furniture, mirrors, clocks, cut glass, fine china, and sterling in an enclosed mini-mall of browsable shops.

A/C—PM. Affordable. Authentication when possible.

Prop. Leona Apostileris   201–295–4333

FRED B. NADLER ANTIQUES, INC., 56 Mount St.

Hours: By appt.

Select collection of Chinese export porcelain and 18th-century English and American furniture. Mr. Nadler is a member of the Art and Antique Dealers Assoc. of America.

A—PM. Selective/Serious collectors.

Prop. Fred B. Nadler   201–295–2055

TURN OF THE CENTURY, 74 Bridge Ave.

Hours: Tues. thru Sun. 11–5

Small pieces of furniture, general line of china and glass, old and new jewelry, mirrors, decorative accessories. "Antiques, Not So Antiques, Gifts." Note the Art Deco, Art Nouveau, and Victorian-type greeting cards in the rear of the shop. Estate sales, appraisals.

A/C—PM. Affordable. Consignments. Authentication.

Prop. Marianne I. Short   201–892–0606

Bayville 08721

THE CLARKS, Hickory Lane. *Also see* Repair and Restoration listing.

Hours: Tues. thru Sun. 10–5

Specializing in oak furniture, decoys, old bottles, Depression glass. Appraisals, liquidations. The Clarks also repair and refinish furniture.

A/C—Some prices marked. Affordable. Consignments. Authentication.

Prop. Ann and Sam Clark   201–269–5181

HANDS OF TIME, 600 Rt. 9 (next to garden center).

Hours: By chance

HANDS OF TIME *continued*

Antique and collectible china, glass, old jewelry, kerosene lamps, some small pieces of furniture.

A/C—PM. Affordable. Authentication.

Prop. D. Z. Enterprises   201–269–1145

Beach Haven Crest 08008

CAPP'S CORNER, Blvd. at Massachusetts Ave. *Also see* Repair and Restoration listing.

Hours: Summer season (June–Sept.): Daily 11–9; off-season: By appt.

Fine antique gold jewelry, porcelain-head dolls, dollhouses and their tiny furnishings, old mechanical toys, Edison reproducing machines, music machines, signed glass, and chandeliers in a spacious and browsable shop. Appraisals. Repair services for antique dolls and mechanical toys.

Λ—PM. Wide range. Consignments. Authentication when possible.

Prop. Irene Lona Capp   609–494–5843

HOUSE OF 7 WONDERS, 7600 Blvd.

Hours: Summer season (June–Sept.): Daily 8–11; off-season (Apr., May; Oct.–Dec.): Sat. & Sun. 8–7

Period furniture from the 1850s on, antique and collectible china, porcelains, and Oriental rugs are specialties. The Arakelians give appraisals and are members of the Post Card Club of New Jersey.

A/C—PM. Affordable. Authentication.

Prop. John and Lucy Arakelian   609–494–9673

THE ROYAL PACK RAT, 7712 Long Beach Blvd.

Hours: Summer season (June–Sept.): Daily 10–10

Interesting collection of original paintings, old and new, from Long Beach Island; general line of fine china and glass, some Victorian furniture, in a combination antique and gift shop.

A/C—PM. Affordable. Authentication when possible.

Prop. Mila B. Smyth   609–494–5209

WIZARD OF ODDS, Culver Ave. and Long Beach Blvd. *Also see* Repair and Restoration listing.

Hours: Summer season (June–Sept.) : Daily 11–10; off-season: Sat. & Sun. 11–10

"Antiques and Such" fill six rooms of a spacious shop—period furniture, stained glass, fine china, antique clothing, jewelry, decorative accessories. A longtime dealer, Mr. Plunkett gives appraisals and is a member of the Nat'l. Historic Trust, the Victorian Soc. of America, and the Nat'l. Music Box Soc. Furniture refinishing, caning and rushing.

A/C—PM. Wide range. Authentication.

Prop. Richard Plunkett   609–296–9373

Beach Haven Gardens 08008

THE ATTIC, 2613 Bay Ave.

Hours: Summer season (June–Sept.) : Daily 10–5

Tastefully arranged shop featuring "interesting old things that are affordable," including small pieces of oak furniture, fine china, glass, decorative accessories. An author of children's books, Mrs. Dahlstedt's latest, Shadow of the Lighthouse, *tells the story of Long Beach Island in the 1870s.*

A/C—PM. Affordable. Consignments. Authentication.

Prop. Marden and Richard Dahlstedt   609–492–1064

Beachwood 08722

COLLECTORS CORNER, 300 Barnegat Blvd. *Also see* Repair and Restoration listing.

Hours: Sat. & Sun. 9–5

General line of furniture, fine china, cut glass, bronzes, nautical antiques. The Schildkrauts are members of the Antique Dealers Assoc. of Ocean County. Repair and restoration of furniture a service.

A/C—PM. Affordable. Authentication.

Prop. Adele and Joseph Schildkraut   201–240–0487

Brick Town 08723

AAA ANTIQUES, 2715 Old Hooper Ave. (Rt. 70).
Hours: Daily 9:30–6
Two floors of a sizable building filled with contents of estates—antique and used furniture, china, glass, old tools, bric-a-brac. Appraisal service.
A/C—PM. Wide range. Authentication.
Prop. Perry and Al Newhaus   201–477–2277

ANTHONY'S ORIENTAL RUGS, Brick Town. *Also see* Repair and Restoration listing.
Hours: By appt.
Antique and used Oriental rugs and a selection of new ones. Cleaning and repairing of Orientals.
A/C—Prices not marked. Wide range. Consignments.
Prop. Anthony Fahmie   201–477–5869

PINE COTTAGE, 525 Glenwood Ave.
Hours: By appt.
"Things old and new"—early iron, wood, glass and china, bric-a-brac, small pieces of furniture.
A/C—PM. Affordable.
Prop. Josephine Morrissey   201–477–1245

Forked River 08731

L & L ANTIQUE TRADERS, 208 Rt. 9. *Also see* Repair and Restoration listing.
Hours: Daily except Tues. 10–5
Mostly oak furniture, wicker, old lamps, prints, mirrors, collectible bottles, china and glassware. Hand-stripping and refinishing of furniture, antique restoration. "Contents of homes and estates bought by the piece or by the house."
A/C—PM. Affordable. Authentication when possible.
Prop. Leonard Parrino   201–269–5769

Harvey Cedars 08006

THE BROKEN OAR, Long Beach Blvd. and 78th St.

Hours: Summer season (June–Sept.): Daily 9–5; off-season: Sat. & Sun. 9–5; or by appt.

All kinds of nautical and railroad items predominate. Tables made from ship hatch covers, railroad memorabilia from lines that have been discontinued, along with primitive and oak furniture, copper pieces, antique tools.

A/C—PM. Wide range. Consignments. Authentication.

Prop. Gilbert Zerbe   609–494–9000

Haven Beach 08008

SNOOPER'S CORNER, 11301 Long Beach Blvd.

Hours: Summer season (June–Sept.): Daily 10–10; off-season: Mon. thru Fri. 12–3; Sat. & Sun. 11–5

An old-time atmosphere in a shop specializing in country and general store items, old kitchen utensils, pine and oak furniture. Nice selection of homemade original patchwork quilts (new), placemats, door stops, pillows.

A/C—PM. Affordable. Authentication.

Prop. Babe Crane   609–492–4032

Lakewood 08701

BLOSSOM ANTIQUES, 200 Clifton Ave. (main st. of town).

Hours: Tues. thru Sat. 9:30–5:30; Nov. 15–Dec. 24: Daily 9:30–5:30

Spacious corner shop with a large selection of antique jewelry, formal American and European furniture, bronzes, fine china, cut glass, Oriental objets d'art. Mrs. Fried designs original pieces of jewelry in gold and silver, gives appraisals, and is a member of the Antique Appraisers Assoc. of America.

A—PM. Selective. Authentication.

Prop. Blossom Fried   201–364–4414

PAULINE C. FERBER ANTIQUES, 1225 Madison Ave.

Hours: By appt.

Sandwich glass, pattern glass, and a general line of fine china.

A/Some collectibles—PM. Affordable.

Prop. Pauline C. Ferber   201–363–1544

LANES MILL ANTIQUES, 1985 Lanes Mill Rd.

Hours: By appt.

"Items of the China trade"—Chinese export porcelain, Canton; paintings and prints in a selective shop. Appraisals for courts and insurance purposes.

A—PM. Selective. Authentication.

Prop. Edith Reilly   201–363–2675

WHAT NOT ANTIQUES, 333 Case Rd.

Hours: By appt.

Specializing in antique and estate jewelry and art glass; a nice selection of antique pocket watches.

A/C—Most prices marked. Consignments. Authentication when possible.

Prop. Joe and Tina Vaccaro   201–364–3155

Loveladies 08008

LOVELADIES GIFTS, OLD AND NEW, Long Beach Blvd. (in the old Coast Guard Station).

Hours: Summer season (June–Sept.): 6 days 10–9; Sun. 10–5; off-season (end of Sept.–Christmas): Sat. & Sun. 10–4; closed in winter

An old Long Beach Island Coast Guard Station, restored in 1952, is the nautical setting for a combined gift and antique shop. Victorian furniture, pressed glass, fine china, mixed in with lots of new gift items. A separate candle room and Christmas shop.

A/C—PM. Affordable. Authentication when possible.

Prop. H. W. Shaner   609–494–2759

Manchester Twp. (Lakehurst P. O. 08733)

GOOD OLD TIMES SHOP, Rt. 571 (700 feet west of Hwy. 70).

Hours: Sat. & Sun. 10–5

Nice selection of primitive, colonial, and Victorian furniture; glass of all types. The Collards buy contents of homes as well as stamps and coins. Appraisal service.

A/C—Most prices marked. Wide range. Authentication if requested.

Prop. Frank and Sally Collard   201–657–5853

New Egypt 08533

THE BARRACKS, 59 Brindletown Rd. (¼ mi. off Main St.). *Also see* Repair and Restoration listing.

Hours: Mon. thru Fri. 10–5; Sat. & Sun. 10–7

Turn-of-the-century furniture a specialty. General line of collectible glass, china, bric-a-brac; some antique jewelry. Hand-refinishing of furniture.

A/C—PM. Affordable. Authentication when possible.

Prop. Carol Reed   609–758–8384

BREAD, WINE & CO., New Egypt Market, Rt. 537 (2 mi. west of Rt. 539).

Hours: Sun. 9–4

Collections of autographs, old deeds, old and rare books, all kinds of "collectible paper."

C/A (some)—PM. Affordable.

Prop. Mel Finn   609–758–2082

COLLECTOR'S CORNER, Bldg. 12W, New Egypt Market, Rt. 537 (2 mi. west of Rt. 539).

Hours: Wed., Sun. 9–4

American primitive furniture, blanket chests, general line of china, glass, bric-a-brac, in a browsable shop inside the bustling Farmer's Market. Appraisals.

A/C—PM. Affordable. Some consignments. Authentication.

Prop. Harold E. Simon   609–758–2082

THE HOBBY HORSE, Bldg. 27, New Egypt Market, Rt. 537 (2 mi. west of Rt. 539).

Hours: Wed., Sun. 9–4; or by appt.

Mostly primitives, early tools, tool boxes, chests, early lamps, chandeliers, some silver pieces, curios and collectibles. Mr. Davis is editor of The Jersey Devil, *a newspaper "about marketeers, for marketeers, by marketeers," published at the New Egypt Market. General appraisals and estate appraisals are services.*

A/C—PM. Affordable. Consignment only on important pieces. Authentication when possible.

Prop. Fritz Davis   609–758–2082

BILL HORNE, Bldgs. 37 and 38, New Egypt Market, Rt. 537 (2 mi. west of Rt. 539).

Hours: Wed., Sun. 9–4

Predominantly furniture, old and not so old—early country pieces, Victorian, used. China, glass, bric-a-brac, decorative items.

A/C—PM. Affordable. Consignments.

Prop. Bill Horne   609–758–2082

KEVIN McMAHON, Bldg. 17, New Egypt Market, Rt. 537 (2 mi. west of Rt. 539).

Hours: Wed., Sun. 9–4; or by appt.

General collection of old glass, old country store items, advertising tins, small pieces of furniture, shown at the market. Nineteenth-century paintings and prints by appointment.

A/C—PM. Affordable. Consignments.

Prop. Kevin McMahon   609–654–5949

SNOOPER'S COOP, 35 Lakewood Rd. (Rt. 528). *Also see* Repair and Restoration listing.

Hours: Daily 7–5

Turn-of-the-century and oak furniture predominate, but there are some nice pieces of early and primitive. "Homesick antiques bought and sold." Repair and restoration of antique furniture.

A/C—PM. Affordable. Authentication when possible.

Prop. C. Edward Tantum   609–758–2673

Pine Beach 08741

NEWTON & SON ANTIQUES, 203 Avon Rd.

Hours: By appt.

All kinds of marine antiques, American primitives, including wood carvings and tools, children's items. Also located in Wiscasset and Owls Head, Maine.

A/Some collectibles—PM. Wide range. Authentication when possible.

Prop. Dayton Newton   201–349–4675

Point Pleasant 08742

GLORIA P. FRAZEE, 626 Ocean Rd. (Rt. 9). *Also see* Auctioneers listing.

Hours: Mon. thru Sat. 9–5

Eighteenth-century country and period furniture, oil paintings, coin silver, clocks, jewelry, decorative accessories, in a spacious building where an auction is held every Friday evening at 8 p.m. Ms. Frazee is an auctioneer and a member of the New Jersey and the National Societies of Auctioneers. Appraisal service.

A/C—PM. Wide range. Authentication.

Prop. Gloria P. Frazee   201–892–2217

OLD BARN ANTIQUES, 2115 Herbertsville Rd. (Spur Rt. 549).

Hours: Daily 11–6

Pewter, bronzes, Early American glass, Wedgwood, Meissen, Limoges, porcelains, brass, copper, silver, some oil paintings, cloisonné, and a general line of furniture shown by a long-experienced dealer. Also some Art Deco, Art Nouveau, Venetian, and Bohemian glass.

A/C—Most prices marked; some coded. Wide range. Consignments. Authentication when possible.

Prop. Cecil Benet   201–899–1163

Point Pleasant Beach 08742

RALPH R. FRAME, 908 Richmond Ave. (Rt. 35 south).

Hours: By appt.

Selective shop specializing in "antiques, books, prints, paintings." Art pottery, period furniture, some collectibles. Appraisal service; house sales conducted.

A/C—PM. Selective. Authentication.

Prop. Ralph R. Frame   201–892–1540

Ship Bottom 08006

THE SHIP'S GRAVEYARD, 16th and Long Beach Blvd.

Hours: Sat. & Sun. 10–5

Two floors of authentic marine antiques—old bulkhead lamps, sextants, ships'

THE SHIP'S GRAVEYARD *continued*

wheels, hatch covers, cabin door locks, cargo blocks. Nautical furniture made from hatch covers.

A/C—PM. Affordable. Authentication.

Prop. Victor Marine   609–494–5667

South Toms River 08753

THE FREIGHT STATION, Rt. 166 and Flint Rd. *Also see* Repair and Restoration listing.

Hours: Through June 1978: Sat. & Sun. 11–5; after June 1978: Daily 11–5

Right on the tracks of an old freight station are a caboose and railroad car filled with nautical artifacts, primitives, early glass, antique dolls. New hand-carved signs and custom-made lamps. Brass polishing, furniture restored and refinished, lamps repaired. The Duriks are members of the Ocean County Antique Dealers Assoc.

A/C—PM. Wide range. Consignments. Authentication when possible.

Prop. Mr. & Mrs. Basil Durik   201–349–0328
                                                          477–3196

SHANTY HOUSE ANTIQUES, 340 Atlantic City Blvd. (Rt. 166).

Hours: Daily 9–5. Closed Wed., Thurs.

"Anything that's old"—period furniture, fine china, silver, bronzes, cut glass, oil paintings, Americana, porcelains, chandeliers. Member Ocean County Antique Dealers Assoc.

A/C—PM. Affordable. Authentication when possible.

Prop. Ann Surgent   201–341–1243

Toms River 08753

THE BENNETTS ANTIQUES, Toms River.

Hours: By appt.

Nice selection of old weathervanes, early tools, antique jewelry, and silver along with fine country and period furniture. The Bennetts are members of the Pennsylvania Antique Dealers Assoc. and do appraisals.

A—PM. Selective. Authentication when possible.

Prop. Betsy Bennett   201–349–5114

MARGARET M. BOOSMAN ANTIQUES, 251 Main St. (at Main Street Antiques).

Hours: Mon., Wed., Fri. 10–4; Sat. 10–2

Antique and collectible china and glass, some furniture and paintings. "Antiques bought and sold." Appraisal service. Member Ocean County Antique Dealers Assoc.

A/C—PM. Affordable. Authentication.

Prop. Margaret M. Boosman   201–349–5764 (bus.)
                                                   597–1143 (res.)

LINDA'S DOLL REPAIR, 1209 Lakewood Rd. (Rt. 166, inside Pettis Clock Shop). *Also see* Repair and Restoration listing.

Hours: Mon. thru Sat. 10–6

Specializing in antique dolls of all kinds and the complete repair and restoration of old dolls.

A/C—PM. Affordable. Consignments. Authentication.

Prop. Linda Clayton   201–349–3311 (bus.)
                                                   341–3905 (res.)

MAIN STREET ANTIQUES, 251 Main St.

Hours: Mon. thru Thurs. 8–10 P.M., Sat. 2–5

Victorian and oak furniture, some period pieces, fine china, glass, antique dolls, paintings, in a large shop with a warehouse in back. "Anything that's old and collectible." Estates purchased and appraised.

A/C—PM. Affordable. Authentication.

Prop. M. Grassia, R. Clayton   201–349–5764 (bus.)
                                                   244–5186 (res.)

THE OAK BARN, 1332 Lakewood Rd. (Rt. 9).

Hours: Tues. thru Sun. 10–5

Furniture of all kinds, especially oak, but some primitive and period pieces in an airy two-room shop.

A/C—PM. Affordable. Occasional consignment. Authentication.

Prop. Barbara Steel   201–341–1975

RICHARDS ANTIQUES, 1830 Lakewood Rd. (Rt. 9).

Hours: Daily 12–5; or by appt.

Cut glass a specialty; also fine china, Staffordshire, antique jewelry, primitives, collectibles. Member Ocean County Antique Dealers Assoc.

A/C—PM. Affordable. Authentication when possible.

Prop. Ruth Richards   201–341–0385

SARAH'S ANTIQUES, 1435 Rt. 9. *Also see* Repair and Restoration listing.

Hours: Tues. thru Sun. 1–5

A general line of furniture, though Victorian predominates; fine china and glass, Victorian jewelry, old clocks. Furniture refinishing specialists.

A/C—PM. Affordable. Consignments. Authentication.

Prop. Sarah Howe   201–244–9841

Tuckerton 08087

BAYBERRY ANTIQUES, 324 East Main St. (Rt. 9). *Also see* Repair and Restoration listing.

Hours: Daily 9–9

Victorian and oak furniture, old trunks, in a small shop to the rear of the main house. Refinishing and restoring of old furniture.

A/C—PM. Affordable. Occasional consignment. Authentication.

Prop. Barry White   609–296–8669

WIZARD OF ODDS, Rt. 9, southbound (also at Beach Haven Crest).

Hours: Sat. & Sun. 11–6; or by appt.

Victorian furniture and appropriate decorative accessories in this second "Wizard of Odds" shop (the original is in Beach Haven Crest). Mr. Plunkett has been a dealer for twenty-five years, gives appraisals, and is a member of the Nat'l. Historic Trust, the Victorian Soc. of America, the Nat'l. Music Box Soc.

A—PM. Wide range. Authentication.

Prop. Richard Plunkett   609–296–9373

Waretown 08758

DIGNIFIED JUNK AND HOMESICK ANTIQUES, Birdsall Rd. (off Rt. 9).

Hours: By chance or appt.

"Varied and interesting collectibles"—thousands of old post cards, nice duck decoys, china, glass, tools, old uniforms, antique clothes, pottery, and crocks in a big old barn. A collector for thirty-five years, Mrs. Rieder is a member of the Ocean County Antique Dealers Assoc.

C/A (some)—PM. Affordable. Authentication when possible.

Prop. Martha Mitchell Rieder   609–693–3659

West Creek 08092

COX'S GENERAL STORE, Rt. 9, southbound.

Hours: Summer season (June–Sept.): Sat. & Sun. 10–5; off-season: By chance or appt.

An old-time general store retains its atmosphere with a large selection of oyster plates, good old pressed glass, Empire washstands, antique dolls, silver, porcelains, pin trays, and country bric-a-brac. Estate sales conducted. Member Ocean County Antique Dealers Assoc.

A/C—PM. Affordable. Consignments. Authentication when possible.

Prop. Ron and Betty Thomas   609–296–8800

PEACEABLE KINGDOM, Rt. 9 at Willets Ave.

Hours: Sat. & Sun. 11–6; or by appt.

Fine selection of duck and goose decoys, including Shourds, at the home of a knowledgeable decoy artisan who has himself won first prize for a confidence decoy in the Ward Foundation World Championship Decoy Competition in Salisbury, Md., April 1977. If you get beyond "folk art at its finest," there are also daguerreotypes, china, glass, country things. Mr. Daley is a member of the Ocean County Antique Dealers Assoc. and does appraisals.

A/C—PM (except on decoys). Affordable. Consignments. Authentication when possible.

Prop. Robert Daley   609–296–3292

WEST CREEK TRADING POST, Rt. 9. *Also see* Repair and Restoration listing.
Hours: Summer season (June–Sept.): Daily 10–5; off-season: Fri. thru Mon. 1–5

Antique clocks bought and sold in a shop that also specializes in antique clock repair. Early lighting devices, including kerosene lamps and chandeliers, and a general line of glassware. Est. 1960. Member Nat'l. Assoc. of Watch & Clock Collectors.

A/C—PM. Affordable. Authentication.

Prop. Charles Rubina   609–296–2555

Framed needlework family record worked by 12-year-old Harriet N. Potter, New Providence, 1843; traced to New Jersey. Potter-Pettit family birth and marriage dates embroidered in wool on linen; grape and leafy vine border in purple, brown, and green. Jotham Potter served in the Militia during the Revolution, was a justice of the peace, and an elder in the Presbyterian Church. *Courtesy Sotheby Parke Bernet Inc., New York*

Queen Anne walnut high chest of drawers with Spanish feet. Pennsylvania or New Jersey, ca. 1750. Ht. 73 in., w. 41½ in., depth 22¼ in. *Courtesy H. & R. Sandor, Inc., New Hope*

Atlantic County

Atlantic City 08401

ABEL'S ANTIQUES, 1833 Boardwalk.

Hours: Summer season (June–Sept.): Daily 10–11; off-season: Daily 10–6

Large Boardwalk shop at the Marlborough-Blenheim Hotel specializes in antique Wedgwood, Royal Worcester, Tiffany, antique silver and jewelry. Many new gift items and collectibles imported from Europe, fine porcelains, wall decorations, decorative pieces. Appraisals of porcelains. Member Wedgwood Soc. of Philadelphia.

A/C—PM. Selective. Authentication.

Prop. William Abel   609–344–6826

DAVID LAWRENCE BAUMAN BOOKS AND ANTIQUES, 14 S. La Clede Pl.

Hours: By appt.

Rare and out-of-print books, paintings and bronzes, some antique furniture, gold and silver pieces. Mr. Bauman is a registered appraiser.

A/C—PM. Wide range. Authentication when possible.

Prop. David Lawrence Bauman   609–344–0763

EDMONDO'S ANTIQUES, 2615 Pacific Ave. (bet. Texas and California Aves.).

Hours: Daily 11–7

"Objects of art, bronzes, collectibles, 'the unusual.' " Gallé, Steuben, art glass, some Orientalia. A search service for collectors; mail-order service.

A/C—PM. Wide range. Occasional consignment. Authentication.

Prop. Edmondo A. Crimi   609–345–9401

HADDON HALL ANTIQUES, Hotel Haddon Hall, N. Carolina and Beach Aves.

Hours: Daily 10–5

Small pieces of formal furniture, Chinese export porcelain, antique silver, cut glass, decorative pieces, in a selective shop. Appraisals. The Carpenters are members of the Atlantic County Antique Collectors Club and the New Jersey Historical Soc.

A—PM. Selective. Authentication.

Prop. Joseph and Beatrice Carpenter   609–344–3003

PRINCETON ANTIQUES, 2917 Atlantic Ave. (main business st.).

Hours: By appt.

Tiffany, 19th- and 20th-century paintings, rare and out-of-print books, crowd two adjoining shops. A stock of over 150,000 books plus a research library of 12,000 volumes aid in a special service—locating rare books for private collectors, universities, and corporations. A third-generation antiques dealer, Mr. Ruffolo is a member of the American Soc. of Appraisers.

A/C—Prices not marked. Wide range. Consignments. Authentication.

Prop. Robert E. Ruffolo II   609–344–1943

Bargaintown (Linwood P. O. 08221)

MILL POND ANTIQUES, Central Ave. at Bargaintown Mill Pond.

Hours: Better to phone ahead

Antiques and collectibles in a charming shop overlooking an old mill pond. Large iron kettles for colonial fireplaces or decorative effect, fine china and glass, good selection of duck decoys and wild-fowl carvings.

A/C—PM. Affordable. Authentication when possible.

Prop. Kate Dilks   609–927–4208

Brigantine 08203

ALADDIN ANTIQUES, Brigantine.

Hours: By appt.

Fine collection of early glass, porcelains, china, jewelry, rare books; selection of formal furniture. Member Wheaton Antique Soc. and the Atlantic County Antique Collectors Club. Appraisal service.

A/C—PM. Wide range. Authentication when possible.

Prop. Andy Zipfel, Harry Marder   609–266–8516
                                                    266–7613

Buena 08310

JONES ANTIQUES, Oak Rd. and Harding Hwy. (opp. Wilmed Glass Co.). *Also see* Repair and Restoration listing.

Hours: Tues. thru Sun. 11–5

Ample space in an old airport hangar for a large collection of furniture, predominantly oak, some wicker; antique lamps of all kinds, decorative accessories. New dollhouses and their diminutive furnishings. Repair and restoration of antique furniture done on premises by Mr. Jones.

A/C—PM. Affordable. Authentication when possible.

Prop. Marie Jones   609–697–0325

English Creek 08330

DEAD HORSE RUN ANTIQUES, Somers Point-Mays Landing Rd. (Rt. 559; 3 mi. east of Gravelly Run). *Also see* Repair and Restoration listing.

Hours: Wed. thru Sun. 10–4

A general line of furniture—all periods—in a spacious shop. Specialists in furniture stripping, refinishing, restoration. Member Bayshore Antique Dealers Guild.

A/Some collectibles—PM. Wide range.

Prop. Susan and John Spurlock   609–927–9173

Hammonton 08037

RAY & ROBERT BANFORD, Box 466, R. D. 6.

Hours: By appt.

Specialists in antique and collectible paperweights and art glass. Glass artists, the Banfords make and sell contemporary paperweights. Appraisals of paperweights; buying for museums.

A/C—PM. Wide range. Authentication.

Prop. Ray and Robert Banford   609–561–7575

MARY'S ANTIQUE SHOP, 629 S. White Horse Pike (Rt. 30; across from Blue Lake Inn).

Hours: Daily 9–5; eves. by appt.

Over 1,000 old bottles on display in a spacious barracks. All kinds of preserving jars, including elderly Mason. Some Early American furniture.

A/C—Some prices marked. Affordable. Occasional consignment.

Mgr. Joseph Mazza, Jr.   609–561–1060

Linwood 08221

COLLECTORS' KORNER ANTIQUES, 208 New Rd. (Rt. 9; across from Central Square Shopping Center). *Also see* Repair and Restoration listing.

Hours: Wed., Thurs., Sat., Sun. 1–4; or by appt.

Country furniture, Victorian, some oak, in a nicely arranged shop. Oriental pieces, cloissoné, china, cut glass, stained glass, copper and brass items, baskets, primitive tools, and kitchen utensils. New Tiffany-type lamps. Services include lamp repair, burnishing, polishing of pewter and silver.

A/C—PM. Affordable. Consignments. Authentication.

Prop. Dorothy Rogowski   609–399–7542

Nesco (Hammonton P. O. 08037)

PHILLIP A. GARUFFI, Pleasant Mills Rd. (Rt. 542; bet. Hammonton and Batsto). *Also see* Auctioneers listing.

Hours: Sat. & Sun. 1–5

Everything from estate sales—furniture of all kinds, glassware, china, lamps,

PHILLIP A. GARUFFI *continued*

*accessories, bric-a-brac. Mr. Garuffi is an auctioneer and conducts auctions every
other Sunday from 3–6 from Nov. to April; every other Monday from 7–10 in
summer.*

A/C—Prices not marked. Wide range.

Prop. Phillip A. Garuffi   609–561–4514

Northfield 08225

JOHNSON'S CLOCK SHOP, 1500 New Rd. (Rt. 9). *Also see* Repair and
Restoration listing.

Hours: Daily 9–5:30

*Antique and new grandfather, mantel, and wall clocks in a selective shop that
also carries a general line of furniture. A "grandfather clock specialist," Mr.
Johnson repairs and restores clocks of all kinds.*

A/C—PM. Wide range. Consignments. Authentication.

Prop. C. Emerson Johnson   609–645–1745

Pleasant Mills (Hammonton P. O. 08037)

BENT CREEK VILLAGE, Rt. 542 (1 mi. south of Batsto).

Hours: Sat. & Sun. 10:30–5:30; or by appt.

*Six clustered shops in a country setting in the pines. A general antique shop with
country furniture; old kitchen equipment, glass, china, primitives in another;
a nautical shop with ships' lights, anchors, wheels; an old bottle shop; lots of
handcrafted decoys in their own place; and a home recreation room shop with
breweriana, tins, and advertising items. Everything from early country to
nostalgia. Appraisal service.*

A/C—PM. Wide range. Authentication.

Prop. Lawrence Ermilio   609–561–4070

Scullville 08330

GREAT EXPECTATIONS, R. D. 1, Box 270, Somers Pt.-Mays Landing Rd.
(Rt. 559).

Hours: Daily 10–6; or by appt.

GREAT EXPECTATIONS *continued*

Fine old home with three rooms of tastefully arranged period furniture, decorative pieces, Staffordshire, flow blue, ironstone, stained glass, quality silver and fine china. Some collectible Depression glass and old toys. An interior designer, Mr. Kelly will do some refinishing and reupholstering through decorators. Member Atlantic County Antique Collectors Club and the Atlantic County Historical Soc.

A/Some collectibles—PM. Selective. Consignments. Authentication when possible.

Prop. Jack and Vicki Kelly   609–927–1225

Smithville 08201

CAPTAIN'S CHEST ANTIQUES, 1478 New York Rd. (Rt. 9). *Also see* Repair and Restoration listing.

Hours: Daily 10–5

An early 1700s house just outside the historic Smithville restoration shows a fine selection of Early American furniture, primitives, appropriate decorative pieces, early china and glass. Naturalists will be interested in the large honey locust tree in front, probably one of the oldest in New Jersey. Mrs. Lingelbach is a member of the Atlantic County Antique Collectors Club. Antique furniture refinished and repaired by Gordon Schell.

A/Some collectibles—PM. Wide range. Authentication when possible.

Prop. Bert Lingelbach, Gordon and Normandie Schell   609–652–1042

Somers Point 08244

DEL ZANE STUDIO, Corner of Atlantic and Groveland Aves.

Hours: Better to phone ahead

Small pieces of elderly furniture, turn-of-the-century washstands, rocking chairs, cut glass, china, silver, and curios in a small, friendly shop. Mrs. Zane does appraisals and is a member of the Bayshore Antique Dealers Guild.

A/C—Prices not marked. Affordable. Authentication.

Prop. Vivian Zane   609–927–5493

Decorated stoneware crock made at Fulper Bro. Co. pottery, Flemington, dated Sept. 27,
1889. *Courtesy The Newark Museum*

HURLEY ANTIQUES, 905 Bay Ave.

Hours: Tues. thru Sun. 11–4

General line of furniture from the late 1800s to the 1940s, antique jewelry, china, cut glass. Antique clothing a specialty, and Mrs. Hurley conducts fashion shows using clothing of bygone times. The Hurleys also manage antiques shows under the name Hurley House.

A/C—PM. Affordable. Consignments. Authentication.

Prop. Tina Hurley   609–927–4317

PLATT'S ANTIQUE ANNEX, MacArthur Blvd. *Also see* Repair and Restoration listing.

Hours: Tues. thru Sun. 12–5

Upholstered Victorian furniture, china, glass, bric-a-brac, some primitives, in an antique shop within a modern retail furniture store. Reupholstering of furniture a service.

A/C—PM. Affordable/Selective.

Prop. David and Celeste Platt   609–927–0372

SOMERS POINT CURIOSITY SHOP, 816 Shore Rd. (Rt. 585).

Hours: Wed. thru Sun. 11–5

Deceivingly small on the outside but large inside and with a warehouse in back, this shop on the main road has Victorian furniture, wicker, a large collection of music boxes, lamps, good cut glass, old china. Appraisals. Member Bayshore Antique Dealers Guild.

A/Some collectibles—PM. Wide range. Authentication.

Prop. John and Sue Conroy   609–927–0805

Ventnor 08406

A & B ANTIQUES, 6504 Ventnor Ave. (main st.).

Hours: Mon. thru Sat. 9–5; or by appt.

Oriental rugs, general line of old furniture, antique jewelry and sterling are specialties. Also fine china, ceramics, paintings, coins, old prints, clocks. Appraisals.

A/C—PM. Wide range. Consignments.

Prop. Adele and Boris Jochebson   609–823–4762

Weekstown (Egg Harbor P. O. 08215)

PINE BARREN PRIMITIVES, Rt. 563 (north of Egg Harbor).

Hours: Sat. & Sun. 10–5; or by appt.

Primitive furniture, old stoves, slipware, and hand-carved decoys in the heart of the Pine Barrens.

A/C—PM. Affordable. Authentication.

Prop. Nelson and Marge Gager   609–965–2516

West Atlantic City 08232

BEACON STREET SHOPS, 510 E. Verona Ave. (Black Horse Pike, Hwys. 322 and 40).

Hours: Sun. thru Thurs. 10–8; Fri., Sat. 10–9

A mixture of old and new in an enormous corner shop that combines antiques with contemporary home accessories. Nice pieces of primitive, Victorian, Empire furniture, along with a candle shop, bath, linen, and lighting shops. Extensive collection of Tiffany-type lamps and hand-crafted leaded shades.

A/C—PM. Wide range. Consignments. Authentication.

Prop. Amelia Arabia   609–646–9382

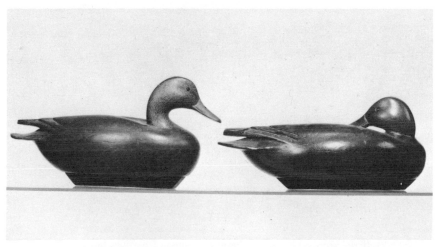

Hand-carved decoys by John McLouglin of Bordentown: (left) graceful Black Duck and (right) fine sleeping Black Duck. *Courtesy Sotheby Parke Bernet, Inc., New York*

Staffordshire dinner serving platter and creamer in tones of purple depicting the residence of the late Richard Jordan of New Jersey. Made by Joseph Heath and Company, ca. 1836–1843. *Courtesy Sotheby Parke Bernet, Inc., New York*

Camden County

Audubon 08106

DÉCOR ANTIQUES, 235 White Horse Pike (Rt. 30).

Hours: Mon. thru Sat. 9–5; or by appt.

Decorative antique accessories attractively displayed. Small pieces of period furniture; mirrors, paintings, china, glass, silver, pewter, antique jewelry, throw rugs, antique dolls. The Krais offer an interior decorating service and are members of the Nat'l. Assoc. of Dealers in Antiques, Inc.

A/Some collectibles—PM. Wide range. Authentication when possible.

Prop. Frank and Jessie Krai   609–547–9055

MULLEN'S ANTIQUE SHOP, 524 White Horse Pike (Rt. 30). *Also see* Repair and Restoration listing.

Hours: Mon. thru Sat. 10–5

Large, bright shop with Oriental porcelains, silks, bronzes, china; period and Victorian furniture, some oak; cloisonné, art glass, including Tiffany and Gallé. Antique clock and watch repair and furniture refinishing services. Member Delaware Valley Antique Dealers Assoc.

A/C—PM. Selective. Consignments "only on exceptionally good pieces." Authentication.

Prop. Marvin and Elaine Mullen   609–546–0507

ONE KINGS HIGHWAY, 1 E. Kings Hwy. (Rt. 41).

Hours: Mon. thru Sat. 10–5:30

Spacious shop carrying a general line of period furniture, fine china, silver, glass.

A/C—PM. Affordable. Authentication.

Prop. Jackie Moon, Neal Page   609–546–0360

Berlin 08009

SALT BOX TREASURES, 11 White Horse Pike. *Also see* Repair and
Restoration listing.

Hours: Thurs. thru Sat. 10–5:30; Sun. 12–5:30

*Interesting groupings of furniture from Early American through Victorian in an
authentically restored saltbox from the mid-1800s. A "little bit of everything" in
china, cut glass, lamps, fireplace equipment. New gift items in the Colonial style.
Electrification of old lamps and a search service are provided.*

A/Some collectibles—PM. Selective. Consignments. Authentication.

Prop. Camille Perotti   609–768–0026

WILMA SAXTON, INC., P. O. Box 218.

Hours: By appt.

*Specializing in china and glass—Heisey, Cambridge, cut and pattern glass;
Royal Doulton; antique jewelry. Mrs. Saxton is a member of the Delaware Valley
Antique Dealers Assoc.*

A/C—PM. Wide range. Authentication.

Prop. Wilma Saxton   609–767–3530

Blackwood 08012

THE GOLDEN KEY, 532 S. Black Horse Pike. *Also see* Repair and Restoration
and Auctioneer listings.

Hours: Wed., Thurs., Sat. 10–5; Fri. 10–9; Sun. 11–5

*Seven showrooms shared by five dealers. Lots of oak furniture, Victorian pieces;
a few country primitives. General line of antique and collectible glass, china,
jewelry, and silver. Repair services include stripping, refinishing of furniture,
clock and watch repair. Once-a-month auctions on last Tuesday of the month.*

A/C—PM. Affordable. Consignments. Authentication.

Prop. Arthur Bailey; Judy Helzel, Mgr.   609–227–9737

Cherry Hill 08003

BETCHEN'S PICTURE FRAMING, Springdale and Greentree Rds. (at Springdale Shopping Center). *Also see* Repair and Restoration listing.

Hours: Daily 8–5:30; Fri. 'til 9:30

Selective shop specializing in antique art, Orientalia, porcelains, "unusual objets d'art." Complete art restoration service and custom framing. Member Delaware Valley Antique Dealers Assoc., Internat'l. Institute of Conservation of Historic and Artistic Works, the Philadelphia Museum of Art.

A—PM. Wide range. Authentication.

Prop. Maury H. and Bessie G. Betchen   609–424–2646

BEVERLY & TOM BOYTIM ANTIQUES, 320 Brookline Ave. *Also see* Repair and Restoration listing.

Hours: Daily 9–5; or by appt.

Unique collection of antique spinning and weaving equipment. Also antique reproductions in miniature. Mr. Boytim repairs antique spinning and weaving equipment when possible.

A— PM. Wide range.

Prop. Beverly and Tom Boytim   609–667 4712

CHERRY HILL ANTIQUES BY BARBARA, LTD., Ellisburg Circle (next to liquor store).

Hours: Tues. thru Sat. 10:30–4:30; eves. by appt.

General line of antique and collectible china and glass, decorative accessories, decorator furniture. Gift certificates and a layaway service. Mrs. Feldman also provides a search service. Member Delaware Valley Antique Dealers Assoc.

A/C—PM. Affordable. Occasional consignment. Authentication.

Prop. Barbara and Gene Feldman   609–428–1533

MARY'S MEMORIES, Cherry Hill.

Hours: By appt.

Antique and collectible jewelry, with emphasis on Victorian and Georgian jewelry; diamonds and gemstones; hand-painted china and patterned flint glass; silver and miniatures of lapis, malachite, gold. Appraisal service; also identifications of gemstones and jewelry. Member Nat'l. Assoc. of Dealers in Antiques, Inc., and the Delaware Valley Antique Dealers Assoc.

A/C—PM. Wide range. Authentication.

Prop. Mary E. Kane   609–429–5931

ROSETTE'S ANTIQUES & COLLECTIBLES, Cherry Hill.

Hours: By appt.

Specializing in a general line of Oriental porcelain, old English glass, cloisonné, Staffordshire china. The proprietor gives informal lectures on cloisonné and is a member of the Delaware Valley Antique Dealers Assoc.

A/C—PM. Affordable. Authentication.

Prop. Rosette   609–428–2172

Clementon 08021

MARLEIGH SCHROEDER ANTIQUES, Clementon. *Also see* Repair and Restoration listing.

Hours: By appt.

Large selection of antique dolls; primitives, old kitchen utensils; toys. Appraisal service. Mrs. Schroeder repairs and restores old dolls. Member Elizabeth Haddon Doll Club.

A/C—PM. Affordable. Authentication.

Prop. Marleigh Schroeder   609–783–2639

Collingswood 08108

THE DIVIS'S ANTIQUES, Collingswood.

Hours: By appt.

General line of antique and collectible china and glass; elderly lamps. The Divis's offer an appraisal service and are members of the Delaware Valley Antique Dealers Assoc.

A/C—PM. Affordable. Authentication.

Prop. The Divis's   609–858–4343

ANTHONY CHARLES SCHMIDT ANTIQUES, 112 E. Linden Ave.

Hours: By appt.

Fine antique oil paintings—American, English, French, Italian, German—from 1800 to 1890. Mr. Schmidt sells to museums and to collectors throughout the country. Appraisal service.

A—Price list given to clients. Serious collectors. Consignments.

Prop. Anthony Charles Schmidt   609–858–4719

THE YESTERYEAR SHOP, 788 Haddon Ave. (main st. of town).

Hours: Tues. thru Fri. 11–4; Sat. 12–4

"Antiques at prices you can afford" in a friendly shop. General line of china, cut glass, art glass, silver; some primitives. Appraisal service and a layaway plan. Member Delaware Valley Antique Dealers Assoc.

A/C—PM. Affordable. Authentication.

Prop. Lois Gilbert, Mary Marsh   609–854–1786

Haddonfield 08033

AMERICANA SHOP, 7 Ellis St. (off Kings Hwy.).

Hours: Mon. thru Sat. 11–4

Specializing in antique and collectible bottles, old Mason jars, advertising tins; glass, fine china; small pieces of furniture. Appraisal service.

A/C—PM. Affordable. Authentication.

Prop. Boyd Hitchner   609–428–5597 (bus.)
                                        429–0863 (res.)

DIANA'S PLACE, 12 Tanner St. (off Haddon Ave.).

Hours: Tues. thru Sat. 11–4:30; and by appt.

Small pieces of decorative furniture to large armoires; nice hanging cupboards; some primitives; Waterford decanters, fine crystal and china fill three rooms of an attractive shop. Some new gift items.

A/C—PM. Affordable.

Prop. Diana Fortin   609–795–1255 (bus.)
                                       667–7343 (res.)

THE G. ANTIQUE SHOP, 3 Tanner St. (off Haddon Ave.).

Hours: Mon. thru Sat. 11–4

Selective shop with period furniture, including Queen Anne, Chippendale; English and French objets d'art; Ridgway pitchers, fine porcelains, cut crystal. The Steinbergs are members of the Nat'l. Assoc. of Dealers in Antiques, Inc.

A—PM. Selective. Authentication.

Prop. Gladys and Raymond Steinberg   609–428–1992
                                                       667–0216

THE GENERAL STORE, 37 Ellis St. (off Kings Hwy.). *Also see* Repair and Restoration listing.

Hours: Mon. thru Sat. 10–5; or by appt.

Five rooms of furniture, particularly Victorian, some Early American; brass lamps, chandeliers, a general line of china and glass. Services include metal polishing and rewiring of lamps, chandeliers, sconces. Note the selection of new dry flower arrangements.

A/C—PM. Affordable. Authentication.

Prop. Lidia Gorohoff   609–428–3707

JUST BRASS ANTIQUES, 314 N. Haddon Ave. *Also see* Repair and Restoration listing.

Hours: Tues. thru Fri. 10–3; Sat. 10–5; Mon. by appt.

Lots of brass pieces, but also bronze, pewter, copper, and silver items, including candlesticks, candelabra, trays, banquet lamps; some Chinese bronzes. Interesting old hardware for restoring period homes. A decorating service, and the Rosens repair and rewire old lamps. Member Delaware Valley Antique Dealers Assoc.

A/C—PM. Wide range. Authentication.

Prop. Carole and Howard Rosen   609–428–4883

PENNY WISE THRIFT SHOP, 23 Mechanic St. (off Haddon Ave.). *Also see* Repair and Restoration listing.

Hours: Tues. thru Sat. 11–4

"A little bit of everything"—some furniture, bric-a-brac, china and glass, decorative accessories. Caning, furniture repair, clock repair.

A/C—PM. Affordable. Consignments. Authentication.

Prop. Doris Staley   609–429–5576

SANSKI ART CENTER, 50 Tanner St. (off Haddon Ave.). *Also see* Repair and Restoration listing.

Hours: Mon. thru Sat. 9:30–5; closed Wed. during June, July, Aug.

Specializing in fine antique paintings from all schools and 19th-century bronzes. Restoration of antique paintings and custom framing. Appraisal service.

A—PM. Selective. Authentication when possible.

Prop. Albert and Karl Sandecki   609–429–2511

ISABELL G. SCHOFIELD ANTIQUES, 218 Hopkins Ave.

Hours: By appt.

Good collection of tin and woodenware, primitives, some antique glassware.

A—PM. Affordable.

Prop. Isabell G. Schofield   609–429–6676

ELEANOR VAIL, 8 Tanner St. (off Haddon Ave.).

Hours: Mon. thru Sat. 10–5

The old Estugh Tavern, established in 1740, is now a combination flower shop and antique shop. Eighteenth-century dried floral arrangements form an appropriate decorative accompaniment to the period furniture and antique and collectible china and glass. Mrs. Vail creates the dried arrangements and custom silk flower arrangements and lectures on the art.

A/C—PM. Affordable. Authentication.

Prop. Eleanor Vail   609–429–4559

THE WOODEN PEG, 9 Ellis St. (just off Kings Hwy.). *Also see* Repair and Restoration listing.

Hours: Mon. thru Sat. 11–4

Nineteenth-century furniture and a few 18th-century pieces; good collection of kitchen and farm primitives; antique clocks and a general line of china and glass in a warm shop shared by two dealers. Appraisals and antique clock and watch repair are services. Member Delaware Valley Antique Dealers Assoc.

A/C—PM. Affordable. Authentication when possible.

Prop. Ruth Stinebring, Noreen Schlitt   609–795–5233

Haddon Heights 08035

HEBE'S ANTIQUES, Haddon Heights.

Hours: By appt.

Victorian furniture a specialty; also antique dolls, cut glass, old silver.

A/C—PM. Affordable/Selective. Authentication when possible.

Prop. Hebe   609–547–2010

Kirkwood 08043

THE CALICO DOLL HOUSE, Gibbsboro Rd. *Also see* Repair and Restoration listing.

Hours: By appt.

Dolls of all ages, antique and collectible; doll-related items. Complete doll repair, including clothes, shoes, and accessories. Member Delaware Valley Antique Dealers Assoc.

A/C—PM. Affordable/Selective. Authentication when possible.

Prop. Jane E. Sheetz   609–784–1292

Laurel Springs 08021

OLDE TYME SHOPPE, 323 White Horse Pike (Rt. 30).

Hours: Tues. thru Sat. 10–5

Two large rooms filled with old oil lamps, antique and collectible glass, fine china, small pieces of furniture, decorative accessories.

A/C—PM. Affordable. Consignments.

Prop. Irene and Les Blore   609–346–0230

Magnolia 08049

ANTIQUES RENAISSANCE, 610 W. Evesham.

Hours: Better to phone ahead

A beautiful old home, the rear section built in 1743 and the front added in 1869, now graciously displays a selective collection of period and primitive furniture; appropriate decorative accessories. Mrs. Eckhardt is a member of the Delaware Valley Antique Dealers Assoc.

A—PM. Selective. Authentication when possible.

Prop. Emile Eckhardt   609–783–7220

Merchantville 08109

THE ANTIQUE CORNER, 2 E. Maple Ave. (Rt. 537). *Also see* Repair and Restoration listing.

Hours: Wed. thru Sat. 11–5; Thurs., Fri. eve. 7–9; Sun. 12–4

THE ANTIQUE CORNER *continued*

A general line of antiques in a large corner shop. Victorian furniture, jewelry, fine china and glass, books, paintings, 1800s clocks, silver, collector's plates. Services include watch and clock repair and caning. Member Delaware Valley Antique Dealers Assoc.

A/C—PM. Affordable. Authentication when possible.

Prop. Audrey Russell   609–663–1200

ANTIQUE JUNCTION, Center and Chestnut Sts. (in old railroad station).

Hours: Tues., Wed., Thurs. 11–4; Sat. 12–4

Primitive, formal, and Victorian furniture, fine china, silver, art glass, antique jewelry, decorative accessories nicely displayed in the old Merchantville railroad station, built in 1885.

A/C—PM. Affordable/Selective. Authentication.

Prop. Stephanie Danik   609–662–2238

DOROTHY BLINDENBACHER ANTIQUES, 18 S. Center St. (main business st.).

Hours: Mon. thru Sat. 12–5; Fri. eve. 7–9

Select shop with choice pieces of fine china and glass—Rudolstadt, belleek, R. M. Prussia, Mettlach, Steuben, Baccarat. All pieces have been researched and are identified on their tags.

A/Some collectibles—PM. Selective. Authentication.

Prop. Dorothy R. Blindenbacher   609–662–6318

CHAPEL ANTIQUES, 26 S. Center St. (main business st.).

Hours: Daily 12–5, except Wed.; Thurs., Fri. eve. 7–9

Sizable shop stocked with an extensive selection of 18th- and 19th-century furniture, including Empire and Victorian; antique clocks, some antique and collectible glass. Appraisal service.

A/C—PM. Wide range. Authentication.

Prop. Bryan McKernan   609–663–9782

Somerdale 08083

GEORGIA FLUHARTY ANTIQUES & BARGAINS, 1118 S. White Horse Pike.

Hours: By appt.

GEORGIA FLUHARTY ANTIQUES & BARGAINS *continued*

Specializing in a general line of antique and collectible china and glass. A large variety, quite affordable. Member Delaware Valley Antique Dealers Assoc.

A/C—PM. Affordable. Authentication when possible.

Prop. Georgia Fluharty   609–627–0693

RICHARD & BARBARA McNULTY ANTIQUES, Somerdale.

Hours: By appt.

Carnival glass a specialty; also antique clocks and fine china. The McNultys are members of the Delaware Valley Antique Dealers Assoc.

A/C—PM. Affordable. Authentication when possible.

Prop. Richard and Barbara McNulty   609–783–4834

Waterford (Hammonton P. O. 08037)

ANTIQUES AND THINGS, Waterford-Blue Anchor Rd. (1 mi. off White Horse Pike at Waterford).

Hours: Better to phone ahead

Antique jewelry, sterling silver, pattern glass, and fine china, some country furniture. Mrs. Davies does appraisals and is a member of the Delaware Valley Antique Dealers Assoc.

A/C—PM. Affordable. Authentication when possible.

Prop. Edith Davies   609–561–3749

BATES MILL ANTIQUES, Waterford. *Also see* Repair and Restoration listing.

Hours: By appt.

Small pieces of turn-of-the-century furniture, oak washstands, tables; general line of antique jewelry, china, and glass; some primitives. Mr. Kelling restores and refinishes furniture.

A/C—PM. Affordable. Occasional consignment.

Prop. Marion Kelling   609–561–3022

Waterford Works 08089

ALICE ESPOSITO, P. O. Box 329. *Also see* Repair and Restoration listing.

Hours: By appt.

ALICE ESPOSITO *continued*

Some pieces of oak and maple furniture, refinished and in-the-rough. Mainly restoration services, caning and rushing, furniture refinishing. Large selection of refinishing products for the do-it-yourselfer.

A/C—PM. Affordable.

Prop. Alice Esposito   609–561–7177

West Berlin 08091

BERTOLINO ART GALLERY, 406 Harrison Ave. *Also see* Repair and Restoration listing.

Hours: Mon. thru Fri. 9:30–5:30; Sat. & Sun. 9:30–1:30

Fine oil paintings, watercolors, drawings, and engravings, antique and collectible. Sculptures in marble, bronze, and terra cotta; selection of art glass. The Bertolinos do custom picture framing and restoration of artwork. Members Nat'l. Assoc. of Dealers in Antiques, Inc.

A/C—PM. Affordable/Selective. Limited consignment. Authentication.

Prop. Charles and Victoria Bertolino   609–767–1006

Westmont 08108

ROSALYN'S ANTIQUES, Westmont. *Also see* Repair and Restoration listing.

Hours: By appt.

Emphasis on the unusual in antique decorator pieces; large selection of silver flatware—sterling and plated. General line of accessories. Mrs. Felheimer is a decorating consultant. Antique clock repair by Mr. Felheimer. Member Delaware Valley Antique Dealers Assoc.

A/Some collectibles—PM. Affordable/Selective. Authentication.

Prop. Rosalyn Felheimer   609–854–0759

THE TREASURE ROOST, 221 Haddon Ave. (Rt. 561).

Hours: Mon. thru Fri. 9–5

Small pieces of country furniture, pressed glass, old tools and bottles, in one room of a local insurance agency.

A/C—PM. Affordable.

Prop. Marie Sulock, Margaret Richter   609–858–8400

Dolls and playthings of the 1900s assembled for auction preview at a Somerset County estate. The doll in the four-poster bed is an Armand Marseille. *Courtesy Elwood Heller, Lebanon. Photo: Ed Schuetz*

Gloucester County

Bridgeport 08014

RACCOON CREEK ANTIQUES, 20 Main St.

Hours: Daily 12:30–4:45; Sun. & eves. by appt. Closed Thurs.

Large collection of Early American pattern glass and "a little bit of everything" in furniture, though emphasis is on country pieces. Decorative accessories and fine china. Est. 1952.

A/C—PM. Affordable. Authentication if history is known.

Prop. The Pedricks   609–467–1141 (bus.)
                                                   467–0247 (res.)

Clayton 08312

THE DEN OF ANTIQUITY, 213 N. Delsea Dr. (Rt. 47).

Hours: Daily 11–5. Closed Fri., Sun.

Spacious shop crammed with antique and collectible South Jersey glass— Wheaton bottles, early Clevenger, old and new paperweights. General line of furniture, large collection of primitive kitchen utensils and old crocks. Member New York Paperweight Collectors Assoc. and South Jersey Heritage Bottle and Glass Assoc.

A/C—PM. Affordable/Selective. Consignments. Authentication.

Prop. E. Wiseburn & Son   609–881–0205

Deptford 08096

KOPPS ANTIQUES, Deptford.

Hours: By appt.

French opalescent crystal and Sabino glass are specialties; also cut glass, china, Oriental porcelains, cloisonné, ivories. The Kopps manage antique shows and are members of the Delaware Valley Antique Dealers Assoc.

A/C—PM. Wide range. Authentication.

Prop. Ann and Jim Kopp   609–845–4599

Fairview (Sewell P. O. 08080)

CHARLES B. SMITH ANTIQUES, 200 Delsea Dr. (Rt. 47).

Hours: Tues. thru Sun. 12–6

A fine collection of antique Wedgwood, general line of fine china, brass, porcelains, Art Nouveau, cut glass, some Durand pieces. A knowledgeable dealer, Mr. Smith is author of "Two Hundred Years of Wedgwood Marks," a booklet published for the Wedgwood Bi-Centennial. Member of the Wedgwood societies of Philadelphia, New York, and England as well as the Appraisers Assoc. of America and the Gemological Institute of America. Appraisals of antiques and precious stones.

A/C—PM. Selective. Authentication.

Prop. Charles B. Smith   609–228–1411

Franklinville 08322

YE OLDE COLONIAL SHOPPE, N. Delsea Dr. (Rt. 47).

Hours: Daily 10–5. Closed Tues.

General line of furniture, from Early American through oak. Also new gift items and dried flower arrangements reminiscent of Colonial times.

A/C—PM. Affordable. Authentication if history is known.

Prop. Eleanor and Eileen Gillespie   609–694–1258

Malaga 08322

SCOTLAND RUN, Harding Hwy. (Rt. 40). *Also see* Repair and Restoration listing.

Hours: Daily 9–6

Period furniture, cut glass, china, paintings, sculpture, primitives, a collection of ABC plates. Large pieces of furniture are in the barn to the rear of the house. Services include furniture restoration, repairing, stripping, and custom finishing.

A/C—PM. Affordable. Consignments (with floater insurance). Authentication when possible.

Prop. Sarah Frank   609–694–3344

VERNE C. STREETER, Harding Hwy. (Rt. 40).

Hours: By chance or appt.

A very large barn filled to the rafters with furniture of various periods, tools, books, paintings, china and glass, fireplace equipment. Mr. Streeter sells mostly to dealers.

A/C—PM. Affordable. Occasional consignment.

Prop. Verne C. Streeter   609–694–4163

Mickleton 08056

THE SPICE BOX, 393 Kings Hwy. (Rt. 551). Also at King's Row, Mullica Hill.

Hours: By appt.

Good Victorian furniture and a general line of antique china, glass, decorative accessories. "All items guaranteed." Long-distance delivery service. Member Delaware Valley Antique Dealers Assoc.

A/C—PM. Wide range.

Prop. C. F. Griffin, M. A. Meyer, P. M. Farren   609–423–6686

MARY B. WARD ANTIQUES, Democrat Road.

Hours: By appt.

"Odd or different" country furniture a specialty. Lots of old tools and kitchen utensils, a general line of fine china, glass, baskets, old books. Mrs. Ward has been a dealer since 1947.

A/Some collectibles—PM. Affordable. Authentication.

Prop. Mary B. Ward   609–423–3093

Mullica Hill 08062

The charming pre-Revolutionary village of Mullica Hill, named for Eric Mullica, who came to the area with a group of Swedish settlers in the mid-1600s, is known now as "Antique Country." A dozen browsable shops and two mini-malls line the main street and offer the collector a pleasant day of antique-hunting. Location: 6 miles south of Woodbury on Rt. 45; 3 miles east of exit 2, N. J. Tpk.

THE ADAMS HOUSE, Rt. 45 and Jefferson (1 mi. north of town).

Hours: Tues. thru Sat. 10–4; Sun. 12–4:30

Early Empire and Victorian furniture a specialty in a tastefully arranged shop. Also fine porcelains, Fenton, Heisey glass, 1800s knife cases, cut glass collection. Appraisals given.

A/Some collectibles—PM. Selective. Authentication when possible.

Prop. Russ and Naomi Adams   609–478–4791

ANTHONY AND ELLEN BARRETT ANTIQUES, South Main St.

Hours: Sat. & Sun. 11–5; weekdays by chance or appt.

"Antiques for the country home"—American painted furniture, folk art, good selection of old quilts, iron for the collector.

A—PM. Selective. Authentication.

Prop. Anthony and Ellen Barrett   609–478–4120 (bus.)
                                                            645–2341 (res.)

CARROLL CHRISTY ANTIQUES, Main St.

Hours: Sat. 11–5; Sun. 1–5; or by appt.

Interesting paint-decorated furniture from the 18th and 19th centuries, related decorative accessories and folk art.

A—PM. Selective. Authentication.

Prop. Carroll Christy   609–478–4755 (bus.)
                                                            825–7553 (res.)

EAGLE'S NEST ANTIQUES, 38 S. Main St.

Hours: 7 days 11–5

Plenty of room in a spacious building for nine dealers to display a wide range of antiques and collectibles.

THE BOARDING HOUSE, Kitty Rudolph.
Early tin and iron, primitives, glass and fine china.

EAGLE'S NEST ANTIQUES *continued*

CAROL BRASS.
Country furniture, kitchen primitives, Depression glass, china, and linens.

THE COBWEB COLLECTIBLES, Daphne Majewski.
Early brass, copper, pewter pieces, crocks, spongeware, primitives.

COLLECTOR TREASURES CHEST, Bea and Richard Murray.
Country furniture, Depression glass, coins, silver, china, spongeware.

GRANDMA'S TREASURES, Betty Jo Servo.
Kitchen primitives, toys, miniatures, antique jewelry, small pieces of furniture, linens, advertising tins, glass, china, old crocks.

HEIRLOOM ANTIQUES, Claire Mullen.
General line—furniture, fine china, glass.

HOMESPUN ANTIQUES, Betty Detzel.
General line of early furniture, china and glass.

HILKA HORVAT.
Early American furniture, kitchen primitives, glass.

SANDY'S ANTIQUE WORLD, Sandy Onofrio.
Advertising tins and boxes, kitchen primitives, jewelry, old tools, post cards.

A/C—PM. Affordable. Authentication.
Prop. Cooperative   609–478–6351

1820 HOUSE, 43 S. Main St.
Hours: Wed., Thurs. 11–4; Sat. 11–5; Sun. 12–5
Eighteenth- and 19th-century period and country furniture predominate in a tastefully arranged 150-year-old home. Sheraton chests, New England step-back cupboards, Pennsylvania pine pie cupboards. The owners offer an interior design service and will also search out fine pieces of furniture.
A—PM. Selective. Authentication when possible.
Prop. Ellie Rexon, Shirley Schwamb   609–478–4311

FIRETHORN ANTIQUES, 13 N. Main St.

Hours: Sat. & Sun. 11–5; eves. by appt.

American country furniture and accessories for the country home; some primitive chests. Delivery up to twenty-five miles.

A/Some collectibles. Selective. Consignments. Authentication.

Prop. Michael and Avis Brangan   609–467–1179

FURNISHINGS FOR THE CONNOISSEUR, 13 N. Main St.

Hours: Fri., Sat., Sun. 1–5; and by appt.

Hepplewhite, Sheraton, and Chippendale furniture and appropriate accessories predominate. Brass beds also a specialty. The Kresslers will work with interior designers and search out pieces of fine furniture. Delivery within fifty miles.

A—PM. Selective. Consignments (limited). Authentication.

Prop. Amelia and Peter Kressler   609–468–7733

KING'S ROW, 44 N. Main St.

Hours: 7 days 11–5

An antiques mini-mall with seven diverse and browsable shops in a large, airy building.

> VIRGINIA ALLEN.
>
> *Country and Victorian furniture, glass, china, bric-a-brac.*
>
> IRK RIVER GALLERY, William Entwisle.
>
> *Antique toys, advertising tins, memorabilia.*
>
> CAROL KEARNEY.
>
> *Early country furniture, cupboards, cobbler's benches, old church pews.*
>
> NANNY'S STUFF, Nancy Gagliardi.
>
> *Art Deco, Art Nouveau, nostalgic items.*
>
> REBECCA'S ANTIQUES, Rebecca Smith.
>
> *Antique silver and glass.*
>
> SERENDIPITY, Joan Egerton.
>
> *Primitives and a general line of elderly accessories.*

KING'S ROW *continued*

THE SPICE BOX, Cecil F. Griffin.

Victorian furniture a specialty; also fine china and glass.

A/C—PM. Affordable. Authentication when possible.

Prop. Cooperative 609–478–4361

KATE AND STAN LAMBORNE ANTIQUES, 34 S. Main St.

Hours: Tues. thru Sun. 11–5

Charming house c. 1842 with hand-hewn beams and a large open fireplace gives an appropriate background to South Jersey antique country furniture, New Jersey sawbuck tables, Ware chairs, country accessories.

A—PM. Affordable/Selective. Authentication.

Prop. Kate and Stan Lamborne 609–478–2484

PATRICIA'S ANTIQUES, Main St.

Hours: Thurs. thru Sun. 11–5

Warm and bustling shop with a very large selection of fine pine country furniture, "at least two dozen dry sinks always," corner cupboards, jelly chests, hand-stripped and hand-rubbed furniture. Nice selection of stoneware and spongeware; pattern glass and flow blue. Mrs. Bunty provides a search service for country furniture. Gift certificates available.

A—PM. Affordable/Selective. Authentication.

Prop. Patricia Bunty 609–478–4737

RAINTREE ANTIQUES, 32 N. Main St.

Hours: Daily 11–5; or by appt.

The pre-Revolutionary Mullica house, finished in 1710 (a beam in the cooking kitchen dates to 1698), forms a perfect setting for 18th- and early 19th-century period and country furniture, decorative accessories, a large collection of New Jersey slipware, oil paintings c. 1830–1840.

A—PM. Selective. Authentication.

Prop. Doris Montgomery Seabrook 609–478–4100

RUSTY NAIL SHOP, Main St.

Hours: Wed., Thurs. 11–4; Sat. 11–5; Sun. 12–5

Early American and Victorian furniture vie for space in a large barn to the rear

RUSTY NAIL SHOP *continued*

of an 1820s home. General line of china, glass, stoneware, agate, and tinware, Victorian and Early American lamps. Appraising service.

A—PM. Selective. Authentication.

Prop. Ella and Harold Mickle   609–478–4379

ROBERT & ANN SCHUMANN ANTIQUES, 56 S. Main St.

Hours: Sun. 1–5; other times by chance or appt.

An early 19th-century barn is home to a collection of country furniture, paint-decorated furniture, folk art, nice selection of spongeware, spatterware, redware. Mr. and Mrs. Schumann both lecture on antiques.

A—PM. Selective. Authentication.

Prop. Robert and Ann Schumann   609–478–2553

THE SIGN OF ST. GEORGE, 54 S. Main St.

Hours: Sat. & Sun. 11–5; other times by appt.

Seventeenth-, 18th-, and early 19th-century period and country furniture nicely arranged with appropriate antique accessories "from the traditional to the unique." Also pewter, stoneware, tinware. The Corderys provide a decorative service and do appraisals.

A—PM. Selective. Consignments (limited). Authentication.

Prop. Jean and Edmund Cordery   609–478–6101

GORDON AND BONNIE WYCKOFF ANTIQUES, 45 S. Main St.

Hours: Wed., Thurs. 11–4; Sat. & Sun. 12–5

A bright, high-ceilinged shop has two large rooms filled with Early American furniture—chests, cupboards, painted pieces; also homespun linens, baskets, and dried arrangements.

A—PM. Affordable/Selective. Authentication when possible.

Prop. Gordon and Bonnie Wyckoff   609–848–1341

Newfield 08344

THE OLD BARN, Northwest Blvd.

Hours: Daily 12:30–5; eves. by appt. Closed Thurs.

Fine old South Jersey pine cupboards and other country pieces, oyster plates c. late 1800s, old tools and kitchenware fill four rooms of an old barn remodeled

*as an antique and gift shop. New painted tinware and a unique collection of
jewelry made from shards of Durand and Kimble glass that Mr. Smith salvaged
in 1966 when the Kimble Glass Company was excavating for a new building.*

A/C—PM. Affordable/Selective. Authentication.

Prop. Mrs. Frank Smith   609–697–3242

Swedesboro 08085

THE SEVEN GABLES, 447 Kings Hwy. (Rt. 551).

Hours: By appt.

*Specializing in formal period furniture and fine oil paintings. Antique
mechanical and live-steam toys, firearms. For the automobile buff, the owners
also have antique European cars.*

A—PM. Selective to serious collectors. Authentication.

Prop. William S. Serri, Jr., William N. Schultz   609–467–2029

Turnersville 08012

TREASURE HUNT, County House Rd. and Black Horse Pike. *Also see*
Auctioneers and Repair and Restoration listing.

Hours: Wed. thru Sun. 10–6; Fri. 'til 8; Mon., Tues. by appt.

*Antiques and collectibles of several dealers upstairs and downstairs in a roomy
setting. General line of furniture from Early American through turn-of-the-
century oak; glass, china, memorabilia. Services include stripping, refinishing,
repairing furniture. Auctions are conducted by Mr. Lucas, member of the
National Auctioneers Assoc.*

A/C—PM. Affordable. Authentication.

Prop. Howard Lucas   609–227–4925

Woodbury 08096

KRACKER BARREL ANTIQUES, 613 N. Broad St.

Hours: By appt.

*Small pieces of primitive and formal furniture, flow blue china, antique clocks,
decorative items attractively arranged in a 200-year-old saltbox on the main street
of town.*

A/Some collectibles—PM. Wide range. Consignments. Authentication.

Prop. Marie Ferrell   609–845–2473

A selection of choice 18th and early 19th-century Wedgwood. *Courtesy Charles B. Smith Antiques, Fairview. Photo: Helga Photo Studio, Inc.*

Salem County

Alloway 08001

DORREL'S ANTIQUES, Lambert and Cedar Sts. *Also see* Repair and
Restoration listing.

Hours: By appt.

*Eighteenth- and 19th-century country furniture, some Victorian pieces, in an
old-time shop. Expert refinishing, restoring, reupholstering; paint-decorated
furniture authentically redone. Appraisal service.*

A—PM. Selective. Authentication.

Prop. Ernest and Olive Dorrel 609–935–4296

JOSIAH M. REEVE HOUSE ANTIQUES, N. Greenwich St. (Rt. 581 to center
of town, rt. at light).

Hours: Sat. & Sun. 1–5; or by appt.

*Distinctive English and American 18th- and 19th-century formal furniture in
an 1826 home being carefully restored by the Culvers. The beautiful all-brick
structure and the one next door at Seven Hearths Antiques, dated 1817, are fine
examples of Federal architecture. Both homes were built by prosperous
shipbuilders in the first half of the 19th century.*

A—PM. Selective. Authentication.

Prop. David and Rebecca Culver 609–935–7020

SEVEN HEARTHS ANTIQUES, N. Greenwich St. (Rt. 581 to center of town, rt. at light).

Hours: Thurs. thru Sun. 1–5; or by appt.

Well-chosen selection of quality American, Irish, and English furniture from the 18th and early 19th centuries in two distinctive shops, one devoted to formal pieces and the other to country furnishings; appropriate decorative accessories. Conversion of antique oil lamps, crocks, and other old items to lamps.

A—PM. Selective. Authentication.

Prop. Edward and Nancy Fogg   609–935–4976

THE TAVERN SHOP, corner of Main and Greenwich Sts.

Hours: Mon. thru Fri. 1–4; or by appt.

A former country tavern provides lots of space for a varied collection of antiques: Victorian furniture, wicker, cane chairs, Ware chairs; selection of Rockingham pottery, fine china and glass, antique dolls, decorative pieces.

A/C—PM. Affordable/Selective. Authentication.

Prop. Alma Yoerger   609–935–1896

Elmer 08318

MADONNIE'S PLACID PINES, Harding Hwy. (Rt. 40, eastbound).

Hours: Tues. thru Sat. 10–5

Small pieces of country furniture; general line of china, glass; chandeliers, old lamps, antique clocks. Member Delaware Valley Antique Dealers Assoc. Appraisal service.

A/C—PM. Wide range. Authentication.

Prop. Louis Madonnie   609–358–2859

THE OLD PINE HUTCH ANTIQUES, 119 S. Main St.

Hours: By chance or appt.

Early American furniture, pine cupboards, chests; some china, cut glass, decorative accessories, nicely arranged in half of a colonial-type corner building; Pfeffer's Bakery adjoins.

A/C—PM. Affordable/Selective. Authentication when possible.

Prop. George C. Pfeffer, Jr.   609–358–6031

Norma 08347

MARY'S ANTIQUES, Box 135.

Hours: Tues. thru Sat. 10–5

Specializing in oak furniture and a general line of china, glass. Also, "usable furniture."

C/A—Most prices marked. Wide range.

Prop. Mary Mason   609–696–3904

Pennsville 08070

HOLLY TREE ANTIQUES, 101 William Penn Ave.

Hours: Tues., Wed., Sat. 1–5; Fri. eve. 7–9

Emphasis on pattern glass in a selective shop; country furniture, fine china, decorative items.

A/Some collectibles—PM. Selective.

Prop. Dorothy and Willard Workman   609–678–7100

Boat landing on Navesink River at Highlands, New Jersey. Early 19th century tinted etching initialled "G. P."; one of a series. Measures 6 in. across × 4½ in. high. *Courtesy The Hudson Shop, Inc., Red Bank*

Carved pine bust of Homer with bronze paint overlay by famed Philadelphia sculptor
William Rush (1756–1833). Ht. 22 in. *Courtesy Daniel Hersh Galleries, New Hope.*
Photo: Sanford Jacobs

Cumberland County

Bridgeton 08302

COUNTRY BUMPKIN, Henry Ave., R. D. 6.

Hours: By appt.

Some country furniture, baskets, folk art, along with hand-painted plaques, tinware, dried flowers, herb plants.

C/A—PM. Affordable. Authentication.

Prop. Barbara Bruno   609–691–3236

THE HITCHING POST ANTIQUES, 81 N. Pearl St. (Rt. 77, east side, directly across from Telephone Dial Building).

Hours: Mon. thru Sat. 2–8; or by appt.

Two rooms in a Victorian home devoted to a general line of china and glass, silver serving pieces, some pieces of primitive and formal furniture; nice cut glass.

A/C—PM. Wide range. Authentication when possible.

Prop. S. F. McKinnie   609–451–2481

THE OLD CURIOSITY SHOP, Cubby Hollow Rd. (Broad St., main business st., to Fayette St., to Cubby Hollow Rd.).

Hours: Wed. thru Sun. 1:30–7:30

Specializing in old kitchen utensils, primitive tables, small pieces of country furniture. "Buy, sell or trade."

A/C—PM. Affordable. Occasional consignment.

Prop. Joan C. Hall   No phone

PICKWICK HOUSE, 710 Shiloh Pike (Rt. 49, westbound).

Hours: Thurs. thru Mon. 12–6

A decorator's antique shop combining antiques with contemporary decorative accessories. Primitive and country furniture, cut glass and china, on two floors of a house that is a scale model of the William Oakford House in Salem County, a hip-roofed brick dwelling c. 1736. Selection of fabrics, wallpapers, gift items.

A/C—PM. Affordable. Consignments. Authentication.

Prop. Patricia and William Mather   609–451–5352

WAGON HOUSE ANTIQUES & GIFTS, R. D. 5, Deerfield-Seeley Rd. (1 mi. south of Deerfield).

Hours: By chance or appt.

Country furniture a specialty; selection of tinware, primitives, baskets, old kitchen utensils. Picture framing, including barn board and pine frames to order.

A/C—PM. Affordable. Authentication when possible.

Prop. Hannah M. Coles   609–451–7014

Dorchester 08316

THE DUSTY DOWRY, Main St. at Hall Rd.

Hours: Mon., Wed., Thurs., Fri. 1–5; Sat. & Sun. 9–5

Old and out-of-print books predominate in a shop that also maintains a book search service. Collectible advertising tins, prints, frames, post cards, general line of glassware, toys, silver.

C/A—PM. Affordable. Authentication when possible.

Prop. Tom and Marie Hugues   609–785–0541

Greenwich 08323

THE GRIFFIN, Ye Greate Street (main thoroughfare).

Hours: Wed. thru Sun. 12–5

Once a general store in historic Greenwich, this authentically restored 1700s saltbox appropriately displays local South Jersey antiques, including Ware chairs, primitive furniture, country pieces. Some formal Chippendale and Empire furniture; decorative accessories, crocks, early brass items. New quality

THE GRIFFIN *continued*

gifts in the colonial tradition and a fine selection of books relating to antiques. Mrs. Watson is president of the Cumberland County Historical Soc.

A/C—PM. Selective. Occasional consignment. Authentication when possible.

Prop. Mrs. Newland Watson   609–451–5867

Heislerville 08324

WOOD PUMP ANTIQUES, Main St. (diagonally across from Post Office). Hours: 7 days 1–5; or by appt.

Nice selection of glass, including an occasional Ralph Barber or John Ruhlander piece, in a friendly country shop. Some primitive and pine furniture, general line of china, old crocks and jugs, elderly lamps. Mrs. Donnelly is a member of the Early American Glass Club, South Jersey Chapter.

A/C—PM. Wide range. Authentication when possible.

Prop. Mrs. John Donnelly   609–785–0237

Mauricetown 08329

COOKHOUSE ANTIQUES, High St. (Rt. 548, eastbound). Hours: By chance or appt.

Fine china, pattern glass, cut glass, small pieces of country furniture, antique toys, collectibles, nicely displayed in the charming cookhouse of an old Victorian home c. 1852.

A/C—PM. Affordable. Authentication when possible.

Prop. Irene and Hammond Ferguson   609–785–1137

MARY'S ANTIQUES, High St. (Rt. 548, westbound). Hours: Mon. thru Sat. 1–5; Sun. 10–6

Specializing in Victorian and oak furniture; general line of fine china, glass, selection of agateware.

A/C—PM. Affordable. Authentication when possible.

Prop. Mary A. Jeffers   609–785–2686

PUMP HOUSE ANTIQUES, High St. (Rt. 548, westbound).

Hours: 7 days 12–5; or by appt.

A general line of antiques and collectibles, including Victorian furniture, antique lamps, china, glass, in the shop and in Mrs. Webb's home.

A/C—PM. Affordable. Consignments. Authentication when possible.

Prop. Caroline Webb   609–785–2246

SEA CAPTAIN ANTIQUES, Second and High Sts. (Rt. 548, eastbound).

Hours: By chance or appt.

A "shop in the house," with nicely displayed primitive furniture, splint baskets, kerosene lamps, china, country accessories.

A/C—PM. Affordable. Consignments. Authentication when possible.

Prop. Vince and Julie Regan   609–785–2416

WAGON WHEEL ANTIQUES, High St. (Rt. 548, westbound).

Hours: 7 days 12–5

Primitives and country furniture predominate in a warm country farmhouse c. 1820; iron, wood, and tin accessories, china and glass. The Webbs are members of the Cumberland County Historical Soc. and the Maurice River Historical Soc.

A/C—PM. Affordable. Authentication when possible.

Prop. Marion and Harry Webb   609–785–0278

Millville 08332

WILLIAM R. BREEDEN, 458 Brenda Terrace.

Hours: Mon. thru Sat. 9–5

Specializing in glass paperweights; also early furniture, fine china and glass.

A/C—Some prices marked. Wide range. Authentication.

Prop. William R. Breeden   609–825–8221

ARTHUR GORHAM PAPERWEIGHT SHOP, Wheaton Village (just off Rt. 47 at Millville; or Rt. 55 to Wheaton exit).

Hours: 7 days 10–5

The shop in historic Wheaton Village, maintained by the nonprofit Wheaton Historical Assoc., features a wide selection of paperweights, both antique and

ARTHUR GORHAM PAPERWEIGHT SHOP *continued*
new, from inexpensive imports to highly collectible Baccarats. Weights by contemporary American artisans as well as those from studios in France, Czechoslovakia, and Italy are available. Search service for collectors.
C/A—PM. Wide range. Authentication.
Prop. Wheaton Historical Assoc. 609–825–6800

MOORE'S ANTIQUES, Millville.
Hours: By appt.
A large collection of early paperweights, fine china, cut glass.
A/C—PM. Affordable.
Prop. Marie and Frank Moore 609–825–5478

Vineland 08360

FOUR NINETEEN ANTIQUE SHOP, 419 Chestnut Ave.
Hours: Mon. thru Sat. 8:30–5:30; Fri. eve. 'til 8:30
Spacious shop crammed with "a little bit of everything": pine and oak furniture, carnival glass, cloisonné, china, decorative accessories.
A/C—PM. Affordable. Authentication when possible.
Prop. Alyce Angelucci 609–691–0991

FRED'S USED FURNITURE & ANTIQUES, 216 W. Wheat Rd.
Hours: Mon. thru Thurs. 9–7; Fri. 9–9; Sat. 9–6
Four tremendous rooms filled with furniture of various periods, some antique, some not so old. Appraisal service.
A/C—Prices not marked. Wide range. Occasional consignment. Authentication.
Prop. Fred R. D'Agistino 609–692–2861

Rockingham-glazed earthenware pitcher depicting volunteer firemen on their way to a fire. Made at the Salamander Works, Woodbridge, ca. 1845. *Courtesy The Brooklyn Museum. The Arthur W. Clement Collection*

Cape May County

Avalon 08202

JONES ANTIQUES, Ocean Dr. at 39th St.

Hours: Summer season (June–Sept.): Daily 10–6; off-season: Sat. & Sun. 10–6

Antique lamps a specialty; small pieces of furniture, wicker and oak; decorative accessories. New dollhouses and their miniature furnishings.

A/C—PM. Affordable. Authentication when possible.

Prop. Marie Jones   609–967–5578

Burleigh 08210

LEMON GROVE, Rt. 9, southbound.

Hours: Daily 11–4:30; better to phone ahead

Sizable shop specializing in Victorian furniture, very large and small pieces; decorative chandeliers, fine china, bric-a-brac.

A/C—PM. Wide range. Authentication when possible.

Prop. William Lemmon   609–465–3135 (bus.)
                                                        522–5170 (res.)

Cape May 08204

ANTIQUES ET AL., 605 Hughes St. (bisects Ocean St.).

Hours: Summer season (June–Sept.): Daily 9–6; other times by appt.

Large selection of English silver and a general line of furniture, some Victorian; fine English china, copper lustre, decorative pieces, in a bright corner shop. History buffs will be interested in the collection of old newspaper engraving blocks of Cape May and environs. Appraisal service.

A/C—PM. Selective. Occasional consignment. Authentication.

Prop. George P. Johnson, Rex E. Ballinger   609–884–2206

CAPE MAY COUNTRY STORE, Columbia Ave. and Jefferson St. (off Lafayette St., main st. of town).

Hours: Summer season (June–Sept.): Daily 10–6, 7–9:30

Mixture of antiques and gifts in a browsable shop. Some small pieces of elderly furniture, nautical items, new and old glassware, china. Hand-dipped candles (made in the shop), crafts.

C/A—PM. Affordable. Consignments.

Prop. The Kurtz's   609–884–8658

NOSTALGIA SHOP, 408 Washington Mall (the Victorian Mall in the center of town).

Hours: Summer season (June–Sept.): Daily 10–5; off-season: Sat. & Sun. 10–5

"Antiques, bric-a-brac, used furniture" in a busy shop on Cape May's Victorian Mall. Old lamps, china and glass, dollhouse accessories.

A/C—PM. Affordable. Authentication.

Prop. Elizabeth Campbell   609–884–7071

PRATLEY'S DOLL HOSPITAL, 1207 Lafayette St. (main st. of town).

Also see Repair and Restoration listing.

Hours: Daily 10–4. Closed Wed.

Specializing in antique dolls, reproductions of old dolls, apple-head dolls, doll kits. Doll repairing and dressing.

A/C—PM. Affordable. Consignments.

Prop. Blanche Pratley   609–884–3551

THE ROADRUNNER, 609–611 Jefferson St. (off Lafayette St., main st. of town).

Hours: Summer season (June–Sept.): Daily 10–5; off-season: Sat. & Sun. 12–5

Two big red barns filled with Early American furniture, Tiffany-type lamps and

THE ROADRUNNER *continued*

domes, "unusual Americana," nautical items, clocks, chandeliers, china, and glass. New giftware.

A/C—PM. Wide range.

Prop. Carol and Bob Gomm   609–884–4563

TRAVIS COVE ANTIQUES, 219 Jackson St. (off Lafayette St., main st. of town).

Hours: Summer season (Memorial Day–Labor Day): Daily 10–5; off-season: Sat., Sun., hols. 10–5

South Jersey pine cupboards, wicker, primitives, china, Orientalia, glassware, and collectibles. "A little bit of everything" at the flea market outside daily from July 4 thru Labor Day, weekends through fall.

A/C—PM. Affordable.

Prop. Jean and Fran Dolbow   609–884–2363

THE VICTORIAN LOOK, 654 Hughes St. (bisects Ocean St.). *Also see* Repair and Restoration listing.

Hours: Summer season (June–Sept.): Daily 10–9; off-season: By appt.

Two floors of a refurbished barn filled with Victorian antiques—furniture and accessories. Fine china and glass. Wicker. Complete interior design service, including documented wallpapers, coordinated materials, and upholstery. Chair caning and furniture refinishing.

A/C—PM. Wide range. Consignment. Authentication.

Prop. Marjorie Forrester   609–884–5360

THE VICTORIAN PINK HOUSE, 33 Perry St. (off the Victorian Mall).

Hours: Summer season (June–Sept.): Daily 10–1:30, 4:30–10. Closed Tues. Appt. advisable after Sept. 15

The Victorian Pink House, built in 1879, is one of the country's most photographed houses. Bright pink with lots of white gingerbread, the small but elegant example of Victorian architecture has been depicted on the cover of The New Yorker, *in travel guides, architectural journals, and is listed in the National Historic Register. The antique and gift shop in the house retains the 1800s atmosphere with nostalgic antique jewelry, art glass, copper, pewter, brass; new gift items include Royal Doulton, Royal Copenhagen, Gorham, quaint music boxes, Victorian-type accessories.*

A/C—PM. Wide range. Authentication.

Prop. Nancy and John Miller   609–884–2525

Cape May Court House 08210

THE PENNY POT GENERAL STORE, Stone Harbor Blvd.

Hours: Fri., Sat. 9–4; Sun. 11–4

Some country and oak furniture, wicker, china, glass, old bottles, along with new giftware.

A/C—PM. Affordable.

Prop. Joanne Nachtigall   609–465–7220

Clermont 08210

CLERMONT COUNTRY STORE, 461 Shore Rd. (Rt. 9, northbound).

Hours: Summer season (June–Sept.): Daily 10–5. Closed Tues. Off-season: By chance or appt.

General line of primitive through Victorian furniture; pattern glass, fine china and glassware, cut glass, clocks, old lamps. "Buy and sell antiques."

A/C—PM. Wide range. Authentication if history is known.

Prop. Doris and Del Simmerman   609–263–8931

THE STATION HOUSE, 494 Shore Rd. (Rt. 9, southbound).

Hours: By chance or appt.

Three rooms of antiques in a beautiful old country home c. 1774. Nice selection of country pine and primitive furnishings from the late 1700s; early pewter, silver, pottery, wooden-, tin- and ironware; china and country baskets.

A—PM. Selective. Authentication if history is known.

Prop. Millie Hall   609–263–3798

THE WALKING STICK, 472A Shore Rd. (Rt. 9, southbound).

Hours: Daily 10–5; Sun. 1–5

Small pieces of furniture, good selection of Heisey and Depression glass, Bavarian and German china as well as Limoges and Nippon attractively arranged in an inviting shop.

A/C—PM. Affordable. Authentication if history is known.

Prop. Margaret Brakefield   609–263–2118

Cold Spring 08204

CAPE MAY FORGE, Old Shore Rd. (½ mi. south of Canal Bridge) *Also see* Repair and Restoration listing.

Hours: Daily 10–5; Sun. 1–5 from April thru Dec.

All kinds of old lamps, kerosene through electrified, a specialty. Small pieces of furniture, decorative accessories. New shades especially designed for old lamps. Lamp repairing, polishing, and buffing, rewiring of lamps and fixtures. The Holmstrups are members of the Victorian Soc. of America, Jersey Cape Chapter. Appraising service.

A/C—PM. Affordable. Consignment (selective). Authentication when possible.

Prop. Gloria and Kenneth Holmstrup   609–884–5397

THE RED BARN, Stimpson Lane and Bayshore Rd. (west of Rt. 9).

Hours: Tues. thru Sat. 10–5; Sun. 1–5

A mixture of old and new in a 200-year-old barn. Small pieces of country furniture, china, crystal, pressed glass, old prints and books, hand-carved canes. New handcrafted jewelry from Cape May "diamonds."

A/C—PM. Affordable. Consignments. Authentication when possible.

Prop. Eleanor and Ray Callahan   609–884–8151

Erma 08204

THE COUNTRY HOUSE ANTIQUES, Rt. 9, southbound. *Also see* Repair and Restoration listing.

Hours: Mon. thru Thurs. 12–5:30; Fri. thru Sun. 10–8

A restored Victorian home c. 1865 crammed with early and Victorian furniture, large collection of fine china and glass, old lamps; some wicker, coins, and antique jewelry. Interesting period pieces from estates. Mr. Brandenburg provides a decorator service and does appraisals. Furniture refinishing of period pieces.

A/C—PM. Wide range. Authentication.

Prop. Dennis Brandenburg   609–884–2381

FIND IT SHOP, Box 130, Rt. 9, southbound. *Also see* Repair and Restoration listing.

Hours: Daily 8–6; or by appt.

FIND IT SHOP *continued*

Victorian and oak furniture and "a bit of everything" in glass, china, clocks, bric-a-brac. Hand-stripping of furniture and caning.

A/C—PM. Affordable. Authentication.

Prop. Robert Dickinson   609–884–8186

HOUSE OF OLD, Rt. 9, northbound. *Also see* Repair and Restoration listing.

Hours: Daily 10–4:30; Sun. 12–4:30. Closed Tues.

General line of Victorian furniture, some oak; large collection of side chairs refinished or in-the-rough; 1800s wood-burning and coal-burning stoves. "Hard to find items." Old stoves repaired, furniture refinished or restored, chairs caned, mirrors resilvered.

A/C—PM. Affordable. Consignments accepted.

Prop. Rose Marie and Bob O'Shea   609–886–3458

Mayville 08210

LITTLE TEACHER ANTIQUES, Rt. 9 at Hereford Ave.

Hours: Summer season (June–Sept.) : Sat. & Sun. 1–5:30

Antique and collectible china, glass, bric-a-brac, small pieces of Victorian furniture in a former old church school. Mrs. Vandepol is a member of the Victorian Soc. of America, Cape May County Chapter, and does appraisals.

A/C—PM. Affordable. Authentication when possible.

Prop. Martha Vandepol   609–465–7552

Ocean City 08226

BARBARA'S ANTIQUES, 918 Asbury Ave. (main st. of town).

Hours: Summer season (June–Sept.) : Mon. thru Sat. 10–4

Antique dolls and antique jewelry are specialties. Also a general line of fine china and silver.

A/C—PM. Affordable. Authentication when possible.

Prop. Barbara Henszey   609–398–1992

JOSEPH'S ANTIQUES, 908 Asbury Ave. (main st. of town).

Hours: Mon. thru Sat. 12–3 year-round; other times by appt.

JOSEPH'S ANTIQUES *continued*

Pattern glass, cut glass, porcelains, fine china, bisque, Orientalia, and a general line of antique accessories.

A/C—PM. Affordable. Consignments. Authentication.

Prop. Caroline Walters 609–399–0839

LOST AND FOUND ANTIQUES, 1324 Asbury Ave. (main st. of town).

Hours: Summer season (May–Sept.) : Daily 9:30–5:30

Specializing in Victorian furniture and appropriate accessories; antique music boxes (when available), art glass, silver. Member of the Music Box Soc. Internat'l. Appraisal service.

A/C—PM. Wide range. Authentication.

Prop. Carol and Joe Lehman 609–399–2934

MOWERY'S ANTIQUES, 3234 Asbury Ave. (main st. of town).

Hours: Mon. thru Sat. 9:30–5:30; July & Aug. 9:30–9

Antique jewelry a specialty; general line of furniture, china, including Meissen, Sèvres, Limoges; old silver.

A/C—PM. Wide range. Authentication when possible.

Prop. Annabelle Mowery 609–399–0552

THE OLD DOLL SHOP, 343 Asbury Ave. (main st. of town). *Also see* Repair & Restoration listing.

Hours: Mon., Wed., Fri., Sat. 1–5

Large selection of antique dolls. Complete repair service for old dolls and dressmaking. "Old dolls bought and sold."

A/C—PM. Affordable.

Prop. Doris H. Maxwell 609–399–0161

THE SUTTONS ANTIQUES, 1741 Asbury Ave. (main st. of town).

Hours: May thru Dec.: Mon. thru Sat. 9:30–5:30

A spacious shop featuring antique furniture from primitive to formal; nice collection of antique silver, jewelry, and watches; pattern glass, art glass, antique china, especially hand-painted china.

A—PM. Selective.

Prop. Lois Sutton 609–399–0552

Ocean View 08230

THE BLUE BARN, Shore Rd. (Rt. 9, southbound).

Hours: Summer season (June–Sept.): Daily 10–5; off-season: Better to phone ahead

Two pleasant rooms in a refurbished barn with tastefully arranged formal and country furniture; pitcher and bowl sets, cut glass, pressed glass; old trunks.

A/C—PM. Affordable. Authentication when possible.

Prop. Cody Holland; Helen Howell, Associate   609–263–8967

ELEANOR & HAROLD POST ANTIQUES, 462 Shore Rd. (Rt. 9, southbound).

Hours: Daily 10–5

Nice selection of country furniture, primitives, pressed and cut glass, antique and collectible china, fill three rooms of a browsable shop to the rear of the main house.

A/C—PM. Affordable. Authentication when possible.

Prop. Eleanor and Harold Post   609–263–8775

STAGE COACH INN ANTIQUES, 140 Shore Rd. (Rt. 9, southbound).

Hours: Daily 10–6. Closed Thurs.

Small pieces of furniture, particularly oak washstands; fine china and old glass, in a charming shop in back of the house.

A/C—PM. Affordable. Consignments. Authentication.

Prop. Major and Mrs. M. G. Vance   609–263–3594

Palermo 08223

FRED PEECH ANTIQUES, 932 Shore Rd. (Rt. 9, southbound).

Hours: Daily 9–5

General line of antique furniture, chests of drawers, side chairs, country cupboards; fine china, glass, coins, old guns, in a sizable barn adjoining an 1830s farmhouse.

A—PM. Affordable/Selective.

Prop. Fred Peech   609–399–5535

Rio Grande 08242

JACK'S BARN, Rt. 47 and Railroad Ave.

Hours: Summer season (June–Sept.): Daily 11–4:30; off-season: Daily 11–4:30. Closed Sun.

Mostly used furniture and contents of homes, but for the diligent collector some oldies among the younger pieces. The enormous dairy barn, "one of the few left in South Jersey," provides lots of room for what-nots, "antiques when we can get them," china, glass, bric-a-brac. Estate appraisals.

C/Some antiques—PM. Affordable.

Prop. Jack Paynter · 609–886–1045

Seaville 08230

THE DUCKS NEST, 2023 S. Shore Rd. (Rt. 9, northbound).

Hours: Daily 10–5. Closed Sun.

A third-generation decoy artisan, Mr. Shourds has a large collection of new and old decoys, including those of his father and grandfather. His own decoys have been in many exhibits and are considered collector's items. Also beautiful hand-carved birds of all kinds in natural settings.

A/C—PM. Affordable/Selective. Authentication.

Prop. Harry V. Shourds · 609–399–0228

SEAVILLE CURIOSITY SHOP, 276 Shore Rd. (Rt. 9, southbound).

Hours: Summer season (June–Sept.): Daily 10–5; off-season: Better to phone ahead

The Corson's Tavern that goes back more than 100 years now houses three rooms of collectible china and glass, some antique furniture, old clocks, new "Gone with the Wind" lamps. A sampling of everything.

A/C—PM. Affordable. Authentication when possible.

Prop. Anne Donovan · 609–263–8044

South Dennis 08245

DENNIS LANDING ANTIQUES, 922 Delsea Dr. (Rt. 47).

Hours: April–Dec.: Daily 1–4. Closed Sun.; other times by appt.

DENNIS LANDING ANTIQUES *continued*

A selective shop with early 19th-century formal and country furniture in an interesting house, the back built in 1801 and joined with the brick front section in 1850. Nice selection of early creamware and soft-paste china. Appropriate prints and accessory pieces.

A/Some collectibles. Selective. Consignments. Authentication.

Prop. Jane and Edgar Van Nuis   609–861–5153

Swainton 08210

NELLIE E. CRAMER ANTIQUES, Rt. 9 (5 mi. north of Cape May Court House).

Hours: Daily 10–5

Mostly antique dolls; some furniture and china; a few Oriental rugs.

A/C—PM. Affordable. Occasional consignment.

Prop. Nellie E. Cramer   609–465–7667

Tuckahoe 08250

FOUR Y'S GENERAL STORE, Rt. 50 and Mosquito Ldg. Rd.

Hours: Summer season (June–Sept.): Mon. thru Fri. 10–6; Sat. & Sun. 10–9; off-season: Better to phone ahead

Many new gift items in an old-time general store, but look for antiques in the back. One of the best collections of oyster plates from 1875 on from a private collection. Pressed glass, Depression glass, old tins, and collectibles.

A/C—PM. Affordable. Authentication when possible.

Prop. Marvin Arnold, Georgette Young   609–628–2721

Magnificent sterling banquet hall candelabrum, originally base or pedestal mounted. French Empire, no later than 1815; one of a set of four. *Courtesy Sterling Silversmiths, Scotch Plains. Photo: Eric G. Mumm*

Across the Delaware
Urbane and Rural Byways

Portrait of a member of the Biddle family by Rembrandt Peale, 1834. Oil on canvas, 35 in. × 30 in. A son of the distinguished American artist Charles Wilson Peale, Rembrandt Peale was born in Bucks County. *Courtesy Daniel Hersh Galleries, New Hope*

Bucks County
Pennsylvania

BRISTOL MART, 316 Mill St. *Also see* Auctioneers listing.

Hours: Mon., Wed. thru Sat. 10–5. Closed Tues. & Sun.

Dolls (1880s to contemporary), early and collectible toys; general line. Monthly auctions conducted by David Reday; mailing list. Member Letitia Penn Doll Club, Phila.

C/A—PM. Affordable. Authentication when possible.

Prop. Marianne Reday   215–788–2621

THE LITTLE NUGGET, 211 Mill St.

Hours: Mon. thru Fri. 11–5:30 or 6; Sat. 'til 5. Mon. & Fri. 'til 9.

Antique furniture, glass, pictures, prints, paintings on glass, bric-a-brac. New imported decorative Italian tiles, marble. Part of a row of frame structures thought to be nearly 300 years old. The ceilings rise to 14 feet.

A/C—PM. Affordable/Wide range.

Prop. Mary M. Chapman   215–788–5652

Buckingham 18912

DUCK & DOLPHIN ANTIQUES, Rt. 202, southbound (at Rt. 313).

Hours: Mon., Thurs., Fri., Sat. 11–5; Sun. 12–5. Closed Tues. & Wed.

Fine 18th-century French and American antiques, decorative accessories, stained glass. Richly carved 19th-century Renaissance furniture; Louis XV carved pieces. Also bronzes, marble statuary, garden appointments (benches, urns). Antiques purchased. Appraisals. A handsome Italianate villa stone residence, completed in 1850.

A—Some pieces marked. Selective to serious collectors. Authentication.

Prop. Paul Cox   215–348–2887

EDNA'S ANTIQUE SHOPPE, at the General Greene Inn, Rts. 263 and 413.

Hours: Mon. thru Sat. 10–5 (flexible); Sun. 12:30–2:30 (call ahead)

General line; pottery, paintings, cut glass, pattern glass, bronzes; "a little bit of everything." At the 200-year-old General Greene Inn. Member Bucks County Antiques Dealers Assoc.

A/C. Affordable.

Prop. Edna Wehmeyer   215–794–7261

Carversville 18913

HOBBY HORSE ANTIQUES, Saw Mill Rd. (off Aquetong Rd.).

Hours: Daily 9–5; and by appt.

American country furniture, primitives. New quilts. Search service. Member Bucks County Antiques Dealers Assoc.

A/also new—PM. Wide range. Authentication.

Prop. Roz Schaeffer   215–345–7719

THE MILL, Carversville.

Hours: 7 days 11–5

Eighteenth-century Continental furniture, American primitives, pottery, kitchenware. Member Bucks County Antiques Dealers Assoc. Also at Lahaska Antiques Centre, Lahaska.

A—PM. Wide range. Authentication.

Prop. Lilias Barger   215–297–5678

MILLER'S STORE ANTIQUES, Aquetong Rd.
Hours: By chance or appt.
Country store items, tin advertising.
C—PM. Affordable. Consignments.
Prop. Elizabeth Miller   215–297–5535

Chalfont 18914

EVELYN'S UPS AND DOWNS, Chalfont.
Hours: By appt.
General line; furniture, clocks, paintings, china, glass, art glass; some pewter, brass, copper, tinware, silverplate, and sterling; costume jewelry, music boxes. Mr. Cooper is a member of the Nat'l. Assoc. of Watch & Clock Collectors. Attractive shop in a 150-year-old wood-pegged barn on "Mounted Route No. 2," dating to an earlier era of rural mail delivery.
A/C—PM. Wide range. Authentication.
Prop. Evelyn B. Cooper   215–822–2812

GUTHRIE & LARASON, 4 E. Butler Ave. (Rt. 202). *Also see* Repair and Restoration listing.
Hours: Daily 10–6; call ahead
Country furniture and accessories, baskets, redware. Antique furniture restored. Member Bucks County Antiques Dealers Assoc., Antiques Dealers Assoc. of Central N. J. A blue and cream trim Victorian facing Chalfont Inn.
A—PM. Affordable/Wide range. Authentication.
Prop. Patti Guthrie, Lew Larason   215–822–3987

Coopersburg 18036

C & E ANTIQUES AND COLLECTIBLES, Rt. 309 (1 mi. south of Coopersburg).
Hours: 7 days 9–6; call ahead suggested
Early through turn-of-the-century furniture, including marble-top pieces, some primitives. Collectibles; beer trays, advertising items, china, glass, Oriental vases, lamps, old prints. Meticulously displayed in five rooms.
A/C—Some prices marked. Affordable. Consignments. Authentication when possible.
Prop. C & E Antiques   215–282–4749

Doylestown 18901

HERITAGE ANTIQUES, 69 E. Oakland Ave.

Hours: Mon. thru Sat. 11–5

Jewelry, 1880 to 1930s; working pocket and ladies' pendant watches, pine mirrors (c. 1835 to late 19th century), Empire and Victorian furniture; china, glass. A gracious shop; prices firm. Matching service for sterling flatware. Member Bucks County Antiques Dealers Assoc. Parking at rear.

A/C—PM. Affordable. Authentication when possible.

Prop. Elizabeth McCain   215–348–4752

Dublin 18917

RHINE'S ANTIQUES AND COLLECTIBLES, 506 Rt. 313 (just west of jct. Rt. 113).

Hours: Wed., Thurs., Fri. 1–5; Sat. 12–5; and by appt.

General line; some primitives. Antiques purchased. Also new stained glass, dried arrangements, pottery, candles. Theorem painting and demonstrations. Pretty shop with red door and large front window, Pennsylvania Dutch design on the shutters.

A/C; also new—PM. Affordable/Wide range. Consignments. Authentication.

Prop. Jan Rhine   215–249–3920

Durham 18039

DURHAM VILLAGE ANTIQUES, Rt. 212. *Also see* Repair and Restoration listing.

Hours: 7 days 9–5

Early and Victorian furniture, oak, lamps; general line. Furniture stripping and refinishing.

C—PM. Affordable; furniture higher. Consignments. Authentication.

Prop. Kenneth Hollingsworth   215–346–7047

Forest Grove 18922

THE OLD—THE UNIQUE, Forest Grove Rd. (4 mi. south of Doylestown).
Hours: Call ahead

Primitives, salt dips, agate; general line. Antiques purchased. Congenial shop; dealers welcome. Member Bucks County Antiques Dealers Assoc.

A/C—PM. Affordable.

Prop. Thelma K. Tomlinson   215–794–8317

Fountainville 18923

RUTH'S WHAT NOT & FURNITURE SHOP, Rt. 313. *Also see* Repair and Restoration listing.
Hours: Tues., Wed. 10–5:30; Thurs., Fri. 10–9

Used furniture, some older pieces; dishes, bric-a-brac. New heavy pine reproduction furniture. Interior decorating. Also to dealers. Refinishing, touch-up work by Ruth Moyer and Bob Roth.

A/C—PM. Wide range.

Prop. Ruth Moyer   215–249–3768

Furlong 18925

THE PINE SHOP, Rt. 263-York Rd.
Hours: Mon. thru Sat. 8–4

Pre-1830 maple, cherry, pine furniture; descriptive tags. Antiques purchased. Appraisals. Member Bucks County Antiques Dealers Assoc. Est. 1945.

A—PM. Wide range/Selective. Authentication.

Prop. Mark Franklin   215–794–8281 (bus.)
                    723–9078 (eves.)

Holicong 18928

HOLICROFT HOUSE (BUCKS COUNTY EMPORIUM), Holicong Rd.
Hours: By appt.

HOLICROFT HOUSE (BUCKS COUNTY EMPORIUM) *continued*

Primitives, copper, brass, mirrors, andirons, small furniture. Member Bucks County Antiques Dealers Assoc.

A—PM. Affordable. Authentication.

Prop. Robert Farnum, Richard Wenick   215–794–7727

Hulmeville 19047

THE GALLERY UPSTAIRS, 521 Main St.

Hours: Daily 9:30–6; Sun. usually 1–6. Closed Wed.

Primitives; jelly and corner cupboards, chairs, tables, blanket chests, primitive tools (including a complete old boring mill). Gallery of contemporary art: original works, signed and numbered prints. Custom framing.

A/C—PM. Selective. Authentication when possible; on request.

Prop. Chris and Bob Stein   215–757–6514

MILL FLEA MART, Trenton and Hulmeville Rds.

Hours: (Shop) Thurs., Fri. 6–10; (Flea Market) Sat. 12–10; Sun. 12–6

Shop and indoor flea market. Antiques, general merchandise; turn-of-the-century oak, late 19th-century cherry, some pine furniture; collectible glass, including art glass and Heisey; china, brass hardware. In the Old Fricke Grist Mill, built in 1881. The three-story mill replaces an earlier structure built on the bank of Neshaminy Creek c. 1740.

C/A—PM. Wide range.

Prop. Kathy Loeffler   215–757–1777

Kintnersville 18930

GAIL ANDREWS, Rt. 611 (jct. Rt. 32). *Also see* Repair and Restoration listing.

Hours: Summer: Daily 10–5; Sun. 1–5. Closed Tues. Winter by appt.

Country and Victorian furniture and accessories; small primitives, baskets, redware, crocks. Good country and period furniture restored; fine cabinetry. In business more than twenty years. Member Bucks County Antiques Dealers Assoc. A Victorian gothic house, built in 1883.

A/C—PM. Wide range. Consignments. Authentication.

Prop. Philip and Gail Andrews   215–847–5177

PICK & POK ANTIQUES, Rt. 611. Mailing address: R. D. 1.

Hours: 7 days 9–5. Winter: weekdays 1–5; weekends 9–5

Turn-of-the-century and Victorian furniture in-the-rough, glass, china, books, small items; "what-is-its," unusual pieces of obscure use. Over 8,000 items in 36 showcases.

C/A—PM. Affordable; glass, books higher. Authentication when possible.

Prop. Joe and Sophie Weiss   215–847–5030

Lahaska 18931

ANTONIO ALBA LTD., Rt. 202, southbound. Mailing address: Box 395.

Hours: Weekdays 10–5:30; Sun. 12–5:30. Closed Tues. & Wed.

Selective antique jewelry, watches, old silver, stained glass; architectural and decorative accessories. Also to dealers, architects, decorators. Antique jewelry remodeling, renovation by appointment. American Express, Master Charge. Member Bucks County Antiques Dealers Assoc., Nat'l. Assoc. of Watch & Clock Collectors. In an 1820 stone inn.

A/C—PM. Wide range. Authentication.

Prop. Antonio Alba   215–794–8228

BENCH AND BOARD ANTIQUES, at 1821 House Antiques. Rt. 202, southbound. Mailing address: Box 173. *Also see* Repair and Restoration listing.

Hours: 7 days 11–5:30

Early furniture; nightstands, benches, blanket chests, mirrors, small tables; kitchen tin and woodenware, boxes. Repair and restoration of primitives, all hand work.

A—PM. Selective. Authentication.

Prop. M. St. James   215–794–8662

COLLECTOR'S DELIGHT, Rt. 263 (opp. Cock & Bull Restaurant).

Hours: Mon. thru Sat. 11–5; Sun. 12–5

Authenticated Edna Hibel and Norman Rockwell lithographs, collector's plates; some furniture. New miniature ceramic animals, giftware. Search service. Master Charge, Visa. Member The Bradford Exchange (worldwide trading in collector's plates).

C; also new—PM. Affordable/Selective (lithographs). Lithographs authenticated.

Prop. Betty Phillips   215–794–5392

DARBY—BARRETT ANTIQUES, Rt. 202, northbound (opp. main entrance to Peddler's Village).

Hours: 7 days 12–5. Closed Christmas.

Primarily decorative pieces and adornments. Antique jewelry (gold, genuine stones—Victorian to the 1930s); Oriental objects, paintings, silver flatware and serving pieces, lamps, old Russian and Japanese items, icons, ivory, bronzes, brass, copper; some signed art glass.

A/C—Some prices marked. Affordable/Selective. Consignments. Authentication when possible.

Prop. Joseph Barrett, Paul Darby   215–794–8277

1821 HOUSE ANTIQUES, Rt. 202, southbound. *Also see* Repair and Restoration listing.

Hours: 7 days 11–5:30

Early rope and canopy beds a specialty. Also dining tables, cupboards, chairs, chests. Repair and restoration of primitive furniture by William Nickel, all hand work. Shares premises with Bench and Board Antiques.

A—PM. Selective. Authentication.

Prop. Helen Nickel   215–794–8662 (bus.)
                                                            646–7643 (res.)

EVELYN'S ANTIQUES, Rt. 202, northbound (next to Solebury Nat'l. Bank). *Also see* Repair and Restoration listing.

Hours: 7 days 9–5:30

American cut glass, 1850 to 1910; kerosene and gas lamps, oak furniture; general line. Lamp rewiring, repair, and restoration. Furniture hand-stripping, repair, restoration, refinishing; oak a specialty. Member Bucks County Antiques Dealers Assoc.

A/C—PM. Wide range. Authentication.

Prop. John Williams   215–794–7385

GOULD'S ANTIQUES, Rt. 202, northbound.

Hours: 7 days 10:30–5:30; call ahead

American farm furniture, glassware; lanterns, tools, country kitchenware. Refinishing. Houseplants from the greenhouse. Very pleasant.

A—PM. Wide range. Authentication.

Prop. Helen Gould   215–794–8395

LAHASKA ANTIQUES CENTRE, Rt. 202, northbound.

Hours: 7 days 11–5; check for Tues. closing

A number of bright and attractive shops in two adjacent buildings. Opposite Peddler's Village and other centers. More room to browse weekdays.

Prop. (Mr.) Von Zelowitz   215–794–7884

DOROTHY AND ABBY BROOKS.

Textiles, quilts, country furniture, primitives, unusual items. Antiques purchased. Member Bucks County Antiques Dealers Assoc.

C (older)—PM. Wide range.

"FOLLIES," Al and Gertrude Hornby.

Cut glass, porcelains, sterling, some jewelry, lamps, old fans, rare walking canes, small furniture (early and Victorian). Attractive, pleasant shop.

A/C—PM. Wide range. Authentication when possible.

GREEN GATE ANTIQUES, Mrs. George Frost.

Glassware, finished trunks, furniture, decorative accessories; selected nice pieces.

C—PM. Affordable.

FAE HAIGHT & LILIAS BARGER.

Decorative antiques. Fine and unusual glass, porcelains, some American period furniture, Continental pieces, primitives, "a splash of Oriental things"; kitchen accessories, woodworking tools. Antiques purchased; estate consultation. Member Early Amer. Industries Assoc. (Ms. Haight), Bucks County Antiques Dealers Assoc. (Ms. Barger). Lilias Barger also at Carversville.

A—PM. Wide range. Authentication when possible.

STANLEY'S ANTIQUES, Eleanor Zebersky.

General line.

A/C—PM. Affordable. Consignments.

K. AND H. STIRNER, Heather Stirner.

Knowledgeable collection of Oriental and ethnographic art. African, Oceanic, pre-Columbian and American Indian objects and adornments;

LAHASKA ANTIQUES CENTRE *continued*

Greek, Roman, Egyptian, and Persian antiquities. Also to decorators and dealers. Appraisals. Member Bucks County Antiques Dealers Assoc.

A/C—Most prices marked. Wide range/Serious collectors. Consignments. Authentication.

215–794–8115

LIPPINCOTT ANTIQUES, Rt. 202, southbound.

Hours: Mon. thru Sat. 10–5

Eighteenth- and 19th-century formal and country furniture. Member Bucks County Antiques Dealers Assoc.

A—PM. Selective to serious collectors. Authentication.

Prop. Carroll Lippincott   215–794–7734

LYNNE-ART'S GLASS HOUSE, INC., Rt. 202, southbound.
Mailing address: Box 242.

Hours: Daily 10–4; eves. by appt.

Specializing in Heisey glass. Authentication service for collectors. A small museum contains a complete Heisey animal collection, including rare trial colors and production patterns. The proprietors are authors of The Heisey Animals, Books I and II, *available direct. Member Bucks County Antiques Dealers Assoc., Pa. Antique Dealers Assoc., charter members Nat'l. Heisey Collectors of Amer.*

C—PM. Wide range. Authentication.

Prop. Lynne Bloch, Art Hartman   215–794–7800

MERNDALE ANTIQUES, Rt. 202, northbound (next to Holiday Inn).
Mailing address: Box 221.

Hours: Tues. thru Sun. 11–5. Closed Mon.

Country and more formal furniture; jelly cupboards, dry sinks, apothecary chests, desks, chairs, hanging and corner cupboards. General line of early Americana; kitchenware, some toys, needlework, prints, tools. Custom lampshades, lamp wiring. Framing. Member Bucks County Antiques Dealers Assoc.

A/C (some)—PM. Wide range. Authentication.

Prop. W. H. Merner   215–598–3354

OAKLAWN METAL CRAFT & ANTIQUES, Rt. 202, southbound (next to Midway Volunteer Fire Company). Mailing address: Box 13.

Hours: Mon. thru Fri. 8–5; Sat. & Sun. 1–5. Closed Sun. July & Aug.

Longtime shop filled with the old and new for collectors. Antique lighting

OAKLAWN METAL CRAFTS & ANTIQUES *continued*

fixtures (and new lighting by Dallas and David John), kerosene lamps, outdoor lanterns; early craftsmen's tools, old hardware, fireplace utensils; crocks, jugs, old tin kitchen molds. A bin with "Things to hang things up." Another with "More things, but cheaper." Handsome new weathervanes cast from old molds, custom-built lanterns; lighting fixtures restored. Member Bucks County Antiques Dealers Assoc., Pa. State Antiques Assoc., Early Amer. Industries Assoc.

A/C; also new—PM. Wide range.

Prop. Dallas, David, and Florence John   215–794–7387

ORIENTAL GALLERY, Rt. 202, northbound (opp. The Yard). Mailing address: Box 304.

Hours: Tues. thru Sun. 12–5. Closed Mon.

Oriental art and antiquities. Ming (1368 to 1644) and Ching Dynasty (1644 to 1912) porcelains, bronzes, carvings.

A/C (some)—PM. Wide range/Serious collectors. Authentication.

Prop. Perry N. Trax   215–794–8583

PEDDLER'S VILLAGE, Rt. 202 and Street Rd.

Hours: Vary with shop

In the heart of Bucks County, a concentration of interestingly browsable and very attractive shops, boutiques, and a restaurant, clustered around a beautifully landscaped commons. Seasonal and holiday events throughout the year. Acres of parking for private vehicles and buses.

KATY KANE, at the Antique and Craft Barn, Street Rd.

Hours: Tues. thru Sun. 12–5

Antique clothing a specialty—Victorian and Edwardian, thru the '30s; 19th-century quilts. Also in the barn, hand-loomed rugs by Kay and Ron Loch.

A/C—PM. Affordable. Authentication.

Prop. Katy Kane   215–357–2683

THE VILLAGE ANTIQUES.

Hours: Mon. thru Sat. 10–5; Fri. 'til 9

American cut glass, fine old lamps, Staffordshire dishes; corner cupboards, cabinets, tables, chairs, chests, one or two chandeliers, andirons, some candlesticks, prints by Currier & Ives and Wallace Nutting. Some new accessory items: enamel art by John Shaw, miniature antique silver

PEDDLER'S VILLAGE *continued*

reproductions by Eugene Kupjack. Reference library. Wiring of decanters, vases, and lamps. Lamps reassembled and mounted; custom shades. Old brass buffed.

A/C—PM. Wide range.

Prop. Mary K. Campbell   215–794–8180

THE YANKEE CLIPPER.

Hours: Mon. thru Sat. 10–5; Fri. 'til 9

Orientals; porcelain, pottery, ivories. Antiques, reproductions; much that's new.

A/C—PM. Wide range.

Prop. Reginald Cornley   215–794–7322

PICTURE FRAME GALLERY, Rt. 202, northbound. Mailing address: Box 75. *Also see* Repair and Restoration listing.

Hours: 7 days 10–5

Old frames, original prints, etchings, engravings, works of art. General line; sterling, china, including Royal Beyreuth and Belleek, cut glass, crocks, some marble-top pieces, a decorative Victorian easel; duplicates from an extensive bell collection. Old frames stocked and restored. Selective new frames; custom and creative framing. Lectures on old bells (c. 2000 B.C. to the 19th century). Member Bucks County Antiques Dealers Assoc., Pa. State Antiques Assoc., Pa. Antiques Appraisers' Assoc., Amer. Bell Assoc.

A/C—PM. Wide range. Authentication.

Prop. Eve Bianco   215–794–7022

STERLING CENTER, Rt. 202, southbound (south of Street Rd.).

Hours: Vary with shop

Antiques, gifts, plants, and a very busy snack bar. A double tier of shops in the popular antiques center of the county. Parking also in adjacent areas.

Prop. Wayne Sterling   215–794–7375

JACQUES' ELEGANT JUNQUE.

Hours: Wed. thru Sun. 12–5

Cut and colored glass, Amberina, cranberry, vaseline; French and English porcelains from 1780; some furniture, primarily English. Old and new.

STERLING CENTER *continued*

Interior design service. Furniture refinishing. Master Charge, Visa.

C; also new/A—PM. Wide range. Authentication.

Prop. John J. McLean   215–794–8055

PARTNERS' CHOICE.

Hours: Tues. thru Sun. 1–5

China, glass, furniture, mirrors. Member Bucks County Antiques Dealers Assoc.

C—PM. Wide range. Authentication.

Prop. Rose Mary Wagner   215–794–8940

PENNINGTON GALLERY.

Hours: Daily 11–5

Large selection of new gifts. Antiques, American cut and pattern glass.

C; new gifts—PM. Wide range.

Prop. Carrie Austin   215–794–7876 (bus.)
                                 609–737–0453 (res.)

STERLING'S.

Hours: Tues. thru Fri. 9–5; Sat. & Sun. 10–6

Eighteenth- and 19th-century country French furniture, reproductions, and decorative accessories. Appraisals. Member Bucks County Antiques Dealers Assoc.

A/C; reproductions—PM. Selective to serious collectors. Authentication.

Prop. Wayne Sterling   215–794–7375

Langhorne 19047

SCHAEFFER'S ANTIQUES, Langhorne-Yardley Rd.

Hours: By appt. or chance

General line; furniture, pattern glass, china; oak, primitives, pine. Layaway plan. Member Atlantic Seaboard Antiques Dealers Assoc. Located in a tenant's home c. 1762, originally a four-room, two-family structure.

A/C—PM. Affordable/Wide range. Authentication on request.

Prop. Janice Schaeffer   215–757–8172

Lumberville 18933

LUMBERVILLE ANTIQUE SHOP, Rt. 32 (River Rd., opp. "1740 House").
Hours: Call ahead. Closed Wed.
Established dealer. Seventeenth-century pieces, early tables, chairs; new brass, copper. The oldest saltbox in Bucks County; put together in 1825 from older houses taken down for construction of the Delaware Canal, a sixty-mile former transportation route from Easton to Bristol.
A/C; also new—PM. Wide range. Consignments. Authentication.
Prop. William V. Woolsey   215–297–5618

GEOFFREY STEELE, Lumberville.
Hours: By appt.
Antiquarian, out-of-print, and rare volumes of architecture and art. Scholarly books, bibliography, references. Appraisals within specialty. Member Middle Atlantic Chapter Antiquarian Booksellers' Assoc. of Amer.
A/C—Most prices marked. Wide range. Authentication.
Prop. Geoffrey Steele   215–297–5187

Morrisville 19067

CHRISTIE LTD., 710 W. Bridge St.
Hours: 7 days 9–5
Furniture—primitive, oak, turn-of-the-century; china, silver. General line.
A/C—PM. Affordable/Wide range. Consignments. Authentication on request.
Prop. Genevieve Sanner   215–295–6666

HELEN MURPHY, 525 Jefferson Ave.
Hours: By appt.
Primitives, country furniture, and accessories; original condition and refinished. Member Bucks County Antiques Dealers Assoc.
A/C. Wide range.
Prop. Helen Murphy   215–295–7628

New Britain 18901

BLUEBERRY MANOR LTD., 326 W. Butler Ave. (Rt. 202, northbound).
Hours: Tues. thru Sat. 10–5

Some antiques, china, primitives. Handcrafted reproduction furniture; gifts, handcrafts. In a farmhouse built in 1809 on a William Penn grant; the 130-year-old addition was a blacksmith shop prior to and thru the Civil War.

A/C; also new—PM. Wide range. Authentication.

Prop. Marie Rosenquist   215–348–9885

ROCKAFELLOW'S ANTIQUES, 609 E. Butler Ave. (Rt. 202).
Hours: Mon. thru Sat. 11–5. Closed Sun.

Nineteenth-century American silverplate, coin silver, and sterling. Primitives. Member Bucks County Antiques Dealers Assoc.

A/C—PM. Affordable/Wide range. Authentication.

Prop. Theodore and Elizabeth Rockafellow   215–345–6709

FRANK J. UDINSON, 134 Iron Hill Rd. (off Rt. 202, southbound; 1 mi. west of Doylestown).

Hours: By appt. or chance

Tiffany, Tiffany-style domes and lamps, old hanging and table lamps. Carriage and country furniture, Jacobean to collectible. Primitives, paintings, corner cupboards, blanket chests, musical instruments, "antiques and objects of art." Very interesting, long-established country shop, belied by outward appearance. Certified, bonded appraisals. Member Bucks County Antiques Dealers Assoc., Pa. Antiques Appraisers' Assoc.

A/C. Wide range.

Prop. Frank J. Udinson   215–345–1725 (bus.)
                                                         348–3295 (res.)

New Hope 18938

THE ANTIQUARY, 40 W. Ferry St.
Hours: Daily year 'round; and by appt.

Antique gas, combined gas and electric lighting fixtures; old prints, frames, 19th-century American country furniture, Oriental export and early Imari china

THE ANTIQUARY *continued*

(pre-1900). "Circa" dates noted for all pieces. Visa, Master Charge. Member Bucks County Antiques Dealers Assoc.

A/C—PM. Wide range. Authentication.

Prop. Ernest and Joan Shandelmier   215–862–5955

AS TIME GOES BY, 7 W. Bridge St.

Hours: Mon. 12–5; Wed. thru Fri. 11:30–5; Sat. 11:30–6:30; Sun. 11:30–6; and by appt. Sat. eve. 7:30–10, during warmer weather.

Fulper, Roseville, Rookwood, Van Briggle art pottery; Art Deco. Antiques purchased. Master Charge, Visa.

C—PM. Affordable. Consignments selectively.

Prop. H. Auerbach, L. Magnus   215–862–2958

COLONIAL ARMS ANTIQUES, The Hamlet at Rolling Fields. Rt. 202, northbound.

Hours: Mon. thru Sat. 10–5. Closed Sun.

Antiques of quality. Seventeenth-, 18th-, and 19th-century American and European paintings; 18th- and 19th-century American, English, and French grandfather clocks. English, French, and American furniture, all periods; china, pewter, decorative accessories. Old platters set into reproduction period table bases. Antiques made into lamps. Also to the trade. Member Bucks County Antiques Dealers Assoc. Complex shared with The Country Shop; ample off-the-road parking.

A—PM. Wide range/Selective (basically). Authentication.

Prop. Frank Mancuso   215–862–2366

THE CORNER, 8 N. Main (cor. Bridge St.). Mailing address: Box 91.

Hours: 7 days 11–4

General line; military items, antique clothing (including wedding gowns, when available), jewelry, primitives, some pattern glass, china, silver, copper, brass, much bric-a-brac, some books, vintage post cards, even a cabinet filled with old sheet music. Member Bucks County Antiques Dealers Assoc.

A/C—PM. Affordable. Authentication.

Prop. Joan Agocs, Anne Delgado   215–862–5480

COUNTRY ROW ANTIQUES, INC., the Country Row Center. Rt. 202, northbound. Mailing address: R. D. 1, Box 84-4.

Hours: Wed. thru Sat. 11–4; or by appt.

Beautiful selection of period country furnishings and accessories. Corner cupboards, Windsor chairs, candlestands, blanket chests; American and English miniature period furniture. Paintings (1750 to early 19th century), Canton export porcelain, candlesticks, quilts, coverlets, 18th- and 19th-century American samplers.

A—PM. Selective to serious collectors. Consignments. Authentication.

Prop. Alyce Conover   215–862–2896

THE COUNTRY SHOP, The Hamlet at Rolling Fields. Rt. 202, northbound. *Also see* Repair and Restoration listing.

Hours: Fri., Sat., Sun. 10–5

Nineteenth-century lamps a specialty. Distinctive student lamps and hanging fixtures; scales, primitives, grandfather clocks, Queen Anne furniture. No reproductions. Polaroid color photos on request. New "Aladdin" lamps and parts. Repair, restoration, and refinishing of table and hanging lamps for museums, collectors, and dealers. Repair and restoration of scales. Lamp appraisals for estates and banks. Member Amer. Antiques Soc.

Of special interest, a large F-sharp bell on permanent display. Made in 1883 by the Clinton H. Meneely Bell Company of Troy, N. Y., for a church in Alpha, N. J., which burned before the bell was used. Clear and resonant in tone, it is a fine example of an old art. The complex is shared by Colonial Arms Antiques; ample off-the-road parking.

A/C—PM. Wide range. Consignments. Authentication.

Prop. George Seemar   215–862–5594 (eves. only)

CROWN & EAGLE ANTIQUES, INC., Rt. 202, northbound (3 mi. south of New Hope; opp. the winery).

Hours: Wed. thru Sun. 12–5:30. Mon. for dealers.

Unusual juxtaposition of artifacts and antiques. American Indian rugs, basketry, beadwork, jewelry; Eskimo carvings, tools, implements; fine American and English furniture, china, weapons, decorative folk art. New jewelry. Authentication service; appraisals of American Indian artifacts. Also to dealers. Establishment of a museum of Indian artifacts, shell, and mineral collections is anticipated.

A/C; also new—PM; coded. Wide range. Consignments. Authentication.

Prop. Lynn Trusdell   215–794–7334
                                                             794–7972

FERRY HILL, 37 Ferry St.

Hours: Mon. thru Fri. 11–5; Sat. & Sun. 11–6.

Copper and brass pots, pans, kettles, utensils, candlesticks; primitives, tables, desks, small pieces of furniture; oil paintings.

A/C—PM. Affordable. Consignments. Authentication.

Prop. Ronald T. Hazzard   215–862–5335 (res).

GARDNER'S ANTIQUES, Rt. 202, southbound.

Hours: Tues. thru Sun. 10:30–5. Closed Mon.

Fine Oriental furniture, porcelains, bronzes, screens; 18th- and 19th-century French, English, and American furniture, including highboys, lowboys, cabinets, grandfather clocks, chandeliers, sconces, brass. Deliveries within 100 miles; shipping worldwide. Member Bucks County Antiques Dealers Assoc.

A—PM. Wide range. Authentication.

Prop. Loren Gardner   215–794–8616

GINSBERG & GINSBERG ANTIQUES, INC., Rt. 202, northbound (at Aquetong Rd.). Mailing address: Box 249, Holicong 18928.

Hours: Daily 11:30–5:30. Closed Tues. & Fri.

Specializing in old stained glass windows and beveled glass doors. Eighteenth- to early 20th-century men's and women's pocket watches, including Fusée (1710–c. 1830); wall and mantel clocks. Windows reframed. Visa, Master Charge.

C—PM. Wide range. Consignments. Authentication (watches, clocks).

Prop. Jay and Cheryl Ginsberg   215–862–2222

THE GOLDEN GRIFFINS, Mechanic St.

Hours: Daily 12–6. Closed Tues.

Spare, softly lighted gallery; Art Deco objets d'art and furnishings. Original Louis Icart (1888–1950) oils, etchings, watercolors, pastels. Visa, Master Charge, American Express, Telecredit.

C—Some prices marked. Selective. Authentication.

Prop. Eugene Schmittle   215–862–2868

DANIEL HERSH GALLERIES, Rt. 202 and Aquetong Rd.

Hours: Sat. & Sun. 11–5; and by appt.

DANIEL HERSH GALLERIES *continued*

Fine 17th-, 18th-, and 19th-century American and European paintings, objets d'art, pre-Columbian artifacts. Appraisals of paintings.

A/C—Prices not marked. Wide range. Consignments. Authentication.

Prop. Daniel Hersh   215–862–9345

GEORGE S. HOBENSACK, JR., Bridge St. (between RR tracks and Ferry St.).
Hours: Mon. thru Sat. 11–6; Sun. 1–5. Closed on Christmas.

Known for garden appointments and old decorative ironwork; gateposts, fences, cast-iron porches, wrought iron fountains; benches, urns, figures, jardinières. New terra cotta statues. General line; Oriental rugs (1885–1950), china, glassware, silver, books, furniture, fireplace mantels. In a sizable old tinsmith shop; much displayed outdoors.

A/C; also new—PM. Wide range. Authentication when possible.

Prop. George S. Hobensack   215–862–2406

LA PETITE GALERIE, Rt. 202. Mailing address: Box 77A.
Hours: Daily 11–5; and by appt.

Primitive and period furniture, rugs. General line; china, baskets, crocks, stained glass. Decorative accessories, from a ship's block to a hat stand, with hats. Several rooms, all filled. Interior design. Congenial and helpful. Member A.S.I.D.

A/C—PM. Affordable/Wide range. Authentication.

Prop. Bunny Greenleaf   215–862–2607

THE LARK, Rt. 202, northbound (bordering Lahaska). Mailing address:
Box A69.
Hours: Wed. thru Sun. 11–5:30. Summer hours: 7 days 11–5:30

General line; small tables, sets of chairs.

A/C—PM. Wide range. Consignments.

Prop. Marcie McCoy, Hannah Cryne   215–794–7871

LAZARUS ANTIQUES, 9 E. Bridge St.
Hours: Tues. thru Sun. 11–5

Clocks and watches (mid-1800s to early 1900s); pre-1890 weapons; early military clothing; nautical items, scrimshaw, ships' wheels, cannon, telescopes. Bonded appraisals. Visa, Master Charge. Pleasant, interesting shop. Member Nat'l. Assoc. of Watch & Clock Collectors.

A/C—PM. Wide range. Authentication.

Prop. Leo and Ermalea Lazarus   215–862–5732

PHILIP F. MURPHY, III ANTIQUES, 36 W. Bridge St.

Hours: 7 days 11–5

General line; reproductions and newer items.

C—PM. Affordable/Wide range.

Prop. Philip F. Murphy, III   215–862–5106

OCHRE HOUSE, 4 Walton Dr. (Rt. 202, northbound; off Reeder Rd.).

Hours: By appt.

Discerning collection of American period, country furniture, primitives; Windsor chairs, early 18th-century ladderbacks. Good early beds, cherry, walnut, painted, canopy, "under-the-eaves." Fluid-burning lamps a specialty; good Sandwich glass lamps, early Betty, and lard oil. Member Bucks County Antiques Dealers Assoc.

A—PM. Selective to serious collectors. Selective consignments. Authentication.

Prop. Manford and Joyce Robinson   215–862–5914

OLDE BOOKS AND THINGS, Rt. 202 (3 mi. west of New Hope).

Hours: Tues. thru Sun. 11–6

Two rooms of old and rare books, prints, maps, deeds, magazines, fine bindings, posters, Americana. English and American authors a specialty; some travel and exploration. "Good books in general."

C/A—Most prices marked. Affordable. Authentication.

Prop. Gene Gustafson   215–794–7073

THE PINK HOUSE, Rt. 179 (old Rt. 202).

Hours: 7 days 10–6

Fine 18th-century Chinese export and English porcelain; French and English 18th- and early 19th-century furniture. Large selection of American quilts. Interior design. Antiques shows managed. Lectures on paintings and prints. In a 1753 blacksmith shop. Member Bucks County Antiques Dealers Assoc.

A—Prices "not always" marked. Selective to serious collectors. Authentication.

Prop. James Gregory, John Puckett   215–862–5947

POOLE ANTIQUES, Rt. 202 and Ingham Rd. (bet. New Hope and Lahaska).

Hours: Mon. thru Fri. 9–5; Sat. & Sun. 12–5; and by appt.

"Painted people," country pine, primitives, wood, tin. Emphasis on kitchen tools, "things that were used." Member Bucks County Antiques Dealers Assoc.

A/C—PM. Affordable/Wide range.

Prop. Frances Poole   215–862–2919

QUÉRIPEL INTERIORS & ANTIQUES, 93 W. Bridge St. (Rt. 179).

Hours: 7 days 10–5; call ahead suggested

Interior design. Selected American and English antiques and decorative accessories; 17th-, 18th-, and 19th-century formal furniture, some country pieces. Emphasis on design adaptability and quality.

A/C (some)—PM. Wide range. Authentication (important pieces).

Prop. William and Louise Quéripel   215–862–5830 (days & eves.)

RED GATE ANTIQUES, INC., Rt. 202, northbound.

Hours: 7 days 10:30–6; call ahead suggested

Meissen, flow blue, nautical and scientific instruments; good early American furniture, early English and Continental pewter. Selective and unusual decorative antiques in a formal shop. American Express. Member Bucks County Antiques Dealers Assoc.

A—PM. Wide range. Consignments. Authentication.

Prop. Thomas M. Davis, Jr.   215–794–8717

H & R SANDOR, INC., Rt. 202 at Reeder Mill Rd. Mailing address: Box 207.

Hours: Mon. thru Sat. 9:30–12, 1–4

Preeminent. Museum quality period furnishings in elegant settings. Fine antique furniture, paintings, decorative accessories; selected less formal pieces. Interiors. Appraisals. Member Appraisers' Assoc. of America. The Ingham Manor, built in 1750.

A—PM. Serious collectors. Authentication.

Prop. Herbert and Richard Sandor   215–862–9181

SHEFFIELD HOUSE, Rt. 202, northbound. Mailing address: Box 52.

Hours: Mon. thru Sat. 10:30–5. Closed Sun.

Pre-1865 Sheffield silver; rugs, furniture. English sporting prints; hand-colored French dogs (contemporary), humorous caricatures—from the original stones.

A/C—PM. Wide range. Authentication.

Prop. Mrs. William D. Barlow   215–862–5467

SIZEMORE ANTIQUES, Country Row Center. Rt. 202 (next to Holiday Inn).
Mailing address: Box 84-D.

Hours: Daily 10–5; Mon. call ahead

SIZEMORE ANTIQUES *continued*

Selected 17th-, 18th-, and 19th-century furniture, primitives, brass, mirrors, paintings, old prints; general line. Some refurbished pieces.

A—PM. Wide range. Authentication.

Prop. Jack and Jean Sizemore   215–862–5727

JOSEPH STANLEY LTD., 181 W. Bridge St. (Rt. 202).

Hours: Wed. thru Sun. 11–5

Formal 17th-, 18th-, and early 19th-century English furniture. Chinese export porcelain; early brass, needlework. In a stately 1816 residence.

A—PM. Selective to serious collectors. Authentication.

Prop. Joseph Stanley   215–862–9300

MIRIAM YOUNG, Rt. 202, southbound (approx. 1 mi. south of Holiday Inn). Mailing address: Box 93.

Hours: Sun. 12–5; appt. advised

Eighteenth- and 19th-century furniture, Oriental rugs, bronzes, early glass, country primitives, decorative pieces in two interesting shops. An established dealer. Also to the trade. A beautiful country setting; the woodland drive winds past an old quarry.

A—Prices not marked. Wide range. Authentication.

Prop. Miriam Young   215–862–5713

Newtown 18940

THE HANGING LAMP ANTIQUES, 140 N. State St.

Hours: Wed. thru Sat. 9:30–5:30; Sun. by appt.

Formal and country furniture, primitives, glass, china. Lamps; custom-made lampshades. Appraisals. In business more than thirty years.

A/C (a few)—PM. Wide range.

Prop. Beatrice and Duane Stump   215–968–2015

REN'S ANTIQUES, 14 S. State St.

Hours: Mon. thru Sat. 10–5; Sun. & eves. by appt.

China, glass, silver, primitives, lamps, "important collectibles," in several rooms of a century-old house. Appraisals. Silver refurbishing; lamp repair; china mending by arrangement. Member Bucks County Antiques Dealers Assoc.

A/C—PM. Wide range. Authentication.

Prop. Mrs. Mitchell Spector   215–968–5511

THE VILLAGE SMITHY, 149 N. State St.

Hours: Daily 9–5. Closed Tues. & Sun.

Eighteenth- and 19th-century furniture, primitives, copper, brass. General line. Antiques purchased. Appraisals. Member Bucks County Antiques Dealers Assoc.

A—PM. Wide range.

Prop. Bud Smith   215–968–2149

Ottsville 18942

THE HISTORY COOP, Rt. 611. *Also see* Repair and Restoration listing.

Hours: Wed. thru Sat. 11–5; Sun. 12–5

American primitive furniture, Civil War items, Kentucky rifles, prints, oil paintings; general line. Consignments (insured). Appraisals. Furniture repair, refinishing; brass and copper polished. Dealers welcome.

A/C—PM. Affordable. Consignments; insured. Authentication.

Prop. Patricia W. Manwaring   215–847–2700

Penndel 19047

AAA ANTIQUES, 164 Durham Rd.

Hours: By appt.

Antique jewelry, diamonds, Oriental rugs (thru the '50s); American paintings, paintings on wood, sketches.

C/A—Prices not marked. Wide range. Authentication.

Prop. Renny Papendick   215–757–2220

Pipersville 18947

ANTIQUES FOR COLLECTORS, at The Rabbit Hole, "Greenhill." Stump Rd., bet. Rt. 413 and Wismer Rd.

Hours: Summers only, July & Aug.; by chance

Collectibles. Jewelry, china, glass, bric-a-brac, crocks, jugs, post cards, inkwells,

ANTIQUES FOR COLLECTORS *continued*

boxes; Americana. Member Long Island Antiques Dealers Assoc. Pleasant country shop; open summers only.

C—PM. Affordable. Authentication when possible.

Prop. Nancy May Greenberg   215–766–7389

MITCHELL & SUSAN BUNKIN, Pipersville.

Hours: By appt.

Known for fine Pennsylvania redware. Early American furniture, iron, quilts; emphasis on Pennsylvania pieces. Bidding at auction, purchases on commission. Member Bucks County Antiques Dealers Assoc.

A—PM. Wide range/Selective. Consignments within specialty. Authentication.

Prop. Mitchell and Susan Bunkin   215–297–8653

Pleasant Valley 18948

BOWER'S ANTIQUES, Rt. 212.

Hours: By appt.

Specializing in Gaudy Dutch, spatterware, and slipware. General line; pressed glass, china, lamps. Member Bucks County Antiques Dealers Assoc.

A—PM. Selective. Authentication.

Prop. Helen Bower   215–346–8295

Plumsteadville 18949

COUNTRY LIGHT SHOP, Rt. 611 and Stump Rd.

Hours: Tues. thru Sun. 11–5

Old lighting fixtures, stained glass, unusual Victorian and oak furniture (most refinished by Mr. Burg). General line, china, glass, bric-a-brac. Antiques purchased. Master Charge. Attractively displayed in an 18th-century tinsmith shop. Next to historic Plumsteadville Inn, built in 1751.

C/A—PM. Wide range. Authentication when possible.

Prop. Lloyd and Diane Burg   215–766–7223

PLUMSTEAD VILLAGE ANTIQUES, Rt. 611, northbound (diag. opp. Plumsteadville Inn). *Also see* Repair and Restoration listing.

Hours: Wed. thru Sun. 12–5

PLUMSTEAD VILLAGE ANTIQUES *continued*

• *Formal French, English, and Italian 18th- and early 19th-century furniture. Large upholstered pieces, armoires, cupboards, mirrors, chandeliers, pedestals, hanging fixtures; decorative old wrought iron furniture. Also to dealers. Antiques restoration by William Bogle; upholstery by arrangement.*

Originally a Presbyterian Church, built in 1839; the rear portion at one time used to restore farm wagons, converted with a 1940s addition to a glove factory.

Ten shops located downstairs, specializing in American primitives; Victorian, oak, and turn-of-the-century furniture; 19th-century farm implements, quilts, small decorative objects. Interestingly browsable.

A/C—PM. Wide range. Consignments. Authentication when possible.
Prop. George Patterson   215–766–0196

Point Pleasant 18950

RIVER RUN ANTIQUES, River Rd. (complex), Rt. 32.
Hours: Wed. thru Sun. 11–5. Closed Mon. & Tues.
Primitives, weapons, some 1920s tin toys. General line, emphasizing "the unusual." Member Bucks County Antiques Dealers Assoc., Pa. State Antiques Dealers Assoc. In the stable behind the "Point Pleasant Hotel," an early 19th-century stopover favored for shad fishing.
A—PM. Wide range. Consignments. Authentication.
Prop. Julia Bartels   215–294–9488 (after 6)

TIME AND TIDE, River Rd. (complex), Rt. 32.
Hours: Sat. & Sun. 9–6
Attractively French. Selective antique and reproduction grandfather clocks (French, c. 1700 thru 20th century); French country furniture and accessories; decorative hand-carved cabinetry doors, old door knockers. New Morbier wag-on-the-wall clocks, some new furnishings crafted of old wood, contemporary French tiles, new hardware and hinges. Member Bucks County Antiques Dealers Assoc.
A/C; also new—PM. Selective to serious collectors (occasional pieces less). Authentication.
Prop. Jacques and Elisabeth Cornillon   215–297–5854

Quakertown 18951

RUSSELL E. HILL, 1465 N.W. End Blvd. (Rt. 309, just north of Unique Gardens).
Hours: Mon. thru Sat. 8–5. Closed Sun.

RUSSELL E. HILL *continued*

Period furnishings beautifully exhibited in room settings. Pennsylvania furniture and folk art, period and country furniture; shelf and tall case clocks, corner cupboards, schranks, redware, slipware, some lighting, paintings, quilts. Member Bucks County Antiques Dealers Assoc.

A—PM. Selective to serious collectors. Authentication when possible.

Prop. Russell E. Hill   No phone

KITTY'S KONOR, 141 E. Broad St. (Rt. 313 west; jct. Rt. 212 east).

Hours: Mon., Tues., Thurs., Sat. 10–5:30; Wed. 10–12; Fri. 10–9

Primarily new and used furniture. Antiques "as they come in." Clocks purchased. Antique clock repair, case refinishing by arrangement. Master Charge, Visa.

C; also new, used—PM. Affordable.

Prop. Robert Roth   215–536–5040

PLANTIQUES, 628 N.W. End Blvd. (Rt. 309, southbound; north of Trainer's restaurant). *Also see* Repair and Restoration listing.

Hours: Tues. thru Sat. 10–6; Sun. 12–6

General line; old and new stained glass, furniture, china, glassware, crocks. Plants to complement. Stained glass repair by Lonny McLaughlin. Visa, Master Charge. Genial shop in upper Bucks County.

A/C—Not all prices marked. Wide range. Consignments.

Prop. Audrey Jennings, Adam Krull, Lonny McLaughlin   215–536–1963

WEBBER'S ANTIQUES, Thatcher Rd.

Hours: By appt. or chance

General line; jewelry, furniture, glass, china, post cards, advertising. Lamps electrified. Member Pa. Antiques Dealers Assoc.

A/C. Affordable. Authentication when possible.

Prop. Mary Webber   215–536–5155

Riegelsville 18077

LITTLE HOUSE ANTIQUES, 250 Linden Lane.

Hours: By appt.

Small early American country furniture and accessories; lamps, pressed glass,

LITTLE HOUSE ANTIQUES *continued*

glass chimneys, mantel clocks. Custom pierced lampshades. Member Bucks County Antiques Dealers Assoc.

A/C—PM. Wide range.

Prop. Gilma Ruth   215–749–2418

LONG SPRING ANTIQUES & INDIAN MUSEUM, Riegelsville.

Hours: By appt.

American Indian objects and artifacts, weaponry, jewelry; military collector's items. The unusual, a British "redcoat's" uniform, Indian beaded buckskin. Member Bucks County Antiques Dealers Assoc.

A/C. Wide range. Authentication when possible.

Prop. Virginia and Lou D. Lovekin   215–346–7659

Solebury 18963

COUNTRY ANTIQUES, Rt. 202, southbound.

Hours: Sat., Sun., Mon., from 1 P.M.; and by appt.

Fine collection of primitives, country furniture, accessories. Tavern, tap, and country worktables, nightstands; utilitarian pieces, dry sinks, benches, tables, chairs, cupboards, lighting. Wall accessories—paintings, mirrors; dolls— primitive, papier-mâché, German, bisque; quilts, coverlets, afghans. Appraisals.

A conversion of use for the landmark Old Solebury Baptist Church. Built in the 1820s, burned, rebuilt in 1851 on "an acre and 16 perches," including the carefully maintained old graveyard.

A—PM. Wide range. Authentication when possible.

Prop. George Keys   215–862–5114

ROBERT C. WHITLEY ANTIQUES, Solebury. *Also see* Repair and Restoration listing.

Hours: By appt.

Small, select choice of American period furniture. Queen Anne, Chippendale, Hepplewhite, Sheritan; a few classical pieces. Specializing in the restoration of fine period pieces for individuals and museums; custom copies. Member American Craftsman's Council, Bucks County Guild of Craftsmen, N. J. Designer Craftsmen.

A—PM. Serious collectors. Authentication.

Prop. Robert C. Whitley   215–297–8452

Spring Valley 18901

RED DOOR, Rt. 202 (3 doors north of Mill Rd. crossroad).

Hours: Tues. thru Sat. 10–5

Specializing in antique whale oil and kerosene lamps; 19th-century American clocks. Custom hand-painted and stencil-cut lampshades. Clocks and lamps repaired. In an attractively restored century-old barn.

A/C—PM. Wide range. Authentication.

Prop. Helen and Arthur H. Naul   215–794–7647

ROBERTSON & THORNTON ANTIQUES, Rt. 202, southbound (midway bet. Doylestown and Buckingham).

Hours: Tues. thru Sat. 10:30–5; Sun. 1–5. Closed Mon.

Diversified collection, formal and informal American antiques. Furniture, some quilts and coverlets; glass, including flint, Sandwich, Pittsburgh, Stiegel-type. Early American glass room and reference library upstairs. A 1780 barn of "rubble" construction. Once separate blacksmith and carriage shops, with a wheelright's shop on the second level. Member Bucks County Antiques Dealers Assoc.

A—PM. Wide range. Authentication.

Prop. Donald H. Robertson, James F. Thornton   215–345–7739

Upper Black Eddy 18972

McCARTY'S ANTIQUES, River Rd. Mailing address: Box 597.

Hours: Fri., Sat., Sun. 9–5, later in summer.

General line; primitives, frames, lamps, scales, brass, copper, iron. Member Bucks County Antiques Dealers Assoc.

A/C—PM. Affordable. Authentication.

Prop. Ann McCarty   215–982–5796

Yardley 19067

ANTIQUES FROM EVE, 40 S. Main St. (small shopping complex; downstairs, rear).

Hours: Tues. thru Sat. 10–5; and by appt.

ANTIQUES FROM EVE *continued*

*Broad selection, with a creative flair. English Victorian furniture (1880–1890),
American turn-of-the-century pieces; Victorian, some Art Deco jewelry; a few
primitives. Of dramatic note, an elaborate traveling theatrical makeup case.
Old jars filled with holiday candy, in season. Layaway plan. Delivery service.
Fabric and lace gift wrappings.*

C/A—PM. Affordable/Wide range. Consignments.

Prop. Evelyn Roth; Linda Dabby, Mgr. 215–493–1468

MEYER TRADING CO., Afton Ave. and Delaware Canal.

Hours: Mon. thru Sat. 10–6. Closed Sun.

*Special interests encouraged. Emphasis on stamps, coins, fine jewelry (1700s to
modern). Good selection of pocket watches (mid-1600s to 1920), objets d'art,
oil paintings; Medieval stained glass windows (late 1400s to mid-1500s). Coins
for young collectors. Private and estate appraisals. Member Amer. Numismatic
Assoc., Amer. Philatelic Soc. In Canal House #10, the oldest continuous store
in Bucks County. The stone and frame structure, built in 1831, was a stop on
the Underground Railroad.*

A/C—PM. Wide range. Consignments. Authentication.

Prop. Robert Meyer 215–493–4118

MILLER-TOPIA DESIGNERS, 41 E. Afton Ave. *Also see* Repair and Restoration listing.

Hours: Mon. thru Sat. 10–5; Sun. 12–4

*Copper, brass, decorative pieces; general line of furniture. Lamps designed;
oil lamps rewired. A distinctive 1750 stone Colonial with bright pink and white
awning and pink shutters.*

C/A (a few)—PM. Affordable/Wide range.

Prop. Arnold and Marnie Miller 215–493–6114

C. L. PRICKETT, Stoneyhill Rd.

Hours: Mon. thru Sat. 10–5. Closed Sun.

*Distinguished collection of pre-1820 American furniture. Queen Anne
highboys, lowboys, tall case clocks, canopy beds. Notable examples of New
Jersey, Pennsylvania craftsmanship.*

A—PM. Selective to serious collectors.

Prop. C. L. Prickett 215–493–4284

Repair and Restoration Specialists

A Art Restoration
C China, Glass, Porcelain
D Dolls, Toys
F Furniture
J Jewelry

L Lamps, Lighting
M Metalwork
MI Musical & Mechanical Instruments
R Rugs, Textiles
T Timepieces

Restoration of a Pennsylvania or New Jersey walnut lowboy, ca. 1730–1740, for display at the Dolley Todd-Madison House, Philadelphia. (Top left) original condition: damage to top and front apron, missing rear left foot, ragged nail and screw holes, addition of 1920s brasses. (Top right) straightening of split top edges in a vise prior to joining. (Bottom left) replacement Spanish foot sculptured in old walnut with ¼ in. gouge chisel. (Bottom right) completed restoration: repairs using old wood conform in grain and color to the original; brasses eliminated since the piece originally bore none. *Courtesy Robert C. Whitley, Solebury. Photos: Robert C. Whitley and Robert C. Whitley, III*

Repair and Restoration Specialists

Sussex County

F, L BETTY GROSCH (Cobweb Corner), Rt. 15, Sparta; 201–383–1952.
Lamps and furniture repaired, restored.

C, F DON and KAREN KIHLSTROM (Bogwater Jim Antiques), Rt. 15 and Beaver Run Rd., Lafayette; 201–383–8170.
Stained glass repair. Caning, rushing; handmade splint baskets.

L, M CY and LORETTA LEWIS (Lamp Lighter Antiques), Rt. 23, Sussex; 201–875–6662.
Oil lamp repairs; brass polishing.

F, T ROBERT POLLARA (Old Colony Antiques), off Rt. 206, Montague; 201–293–7312 (bus.), 293–7359 (res.).
Clocks and antique furniture repaired, restored. Member Nat'l. Assoc. of Watch & Clock Collectors.

C VITO and MARY ELLEN SICO (Cameo Antiques), 44 Main St., Stanhope; 201–347–8181.
Porcelain repair.

F DAN WELDON (The Furniture Emporium, Inc.), 139 Main St., Andover; 201–786–5118.
Furniture repair, restoration; cabinetry. Antique architectural woodworking repaired or copied.

Warren County

F DIANNE and HENNING JOHANSSON (Whispering Pines Antiques), Rt. 57, Beattystown; 201–852–2587.
Caning; rushing.

F WILLIAM P. THOMAS, Mountain Lake Rd., Belvidere; 201–475–4818.
Furniture repair, refinishing, restoration; cabinetmaking for more than thirty years.

F TOM and ELSIE YOUNG, Rt. 519, Roxburg; 201–475–2648.
Furniture refinishing; rushing, caning.

Morris County

F ARCH GALLERIES CORP., 629 Rt. 23, Pompton Plains; 201–835–5034.
Furniture refinishing and repairing, reupholstering; caning, rushing.

L, M A. BERTELO (The Gazebo), 21 Brook Valley Rd., Towaco; 201–334–0361.
Converting, electrifying, repairing chandeliers, sconces, lanterns; brass burnishing, silver plating.

F JOSEPH and MARGE COOK (Treasure Trove), Florham Park; 201–377–6279.
Furniture refinishing; caning.

MI LOU DE CICCO, DON DONAHUE (The Olde Tyme Music Scene), 917 Main St., Boonton; 201–335–5040.
Repair and restoration of old phonographs.

F GAIL FATUM, 42 Old Shunpike Rd., Mt. Freedom; 201–895–4019.
Antique furniture restored, refinished; touch-up work; pickup and delivery.

D MARY FLANAGAN (The Emporium), 71 Main St., Chester; 201–879–7751.
Doll repairing and dressing.

F, T DON FRAYKO (Wagon Wheel Antiques), Rt. 23, Newfoundland; 201–697–6927.

Clock repair and restoration; furniture repair.

T GREGORY GRANT (Antiques Unlimited of Morristown), 17 Elm St., Morristown; 201–267–0994.

Repair and restoration of clocks and watches.

F CATHERINE HAYNES, SUSAN STOCKNOFF (Grandma's Attic), 69 W. Blackwell St., Dover; 201–366–8230.

Furniture refinishing; caning.

F KAREN KINNANE (White House Antiques), 215 Myrtle Ave., Boonton; 201–335–4926.

Splint seats replaced.

F GENE LEONCAVALLO (Antique Chair Shop), 6 Hilltop Rd., Mendham; 201–543–2164.

Antique restoration on all periods and styles of furniture; refinishing and upholstering; gold leaf, Chinese lacquer.

T GARY LESTER (Yesterday Once More Shoppe), Morris County Mall, Ridgedale Ave., Cedar Knolls; 201–539–6449.

Antique clock and watch repair; grandfather clocks delivered and set up free.

T THOMAS McDONALD, BARRY MARKE (Father Time), 1 E. Main St., Mendham; 201–543–6446.

Antique clock and watch repair and restoration.

T A. G. MASON, 1 Knollwood Dr., Mendham; 201–543–2174.

American wall clocks repaired and restored.

M GEORGE MORTAT (Chatham Silversmiths), 248 Main St., Chatham; 201–635–8505.

Silver plating, polishing, repairing.

F ERNEST R. NORDBERG, 71 McGregor Ave., Mt. Arlington; 201–663–3677.

Furniture refinishing, restoring; caning, rushing.

F WILLIAM PLUMMER, 203 Meyersville Rd., Chatham; 201–635–6228.

Antique furniture refinishing.

D NANCY RESCH (The Pigwidgeon's Niche), 26A Diamond Spring Rd., Denville; 201–625–5610.

Antique doll repairing.

F MARIAN RILEY (Country Girl Antiques), 189 Ridgedale Ave., Florham Park; 201–377–5440.

Furniture refinishing; caning, rushing, splint seats.

D MARVIN SILVERSTEIN (Marvin's Crackers), 24 Minton Ave., Chatham; 201–635–6260.

Restoration of antique toys.

F CARL W. SUNDBERG (The Restore), 253 Main Ave., Stirling; 201–647–0613.

Hand-stripping and finishing of furniture; restoration; caning.

F, T HAROLD B. THORPE, JR., Mt. Kemble Ave., Harding Twp.; 201–766–1334.

Restoration of antique furniture; clock repair.

F MARTIN D. URBANSKI (Trading Post Antiques), 211 Hickory Tavern Rd., Meyersville; 201–647–1959.

Antique furniture repair and restoration; caning, rushing.

F HAROLD VALENTINE (Bread Board Country Store), 50 E. Main St., Chester; 201–879–7188.

Furniture refinishing.

Passaic County

F, T ROSANNE and LARRY GUIZIO (Century Antiques), 565 Clifton Ave., Clifton; 201–365–1592.

Furniture repair, restoration, hand work; free estimates. Clock repair. Caning. Supplies; advice. Members Appraisers' Assoc. of America.

F EWALD POEHLER, JR. (Dukes Corner Shoppe), 4 Broad St., Pompton Lakes; 201–839–3880.

Furniture refinishing, antique restoration; gold leaf work, chair regluing. Caning; genuine rush and ash splint weaving.

F JIM RUDI (Nostalgic Attic), 322 Ringwood Ave., Pompton Lakes; 201–835–9397.

Furniture hand-stripping, repair, restoration, refinishing.

F, MI TERRY and JAN WORDEN (Then & Now Shoppe), 169 Rt. 23, Singac; 201–256–8413 (bus.), 201–226–2149 (res.).

Chair caning, rushing. New piano rolls to order.

Bergen County

J, T PHILIP BADER (Phillys Dillys), Village Square, Bergen Mall, Rt. 4, Paramus; 201–843–0466.

Watch, clock, and jewelry repairs.

F KAY and KEN BLAIR (Unicorn Antiques), 108 Harrison Ave., Garfield; 201–340–1454.

Caning; refinishing.

F RICHARD BRANDMAYR, 235 Prospect Ave., Hackensack; 201–342–4810.

Furniture repair, restoration, refinishing; hand-rubbed finishes.

F A. P. CHURUTI (Churuti Upholstery), 23 Emerson Plaza E., Emerson; 201–265–8090.

Furniture repair, reupholstering.

F, L L. COHEN (Treasure Chest Antiques), Montvale Antique Mall, 30 Chestnut Ridge Rd., Montvale; 914–354–4205.

Furniture, lamps, chandeliers repaired, restored, refinished. Lamps and chandeliers rewired.

C BORIS M. CUMPELIK (Bohemian Glass Engravers), 41 Lincoln Terr., Hillsdale; 201–664–3504 (eves. only).

Fine glass repair; by appt. Old crystal, Tiffany, early American glass restored. Cracked, partly broken glassware salvaged; new teeth cut, chipped or scratched areas removed; acid work. Individually designed paperweights made to order, signed.

F FLORENCE DANIEL (Florence Daniel Interiors, Inc.), 621 Godwin Ave., Midland Park; 201–445–2828.

Restoration of antique furniture, upholstering; workroom on premises.

F HELEN FISHER (The Antique Place), 10 West St., Englewood; 201–567–9493.

Furniture stripping, refinishing.

J   AL and FRAN FROHMAN (Frohmans Antique Jewelry), Village Square, Bergen Mall, Rt. 4, Paramus; 201–843–3113.

Repair of antique jewelry.

F   DENNIS GRACE (Oakwood Antiques), 1079 Washington Ave., Old Tappan; 201–666–3535.

Oak furniture refinished. Caning.

A   VICTOR GRACE (Grace Galleries, Inc.), 75 Grand Ave., Englewood; 201–567–6169.

Conservators of oil paintings, canvas and panel; fine art restoration. Member Institute for Conservation and Restoration of Historical Works of Art.

F   S. R. GUERRA, 259 Passaic St., Hackensack; 201–342–6883.

Repair and restoration of antiques; complete furniture repair and refinishing.

F   JAN HIEMINGA, R. L. BOGERT (Bogert Built Furniture, Since 1820), 25 Blvd., P. O. Box 59, Westwood; 201–664–0103.

Antique restoration, refinishing.

F   JOAN LAST (Antiques At Last), 5–02 Fair Lawn Ave., Fair Lawn; 201–278–7468.

Caning.

F   THOMAS C. LaVECCHIO (Milford Furniture Shop), 580 Maple Ave., Ridgewood; 201–444–4040.

Furniture repair, restoration. Also 18th-century English, American, and French reproductions.

MI   PAUL MANGANERO, 121 Valley Brook Ave., Lyndhurst; 201–438–0399.

Automatic musical instruments repaired, restored. Member Music Box Soc.

F, T   BILLIE and DAVE MARSHALL (Knock On Wood), 33 S. Kinderkamack Rd., Montvale; 201–391–1414.

Furniture hand-stripping, repair, custom refinishing; upholstering. Caning, rushing. Antique clocks repaired, restored.

J, R MARGUERITE MORGAN (Studio I), 6 Highland Cross, Rutherford; 201–939–7222.

Antique clothing, tapestries, hangings restored. Beads restrung. Member Internat'l. Old Lacers.

F HENRY MULLER (Stable Antiques), 116 E. Saddle River Rd., Saddle River; 201–327–0646.

Turn-of-the-century furniture hand-stripped, refinished.

F BART J. PALAMARO (Palamaro Furniture Decorators), 196 Kipp Ave., Elmwood Park; 201–797–5070.

Restoration of antique furniture. Refinishing; raised Chinese lacquering, tortoise shell, marbleizing, gilding, etc.

L R. and M. POLLA (Country Lamps & Antiques), 290 Godwin Ave., Wyckoff; 201–891–0044, 337–4310 (eves.).

Lamps repaired, restored; new replacement parts. Custom early American shades.

MI TONY PROVENZANO (Pro Antiques), Brownstone Mill, 11 Paterson Ave., Midland Park; 201–652–7453 (bus.), 445–7898 (res.).

Repair of wind-up phonographs, old radios.

F GIANNINI RICCI (Michele Decorators, Inc.), 102 W. Palisade Ave., Englewood; 201–569–8386.

Antique furniture restored, refinished; "anything concerning wood." Complete home decorating.

D, T ROBERT SLATER (Past In Present), Barnstable Ct., E. Allendale Ave., Saddle River; 201–327–0229.

Clock and doll repairs.

F EILEEN M. SMITH, CHARLES B. ROEDER (Roeder Smith Associates), 409 Ramapo Valley Rd., Oakland; 201–337–4500 (bus.), 337–0458 (res.).

Furniture repair, restoration.

A LORENE SLATER STEINBERG (Past In Present), Barnstable Ct., E. Allendale Ave., Saddle River; 201–327–0229.

Oil paintings cleaned, restored.

J, T BURT STERN (Barrett Jewelers), 185 E. Ridgewood Ave., Ridgewood; 201–445–3060.

Watch and jewelry repair.

F The STOCKNOFF's (Strip 'n Browze), 591 Broadway, Westwood; 201–666–3218.

Furniture repair, restoration; hand- and vat-stripping, veneer repair, hand finishing; touch-ups, polishing.

A STEPHEN VAN CLINE, MICHAEL SOUTHEBY DAVENPORT (Franklin Lakes Galleries), 792 Franklin Ave., Franklin Lakes; 201–891–4588.

Paintings, frames restored. Member American Assoc. of Conservators and Restorers.

F ED ZIPFEL (Habitat Antiques), 286 Terrace Ave., Hasbrouck Heights; 201–288–4180.

Furniture restoration, refinishing; caning, wicker reweaving.

Hudson County

F PETER CANARIS (Antiques by Canaris), 60 Harrison Ave., Jersey City; 201–333–2840, 332–0252.

Furniture restoration, repair.

M DAVE CIOCHER (Gés Fine Metal Finishing), 7013 Park, Guttenberg; 201–869–0033.

Metal repair, restoration; patinas a specialty.

F MICHAEL HULING, 3524 Kennedy Blvd., Jersey City; 201–659–6863.

Furniture repair, restoration.

F ROLF O'HALL (Hall Finishers), 133–38 St., Union City; 201–864–2592.

Antique repair, restoration; gold leaf work. Antiques copied. Chair caning, rushing. Planters designed for indoor trees and large houseplants.

Essex County

C, F JOHN and LUCY ARAKELIAN (House of 7 Wonders), 759 Springfield Ave., Irvington; 201–373–5618.

China repair; furniture refinishing, repairing; caning.

A ROBERT E. BROVACO (Brovaco Gallery), 436 Bloomfield Ave., Montclair; 201–744–3111.

Restoration of oil paintings.

F GLENN GABRIEL (Glenn Gabriel Antiques), 63 Main St., Millburn; 201–379–7292.

Restoration of antique furniture; painted finishes.

MI LESLIE GOULD, 391 Tremont Pl., Orange; 201–672–4060.

Repair and restoration of mechanical musical instruments, player pianos, music boxes, phonographs.

F WILLIAM D. GROSS, 1266 Springfield Ave., Irvington; 201–373–1753.

Furniture refinishing, restoring.

T ALEX KARR (Alex's Clock Shop), 133 Bloomfield Ave., Verona; 201–239–5025.

Repair of antique clocks and watches. Member Nat'l. Assoc. of Watch & Clock Collectors.

F SAM MERCER (The Old Smuggler), 592 Rt. 46, Fairfield; 201–227–6665.

Furniture stripping, refinishing.

F,M RICK MORDWIN (Poor Richard's), 69 N. Willow St., Montclair; 201–783–5333.

Furniture stripping, refinishing, reupholstering; caning, rushing, wicker repair; metal stripping, repairing, replating.

F KEVIN MURPHY (Chem-Clean), Liberty St., West Orange; 201–736–2011.

Furniture stripping, refinishing, restoring.

F JAMES ROSE, 72 Harrison Ave., West Orange; 201–325–3364.

Stripping, restoring, reupholstering antique furniture.

F WILLI F. ROSENGART (Little Cabinetmaker Shop), 195 Bellevue Ave., Upper Montclair; 201–746–0040.

Repair and restoration of antique furniture; caning and natural rush seating.

F, M J. ROSSER (A Touch of Oak), 618 Freeman St., Orange; 201–673–1551.

Furniture refinishing and restoration; caning, Victorian wicker woven; metal polishing.

J ALVIN and SELMA SCHLOSSBERG (The Lennards Antiques), 358 Millburn Ave., Millburn; 201–376–7274.

Antique jewelry repair.

R BEN JOSEPH SETAREH (Ben Joseph Oriental Rugs), 530 Valley St., Maplewood; 201–762–2087.

Oriental rug repair.

J, L, T S. J. SMITH and S. H. FEINGOLD (F & S Antiques), 32A Church St., Montclair; 201–744–2622.

Antique jewelry repair; lamp repair; watch and clock repair.

Hunterdon County

D ROBERT and JEAN BACH (Raggedy Ann Doll Hospital & Museum), 171 Main St., Flemington; 201–782–1243.

Hospital for dolls of "reasonably good quality"; new clothes of older fabric. Member United Fed. of Doll Clubs, N.Y.C. Doll and Toy Collectors Club, patron Nat'l. Institute of American Doll Artists.

F, T WILLIAM E. and KATHERINE S. BIEG (Web Cabinet Shop), 160 Main St., Flemington; no phone.

Furniture repair, restoration, refinishing; carving, inlay, and custom work. Clock repairs.

F ANDY and JACKIE BURACHYNSKI (Andjac Antiques), R. D. 1, Box 42, Pittstown; 201–735–7569.

Natural chair caning, splint weaving. Custom refinishing; also taught at adult school courses.

F DALE DALRYMPLE (What-Da-Ya-Want?), 152 Main St., Lebanon; 201–236–2849.

Furniture stripping, refinishing.

D ROBERT DANKANICS (The Dollhouse Factory), 157 Main St., Lebanon; 201–236–6404.

Consultation on dollhouse construction. Repair and restoration service.

A JOAN DARLING (Tobermory Antiques), R. D. 1, Ringoes; 201–782–5610.

Tole restoration.

L CARL H. DILTS (Ye Olde Lamp Shop), 55 Main St., Lebanon; 201–236–2345.

"Lamps out of anything"; electrified, repaired, restored; mountings.

M BERNARD FRANCFORT (Buttonwood Forge Antiques), 83 Beaver Ave., Annandale; 201–735–5235.

Design; restoration of early iron.

F RONALD GYURO (Long House Antiques), 16 W. Main, Clinton; 201–735–4838 (bus.), 735–7994 (res.).

Furniture repair, refinishing.

C CHARLES D. HANNAH (Studio Hannah), Star Rt. A, Flemington; 201–782–7468.

Repair of fine old paperweights; faceting of new paperweights.

F MARCY HEDGEPETH, Rt. 179 and Boss Rd. Mailing address: R. D. #2, Box 17, Ringoes 08551; 201–782–8392.

Furniture refinishing; hand work. Chair caning, natural rushing, splint weaving.

F MONROE and BEVERLY HOFFMAN, 51 E. Main St., High Bridge; 201–638–6466.

Furniture refinishing.

C WILLIAM IORIO (Iorio Glass Shop), S. Main St., Flemington; 201–782–5311.

Custom glass cutting, engraving, glass blowing. Repair and restoration of blown glass and china. Lamp repair, restoration; parts. Member Early American Glass Collector's Club, American Paperweight Assoc. Mr. Iorio is a third-generation artisan. Iorio glass is represented in museum collections.

F JACK LEWIS (Jack Lewis Ltd.), Rt. 31, Lebanon; 201–735–7444.

Fine antique restoration; custom cabinetmaking. Hand-stripping, furniture repair, veneer work. Mr. Lewis is a craftsman trained in Great Britain; apprentices.

F PAUL F. RAYWOOD, BEATRICE RAYWOOD (North Country Antiques), 10 N. Union St., Lambertville; 609–397–2177.

Furniture refinishing, restoration.

F ANNE and STEPHEN SOODUL (A & S Antiques), 163 Main St., Flemington; 201–782–5270.

Furniture repair, restoration; hand-stripping.

A LLOYD K. SWANSON, JR. (Swanson Fine Art Restoration), 35 Main St., High Bridge; 201–638–4224, 638–8539.

Conservation and restoration of paintings, prints, maps, photographs, frames, sculpture, furniture; gold leaf gilding. Quality custom framing.

F WAYNE and SUE TIMPSON (Whitehouse Manor Antique Center), Rt. 22, Whitehouse; 201–534–9904.

Furniture repair, restoration; caning, rushing.

MI MARGARET MARY WILSON (One Sutton Place), Main St. and Sutton Pl., Lebanon; 201–236–6200.

Telephone restoration.

Somerset County

F JOSEPH CHERUBINO (Cherubino Upholstery), 339 Somerset St., North Plainfield; 201–756–4950.

Upholstering of antique furniture.

A PHILLIP FICO (The Connoisseur), 20 Claremont Rd., Bernardsville; 201–755–1139.

Restoration and conservation of paintings.

C ALAN GLENN (Alteg Poly Marble), 73 Second St., Somerville; 201–526–2777.

Porcelain tub and tile resurfacing.

F BIFF HEINS (The Country Shop), Canal Rd., East Millstone; 201–844–2640.

Restoration of antique furniture; restoring surfaces of old painted and decorated furniture.

F, M GARY HOOK, 79 Wilson Ave., North Plainfield; 201–753–6166.

Furniture refinishing and restoration; brass beds polished.

F GARY JOHNSON (Looking Back), 93 Somerset St., North
Plainfield; 201–753–1020.

Furniture repair and restoration.

F GREG McCLEARY (The Big Dipper), Rt. 206, Bedminster;
201–234–2511.

Furniture stripping and refinishing; caning, wicker repair.

F ALEXANDRA PUNNETT (The Wood Shed Furniture Stripping),
Bridgepoint Rd., Belle Mead; 201–359–2727

Chem-Clean furniture stripping, refinishing, including colored lacquer,
antique finishes.

F, M EDWARD RAYMOND (The Mad Stripper), 126 Mt. Bethel Rd.,
Warren; 201–755–3238.

Furniture stripping, refinishing, repairing; metal stripping.

L ELIZABETH RICHARDS (The Acorn Shop), 31 S. Finley Ave.,
Basking Ridge; 201–766–5776.

Lamp repair and conversion.

F ALBERT SCARINCI (Scarinci Brothers), Rt. 22, Green Brook;
201–968–7270.

Antique furniture refinishing, hand-stripping; caning and rushing.

T RICHARD C. SCHWARTZ (Collector's Corner), 326 Somerset St.,
North Plainfield; 201–753–2650.

Clock and watch repair. Member Nat'l. Assoc. of Watch & Clock
Collectors.

F, L, M VERN SPENCE (Bell Post Antiques), R. D. 2, Dutchtown Rd.,
Belle Mead; 201–359–6730.

Furniture refinishing; lamp conversions, chandeliers rewired; brass
polishing; casting.

T CARL TONERO (The Mountain House), Martinsville;
201–469–2195.

Antique clock restoration. Member Nat'l. Assoc. of Watch &
Clock Collectors, American Watchmakers Institute.

Union County

M ANTHONY BRUNO (Sterling Silversmiths), Stage House Village, Front St., Scotch Plains; 201–322–5854.

Known for fine silver repair, restoration, plating. A craftsman for more than forty years.

F GEORGE BUSSINGER (Old World Craftsman), 1927 Rt. 22, Scotch Plains; 201–322–7514.

Fine antique repair, refinishing, restoration; inlay work, gold leafing, reupholstering. Cabinetmaking. Hand- and press-caning.

D ELIZABETH and JIM CONNORS (Good Fairy Doll Hospital & Museum), 205 Walnut Ave., Cranford; 201–276–3815.

Doll hospital. Member Keepsake Doll Club, Fanwood.

F ROSEMARY and JOHN DeLUCA (Aviary Antiques), Murray Hill Square, Floral Ave., Murray Hill (New Providence); 201–464–8422.

Repair and restoration of antique furniture; hand work.

F GILBERT FOSTER, 635 Glen Ave., Westfield; 201–232–2577.

Hand-stripping; old wood employed in restorations.

M JACK LOGAN (Brakes Unlimited), 354 North Ave., Garwood; 201–789–1227.

Metal cleaning; antiques, iron beds, sewing machines, car parts, etc. Brakes relined on antique cars.

F DON MAXWELL, 885 Mountain Ave., Mountainside; 201–232–0226.

Furniture refinishing, restoration, upholstering; extensive repair shop. At this location since 1926.

D YVONNE MILLER, LEE PAARDECAMP (The Doll's Corner), 115 Martine Ave., Fanwood; 201–388–1869, 322–1774.

Complete doll hospital service.

F SHIRLEY NICHOLS (Shir-Norm Antiques), 1308 E. Front St., Plainfield; 201–561–3640.

Furniture repair, refinishing.

A, C PHILIP ORLANDO, Plainfield; 201–755–1695.

Restoration of fine art, sculpture, porcelains. Lost wax casting of parts in bronze or pewter. The bronze statue in Raritan, N. J., honoring World War II hero John Basilone, was sculpted by Mr. Orlando, as were relief panels and other works adorning the National Council of State Garden Clubs building in St. Louis. Sculpture, paintings, and bronzes by Mr. Orlando are exhibited at Gallery 52, South Orange.

L BOB ROYER (Lamp Clinic, Inc.), 513 Morris Ave., Summit; 201–273–1323.

Lamp wiring, refinishing; mountings. Custom lampshades.

A WALTER SWAIN (Swain's Art Store), 300 E. Front St., Plainfield; 201–756–1707.

Fine art restoration, oil paintings. Restoration of antique frames; repair, regilding, gold leaf work. Associate member American Soc. of Appraisers. A venerable business, now in its fourth generation; founded 1868.

T ETHEL and ROBERT WILEY (The Odds and Ends Shop), Rahway; 201–382–1145.

Complete clock repairs, restoration. Member Nat'l. Assoc. of Watch & Clock Collectors.

T LAWRENCE YOUNG (Colonial Arms Antiques), Union; 201–688–3932.

Clock repair, restoration. Member Nat'l. Assoc. of Watch & Clock Collectors.

F JOSEPH ZICHICHI (Joseph Zichichi & Sons, Inc.), 474 Morris Ave., Summit; 201–277–1402.

Furniture repair, restoration, refinishing.

Middlesex County

T CONSTANCE BOLTON (Browse Around Antiques), 563 Bound Brook Rd., Middlesex; 201–968–7220.

Antique clocks repaired.

MI, T GARY CLEVELAND, BENTLEY TERRACE (Resurrected Recollections), 1903 Village Dr., Avenel; 201–574–9281.

Complete restoration service; timepieces, music boxes. Member Nat'l. Assoc. of Watch & Clock Collectors; Music Box Soc. of Gt. Brit., American Music Box Soc.

T ANN GESCHLECHT (Boro Art Center), 505 Middlesex Ave.,
Metuchen; 201–549–7878.

Clock repair, restoration, cleaning. Member Nat'l. Assoc. of Watch &
Clock Collectors.

F STEVE HASSELBACH, Rt. 130, Box 275, Cranbury; 609–395–1920,
448–6771.

Complete woodworking and finishing, by appt. Wood carving, bending,
veneering. Caning. Woodworking and finishing for antique automobiles.
Third generation.

F BOB KUBIAK (Ye Bygone Years Antiques), 462 Amboy Ave.,
Perth Amboy; 201–826–2628.

Furniture stripping, repair, refinishing.

F ED KULDINOW (Ed's Upholstery Shop), 43 French St., New
Brunswick; 201–828–7144.

Furniture repair, restoration, refinishing, reupholstering; all services.

F LOIS MAZZA (Brass Lantern Antiques), 327 Main St., Metuchen;
201–548–5442.

Furniture hand-stripping, repair, restoration.

F BRENT NIELSEN (Trash or Treasure Shop), Old Bridge-
Englishtown Rd., Old Bridge; 201–446–6572.

Repair, restoration of fine furniture; hand work.

F RICH PARELLA (Attics & Cellars), 177 Main St. (historic section
of Old Bridge), East Brunswick; 201–238–3838.

Hand-stripping, furniture repair, restoration, refinishing. Hand-
pressed caning; rushing.

F JUSTIN and SANDRA SWEENEY, 891 King George Rd., Edison;
201–738–0636.

Complete restoration service: regluing, repairing, veneer repair or
replacement. Woven, pressed, and French caning, splint and reed; fiber
and natural rush.

T VICAI'S FRENCH ANTIQUES & CLOCKS, 10 Morningside Dr.,
Colonia; 201–381–3374.

Specializing in repair of 18th- and 19th-century French clocks, primarily
mantel, wall clocks.

Monmouth County

F BOB ADAMS (Adams' Refinishing), 142 Memorial Pkwy., Atlantic Highlands; 201–872–0656.

Antiques, general furniture repair, refinishing, restoration.

F GEORGE BENFANTE (Furniture Craftsman, Inc.), 415 Shrewsbury Ave., Shrewsbury; 201–842–0055.

Complete repair, restoration, refinishing; upholstering. Third-generation.

F JANE and ROBERT FITZGERALD (Fitzgerald's Antiques), 44 Academy, Farmingdale; 201–938–5591. Shop at Squankum-Yellow Brook Rd.,Howell Twp.

Furniture repair, restoration. Hand-stripping, gluing, veneer work; spoke and spindle replacement. Caning, rushing.

F GEORGE HOWER, 35 N. Bridge Ave., Red Bank; 201–747–5499.

Furniture repair, restoration.

F DICK and CAROL LACKMAN (Woods Edge Antiques), 655 Broad St., Shrewsbury; 201–842–9219.

Restoration of antique furniture.

L ED LUZZI (Woods Edge Shoppes), 655 Broad St., Shrewsbury; 201–842–9219.

Lamp repair; wiring, polishing, lacquering.

D PHIL MAY, HERB BACHMANN (Dahlrose Antiques), Antiques Center of Red Bank, Bldg. II (Annex), 195 W. Front St., Red Bank; 201–842–3393.

Doll hospital. Member Nat'l. Doll Federation.

F LOU NEEVERS-SCHOLTE (Lou's Thrift Shop), 716 Main St., Bradley Beach; 201–776–9080.

Rockers repaired, restored to usable condition. Porch rockers a specialty. Old pieces hand-stripped, reupholstered.

F GARY NIELSEN, Antiques Center of Red Bank, Bldg. III, 226 W. Front St., Red Bank; 201–842–4336.

Furniture restoration, refinishing; hand-carving. Handmade country furniture.

F MARIAN OLSON (Antiques An'non), 400 Higgins Ave., Brielle; 201–528–5943.

Hand- and pressed caning; rushing.

C DAMIEN PEDUTO, 55 Brighton Ave., West End; 201–229–6492.

Tiffany restorations using genuine Tiffany glass. Art Nouveau stained glass windows repaired, restored.

J, T DON PONS (Don Pons, Jewelers), 799 River Rd., Fair Haven; 201–842–6257.

Jewelry design, remodeling, repair. Antique clocks repaired; grandfather clocks serviced. Member Nat'l. Assoc. of Watch & Clock Collectors.

F MR. and MRS. RONALD SNYDER (Chem-Clean Restoration Center), Matthews Rd., Farmingdale; 201–938–2303.

Furniture stripping, refinishing, restoration; veneering. Caning. Patented chemical stripping; no water used. Materials and supplies for home application.

F MARY ELLEN THOMPSON (The Country Kitten Antiques), 26 Thomas Ave., Shrewsbury; 201–747–1286.

Caning; lessons.

F MARY and CHRISTINE VANDERBILT ("R" Barn), 640 W. Front St., Red Bank; 201–747–9226.

Furniture refinishing; caning.

F, M AL ZABRISKIE (American Craftsman/Yankee Stripper), 819 Rt. 35, Wanamassa; 201–988–1414.

Furniture repair, custom modification; decorator lacquer work. Restoration of structural elements and finish for collectors and museums. Caning, rushing, reed work. Brass and copper polishing, repair. More than twenty-five years of restoration experience.

Mercer County

C BROOKE BAUMANN, DAURELLE GOLDEN (Stained Glass Studio of Hopewell), 25–29 Railroad Pl., Hopewell; 609–466–3747.

Repair and restoration of stained glass, in the shop or on site; glass bending.

F, J, T LIZ BENEDIK (House of Treasures Antiques), Rt. 1, R. D. 4, Princeton; 609–452–1234.

Furniture repairing; watch and jewelry repair.

F KATHLEEN CHRISTIANSEN, 145 Ward St., Hightstown; 609–443–4508.

Furniture refinishing and restoration.

F DOMINICK and THOMAS GIRALDI, Bow Hill Ave. and Reed Ave., Trenton; 609–392–7200.

Reupholstering, refinishing, restoring of antique furniture.

F KARL GUUSSER, River Dr., Titusville; 609–737–0800.

Antiques and fine furniture restored by craftsman who also lectures on antiques and appraises antique furniture.

F JAMES and OLGA HALL, 3640–44 Nottingham Way, Hamilton Square; 609–890–0926. *Also see* Auctioneers listing.

Furniture repairing, refinishing, restoring.

F, M CLARENCE J. HANEY (Castaways), 215 Woodside Ave., Trenton; 609–393–6103.

Furniture restoration and repair, hand-stripping and refinishing; caning, turning; mirrors resilvered, brass polished.

F MILHOLLAND & OLSON, INC., 8 Stockton St., Princeton; 609–924–2175.

Complete care and restoration of furniture.

M ALEX PARUBCHENKO (Blacksmith and Tool Shop of Trenton), 334 N. Olden Ave., Trenton; 609–396–9583.

Repair and duplication of metalwork, old farm equipment, mills; period hardware. Work by master blacksmith and apprentice.

F PAUL A. PUSECKER, 219 Ingleside Ave., Pennington; 609–737–0665.

Antique furniture restoration.

F, L STANLEY J. SREDINSKI (S & S Collectibles), 1520 Princeton Ave., Trenton; 609–599–1520.

Furniture repairing; lamp refinishing.

F DIANE and STEWART SURICK (D. C. Treasure Cove), 44 Spring St., Princeton; 609–924–8585.

Furniture repair and restoration. *Also see* Auctioneers listing.

T BARRY WEISSMAN, 203 South Lane, West Windsor; 609–443–3551.

Repair and servicing of all types of antique clocks.

D LUELLA WHEELING, Box 155, Hopewell; 609–466–2411.

Antique dolls repaired and restored.

Burlington County

C MIRIAM ARMSTRONG (Potpourri), 301 Stokes Rd., Medford; 609–654–7011.

Repair of old and new stained glass.

F, M KEN BITTNER, PETER CLARKE (Precious Pieces), Old Marlton Pike and Hartford Rd., Medford; 609–654–8555.

Stripping, refinishing, repairing furniture; brass and copper polishing; mirror resilvering.

D MARY BITTNER (Granny's Doll Shop and Hospital), Lakes Shopping Center, Medford Lakes; 609–654–4727.

Doll repair and restoration.

M GENE BOHN (Cassidy's Corner), Rts. 38 and 206, Vincentown; 609–261–2230.

Mirror resilvering.

F JACK COONEY (Jack & Mary's), Main St., Crosswicks; 609–298–2035.

Stripping, refinishing furniture; caning, rushing.

F, M TOM De FUSCO (Lakeside Antiques), 149 Chippewa Trail, Medford Lakes; 609–654–5194.

Stripping, upholstering; caning, rushing; brass polishing.

D NANCE GAMBACORTA (Rocky & His Friends), 18 N. Main St., Medford; 609–654–7592.

Doll repair and dressing.

T RANDI and ROBERT GOMEL (Yesterday & Today), Lakes Shopping Center, Medford Lakes; 609–654–7786.

Clock repair.

D VIRGINIA GREENWOOD (The Carpetbaggers), Creek Rd., Rancocas Woods; 609–234–5095.

Doll repair and restoration.

L URSULA HOLMAN (The Duck Blind), R. D. 2, Lower Bank; 609–965–2902.

Lamp repair and restoration.

F, L, M RUTH ISGRO (Stone Hearth Antiques), Wynwood Dr.-Arney's Mount, Pemberton; 609–267–6919.

Furniture refinishing; lamp restoration; pewter repair.

F, M, T CHUCK and CHARLIE JOHNSON (The Browse Around Shop, Inc.), R. D. 2, Rt. 38, Mt. Holly; 609–261–0274.

Furniture refinishing and restoration; clock repair; reburnishing and lacquering of metals; resilvering mirrors.

F, M ROBERT and VIRGINIA LEES (The Country Workshop), Chatsworth Rd., Tabernacle; 609–267–1200.

Furniture repair and restoration; caning, rushing; stenciling; brass polishing; mirror resilvering.

F CHARLES R. SMITH, HARVEY V. CLARK, 87 Mill St., Mt. Holly; 609–267–1870.

Furniture refinishing; rushing, caning; cabinet work.

F TONY and JUNE WELLS, Lumberton; 609–261–2922.

Furniture refinishing; caning, rushing, reeding; wicker repair.

M, T MARY and JACK WELSH (Welsh Jewelers), 115 S. Church St., Moorsetown; 609–234–2445.

Clock and watch repairs; brass polishing, silver plating.

Ocean County

D, J BUD and IRENE CAPP (Capp's Corner), Blvd. at Massachusetts Ave., Beach Haven Crest; 609–494–5843.

Doll and mechanical toy repair; antique jewelry repair.

F SAM CLARK (The Clarks), Hickory Lane, Bayville; 201–269–5181.

Furniture stripping and refinishing.

D LINDA CLAYTON (Linda's Doll Repair), 1209 Lakewood Rd., Toms River; 201–349–3311.

Antique doll repair.

F, L, M BASIL DURIK (The Freight Station), Rt. 166 and Flint Rd., S. Toms River; 201–349–0328 or 477–3196.

Furniture refinishing and restoration; lamp repair; brass polishing.

R ANTHONY FAHMIE (Anthony's Oriental Rugs), Brick Town; 201–477–5869.

Oriental rugs cleaned and repaired.

F SARAH HOWE (Sarah's Antiques), 1435 Rt. 9, Toms River; 201–244–9841.

Furniture refinishing.

F, M CRAIG MITCHELL (The Strip Joint), Rt. 37, Toms River; 201–244–8585.

Hand-stripping of furniture, refinishing; caning; metal stripping.

F LEONARD PARRINO, 208 Hwy. 9, Forked River; 201–269–5769.

Hand-stripping, refinishing, restoration of furniture.

T PETTIS CLOCK SHOP, 1209 Lakewood Rd., Toms River; 201–349–3311.

Repair and restoration of antique clocks and pocket watches.

F RICHARD PLUNKETT (Wizard of Odds), Long Beach Blvd. and Culver Ave., Beach Haven Crest; 609–296–9373.

Furniture refinishing; caning, rushing.

F CAROL REED (The Barracks), 59 Brindletown Rd., New Egypt; 609–758–8384.

Hand-refinishing of furniture.

T CHARLES RUBINA (West Creek Trading Post), Rt. 9, West Creek; 609–296–2555.

Antique clock repair. Member Nat'l. Assoc. of Watch & Clock Collectors.

F JOSEPH SCHILDKRAUT (Collectors Corner), 300 Barnegat Blvd., Beachwood; 201–240–0487.

Furniture repair and restoration.

F C. EDWARD TANTUM (Snooper's Coop), 35 Lakewood Rd., New Egypt; 609–758–2673.

Furniture repair and restoration.

F HENRY TAWYEA (Heritage House Antiques), 408 Main St., Barnegat; no phone.

Furniture repair and restoration.

F STANLEY WASILEWSKI (The Sampler), 708 Broadway, Barnegat Light; 609–494–3493.

Furniture refinishing, repair, restoration, reupholstering.

F BARRY WHITE (Bayberry Antiques), 324 E. Main St., Tuckerton; 609–296–8669.

Furniture refinishing, restoration.

Atlantic County

T C. EMERSON JOHNSON (Johnson's Clock Shop), 1500 New Rd., Northfield; 609–645–1745.

Clock repair and restoration.

F LEONARD JONES (Jones Antiques), Oak Rd. and Harding Hwy., Buena; 609–697–0325.

Refinishing and restoration of antique furniture.

F DAVID C. PLATT (Platt's Antique Annex), MacArthur Blvd., Somers Point; 609–927–0372.

Furniture upholstering.

L, M DOROTHY ROGOWSKI (Collectors' Korner Antiques), 208 New Rd., Linwood; 609–399–7542.

Lamp repair; burnishing of copper and brass; polishing of silver and pewter.

F GORDON SCHELL (Captain's Chest Antiques), 1478 New York Rd., Smithville; 609–652–1042.

Refinishing and repairing of antique furniture.

F JOHN SPURLOCK (Dead Horse Run), Somers Point-Mays Landing Rd., English Creek; 609–927–9173.

Furniture stripping, refinishing, restoration.

Camden County

C, L MAX BAER (Baer Specialty Shop), 32 Brown Ave., Bellmawr; 609–931–0696.

China and glass repair, chipped crystal smoothed and polished; lamps mounted. Over thirty years' experience.

A CHARLES BERTOLINO (Bertolino Art Gallery), 406 Harrison Ave., West Berlin; 609–767–1006.

Restoration of paintings.

A MAURY H. BETCHEN (Betchen's Picture Framing), Springdale and Greentree Rd., Cherry Hill; 609–424–2646.

Art restoration.

F TOM BOYTIM, 320 Brookline Ave., Cherry Hill; 609–667–4712.

Repair of antique spinning and weaving equipment.

F ALICE ESPOSITO, P. O. Box 329, Waterford Works; 609–561–7177.

Furniture refinishing; caning, rushing.

T CY FELHEIMER (Rosalyn's Antiques), Westmont; 609–854–0759.

Clock repair.

F JOHN GIGLIO (The Collingswood Upholstery Shop), 713 Haddon Ave., Collingswood; 609–854–6897.

Furniture refinishing, repair, reupholstering.

F THE GOLDEN KEY (Arthur Bailey), 532 S. Black Horse Pike, Blackwood; 609–227–9737.

Furniture stripping, refinishing.

L LIDIA GOROHOFF (The General Store), 37 Ellis St., Haddonfield; 609–428–3707.

Polishing, rewiring of lamps, chandeliers, sconces.

F TERRY HOWARDS (Philadelphia Furniture Repair Service), 1802 Winding Way, Clementon; 609–784–1200.

In-home furniture restoration. Travel within 75-mile radius of Philadelphia.

F CHARLES KELLING (Bates Mill Antiques), Waterford; 609–561–3022.

Furniture refinishing and restoration.

F WILLIAM B. McCURDY, 1115 Chews Landing Rd., Laurel Springs; 609–783–1074.

Touch-up of damage on antique furniture—scratches, digs, white marks; complete resurfacing.

F MARVIN MULLEN (Mullen's Antique Shop), 524 White Horse Pike, Audubon; 609–546–0507.

Furniture refinishing.

F REALE, 308 5th Ave., Glendora; no phone.

Furniture refinishing, repair, and restoration.

L CAROLE and HOWARD ROSEN (Just Brass Antiques), 314 N. Haddon Ave., Haddonfield; 609–428–4883.

Lamp rewiring.

F, T AUDREY RUSSELL (The Antique Corner), 2 E. Maple Ave., Merchantville; 609–663–1200.

Caning; antique clock and watch repair.

A ALBERT and KARL SANDECKI (Sanski Art Center), 50 Tanner St., Haddonfield; 609–429–2511.

Restoration of antique paintings.

D JANE E. SHEETZ (The Calico Doll House), Kirkwood; 609–784–1292.

Antique doll repair and dressing.

D MARLEIGH SCHROEDER (Marleigh Schroeder Antiques), Clementon; 609–783–2639.

Antique doll repair.

F DORIS STALEY (Penny Wise Thrift Shop), 23 Mechanic St., Haddonfield; 609–429–5576.

Furniture repair.

F E. R. SWITZER, 1001 Line St., Camden; 609–964–3198.

Restoration and upholstering of quality antiques for the trade and retail.

F TROSO BROTHERS UPHOLSTERING (Leo J. Troso), 6315 Westfield Ave., Pennsauken; 609–662–4403.

Reupholstering and refinishing of sofas and chairs.

F JEROME and SHAULA WRIGHT, 1743 Old Cuthbert Rd., Cherry Hill; 609–429–2790.

Furniture refinishing and repair.

Gloucester County

F KENNETH R. CUNDIFF (The Nip and Tuck Shop), 407 S. Broadway, Pitman; 609–589–9623.

Antique furniture refinishing, reupholstering, restoring.

F LEE S. FONTANA (Scotland Run), Rt. 40, Malaga; 609–694–3344.

Furniture stripping, refinishing, restoration.

F HOWARD LUCAS (Treasure Hunt), County House Rd. and Black Horse Pike, Turnersville; 609–227–4925. *Also see* Auctioneers listing.

Furniture stripping, refinishing, repairing.

M WILLIAM SPENCER, Salem Ave. and Weymouth Rd., Newfield; 609–696–0359.

Brass and copper polishing, burnishing, lacquering; electrostatic spray system and baking process. Est. 1897.

Salem County

F ERNEST DORREL (Dorrel's Antiques), Lambert and Cedar Sts., Alloway; 609–935–4296.

Refinishing, restoring of antique furniture; paint-decorated furniture a specialty.

F DAVE STRONG, R. D. 2, Salem; 609–935–0868.

Victorian furniture restoration; refinishing, repairing, upholstering, hand-tufting; caning.

Cumberland County

F RICHARD KOERNER, 3192 S. Main Rd., Vineland; 609–691–8520.
Furniture stripping, repairing, refinishing; caning.

Cape May County

F DENNIS BRANDENBURG (The Country House Antiques), Rt. 9,
Erma; 609–884–2381.
Furniture refinishing.

F ROBERT DICKINSON (Find It Shop), Rt. 9, Erma; 609–884–8186.
Furniture stripping; caning.

F C. DEAN EWEN (Dean's Furniture Stripping & Refinishing), Rt. 9,
Ocean View; 609–263–2785.
Furniture stripping, refinishing, restoration.

F MARJORIE FORRESTER (The Victorian Look), 654 Hughes St.,
Cape May; 609–884–5360.
Furniture refinishing; caning.

L, M KENNETH HOLMSTRUP (Cape May Forge), Old Shore Rd.,
Cold Spring; 609 884 5397.
Lamp and fixture repair; copper and brass cleaning, buffing,
lacquering.

D DORIS H. MAXWELL (The Old Doll Shop), 343 Asbury Ave.,
Ocean City; 609–399–0161.
Doll repair and dressmaking.

F, M ROBERT O'SHEA (House of Old), Rt. 9, Erma; 609–886–3458.
Furniture refinishing, restoration; caning; old stoves repaired.

D BLANCHE PRATLEY (Pratley's Doll Hospital), 1207 Lafayette St.,
Cape May; 609–884–3551.
Antique doll repair and dressing.

Bucks County, Pa.

F PHILIP and GAIL ANDREWS, Rt. 611 Kintnersville; 215–847–5177. Good country and period furniture restored; fine cabinetry. In business more than twenty years.

A EVE BIANCO (Picture Frame Gallery), Rt. 202, Lahaska; 215–794–7022.

Custom and creative framing; old frames restored. Member Pa. Antiques Appraisers' Assoc.

F WILLIAM BOGLE (Plumstead Village Antiques), Rt. 611, Plumsteadville; 215–766–0196.

Antiques restored; upholstering by arrangement.

F LAWRENCE GIAMBRONE, Box 435, Kintnersville; 215–847–5836. Sixteenth- thru 18th-century American and English furniture restored, refinished; furniture reproductions.

F PATTI GUTHRIE and LEW LARASON (Guthrie & Larason), 4 E. Butler Ave. (Rt. 202), Chalfont; 215–822–3987. Restoration of antique furniture.

F KENNETH HOLLINGSWORTH (Durham Village Antiques), Rt. 212, Durham; 215–346–7047.

Furniture stripping, refinishing.

F L. ROBERT KLING (Carversville Cabinet Shop), Carversville; 215–297–5878.

Furniture repair, refinishing, restoration; fine finish work, "strictly by hand." Chair seats recaned. Family business; est. 1947.

F, M PATRICIA MANWARING (The History Coop), Rt. 611, Ottsville; 215–847–2700.

Furniture repair, refinishing. Brass and copper polished.

C LONNY McLAUGHLIN (Plantiques), 628 N. W. End Blvd. (Rt. 309), Quakertown; 215–536–1963.

Stained glass repair.

L ARNOLD and MARNIE MILLER (Miller-Topia Designers), 41 E. Afton Ave., Yardley; 215–493–6114.

Lamp design; oil lamps rewired.

F RUTH MOYER, BOB ROTH (Ruth's What Not & Furniture Shop),
Rt. 313, Fountainville; 215–249–3768.

Furniture refinishing, touch-up work.

F WILLIAM NICKEL (1821 House Antiques), Rt. 202, Lahaska;
215–794–8662, 646 7643 (res.).

Repair and restoration of primitive furniture; hand work.

F M. ST. JAMES (Bench and Board Antiques), at 1821 House
Antiques, Rt. 202, Lahaska; 215–794–8662.

Repair, restoration of primitives; hand work.

L, MI GEORGE SEEMAR (The Country Shop), The Hamlet at Rolling
Fields, Rt. 202, New Hope; 215–862–5594 (eves. only).

Repair, restoration, refinishing of table and hanging lamps for
museums, collectors, and dealers. New "Aladdin" lamps and parts.
Repair and restoration of weighing scales.

F ALBERTUS W. VANDER MEER (The Yardley Cabinet Makers),
174 S. Main St., Yardley; 215–493–2654.

Antiques restored, refinished; sold. Furniture restored, refinished for
home or office.

F ROBERT C. WHITLEY, Solebury; 215–297–8452.

Restoration of fine period pieces, including brass work and forging.
Custom copies of antiques (no commercial reproductions as such).
Member American Craftsman's Council, Bucks County Guild of
Craftsmen, N. J. Designer Craftsmen.
A master artisan, Mr. Whitley made the four Queen Anne chairs in
the Governor's Council Chamber, Independence Hall, Phila.; a copy
of the chair in which Thomas Jefferson wrote the Declaration of
Independence, for the Graf House museum (Jefferson's rented rooms)
at 7th and Market Sts., Phila.; the copy of Benjamin Franklin's electric
experimentation machine (predominantly of wood) in Franklin Court.
At the request of the Nat'l. Park Service, Mr. Whitley reproduced a
documented 6′ × 12′ c. 1835 billiard table for the reconstructed
old Bent's Fort trading post on the Arkansas River in La Junta,
Colorado.

F, L JOHN WILLIAMS (Evelyn's Antiques), Rt. 202, Lahaska;
215–794–7385.

Lamp rewiring, repair, restoration. Furniture hand-stripping; repair,
restoration, refinishing. Oak a specialty.

"What am I bid?" Scene at a country auction, one of many scheduled each week during warmer weather. Auction barns and galleries conduct sales year 'round. Pictured at left, Robert Heller, assisted by Barbara Trumble (rear). *Courtesy Elwood Heller, Lebanon. Photo: Andrew Jacobs*

Auctioneers

Auctions in the Garden State go back a long way—
the first of note having taken place in 1682 when the
trustees for Lord Cartaret auctioned the entire
province of East Jersey to William Penn and eleven
associates for £3,400.

My wish is that my drawings, my prints, my
curiosities, my books—in a word, those things of art
which have been the joy of my life—shall not be
consigned to the cold tomb of a museum, and
subjected to the stupid glance of the careless
passer-by; but I require that they shall all be
dispersed under the hammer of the auctioneer, so
that the pleasure which the acquiring of each one of
them has given me shall be given again, in each case,
to some inheritor of my own tastes.

Edmond de Goncourt, Will (1896)

Farm scene whirligig, carved and painted wood. Probably New Jersey, late 19th century.
Courtesy Sotheby Parke Bernet Inc., New York

Auctioneers

New Jersey Auctioneers

RICHARD P. ALLEN, Vincentown-Lumberton Rd., Vincentown, Burlington C.; 609–267–8382.

Auctioneering of antiques and general merchandise. Auction barn.

JIM ANDERSON (Andy's Plaza), Rt. 9, Freehold, Monmouth C.; 201–431–3212.

Weekly consignment auctions; Sat., 7:30 P.M.

EDWARD F. BARBER, Black Horse Pike and Poplar St., Williamstown, Gloucester C.; 609–629–3500.

General auctioneering.

EDWARD BERMAN (Berman's Auction Barn), 4 Dewey St., Dover, Morris C.; 201–361–3110.

Auctions on 2nd and 4th Sat. eves., 7:30 P.M.; middle Wed. eves., 7:30 P.M. Sat. auctions quality antiques; Wed. collectibles and household contents. Specializing in cut glass, art glass, steins. Estate auctions. Mailing list. Member N. J. State Soc. of Auctioneers, Nat'l. Auctioneers Assoc., Nat'l. Auctioneers Guild.

JIM BISHOP (Five Acres Antique Auction Gallery), Rt. 46, Belvidere, Warren C.; 201–475–2572.

Antiques auctions Sun., 1–6 or 7 P.M. Newspaper notices.

NOËL and RALPH CANNITO (Washington's Headquarters), 27 Belvedere Ave., Washington, Warren C.; 201–689–2025, 201–689–6020.

Auctions. Member American Numismatic Soc., American Numismatic Assoc., Numis. Internat'l.

DON CASTNER, Branchville, Sussex C.; 201–948–3868.

Auctioneer; appraisals. Real and personal estate broker.

B. G. COATS & ASSOCIATES, 45 W. River Rd., Rumson, Monmouth C.; 201–842–4033.

Complete auction service; specializing in estate liquidations.

WILLIAM COLLINS (Collins Corner), Dumont Rd., Far Hills, Somerset C.; 201–234–0995.

Complete auctioneer service.

RICHARD J. CONTI (Conti Realty and Auction Service), 116 Youngs Rd., Trenton, Mercer C.; 609–586–9202.

Estate and antiques auctions.

ROD DAVIS (Davis Associates), Antiques Center of Red Bank, Bldg. II (Annex), 195 W. Front St., Red Bank, Monmouth C.; 201–842–3393.

Member Nat'l. Auctioneers Assoc., N. J. State Soc. of Auctioneers.

JOHN DENNIS (John Dennis Auction Gallery), Rt. 31, Hampton, Warren C. Mailing address: 631 Oxford St., Belvidere 07823; 201–537–2881.

Antiques, general merchandise auctioned Wed. eves., 7 P.M. sharp. Mailing list. Member N. J. State Soc. of Auctioneers.

TOM DWYER, ROBERT LARSEN (Lakeland Galleries), Rt. 206, Andover, Sussex C.; 201–786–6004.

Antiques auctioned monthly indoors; general merchandise weekly outside.

FAIRGROUND FLEA AND FARMERS MARKET, 1690 Nottingham Way, Rt. 33, Trenton, Mercer C.; 609–586–2326.

Two antiques auctions Sat., 7 P.M., one sit-down and one tailgate.

GLORIA FRAZEE (Willinger's, Inc.), 626 Ocean Rd., Point Pleasant, Ocean C.; 201–892–2217.

Auction every Fri., 8 P.M. Member Nat'l. Auctioneers Assoc., N. J. State Soc. of Auctioneers.

PHILLIP A. GARUFFI, Weymouth Rd., Hammonton, Atlantic C.; 609–561–4514.

Estate auctions Sun., 3–6 P.M. (Nov.–April); Mon., 7–10 P.M. (May–Sept.).

GEORGE'S AUCTION ROOMS, INC., 83 Summit Ave., Summit, Union C.; 201–277–0996.

Auctions on premises; mailing list. Member Appraisers' Assoc. of America.

JIMMY and OLGA HALL (Jimmy Hall's Auction), 3640–44 Nottingham Way, Hamilton Square, Mercer C.; 609–890–0926.

Antiques and general auctions 1st and 3rd Wed., 7 P.M., exhibit 1 P.M. Mailing list. Bonded auctioneer. Member N. J. State Soc. of Auctioneers.

ARTHUR HANNA, Bellis Rd., R. D. 2, Bloomsbury, Hunterdon C.; 201–993–7862.

Auctioneer; antiques, household, farm. Newspaper notices. Member N. J. State Soc. of Auctioneers.

JOHN HEDGEPETH (Frenchtown Auction), Bridge St., Frenchtown, Hunterdon C.; 201–782–8392 (res.). Mailing address: R. D. 2, Box 17, Ringoes 08551.

Weekly auction sales; Thurs., 6:30 P.M. Consignments welcome Mon., 6–9 P.M. Mailing list. Appraisals. Member Nat'l. Auctioneers Assoc., Consumer Bureau, Princeton.

ELWOOD G. HELLER, 152 Main St., Lebanon, Hunterdon C.; 201–236–2195 (bus.), 725–8973 (res.).

Specializing in antiques. Complete estate service; appraisals. Auctions every Mon., 9:30 A.M. at the "Old Mill," above address; consignments accepted. Estate sales on location throughout the year. Mailing list for specialty items. Member Nat'l. Auctioneers Assoc., N. J. State Soc. of Auctioneers.

JOHN P. KACHMAR, R. D. 2, Flemington, Hunterdon C.; 201–782–4271.

Complete auction service; estate sales, business liquidations. Member N. J. State Soc. of Auctioneers, Nat'l. Auctioneers Assoc. Est. more than 20 years.

GEORGE VLADIMIR KEDROWSKY, Antiques Center of Red Bank, Bldg. II (Annex), 195 W. Front St., Red Bank, Monmouth C.; 201–842–3393.

Complete auctioneer services. Member American Philatelic Soc.

EDMOND KIAMIE (Carrie Ann Antiques), 10 North Ave. E., Cranford, Union C.; no phone.

Antiques auctions.

EDWARD R. and DORIS KIBBLE (The Collectors), 83 Main St., Matawan, Monmouth C.; 201–583–3222.

Auctions; mailing list. Member N. J. State Soc. of Auctioneers.

ANDREA LICCIARDELLO (Andrea's Auction), Harrisonville-Pedricktown Rd., Swedesboro, Gloucester C.; 609–467–1165.

Consignment auctions Thurs., 6:30 P.M. Estate auctions. Member Nat'l. Auctioneers Assoc., N. J. State Soc. of Auctioneers.

LINCOLN MAYFLOWER STORAGE WAREHOUSES, 225 Scotland Rd., Orange, Essex C.; 201–677–2000.

Estate auctions, appraisals.

HOWARD LUCAS, County House Rd. and Black Horse Pike, Turnersville, Gloucester C.; 609–227–4925.

General auctioneering. Member Nat'l. Auctioneers Assoc.

PAT LUSARDI (Lusardi's Auction Gallery), Rt. 46, Belvidere, Warren C.; 201–475–3438.

Monthly antiques auctions; weekend eve. mid-month. Mailing list.

ROBERT MANNING (Manning's Auction), Main St., Peapack, Somerset C.; 201–234–9824.

Consignment auctions Fri. eves., 7 P.M. Newspaper notices.

COL. JAMES A. MOORE, 101 Main St., Farmingdale, Monmouth C.; 201–938–2648.

Full auction sales service; estates. Mailing list.

NEW EGYPT AUCTION AND FARMERS MARKET, Rt. 537, New Egypt, Ocean C.; 609–758–2082.

General auctions Sun., 2 P.M., Thurs., 6:30 P.M.

DAN A. NORDBERG, Belcher Rd., R. D. 1, Blairstown 07825, Warren C.; 201–362–8679, 201–362–6309.

Antiques, farms, heavy equipment dispersal, on location. Mailing list. Annual antiques auction April or Sept. Member N. J. Auctioneers Assoc.

ARTHUR PETROVIC (Tony Art Galleries), 120 Grand Ave., Englewood, Bergen C.; 201–568–7271.

Member N. J. State Soc. of Auctioneers.

COL. JASON RAHM (Auction 'Round the Back), W. Main St., Clinton, Hunterdon C. Mailing address: P. O. Box 5331, Clinton 08809; 201–735–9362. Auctions Fri. eves., 7 P.M. (every two or three wks.), above address. Also on location. Mailing list or see newspaper notices.

GORDON ROGERS, P. O. Box 501, Atlantic City, Atlantic C.; 609–822–2921. Complete auction service.

VALENTINO ROMAGNOLI (Val's Auction), Alpha Industrial Park, Alpha, Warren C.; 201–454–4145. Complete auction service. Sales every Sat., 7 P.M.

J. SARTOR (Sartor Auction Sales), 437 W. Clinton St., Dover, Morris C.; 201–361–6877. Complete auction service, estate sales. Special consideration to nonprofit groups. Phone for auction information.

COL. GEORGE WASHINGTON SCHUELER, 1315 Allaire Ave. and Rt. 35, Wanamassa, Monmouth C.; 201–531–4488. Auctions; antiques and U. S. coins a specialty (also purchased).

JOHN SIEGFRIED (Village Shops), Rt. 31, Buttzville, Warren C.; 201–453–2727. Auctioneer; mailing list.

GEORGE SIMON (Simon Sez Auction Gallery), Rt. 15, Lake Hopatcong, Morris C.; 201–663–0276. Antiques auctions 1st and 3rd Sat., 7:30 P.M., exhibit 1 P.M. Estate auctions.

SKIP & STONEY & BLEW AUCTIONEERS, INC., R. D. 2, Woodstown, Salem C.; 609–769–3000. General auctioneering.

LESTER and ROBERT SLATOFF, INC., 777 W. State St., Trenton, Mercer C.; 609–393–4848. Estates appraised, auctioned, bought or sold. Consumer Bureau registered. Member N. J. State Soc. of Auctioneers.

DALLAS R. SMITH III AND ASSOCIATES, N. Main St., Woodstown, Salem C.; 609–769–1319. Complete auction service, estates, personal property. Director N. J. State Soc. of Auctioneers, member Nat'l. Auctioneers Assoc.

EILEEN M. SMITH, CHARLES B. ROEDER (Roeder Smith Associates),
409 Ramapo Valley Rd., Oakland, Bergen C.; 201–337–4500 (bus.),
337–0458 (res.).

Auctions at least once a month; mailing list. Member Nat'l. Soc. of Auctioneers,
N. J. State Soc. of Auctioneers.

GARRY SMITH, 841 E. 29th, Paterson, Passaic C.; 201–523–3035.

Member N. J. State Soc. of Auctioneers.

MAC SPAULDING, 34A Wilson Rd., Sussex, Sussex C.; 201–875–7078.

Auctioneer; appraisals.

GERALD STERLING (Sterling Auction Gallery), 62 N. Second St., Raritan,
Somerset C.; 201–685–9565, 464–4047.

Auctions, appraisals, tag sales; estate and antiques auctions. Member Appraisers'
Assoc. of America, N. J. State Soc. of Auctioneers, Nat'l. Auctioneers Assoc.
Monthly public auctions. Mailing list.

DIANE SURICK (D. C. Treasure Cove), 44 Spring St., Princeton, Mercer C.;
609–924–8585, 448–5107.

General auctions Mon., 7:30 P.M., exhibit 1 P.M. Mailing list. Member N. J.
State Soc. of Auctioneers.

JOHN TORLISH (Towne Antique Auction, Inc.), 56 W. Somerset St.,
Raritan, Somerset C.; 201–722–2280.

General auctioneering. Member N. J. State Soc. of Auctioneers.

WEB & ASSOCIATES, 1101 E. Broad St., Cinnaminson, Burlington C.;
609–829–2033.

Antiques and estate auctions; appraisals.

HOWARD E. WIKOFF (New Jersey Auction Service), 123 W. Saddle River
Rd., Saddle River 07458, Berger C.; no phone.

Bucks County Auctioneers

J. BELLI, B. GIMELSON (611 Auction Gallery), Rt. 611, Pipersville;
215–766–8802.

Specializing in auctions of antiques, oil paintings. Five catalog sales a year.

KENYON B. BROWN (Brown Bros.), 2455 Rt. 413, Buckingham;
215–794–7630.

Auctions of antiques, general household effects. Est. 1915.

Set of carved ivory Japanese okimono (shelf or alcove figures) representing the Rokkasen or Six Poetic Immortals of the Fujiwara period. Signed "Sosai"; probably late 18th century. *Courtesy J. Turk Antiques, Little Silver. Photo: Dorn's Inc.*

J. J. MATHIAS, 863 Bristol Pike, Andalusia 19020.

Antiques auctions.

ANDREW J. OSER (Andy's Auction), 1561 Woodbourne Rd., Levittown; 215–945–3765.

Antiques auctions; mailing list. Licensed auctioneer.

DAVID REDAY (Bristol Mart), 316 Mill St., Bristol; 215–788–2621.

Monthly auctions; mailing list.

French antiques displayed for sale at a show. From rear, clockwise: cherry "vaisselier" with lovely inlay and carving, original hardware, Louis XV style panels and feet, ca. 1740; early Morbier clock, decorated pine with enameled face, brass lyre pendulum, ht. 7 ft. 2 in.; child's rush seat feeding chair with lift-up tray, mid-19th century; a unique cradle of aristocratic lineage from Provence, mid-19th century. *Courtesy Time and Tide, Point Pleasant, Pa. Photo: Christian Mattheson*

Principal Antiques Shows

South Jersey pitchers: (left) dark olive-amber with heavy ribbing, baluster base and plain foot, ht. 6 in.; (right) cobalt blue with threaded lip and lily pad decoration and applied crimped foot, ht. 9¼ in. Both 19th century. *Courtesy Sotheby Parke Bernet Inc., New York*

Principal Antiques Shows

January

RIDGEWOOD (Bergen C.): Church Women's Guild Antiques Show and Sale. Parish Hall, Christ Church, 105 Cottage Pl.

YARDLEY, PA. (Bucks C.): Yardley Antiques Show. Yardley Community Center, 64 S. Main St.

February

ATLANTIC CITY (Atlantic C.): Autorama & Antique Mini-Mart. Convention Hall.

BRIDGEWATER (Somerset C.): Temple Sholom Antiques Show & Sale. Temple Sholom, N. Bridge St.

GLEN RIDGE (Bergen C.): Antiques Show and Sale. Congregational Church, 195 Ridgewood Ave.

RUMSON (Monmouth C.): Sisterhood Antiques Show and Sale. Congregation B'nai Israel, Hance and Ridge Rds.

SUMMIT (Union C.): Nat'l. Council of Jewish Women Antiques Show & Sale. Temple Sinai, 208 Summit Ave.

March

BRANCHBURG TWP. (Somerset C.) : Branchburg Rescue Squad Aux. Antiques Show & Sale. Branchburg Rescue Squad Bldg., off Rt. 202 (3 mi. south of Somerville traffic circle).

COLTS NECK (Monmouth C.) : Colts Neck Hist. Soc. Spring Antiques Show and Sale. Cedar Drive School, Cedar Dr.

ELIZABETH (Union C.) : Deborah League of Elizabeth Antiques Show. Masonic Temple, 668 N. Broad St.

HACKENSACK (Bergen C.) : Temple Beth El Antique Show. Temple Beth El, 280 Summit Ave.

MONTCLAIR (Essex C.) : Montclair Women's Club Show & Sale. 82 Union St.

PENNSAUKEN (Camden C.) : West Jersey Hospital Antiques Show & Sale. Washington Rm., Ivystone Inn, Rt. 130.

PRINCETON (Mercer C.) : Wellesley Club of Central N. J. Antiques Show. Princeton Day School, The Great Rd.

RIDGEWOOD (Bergen C.) : Junior Women's Club Antique Show. 215 W. Ridgewood Ave.

SELLARSVILLE, PA. (Bucks C.) : The Twiglings, Quakertown Community Hospital Antiques Show. V.F.W. Hall, Old Bethlehem Pike.

SPRINGFIELD (Union C.) : Springfield Antique Show and Sale. Parish House, Historic Presbyterian Church, 37 Church Mall.

TURNERSVILLE (Gloucester C.) : Antique Bottle Show, S. Jersey Bottle & Glass Club. Whitman Sq. Fire Hall, Rt. 42 and Johnson Rd.

WESTFIELD (Union C.) : Ladies Aux. Antiques Show and Sale. Holy Trinity Greek Orthodox Church, 250 Gallows Hill Rd.

WESTWOOD (Bergen C.) : Antiques Show and Sale. Grace Episcopal Church, 9 Harrington Ave.

April

BERKELEY HEIGHTS (Morris C.) : Diamond Hill Community Church, 105 Diamond Hill Rd.

BRIDGEWATER (Somerset C.) : Somerset Hospital Antiques Show. Somerset County Vocational Technical School, off Rt. 22, westbound at Somerville Inn exit; ½ mi. north.

DOYLESTOWN, PA. (Bucks C.): Bucks County Antiques Dealers Show. Warrington Country Club, Almshouse Rd., off Rt. 611 (3 mi. south of Doylestown).

LIVINGSTON (Essex C.): Newark Academy Antiques Show. Newark Academy, 91 S. Orange Ave.

MORRISTOWN (Morris C.): Assoc. Antiques Dealers of N. J. Spring Antiques Show and Sale. Grand Ballroom, Governor Morris Inn, 2 Whippany Rd.

MORRISTOWN (Morris C.): Morristown Antiques Fair & Sale. Nat'l. Guard Armory, Western Ave.

NEWTOWN, PA. (Bucks C.): Amer. Heart Assoc. Heart of Bucks Antiques Show & Sale. Council Rock High School, Swamp Rd.

RED BANK (Monmouth C.): Red Bank Antiques Show & Sale. Trinity Episcopal Parish House, W. Front St.

May

BASKING RIDGE (Somerset C.): Basking Ridge Antiques Show & Sale. Methodist Church, S. Finley Ave.

GLASSBORO (Gloucester C.): Antiques Show and Sale. St. Thomas' Parish House (across from school), St. Thomas' Episcopal Church, Delsea Dr.

MILLINGTON (Morris C.): Bonnie Brae May Benefit & Antiques Show. Bonnie Brae, Valley Rd.

NEW HOPE, PA. (Bucks C.): New Hope Hist. Soc. Antiques Show & Sale. High School Auditorium, Rt. 179 (old Rt. 202).

PRINCETON (Mercer C.): Princeton YMCA Antiques Show. Princeton YMCA, Avalon Pl.

RAMSEY (Bergen C.): Antiques Show & Sale. Don Bosco High School, N. Franklin Tpk.

SPRING LAKE (Monmouth C.): Jersey Coast Antique Show & Sale. Essex & Sussex Hotel, 700 Ocean Ave.

WAYNE (Passaic C.): Wayne Antiques Show & Sale. Preakness Reformed Church, 131 Church Lane (bet. Hamburg Pike and Ratzer Rd.).

WESTFIELD (Union C.): Kiwanis Antiques Show & Sale. Elm St. Field.

June

BUCKINGHAM, PA. (Bucks C.): Buckingham Antiques Show. Tyro Grange Hall, Rts. 202 and 413.

GREAT MEADOWS (Warren C.): Antiques Show & Sale. SS. Peter and Paul R. C. Church (SS. Peter and Paul Hall), Rt. 46, corner Hope Rd.; 6 mi. west of Hackettstown.

GREENWICH (Cumberland C.): Cumberland County Historical Soc. Antique Show & Sale. Morris Goodwin School, Main St.

MOORESTOWN (Burlington C.): Moorestown Antiques Show. Moorestown "Y" Men's Club, Church and Second St. Gym.

MORRISTOWN (Morris C.): American Heart Assoc. Antiques Show. Nat'l. Guard Armory, Western Ave.

July

HOPE (Warren C.): Hope Historical Soc. Antiques Show and Sale. Hope Community Center.

NEW HOPE, PA. (Bucks C.): New Hope Historical Soc. Antiques Show & Sale. High School Gym, Rt. 179 (old Rt. 202).

POTTERSVILLE (Somerset C.): Pottersville Fire Co. Antiques Show & Sale. School House and Firehouse.

SPARTA (Sussex C.): Antiques Show & Sale. First Presbyterian Church, Main St.

STONE HARBOR (Cape May C.): Women's Civic Club Antiques Show and Sale. Elementary School, 93rd and 3rd Aves.

WARREN (Somerset C.): Country Antiques Show & Sale, Community Vol. Fire Co. and Ladies Aux. American Legion Hall, Community Dr.

August

BAY HEAD (Ocean C.): St. Paul's United Methodist Church, corner Bridge and West Lake Aves.

DOYLESTOWN, PA. (Bucks C.): Bucks County Antiques Dealers Association Outdoor Antiques Show, Memorial Field on Rt. 202.

OCEAN CITY (Cape May C.): Saint Augustine's School Antiques Show, St. Augustine's School, 17th and Simson Aves.

SURF CITY (Ocean C.): Southern Ocean County Hospital Auxiliary Antiques Show & Sale, Ethel Jacobsen School, Barnegat Ave. and South Third St.

September

CLINTON (Hunterdon C.): Hunterdon Art Center, Old Stone Mill.

FRANKLIN LAKES (Bergen C.): Rosary Altar Society Antiques Show, Most Blessed Sacrament School, Franklin Lakes Rd.

GREEN BROOK (Somerset C.): Green Brook Rescue Squad Antiques Show & Sale, Rescue Squad Bldg., 101 Green Brook Rd.

HIGHTSTOWN (Mercer C.): Hightstown Women's Club Antiques Show & Sale, St. Anthony's Church Hall, Maxwell Ave.

HOHOKUS (Bergen C.): Saint Bartholemew's Episcopal Church Antiques Show, 70 Sheridan Ave.

MORRISTOWN (Morris C.): Original Morristown Antiques Show, National Guard Armory, Western Ave.

PARSIPPANY-TROY HILLS (Morris C.): Country Peddlers' Antiques Show, Morris Grange Grounds, S. Beverwyck Rd. at Rts. 10 and 78.

RIDGEWOOD (Bergen C.): Ridgewood Antiques Show, First Presbyterian Church, East Ridgewood and Van Dien Aves.

SHREWSBURY (Monmouth C.): Shrewsbury Corners Antiques Show & Sale, Presbyterian Church House, 352 Sycamore Ave.

SUMMIT (Union C.): Summit Outdoor Antiques Show, Brayton School Grounds, Tulip St. and Ashland Rd.

October

DOYLESTOWN, PA. (Bucks C.): Bucks County Antiques Dealers Association Show, Warrington Country Club, Almshouse Rd. off Rt. 611.

EWING TWP. (Mercer C.): The Greater Trenton Antiques Show & Sale, Jewish Community Center, 999 Lower Ferry Rd.

FLEMINGTON (Hunterdon C.): Antiques Dealers Association of Central New Jersey Antiques Show & Sale, American Legion Hall, Rt. 31.

MILLTOWN (Middlesex C.): Milltown Historical Society Antiques Show & Sale, Joyce Kilmer School, Rts. 1 & 9.

MORRISTOWN (Morris C.): Morristown Antiques Fair & Sale, National Guard Armory, Western Ave.

NEW PROVIDENCE (Union C.): Antiques Show & Sale, United Methodist Church, 1441 Springfield Ave.

PATERSON (Passaic C.): Antiques Show & Sale, Nathan Barnert Memorial Temple, Derrom and Wall Aves.

PENNSAUKEN (Camden C.): Antiques Show & Sale, Benefit of the West Jersey Hospital, Ivystone Inn, Rt. 130.

PLAINFIELD (Union C.): Monday Afternoon Club Antiques Show, Monday Afternoon Club Clubhouse, 1127 Watchung Ave.

SCOTCH PLAINS (Union C.): All Saints Episcopal Church Antiques Show, Parish House, All Saints Episcopal Church, 559 Park Ave.

SHORT HILLS (Essex C.): Short Hills Antiques Show, Community Congregational Church, Parsonage Hill Rd.

TENAFLY (Bergen C.): Antiques Show, Greek Orthodox Church, E. Clinton Ave.

UPPER SADDLE RIVER (Bergen C.): Antiques Show & Sale, Religious Education Building, The Old Stone Church, East Saddle River Rd. and Weiss Rd.

VINELAND (Cumberland C.): Delaware Valley Antiques Show, Armory, S. Delsea Dr.

WESTFIELD (Union): Kiwanis Club Antiques Show, Elm St. Field.

WYCKOFF (Bergen C.): Valley Hospital Auxiliary Antiques Show, Eisenhower School, 344 Calvin Court.

November

BRIDGEVILLE (Warren C.): White Township Historical Society Antiques Show & Sale, White Township School Gym, Rts. 46 and 519.

CHATHAM (Morris C.): Ogden Memorial Presbyterian Church Antiques Show & Sale, Church School Bldg., Main St. and Elmwood Ave.

CHERRY HILL (Camden C.): Women's Auxiliary to the Institute for Medical Research Antiques Show, Cherry Hill Armory, Park Blvd. and Grove St.

FAIR LAWN (Bergen C.): Sisterhood, Fair Lawn Jewish Center Antiques Show, Fair Lawn Jewish Center, Norma Ave.

FLEMINGTON (Hunterdon C.): Hunterdon Central High School Boosters Club and Band Parents Antiques Show & Sale, Hunterdon Central High School, New Field House, Rt. 523.

MOORESTOWN (Burlington C.): Moorestown Friends School Alumni Association Antiques Show, Moorestown Friends School, Main St.

Antiquing in New Jersey & Bucks County, Pa.   Rutgers Univ.   (G)   141

MOUNT HOLLY (Burlington C.): Burlington County Antique Dealers Association Antique Show & Sale, National Guard Armory, Rt. 38, east of Pine St.

NEW HOPE, PA. (Bucks C.): New Hope Historical Society Antiques Show, High School Gym, Rt. 179 (old Rt. 202).

NEWTOWN, PA. (Bucks C.): Newtown Antiques Show & Sale, Newtown Legion Home, Linden Ave. off Richboro Rd.

NORTH BERGEN (Hudson C.): Schuetzen Park Antiques Show, Kennedy Blvd. and 32nd St.

OAKLAND (Bergen C.): Antique Bottle Show, North Jersey Antique Bottle Association, Valley Middle School.

RIDGEWOOD (Bergen C.): The College Club of Ridgewood Antiques Show, Benjamin Franklin Junior High School, corner N. Van Dien and Glen Aves.

RUMSON (Monmouth C.): Rumson Antiques Show, Holy Cross School, Rumson Rd.

SALEM (Salem C.): The Women's Club of Salem Antiques Show & Sale, Salem High School, Walnut Street Rd.

SHORT HILLS (Essex C.): B'nai Brith Women of Short Hills Antiques Show, Temple B'nai Jeshurun, 1025 South Orange Ave.

WHIPPANY (Morris C.): Annual Christmas Antiques Show & Sale, Birchwood Manor, North Jefferson Rd.

December

BUCKINGHAM, PA. (Bucks C.): Buckingham Antiques Show, Tyro Grange Hall, Rts. 413 and 202.

COLTS NECK (Monmouth C.): Colts Neck Historical Society Christmas Antiques Show & Sale, Cedar Drive School, Cedar Dr.

FAIR LAWN (Bergen C.): Cardozo Lodge, Knights of Pythias Antiques Show, Fair Lawn Senior High School.

MANVILLE (Somerset C.): Somerset County Unit, New Jersey Association for Retarded Children, Inc., Antiques Show, VFW Hall, 600 Washington Ave.

NORTH PLAINFIELD (Somerset C.): Annual Antiques Show & Sale, The Church of the Holy Cross, Washington and Mercer Aves.

PARAMUS (Bergen C.): Women's Alliance Antiques Show, Unitarian Church, 156 Forest Ave.

Selected Bibliography

General References

Cole, Ann Kilborn. *Antiques*. New York: Collier Books, 1957.

Corlette, Suzanne. *The Fine and Useful Arts in New Jersey 1750–1800*. Trenton: New Jersey Historical Commission, 1975.

Deetz, James. *In Small Things Forgotten*. Garden City, New York: Doubleday, Anchor, 1977.

Drepperd, Carl W. *A Dictionary of American Antiques*. Boston: Charles T. Branford Company, 1952.

Guild, Lurelle Van Arsdale. *The Geography of American Antiques*. Garden City, New York: Doubleday, Doran & Company, 1935.

Michael, George. *George Michael's Treasury of Federal Antiques*. New York: Hawthorn Books, 1972.

Peterson, Harold. *How Do You Know It's Old?* New York: Charles Scribner's Sons, 1975.

Ramsey, L. G., ed. *The Complete Encyclopedia of Antiques*. New York: Hawthorne Books, 1962.

Revi, Albert Christian, ed., and the staff of *Spinning Wheel* magazine. *The Spinning Wheel's Complete Book of Antiques*. New York: Grosset & Dunlap, 1949–1972, inclusive.

Stillinger, Elizabeth, *The Antiques Guide to Decorative Arts in America*. New York: Straight Enterprises, 1972.

Van Hoesen, Walter Hamilton. *Crafts and Craftsmen of New Jersey*. Fairleigh Dickinson University Press, 1973.

Weygandt, Cornelius. *Down Jersey.* New York: D. Appleton-Century Company, 1940.

White, Margaret E. *The Decorative Arts of Early New Jersey.* Princeton: D. Van Nostrand Company, 1964.

Winchester, Alice, ed., and the Staff of *The Magazine Antiques. The Antiques Book.* New York: A. A. Wyn, 1950.

Glass

Downer, John B. "Caspar Wistar's Glass Works." Manuscript compiled from the *Glassboro Enterprise.* Glassboro, New Jersey, 1920.

Gribble, W. Griffin. "Pairs in New Jersey Glass." *Antiques* magazine, November 1934.

Knittle, Rhea Mansfield. *Early American Glass.* New York: D. Appleton-Century Company, 1935.

McKearin, George S. "Wistarberg and South Jersey Glass." *Antiques* magazine, October 1926.

McKearin, George S., and McKearin, Helen. *American Glass.* New York: Crown Publishers, 1941.

————. *Two Hundred Years of American Blown Glass.* New York: Crown Publishers, 1958.

Maxwell, Florence C. "Wistarberg, Yesterday and Today." *Antiques* magazine, September 1951.

Minns, Edward W. "Paperweight Making as Done at Millville." *American Collector* magazine, November and December 1938.

Pepper, Adeline. *The Glass Gaffers of New Jersey and Their Creations from 1739 to the Present.* New York: Charles Scribner's Sons, 1971.

Polak, Ada. *Glass: Its Tradition and Its Makers.* New York: G. P. Putnam's Sons, 1975.

Sicard, Hortense Fea. "Sidelights on the Wistars and Their Glass-House." *Antiques* magazine, October 1926.

Pottery and Porcelain

Barber, Edwin Atlee. *The Pottery and Porcelain of the United States.* Philadelphia, 1901.

————. *Tulip Ware of the Pennsylvania-German Potters.* Philadelphia: The Pennsylvania Museum and School of Industrial Art, 1903.

Clark, William H. "Pottery and Potters." *Americana* magazine, vol. 32, no. 3, July 1938.

Cox, Warren E. *The Book of Pottery and Porcelain,* vol. 2. New York: Crown Publishers, 1944.

"The Editor's Attic." *Antiques* magazine, vol. 62, July 1952.

Exhibition pamphlet, *New Jersey Pottery to 1840.* Trenton: The New Jersey State Museum, 1972.

Holmes, George Sanford. *The Story of Walter Scott Lenox.* Privately printed, 1924.

Lichten, Frances. *Folk Art of Rural Pennsylvania.* New York: Charles Scribner's Sons, 1946.

Mills, Flora Rupe. *Potters and Glassblowers.* San Antonio: The Naylor Company, 1963.

Ramsay, John. *"East Liverpool* vs. *Bennington."* *Antiques* magazine, Jan. 1946.

Spargo, John. *Early American Pottery and China.* New York: The Century Company, 1926.

Stiles, Helen E. *Pottery in the United States.* New York: E. P. Dutton and Company, 1941.

Thorn, C. Jordan. *Handbook of Old Pottery and Porcelain Marks.* New York: Tudor Publishing Company, 1947.

Watkins, Lura Woodside. "Henderson of Jersey City and His Pitchers." *Antiques* magazine, December 1946.

Clocks

Allen, Alex B. "Joachim Hill, Clock Maker." Flemington: *The Jerseyman,* vol. 2, no. 2, May 1905.

Bailey, Chris. *Two Hundred Years of American Clocks and Watches.* Englewood Cliffs: Prentice-Hall, A. Rutledge Books, 1975.

Drost, William E. *Clocks and Watches of New Jersey.* Elizabeth: Engineering Publishers, 1966.

Henry Hogeland & Catherine, his wife, to Joakim Hill. Deed, 1830. Archives, Flemington Historical Society, Flemington, N. J.

"A Man of Note Was Joachim (*sic*) Hill." Flemington: *Hunterdon County Democrat,* December 14, 1922.

Palmer, Brooks. *The Book of American Clocks.* New York: Macmillan Publishing Co., 1928, 1950.

Furniture

Bjerkoe, Ethel Hall. *The Cabinetmakers of America.* Garden City, New York: Doubleday & Company, 1957.

Drepperd, Carl W. *Handbook of Antique Chairs.* Garden City, New York: Doubleday & Company, 1948.

Early Furniture Made in New Jersey 1690–1870. Exhibition pamphlet. Newark: The Newark Museum, 1958.

Horner, W. M., Jr. "Three Generations of Cabinetmakers." *Antiques* magazine, vol. 14, September, November 1928.

Nutting, Wallace. *Furniture Treasury,* vol. 3. New York: The Macmillan Company, 1949.

Powers, Mabel Crispin. "The Ware Chairs of South Jersey." *Antiques* magazine, vol. 9, no. 5, 1926.

White, Margaret E. "Further Notes on Early Furniture of New Jersey." *Antiques* magazine, vol. 78, August 1960.

Winchester, Alice, ed., and the staff of *Antiques* magazine. *The Antiques Treasury of Furniture and Other Decorative Arts.* New York: Galahad Books, 1951.

Commercial Weaving

Brückbauer, Frederick. *The Kirk on Rutgers Farm.* Fleming H. Revell Company, 1919.

Crosby, Ernest H. *The Rutgers Family of New York.* New York: Trow's Printing & Bookbinding Co., 1886. (Reprinted from The New York Genealogical Record, April 1886.)

Demarest, William H. S. *A History of Rutgers College.* New Brunswick, N. J.: Rutgers College, 1924.

Federal Writers' Project of the Works Progress Administration for the State of New Jersey. American Guide Series. *New Jersey—A Guide to Its Present & Past.* New York: Hastings House, 1939.

Fisher, the Rev. Samuel, D. D. "Census of Paterson, N. J. 1827–32."

Gordon, Thomas F. *The History of New Jersey from Its Discovery by Europeans to the Adoption of the Federal Constitution.* Trenton: Daniel Fenton, 1834.

McCormick, Richard P. *Rutgers: A Bicentennial History.* New Brunswick, N. J.: Rutgers University Press, 1966.

McMahon, Ernest E., and Miers, Earl Schenck. *The Chronicles of Colonel Henry.* New Brunswick, N. J.: Thatcher-Anderson Company, 1935. (Limited Edition, 100 copies.)

Myers, William Starr, ed. *The Story of New Jersey,* vol. 3. New York: Lewis Historical Publishing Company, 1945.

Henry Rutgers. Will. Surrogate's Court, City of New York, August 1830.

Schwartz, Esther I. "Notes From A New Jersey Collector." *Antiques* magazine, vol. 74, October 1958.

Trumbull, L. R. *History of Industrial Paterson.* Paterson, N. J.: Carleton M. Herrick, Book & Job Printer, 1882.

Firearms

Boothroyd, Geoffrey. *Guns through the Ages.* New York: Bonanza Books, 1961.

Chapel, Charles Edward. *The Gun Collector's Handbook of Values.* New York: Coward, McCann & Geoghegan, 1975.

Haven, Charles T., and Belden, Frank A. *A History of the Colt Revolver.* New York: Bonanza Books, 1940.

Pollard, Maj. H. B. C. *A History of Firearms.* Boston and New York: Houghton Mifflin Company, 1927.

Russell, Carl P. *Guns on the Early Frontiers.* Berkeley and Los Angeles: University of California Press, 1957.

Sutherland, R. Q., and Wilson, R. L. *The Book of Colt Firearms.* Kansas City, Mo.: Robert Q. Sutherland, 1971.

Trumbull, L. R. *History of Industrial Paterson.* Paterson, N. J.: Carleton M. Herrick, Book & Job Printer, 1882.

Bird Decoys

Bauer, Edwin A. *The Duck Hunter's Bible.* Garden City, New York: Doubleday & Company, 1965.

Burk, Bruce. *Game Bird Carving.* New York: Winchester Press, 1972.

Mackey, William J., Jr. *American Bird Decoys.* New York: E. P. Dutton & Company, 1965.

Webster, David, and Kehoe, William. *Decoys at the Shelburne Museum.* Shelburne, Vermont: Museum Pamphlet Series No. 6, 1962.

Dolls

Anderton, Johana Gast. *More Twentieth Century Dolls.* North Kansas City: Athena Publishing Company, 1974.

Blasberg, Robert. *Spinning Wheel* magazine, October 1973.

Coleman, Dorothy S.; Coleman, Elizabeth A.; Coleman, Evelyn J. *The Collector's Encyclopedia of Dolls*. New York: Crown Publishers, 1968.
Eaton, Faith. *Dolls in Color*. New York: Macmillan Publishing Co., 1975.
Fulper Pottery Company. *Fulper Pottery and Porcelaines*. Flemington, undated.
Young, Helen. *The Complete Book of Doll Collecting*. New York: G. P. Putnam's Sons, 1967.

Index of Dealer Specialties

Index of Towns

List of Antiques Centers and Malls by County

Response Card

If you wish to be included in subsequent editions or would like to update the information in your listing, please fill out and return the form below to

Antiquing in New Jersey & Bucks County, Pa.
Rutgers University Press
30 College Avenue
New Brunswick, N. J. 08903

Name

Address

Town   Zip

County

Business hours

Check where applicable

☐ New business   ☐ Dealer

☐ Change of address   ☐ Repair & restoration specialist

☐ No change   ☐ Auctioneer

Information change or comments
